SIMULATIONS AND STUDENT LEA

Edited by Matthew A. Schnurr and Anna MacLeod

Simulation-based education (SBE) is a teaching strategy in which students adopt a character as part of the learning process. SBE has become a fixture in the university classroom based on its ability to stimulate student interest and deepen analytical thinking.

Simulations and Student Learning is the first piece of scholarship that brings together experts from the social, natural, and health sciences in order to open up new opportunities for learning about different strategies, methods, and practices of immersive learning. This collection advances current scholarly thinking by integrating insights from across a range of disciplines on how to effectively design, execute, and evaluate simulations, leading to a deeper understanding of how SBE can be used to cultivate skills and capabilities that students need to achieve success after graduation.

MATTHEW A. SCHNURR is an associate professor in the Department of International Development Studies at Dalhousie University.

ANNA MACLEOD is a professor in the faculties of Medicine and Graduate Studies at Dalhousie University and holds academic appointments at St. Francis Xavier University, Acadia University, and the University of Toronto.

Simulations and Student Learning

EDITED BY MATTHEW A. SCHNURR
AND ANNA MACLEOD

UNIVERSITY OF TORONTO PRESS
Toronto Buffalo London

© University of Toronto Press 2021
Toronto Buffalo London
utorontopress.com
Printed in the U.S.A.

ISBN 978-1-4875-0773-2 (cloth)   ISBN 978-1-4875-3684-8 (EPUB)
ISBN 978-1-4875-2533-0 (paper)   ISBN 978-1-4875-3683-1 (PDF)

Library and Archives Canada Cataloguing in Publication

Title: Simulations and student learning / edited by Matthew A. Schnurr and
   Anna MacLeod.
Names: Schnurr, Matthew A., editor. | MacLeod, Anna, 1976– editor.
Description: Includes bibliographical references.
Identifiers: Canadiana (print) 20200331604 | Canadiana (ebook) 20200331663 |
   ISBN 9781487525330 (softcover) | ISBN 9781487507732 (hardcover) |
   ISBN 9781487536831 (EPUB) | ISBN 9781487536848 (PDF)
Subjects: LCSH: Education – Simulation methods.
Classification: LCC LB1029.S53 S56 2020 | DDC 371.39/7 – dc23

This book has been published with the help of a grant from the Federation
for the Humanities and Social Sciences, through the Awards to Scholarly
Publications Program, using funds provided by the Social Sciences and
Humanities Research Council of Canada.

University of Toronto Press acknowledges the financial assistance to its
publishing program of the Canada Council for the Arts and the Ontario Arts
Council, an agency of the Government of Ontario.

Canada Council
for the Arts

Conseil des Arts
du Canada

ONTARIO ARTS COUNCIL
CONSEIL DES ARTS DE L'ONTARIO

an Ontario government agency
un organisme du gouvernement de l'Ontario

Funded by the   Financé par le
Government   gouvernement
of Canada   du Canada

This book is dedicated to the next generation of learners, especially Louis, Evan, and Mary Claire.

Contents

Figures and Tables

Figures

Tables

Acknowledgments

This volume is the product of and a testament to the power of informal conversations among colleagues. These contributions evolved out of discussions with faculty from multiple disciplinary backgrounds at Dalhousie University with shared interests in simulation-based education (SBE). We are grateful to our collaborators, who shared their thoughts and experiences as part of this community of practice: Alex Brodsky, Meinhard Doelle, Brenda Merritt, and Binod Sundararajan. These informal conversations eventually led to a SSHRC Connections Grant, which enabled us to convene a one-day workshop on simulations and student learning in Halifax, and a travelling roadshow that allowed us to interact with colleagues at partner institutions across Atlantic Canada. We thank every one of these participants for sharing insights that helped to sharpen our thinking on the value of transdisciplinary thinking in SBE.

Our colleagues and friends at Dalhousie's Centre for Learning and Teaching were supportive of our endeavours and generous with their time. Thanks are due to Brad Wuetherick, Suzanne Le-May Sheffield, Chad O'Brien, and Jill McSweeney, who all added tremendous value to the final product. Meghan Ruston designed the excellent graphic for the simulation life cycle. Meg Patterson and Leah Connor from University of Toronto Press were wonderful to work with. Alanna Taylor served as the research coordinator for the *Simulations and Student Learning* project from beginning to end. Her thoughtfulness, diligence, and attention to detail are embedded throughout the volume.

On a personal note, MS thanks his family for their unwavering support: parents Brian and Annalee, sister Jessica and bonus brother Mike, and family-in-law Margo, Frank, and Lisa. Special thanks to Natalie, Louis, and Evan for always believing in me. AM is grateful to her MacLeod and Muzika families, especially her parents, Jo-Anne and Gregor, and her brother Peter. Most of all, AM thanks Greg and Mary Claire for making her world a better place, every single day.

Abbreviations

AP	Advanced Placement
ASPE	Association of Standardized Patient Educators
CEL	Complex experiential learning
CIHC	Canadian Interprofessional Health Collaborative
CMS	Course management systems
CRM	Crew (crisis) resource management
DBER	Discipline-based education research
DC	Direct current
EES	Earth and environmental sciences
ERP	Enterprise resource planning
FCI	Force Concept Inventory
FDM	Finite difference method
FIFE	Feelings, ideas, effect on function, and expectations
IP	Interprofessional
IPC	Interprofessional collaboration
IPE	Interprofessional education
LO	Learning objective
MSE	Materials science and engineering
MSW	Master of social work
MQI	Mid-quarter inquiry
NCCSTS	National Centre for Case Study Teaching in Science
NGSS	Next Generation Science Standards
OSCE	Objective structured clinical examination
PEARLS	Promoting Excellence and Reflective Learning in Simulation
RTTP	Reacting to the Past
SBE	Simulation-based education
SBIRT	Substance use screening, brief intervention, and referral to treatment

SBME	Simulation-based medical education
SERC	Science Education Resource Centre
SO	Student outcome
SOBP	Standards of Best Practice
SP	Simulated participant/patient
SSI	Socio-scientific issues
STEM	Science, technology, engineering, and mathematics
VAC	Virtual aluminium castings system

Introduction
The Promise of Simulation-Based Education

MATTHEW A. SCHNURR AND ANNA MACLEOD

Simulation-based education (SBE) – in which learners adopt a character and represent this role within an approximation of real life as part of the learning process – has become a fixture of university pedagogy. Lauded as teaching strategies that recreate complex realities in a simplified and condensed manner, simulations have been shown to help stimulate student interest (Druckman & Ebner, 2007; Schnurr et al., 2015), enhance the mastery of course materials (Rivera & Simons, 2008; Tawalbeh & Tubaishat, 2014), deepen clinical, analytical, and critical thinking skills (Jorm et al., 2016; Murdoch, Bottorff, & McCullough, 2014), and foster communication and collaboration skills (Dohaney, Brogt, Kennedy, Wilson, & Lindsay, 2015; Gordon & Thomas, 2018; Russ & Drury-Grogan., 2013). Simulations also help learners appreciate the complexity intrinsic in real-world scenarios (Dengler, 2008; Gordon & Thomas, 2018; Paschall & Wüstenhagen, 2012), acquire and apply course-based knowledge (Asal & Blake, 2006; Shellman & Turan, 2006), and gain a sense of preparedness for situations they'll encounter as professionals (Wright et al., 2018).

Simulations are one of a series of options that fall within the umbrella of experiential learning, alongside work-integrated learning, field-based instruction, undergraduate research, and study abroad programs. Simulations are unique within this landscape in that they recreate fictionalized or hypothetical scenarios and are embedded within existing courses or curriculum. The viability of such experiential opportunities is under threat within the current era of exceptional austerity, given tight budgetary constraints and the need to scale up these interventions to reach ever-greater numbers of learners. Simulations are uniquely positioned to enable the attainment of both knowledge and skills-based learning outcomes, without many of the costs associated with other forms of experiential learning. In this way, simulations represent a cost-effective and scalable pedagogical strategy that can offer learners direct, hands-on experience in order to develop capacities they will need to thrive in an evolving labour market (Association for Experiential Education, 2015).

This volume originated in conversations among six instructors from different faculties at Dalhousie University in Halifax, Nova Scotia, Canada, all of whom use simulation-based techniques in their teaching practice. Drawing from our respective appointments in the Faculties of Arts and Social Science, Law, Management, Computer Science, Health, and Medicine, the six of us began meeting regularly to share our experiences and learn more about how these immersive techniques are used across these very different teaching contexts. Over time, these informal conversations evolved into a transdisciplinary community of practice, providing a forum for continual exchange around how to better conceptualize, structure, and deliver this pedagogical strategy. This multi-directional knowledge sharing became so enriching that we decided to open it up to reach a wider network of researchers and instructors. An application to the Social Sciences and Humanities Research Council of Canada Connections Grant competition enabled us to convene a symposium, embark upon a travelling roadshow, and create an online hub, which together were designed to build reciprocal relationships among researchers and instructors committed to understanding how such experiential learning techniques can improve student learning. This edited volume represents the final phase in the trajectory of this collaboration.

The pages that follow represent the first piece of scholarship that brings together experts from the social, natural, and health sciences in order open up new opportunities for learning about different strategies, methods, and practices of immersive learning. This collection advances current scholarly thinking by integrating insights from across a range of disciplines on how to effectively design, execute, and evaluate simulations, leading to a deeper understanding of how this delivery mechanism can be utilized to cultivate skills and capabilities that learners will require to achieve success after graduation. Framing this conversation in transdisciplinary terms serves to widen instructor knowledge of what a simulation is, what it could be, and how to maximize its effectiveness. In seeking to recreate real-life scenarios, simulation-based learning is by its very nature transdisciplinary. Yet, as Ellett, Esperanza, and Phan (2014) observe, "the literature often implicitly states the way in which simulations require students to think across disciplines, but encouragement and instruction of how to tackle an interdisciplinary problem is rarely explicitly stated as a goal" (p. 131). This volume aims to address this critical gap.

This collection employs a tripartite structure to explore simulation-based learning across the social, natural, and health sciences. Each of the three subsections is anchored by a short framing piece that reflects on the particular opportunities and challenges for simulation-based teaching in the respective field. Each subsection is then rounded out by four empirical chapters prepared by scholars across different disciplines within that field that survey the utility of simulation-based learning in the scholars' own teaching context and evaluate its impact on student learning. The conclusion reflects on how the transdisciplinary insights generated throughout the volume can be used to develop faculty development resources to enhance and enrich the delivery of these immersive techniques.

This introduction offers an overarching synthesis of the current state of knowledge and practice on employing simulation-based learning across different disciplinary settings by outlining the value generated by examining such questions in a transdisciplinary context. It then shifts toward an emphasis on teaching practice by introducing a simulation project cycle that can act as a blueprint for instructors and researchers seeking to expand or enrich their use of simulation-based learning. Finally, it synthesizes the major insights from each of the volume contributors and evaluates the transdisciplinary perspectives generated as they relate to each of the six steps in the project cycle: conceptualizing a simulation, creating an immersive environment, integrating technology, simulation assessment, debrief, and evaluating student learning outcomes. Taken together, the chapters in this volume offer the first transdisciplinary assessment on how to effectively design, execute, and evaluate simulations, leading to a deeper understanding of how this delivery mechanism can be utilized to cultivate skills and capabilities that students will require to achieve success after graduation.

The Value of Transdisciplinarity

Scholarship on how SBE can benefit student learning has taken place almost entirely within, rather than across, disciplinary settings. This is not all that surprising. Teaching, even more than research, remains bound within the silo model of higher education; faculty members are often reticent to talk about teaching-based practice with their own departmental colleagues, let alone colleagues in disparate fields. The scholarship on simulation-based teaching perpetuates this compartmentalized approach, and tends to be restricted to activities taking place within respective disciplines. For example, volumes in the health sciences, including *The Comprehensive Textbook of Healthcare Simulation* (Levine,

DeMaria, Schwartz, & Sim, 2014), *Defining Excellence in Simulation Programs* (Palangas, Maxworth, Epps, & Mancini, 2014), and *Healthcare Simulation Education: Evidence, Theory and Practice* (Nestel, Kelly, Jolly, & Watson, 2018), offer convincing and compelling justification for healthcare simulations. But these are inward looking, focusing exclusively on healthcare providers and emphasizing best practices and implementation strategies. Volumes in the social sciences similarly restrict their scope to their own disciplines (see, e.g., volumes on *Reacting to the Past* [RTTP] initiatives such as *Minds on Fire: How Role-Immersion Games Transform College* [Carnes, 2014] and *Playing to Learn with Reacting to the Past: Research on High Impact, Active Learning Practices* [Watson & Hagood, 2018]), while existing volumes in the natural sciences tend to revolve around individual simulations and remain bound within narrow disciplinary boundaries (e.g., *Learning Science Through Computer Games and Simulations* [Honey, Hilton, & National Research Council, 2011], *Impact of Visual Simulations in Statistics: The Role of Interactive Visualizations in Improving Statistical Knowledge* [Iten, 2015]).

So what value is gained by examining such immersive technologies across – as opposed to within – disciplinary boundaries? We see three layers of benefits. The first layer accrues to the instructors themselves. At the one-day symposium dedicated to bringing together scholars and practitioners from across the social, natural, and health sciences, participants repeatedly emphasized how broadening the conversation around immersive teaching created new opportunities for innovation and refinement of pedagogical strategies. Colleagues valued learning about different strategies, methodologies, and best practices from outside disciplines, which they could then incorporate into their own teaching. We all get stuck in our own way of doing things, and these preferences and proclivities are often shaped foundationally by the discipline we inhabit. Transdisciplinary exchanges among instructors serve to challenge these accepted truths, exposing us to ideas and approaches that could spark a new direction in our teaching practice.

The second layer of benefits accrues to learners. Transdisciplinary perspectives on teaching and learning translate into educational interventions that expose learners to knowledge and processes that extend beyond their primary area of study. Conversations across disciplines can create opportunities for collaborative simulations that straddle disciplinary boundaries (Tivener & Gloe, 2015; Willhaus, 2010). Simulation-based learning is founded upon the mirroring of real-world processes, and the real world does not operate within disciplines. Integrating knowledge from outside one's discipline into the conceptualization or execution of a simulation serves to better replicate real-world processes and widens student exposure to outlooks that might otherwise have gone unnoticed (Balsiger, 2015). A transdisciplinary approach can further underline the transportability of the skills or knowledge imparted in the simulation: "The fungibility of these tools is rendered visible to learners when they are exposed to case studies that explicitly link two or more disciplines" (Ellett, Esperanza, & Phan, 2014, p. 132). It is no accident that simulations make up an increasingly important part of teaching and learning within topics that are themselves foundationally transdisciplinary, such as environmental sustainability (Dieleman & Huisingh, 2006), terrorism, crisis and emergency management (Brynen, 2010; Dohaney et al., 2015), social work (Dennison, 2011), climate change (Paschall & Wüstenhagen, 2012), water resource management (Hoekstra, 2012), conservation biology (Schedlbauer, Nadolny, & Woolfrey, 2016), and patient care (Fernandez, Parker, Kalus, Miller & Compton, 2007). Broadening simulations to increase their transdisciplinary content makes these undertakings more accurate, more realistic, and more credible. In this way, a transdisciplinary approach enhances student learning.

The final set of benefits relates to the enrichment of the scholarship of teaching and learning. Comparing and contrasting disciplinary principles and practices reveal important distinctions that advance our understanding of this immersive technique as a pedagogical tool. For example, measurements of learning outcomes reveal significant disparities in terms of what learners take away from simulations: management and health sciences emphasize the professional benefits of targeted skill development (Auchter & Kriz 2014; Bradley, Whittington & Mottram, 2013; Smolinski & Kesting, 2012), while assessments in the social sciences underline the simulation's value in decreasing self-reported competencies, which they attribute to a sort of humbling (Schnurr, De Santo, & Green, 2014; Youde, 2008). Contributions in this volume echo this fundamental distinction in purpose between those disciplines that utilize simulations as tools to augment or accelerate professional competencies (medicine, social work, law, management) and those that utilize simulations as a tool to illuminate particular concepts, knowledge, or competencies (political science, chemistry, physics, environmental science).

A transdisciplinary analysis offers crucial insights that can help to categorize different types of simulations that cater to different types of learning objectives, which can in turn lead to more specialized faculty development resources (a point we expand upon in the conclusion). De-aggregating our understanding of simulation-based learning can lead to more nuanced educational development and to instructional design that is better able to match the immersive exercise with the desired learning outcome. As Fowler (2009) notes, transdisciplinary conversations lead to a "cross-pollination of ideas" (p. 352), which can generate important insights on how to maximize the learning benefits associated with simulation-based learning.

Doing Simulations Across Disciplines

Our years of transdisciplinary conversations have revealed crucial insights regarding the similarities and differences of executing immersive learning techniques in different disciplinary contexts. We used these exchanges as the building blocks for the generation of a simulation life cycle, which can serve as a template for instructors wishing to expand or enrich their use of simulation-based learning in most (but certainly not all!) disciplinary contexts. When instructors were asked about the constraints they face in implementing such active learning techniques, the number one response related to time and workload: many expressed a desire to experiment with novel techniques or to evaluate the effectiveness of their teaching interventions, but lacked the time to prioritize this and reverted instead to tried and true teaching methods that required less preparation and less experimentation.

The project cycle was designed to address this constraint (see Fig. I.1). It is housed on Dalhousie's Simulation and Student Learning Website (https://www.dal.ca/dept/clt/simulation.html), which comprises a series of "just-in-time" web-based resources that offer instructors a step-by-step guide to creating an engaging and effective simulation, including worksheets, annotated bibliographies, and short videos showcasing simulations across various disciplines. Here, we eschew the "how-to" focus of the website and employ the simulation life cycle as a heuristic tool that comprises an iterative pathway for integrating or deepening simulation-based learning. In this section we introduce each step in turn, synthesizing the insights generated by this volume's contributions in order to highlight how transdisciplinary perspectives can enrich our knowledge about and implementation of these experiential techniques throughout their life cycle.

Step 1: Conceptualizing a Simulation

Contributors agree that simulation-based learning needs to begin by instructors conceptualizing how this activity will help to achieve the course learning objectives. Raymond (Chapter 1) puts it bluntly: "The worst mistake an instructor can make in this regard is to use a simulation without having specific reasons for doing so" (p. 26). Contributors

Figure I.1. The Simulation Life Cycle.

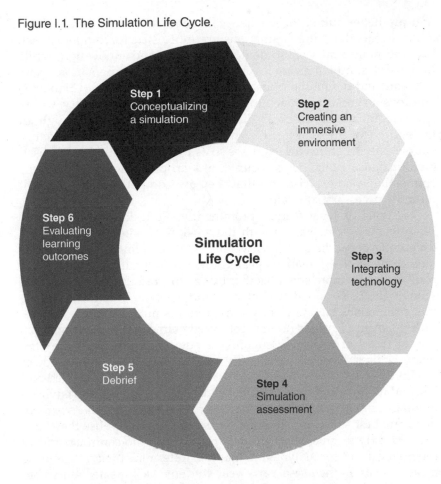

offer a slew of reasons for why they opted to embark upon simulation-based teaching: to recreate situations of professional practice, to apply knowledge learned in class, to provide learners with alternative perspectives, to stimulate interest, and to spur knowledge retention. The relative weight of these priorities is governed primarily by disciplinary orientation and course-specific learning outcomes.

In addition to learning outcomes, other more practical considerations such as scale, level, and student numbers figure prominently throughout the volume. Drawing on their experience in the field of law, Donohue and Forcese (Chapter 3) distinguish between micro-simulations, one-off exercises that they contend are better suited to larger-scale lectures, and longer-term immersive simulations that are better suited for smaller-scale seminars. Their emphasis on scale reveals that mini-simulations are more structured and as such provide more limits on student creativeness and innovation, while immersive simulations are less defined and give learners more room to create and define the rules of the game. Chamberlain (Chapter 7) employs a similar approach to scale in the field of chemistry, where she integrates a series of 23 different mini-simulations throughout the entirety of the semester. Given the setting of a large, introductory course, she structures the exercises so as to limit the number of possible outcomes, which helps ensure that learners understand the logic connecting each exercise and that they are competent and confident with the necessary software.

Questions of level feature prominently alongside those of scale. Many contributors grapple with the tension of tailoring simulations differently depending on large versus small enrolments, and the difference between simulations geared toward foundational, entry-level courses versus more specialized offerings in graduate or professional schools. Both Raymond (Chapter 1) and Paetkau (Chapter 9) agree that simulations targeting early-year students must be managed carefully to ensure learners do not feel overwhelmed. Paetkau articulates this in terms of managing cognitive loads; otherwise there are "too many choices, too much ambiguity, and too much processing power required" (p. 152), which can lead to students feeling intimidated and lost and ultimately disengaging. In the disciplines of earth and environmental sciences, Ryan and Gass (Chapter 10) argue that upper-year students are best suited for simulation-based learning because they have the necessary technical background and are ready to confront some of the political and social dynamics that will determine their outcomes as professionals. In their case, early-year students lack the necessary content and analytical sophistication to develop the degree of geo-scientific argumentation needed for the immersive exercise to succeed.

Step 2: Creating an Immersive Learning Environment

Simulations work only if learners buy into the premise. As such, one of the key challenges associated with building a successful simulation is crafting a learning environment that promotes student investment in the experience. In clinical fields, questions of authenticity are paramount. Many of the simulations in professional schools are designed to offer learners a window into the interactions they will encounter upon graduation; as such, their success as pedagogical interventions hinges on their ability to accurately replicate these real-world interactions.

In the field of social work, for instance, Bogo (Chapter 4) recounts the limitations of simulations where students lack the professional insights to portray accurately situations presented by patients. Some tend to help out their peers when the material becomes too taxing or emotional, while other feel judged by their peers, which has negative implications for future classroom dynamics. For these reasons, Bogo's department made the decision to employ human actors to create more authentic simulations that nurture the core competencies that students would need in future field-based modules. Bogo unpacks the process of creating authentic simulations by integrating perspectives from both practitioners and clients – both ends of the real-world relationship – in the conceptualizing and planning phase, as well as pilot testing the simulation with a standardized client. The added value of enlisting professional actors is explored further by McNaughton and Nester (Chapter 13), who argue that simulated patients can enhance fidelity by contributing to the emotional and affective realism of a clinical interaction. In the field of medical education, Picketts and MacLeod (Chapter 14) grapple with the challenge of creating authentic simulation experiences that avoid the pitfall of being enacted in a ritualistic or performative manner. Their results expose one of the underreported dangers of simulation-based learning – that it can reinforce a formulaic, rehearsed clinical interaction that can serve to undermine the openness and flexibility crucial to the delivery of high-quality patient care. This chapter tackles the limitations of the simulated clinical context, with important implications for creating pedagogy that enables learners not just to play the role of the physician, but to actually become a physician.

Attaining a high degree of authenticity tends to be more challenging in the social sciences and humanities, where the degree of separation between reality and its simulated representation is much more entrenched. Students enrolled in more generalist undergraduate studies are far more removed from the real-world contexts targeted via simulations than their professional colleagues training to be nurses, doctors, or physiotherapists. Clinical fields also have at their disposal tools that are largely unimaginable to social scientists, including infrastructure designed to mirror clinical practice, paid simulated patients, and video labs where every interaction can be broken down and analysed. Social scientists tend to operate simulations in the same lecture hall where all other course activities have taken place. This spatial continuity can undermine student buy-in if it doesn't allow flexible arrangements of desks and chairs, and it further constrains student imagination by blurring the distinction between this immersive teaching activity and the non-immersive teaching that preceded it. In order to achieve student buy-in, instructors must be resourceful: Donohue and Forcese (Chapter 3) reveal the amount of background research necessary when utilizing simulations in the field of law, where "storylines are assiduously researched, sourced, and validated to ensure plausibility" (p. 61). They must also be creative: Brynen (Chapter 2) recounts his use of game show simulations, replete with theme music, contestant interviews, and other "appropriate gimmicks" (p. 39) designed to keep students engaged. Brynen provides a second example that exemplifies how much work it can be for one individual to take responsibility for creating a realistic simulated environment. In a course on international peacekeeping, one hundred students spend an entire week representing roles related to the dissolution of the country Brynania. Brynen holes up in his basement for an entire week filled with 12 hours of continuous gameplay per day, in which he serves as Control (i.e., God) in order to ensure a realistic and successful unfolding.

The learning context seems less important in the natural sciences, where simulations are used predominantly to illuminate processes or phenomena that are difficult for learners to access within the classroom. This emphasis on visualizing microscopic processes – as opposed to mimicking human-scale ones – alleviates the necessity of investing in setting. Laboratories have long been revered as the hands-on application of simulated interactions, which has, in certain disciplines, provoked some resistance to embracing a wider view of digital simulations that are unable to fully replicate the physical properties of material reality. Yaron (Chapter 6) views simulations as virtual laboratories that allow learners to interact and gain experience with phenomena that occur at scales outside those of everyday experience, including spatial scales that range from the molecular up through the astrophysical, and time scales that range from the vibrational period of a molecule up through the life cycle of a star. Paetkau (Chapter 9) articulates this emphasis on abstraction in terms of representational fluency; that is, the value of simulation-based learning is the ability to create and jump between multiple contextual representations of a phenomenon – including graphs, numbers, pictures, et cetera. Underlining both the connections between these different representations and their connection to the real world constitutes one of the simulation's most valuable lessons.

Step 3: Integrating Technology

The strategic use of e-learning resources can enhance a simulation's ability to meet its learning objectives. Technology can make simulations more realistic and more interactive, and can help to overcome spatial or temporal constraints (Jones, Passos-Neto, & Braghiroli, 2015). Increasingly, educators are incorporating computer-mediated tools alongside traditional classroom methods in order to create new opportunities for collaboration, assist in knowledge building, and intensify feelings of community among students (Bonk & Graham, 2006; Littlejohn & Pegler, 2007; Serby, 2011; Schnurr, De Santo, & Craig, 2013).

Contributors to this volume highlight how differently these dynamics around technology play out across disciplinary contexts. Contributors in the social and natural sciences tend to favour simulations that are primarily or exclusively face to face. Donohue and Forcese (Chapter 3), Bogo (Chapter 4), and Sundararajan (Chapter 5) all describe simulations that privilege in-person over online interactions. But, as Mark Carnes (2014) reminds us, this does not mean they are any less innovative; indeed, the in-person interactions depicted in these chapters successfully create a sense of community and theatre that is difficult to recreate with e-learning technologies, providing important lessons on how to stem the tide of the "online tsunami" that is computer gaming (p. 288).

Others are more bullish on the power of technology to enhance simulation learning. Brynen (Chapter 2) creates an entire online world, immersing students in a week-long, real-time peacekeeping simulation that redresses the fallout from the breakdown of the fictitious country of Brynania. Brynen underlines the value of integrating e-learning technology in policy-based simulation as tools that can help to replicate the pressures and constraints shaping real-world decision-making, allow students to engage with simulation outside of class time, and enable them to hone precise and nuanced policy writing. Chamberlain (Chapter 7) reviews online repositories of simulations in chemistry, in which technology allows students to visualize non-observable processes at the molecular or the atomic level. Yaron (Chapter 6) argues that technology is crucial to enabling learners to grasp how altering rules impact emergent properties, such as how changes in the mass of a planet impact the size of an orbit or how changes in the forces between molecules impact a substance's boiling point. Elsewhere, we have highlighted another advantage of e-learning technologies: they provide alternative forums for engaging learners who might otherwise have lacked the confidence or the comfort level to participate in face-to-face forums, and can thus create more inclusive classroom experiences (Schnurr, De Santo, & Green 2014).

Other contributions highlight some of the challenges that accompany heavy reliance on technology. Brynen (Chapter 2) talks about the black box of causality, where digital platforms can serve to obscure the very dynamics that the instructor wishes students to understand. Paetkau (Chapter 9) discusses lack of software familiarity as a potential barrier to SBE in physics and the importance of carefully layering complexity to ensure that students' cognitive loads are not overly taxed. Gentry (Chapter 8) relays some of the difficulties of utilizing computer-based simulations in an engineering undergraduate curriculum, where differences in incoming skill level and competency make it difficult to reach students at both the top and the bottom. All of these authors emphasize the importance of scaffolding in order to ensure that learners have the necessary proficiency for technology to act as an enabler, and not a barrier, to student learning.

Nowhere is technology emphasized more than in the health sciences. The predilection for technological interventions is evident in McNaughton and Nestel's chapter (13), where they reflect on the limitations of simulated patients in terms of their human materiality and mortality – that is, their "living bodies that are unable to enact more complex physical findings or take part in invasive clinical procedures" (p. 221). Hamstra (Chapter 12) recounts his work establishing multiple simulation centres, which, in his extensive experience, are most often borne out of enthusiasm for a new, cutting-edge technology, which leads to a medical education approach that is increasingly specialized, siloed, and compartmentalized. Such centres are extremely proud of their technological prowess. But he recounts encountering high-tech simulations that were either underused or broken down, due either to lack of structured time for learners to take advantage of the technology in question or insufficient funds allocated to repair and replacement. He delves further into the sticky issue of cost-effectiveness, reporting studies that have relied on relatively simple training materials and yet produced learning outcomes comparable to more complex and costly technological options. His chapter is an important reminder that technology itself is not a solution to educational challenges, and that even the best technologies will flounder if not supported by thoughtful instructional design and sustained investment in operational support.

Step 4: Simulation Assessment

Assessment is a process that measures student improvement over time, motivates students to study, evaluates the effectiveness of teaching methods, and ranks student performance in comparison to their cohort (Jabbarifar, 2009). In SBE, assessments offer learners the opportunity to integrate knowledge, practise their skills, exhibit professional competency, and show that they are ready to handle real-life situations.

Assessment in more generalist, undergraduate courses focuses on specific modules designed to evaluate targeted knowledge or skills. The most frequently used mechanisms are written assignments, which are most usefully classified into two categories: an in-role piece of writing, frequently comprising background research or articulating the student's particular negotiating position, or out-of-role, which includes reflective assignments that ask students to consider what they learned through the simulation exercise (Prinsen & Overton, 2011). Assessment tools should be selected based on what is best suited to target students' desired learning objectives, with multiple forms of assessment being used – ideally both in- and out-of-role.

Raymond (Chapter 1) advocates an approach to assessment that views it as part of a feedback loop that helps trigger higher-order thinking. He further urges instructors to consider that undergraduate students tend to feel intimidated or overwhelmed when encountering experiential pedagogy; to minimize this, instructors should strive to create assessments that are as transparent, consistent, and accessible as possible. Gentry (Chapter 8) exemplifies this commitment to clarity and transparency in a case study taken from material sciences and engineering that utilizes a scaffolded combination of scenario-based assignments, quizzes, and exams to create carefully crafted assessments that match up directly with course learning objectives. She narrates the evolution of these assessments, which were revised and refined to create preparatory materials and skill modules designed to alleviate cognitive overload and ensure struggling students had the computational competency to handle the scenarios. Chamberlain (Chapter 7) similarly mobilizes a suite of different forms of assessment in a large, introductory chemistry course, including written assignments, homework reviews, pre-lab assignments, and exam questions. Her follow-up research found that student uptake of these various tools hinged largely on whether the assessment was for credit: participation increased threefold when an assessment was graded. Her experience suggests that carefully integrating evaluative components might be the single most important motivator for undergraduates to utilize a simulation.

In the context of health professions education, high-stakes assessments often involve a simulation-based component. The gold standard, the Objective Structured Clinical Examination, is designed to evaluate clinical skills, including communication and procedural skills, and hinges largely on simulated participants, as described by McNaughton and Nestel (Chapter 13) and Picketts and MacLeod (Chapter 14), performing the patient role. Candidates are observed by examiners as they cycle through a series of simulated clinical scenarios, and must demonstrate their competence in a variety of clinical skills – everything from breaking bad news to taking a medical history to conducting a physical examination. Examiners make judgments about learners' abilities based on their performance in the simulation-based examinations – the idea being that skills transfer from simulation to real life.

Step 5: Debrief

A debrief is a critical reflection that provides an opportunity for students to engage in thoughtful introspection on what they learned from the simulation and/or receive specific feedback on their performance. Debrief can take many forms. The most common remains the structured, instructor-led, face-to-face model, where guiding questions help students to engage with key learning outcomes. Increasingly, instructors are embracing a mixed model, incorporating self-directed debrief via written assignments, video-assisted debriefs, and peer-led debriefing. The existing scholarship suggests no significant differences associated with these distinct modes of debrief. The most important factor determining the outcome of the debrief is that the instructor creates a safe and structured context that is inclusive enough to allow different types of learners to have their voices heard (Hall & Tori, 2017; Grant, Robinson, Catena, Eppich, & Cheng, 2018).

For contributors in professional schools, the importance of debriefing centres on its ability to provoke critical self-reflection, which translates into enhanced professional awareness and proficiency. Bogo (Chapter 4) reflects on the notion of holistic competence in the field of social work, arguing that it comprises both procedural competencies, which can be observed, and meta-competencies, which include subconscious tendencies, assumptions, and cognitive biases that are internal to the student and often hidden to the instructor or evaluator. She recommends combining techniques of reflection-in-action and reflection-on-action to access this concealed layer of student self-awareness. LeBlanc (Chapter 11) views the value of debriefing in medical education in similar terms: debrief stimulates reflection, identifies performance gaps, and sparks the formulation of improvements. She dwells on the question of timing, mobilizing evidence to suggest that terminal (summative) feedback is more effective than concurrent (formative) feedback for enhancing skill development.

Other contributors view debriefing in more utilitarian terms, as a tool that provides feedback and provokes improvement at the level of pedagogical intervention. Brynen (Chapter 2) understands debriefing as a two-way process that allows the instructor the opportunity to underscore key lessons for students, and to gather feedback from the perspectives of those who lived it, which can in turn be used to enhance the pedagogical delivery in future iterations. Forcese (Chapter 3) relies on a process of constant feedback that allows him to circle back and address areas where students are struggling. Gentry (Chapter 8) presents a series of simulations in the material sciences and engineering that prioritize nimbleness and flexibility. What she describes in her chapter is an iterative model of delivery, with structured opportunities to revise and refine the mechanics of the simulation based on student feedback both within and across semesters. In these cases, debrief is used as much for the instructor as for the student, a mechanism of embedding feedback as a mode of constant tinkering that allows the instructor to be more responsive to the student learning experience.

One practice that has been embraced across disciplines as a means of deepening self-reflection is having students rotate through multiple roles in a single simulation so they can experience the same interaction from divergent perspectives. In social work, Bogo (Chapter 4) explains that she requires students to each play the role of the practitioner, the client, and the evaluator in order provoke introspection. Using an example from earth and environmental science, Ryan and Gass (Chapter 10) argue that learning is heightened when students rotate among the three simulation roles of mining company, community member, and environmental expert because they learn to appreciate the diversity and complexity of positions involved in localized, public scientific debates. Sundararajan (Chapter 5) created a role-play seminar for upper-year business students that exposes them to various roles within a series of corporate communications crises, enabling students to gain both an inside-out and outside-in perspective on how corporate organs cope with crisis. In his words: "this cross-pollination of roles, perspectives, and contexts will begin to provide glimpses of the big picture and the minutiae surrounding organizational practices and strategies" (p. 91).

Alyshah Kaba (Chapter 15) presents the most sustained engagement with debriefing. Operating in the field of interprofessional health education, she advocates for shifting the scale of debriefing from an individual to a collective emphasis: "In a debrief on role clarity following an IP [interprofessional] simulation, the focus of the debrief moves from team members being individually competent in their given roles (i.e., giving medications, airway management, etc.) to understanding all roles on the team and how they work together to achieve a common collective goal" (p. 257). This emphasis on collective competencies is particularly important in team settings, where debriefing is uniquely positioned to draw awareness to a phenomenon of group conformity bias where individuals prefer to remain silent rather than question the majority consensus. She offers specific recommendations for how to enhance debrief effectiveness, including scheduling the debrief right after the simulation, allotting twice the amount of time allocated to the simulation itself, and bringing in specialized educators to co-lead the debrief alongside the instructor or team member. These suggestions challenge long-standing practices within SBE, particularly the emphasis on individual versus collective debrief, and the tendency to tack on debrief rather than allot it the conceptual and temporal space needed to draw out key learning outcomes.

Step 6: Evaluating Learning Outcomes

An evaluation is an appraisal of the simulation designed to identify its strengths and weaknesses and measure whether the simulation succeeded in achieving its core learning objectives. The evaluation phase provides an opportunity for instructors to gauge whether the simulation achieved its pedagogical goals and to incorporate improvements to ensure greater success in future iterations (Murray et al., 2008). Despite these efforts, there remains an absence of systematic assessments of whether the specific learning outcomes associated with a simulation exercise have been achieved (Raymond & Usherwood, 2013).

Much has been written about how to best create robust assessments of simulated learning exercises. While the descriptive literature on case-study approaches to doing SBE is quite rich in the social sciences, few studies rigorously investigate the precise mechanisms through which such techniques impact student learning. The three most popular methods are contrasting participation in a simulation with academic performance (Chasek, 2005), using comparisons with control groups of students who do not participate in the simulation (Krain & Lantis, 2006), and employing pre- and post-surveys to identify students' self-perceived changes in learning (Schnurr, De Santo, & Green, 2014).

Raymond (Chapter 1) champions control groups as the gold standard for rigorous and robust evaluation of learning outcomes and warns against relying on student self-reported learning outcomes. Other contributors express reservations about implementing such a structured experimental design (Forcese and Donohue, Chapter 3), while still others mobilize self-reported learning outcomes in quite illuminating ways (see, e.g., Brynen, Chapter 2, and Chamberlain, Chapter 7). Paetkau

(Chapter 9) reviews the value of various methodological approaches employed in physics education, exposing their relative merits and deficiencies, including the use of course grading as a proxy for learning. He also explores the potential value of emerging technologies like eye-capture, which offer exciting opportunities for charting the precise course of student learning trajectories.

The evaluation of learning outcomes is most developed in the health sciences. LeBlanc (Chapter 11) narrates the evolution of this knowledge base, which began with descriptive studies, progressing through justification studies to more comprehensive measures. These more recent evaluations suggest that the success of a simulation hinges on its instructional design, underscoring the need for thoughtful and reflexive practice on the part of practitioners. LeBlanc shines a light on how important robust scholarship is for exposing what works and what does not within simulations. She relays results from one meta-study showing that only half of the studies comparing SBE with a control group were able to demonstrate additional gains in knowledge, critical thinking, or perceived clinical confidence or satisfaction, underlining how little we really know about how and whether simulations actually enhance student learning (Cant & Cooper, 2010).

Conclusion: Operationalizing the Simulation Life Cycle

The contributors to this volume hail from 13 disciplines spanning the social, natural, and health sciences. Comparing their analytical engagement with simulations drawn from their individual teaching practice underscores the range and variation within simulation-based teaching in higher education. Despite these differences, what is common among all of these perspectives is a deep commitment to an iterative approach that is nimble and flexible enough to respond to student feedback and instructor observation. The simulation life cycle is designed to embrace this flexibility. It is designed not to be prescriptive, but rather to capture what we believe to be the core components of SBE in an iterative process that allows for constant revision and refinement. It is designed not to be linear; some practitioners will encounter these steps out of order, or will collapse multiple steps into one, or skip steps altogether. What is most crucial to this approach to SBE is the constant tinkering and tweaking. The project cycle presents the simulation as an experiment, one that requires multiple iterations, sustained self-reflection, and rigorous evaluation of learning outcomes in order to accomplish its intended goals. Such requirements can prove daunting for the uninitiated. This volume is designed as a resource for those wishing to engage with or enhance their use of simulation-based teaching, for when it is done right it is a tool that can create profound learning opportunities for learners and instructors alike.

REFERENCES

Asal, V., & Blake, E.L. (2006). Creating simulations for political science education. *Journal of Political Science Education*, 2(1), 1–18. https://doi.org/10.1080/15512160500484119

Association for Experiential Education. (2015). *What is experiential education?* Retrieved from http://www.aee.org/what-is-ee

Auchter, E., & Kriz, W.C. (2014). The impact of business simulations as a teaching method on entrepreneurial competencies and motivation – A review of 10 years of evaluation research in entrepreneurship education. *Proceedings of the 45th Conference of the International Simulation and Gaming Association, Dornbirn*, 55–65. Available at https://s3.amazonaws.com/

Balsiger, J. (2015). Transdisciplinarity in the classroom? Simulating the co-production of sustainability knowledge. *Futures, 65*, 185–194. https://doi.org/10.1016/j.futures.2014.08.005

Bonk, C.J., & Graham, C.R. (2006). *The handbook of blended learning: Global perspectives, local designs*. San Francisco, CA: Pfeiffer.

Bradley, G., Whittington, S., & Mottram, P. (2013). Enhancing occupational therapy education through simulation. *British Journal of Occupational Therapy, 76*(1), 43–46. https://doi.org/10.4276/030802213x13576469254775

Brynen, R. (2010). (Ending) civil war in the classroom: A peacebuilding simulation. *PS: Political Science and Politics, 43*(1), 145–149. https://doi.org/10.1017/S1049096510990719

Cant, R.P., & Cooper, S.J. (2010). Simulation-based learning in nurse education: Systematic review. *Journal of Advanced Nursing, 66*(1), 3–15. https://doi.org/10.1111/j.1365-2648.2009.05240.x

Carnes, M. (2014). *Minds on fire: How role-immersion games transform college*. Cambridge, MA: Harvard University Press.

Chasek, P.S. (2005). Power politics, diplomacy and role playing: Simulating the UN Security Council's response to terrorism. *International Studies Perspectives, 6*(1), 1–19. https://doi.org/10.1111/j.1528-3577.2005.00190.x

Dengler, M. (2008). Classroom active learning complemented by an online discussion forum to teach sustainability. *Journal of Geography in Higher Education, 32*(3), 481–494. https://doi.org/10.1080/03098260701514108

Dennison, S.T. (2011). Interdisciplinary role play between social work and theater students. *Journal of Teaching in Social Work, 31*(4), 415–430. https://doi.org/10.1080/08841233.2011.597670

Dieleman, H., & Huisingh, D. (2006). Games by which to learn and teach about sustainable development: Exploring the relevance of games and experiential learning for sustainability. *Journal of Cleaner Production, 14*(9), 837–847. https://doi.org/10.1016/j.jclepro.2005.11.031

Dohaney, J., Brogt, E., Kennedy, B., Wilson, T., & Lindsay, M. (2015). Training in crisis communication and volcanic eruption forecasting: Design and evaluation of an authentic role-play simulation. *Journal of Applied Volcanology, 4*(1), 1–26. https://doi.org/10.1186/s13617-015-0030-1

Druckman, D., & Ebner, N. (2007). Onstage or behind the scenes? Relative learning benefits of simulation role-play and design. *Simulation & Gaming, 39*(4), 465–497. https://doi.org/10.1177/1046878107311377

Ellett, R.L., Esperanza, J., & Phan, D. (2016). Fostering interdisciplinary thinking through an international development case study. *Journal of Political Science Education, 12*(2), 128–140. https://doi.org/10.1080/15512169.2015.1071263

Fernandez, R., Parker, D., Kalus, J., Miller, D., & Compton, S. (2007). Using a human patient simulation mannequin to teach interdisciplinary team skills to pharmacy students. *American Journal of Pharmaceutical Education, 71*(3), 51. https://doi.org/10.5688/aj710351

Fowler, M.R. (2009). Culture and negotiation: The pedagogical dispute regarding cross-cultural simulations. *International Studies Perspectives, 10*(3), 341–359. https://doi.org/10.1111/j.1528-3585.2009.00380.x

Gordon, S., & Thomas, I. (2018). "The learning sticks": Reflections on a case study of role-playing for sustainability. *Environmental Education Research, 24*(2), 172–190. https://doi.org/10.1080/13504622.2016.1190959

Grant, V., Robinson, T., Catena, H., Eppich, W., & Cheng, A. (2018). Difficult debriefing situations: A toolbox for simulation educators. *Medical Teacher, 40*(7), 703–712. https://doi.org/10.1080/0142159X.2018.1468558

Hall, K., & Tori, K. (2017). Best practice recommendations for debriefing in simulation-based education for Australian undergraduate nursing students: An integrative review. *Clinical Simulation in Nursing, 13*(1), 39–50. https://doi.org/10.1016/j.ecns.2016.10.006

Hoekstra, A.Y. (2012). Computer-supported games and role plays in teaching water management. *Hydrology and Earth Systems Science, 16*(8), 2985–2994. https://doi.org/10.5194/hess-16-2985-2012

Honey, M.A., Hilton, M.L., & National Research Council. (Eds.). (2011). *Learning science through computer games and simulations.* Washington, DC: The National Academies Press.

Iten, G. (2015). *Impact of visual simulations in statistics: The role of interactive visualizations in improving statistical knowledge.* Basel: Springer.

Jabbarifar, T. (2009). The importance of classroom assessment and evaluation in educational system. *Proceedings of the 2nd International Conference of Teaching and Learning, Malaysia, 1–9.* Retrieved from https://pdfs.semanticscholar.org/db8c/4d3e5e56aa80c220e17eeac25183acaaa43d.pdf

Jones, F., Passos-Neto, C.E, & Braghiroli, O. F.M. (2015). Simulation in medical education: Brief history and methodology. *Principles and Practice of Clinical Research, 2*(1), 56–63

Jorm, C., Roberts, C., Lim, R., Roper, J., Skinner, C., Robertson, J., ... Osomanski, A. (2016). A large-scale mass casualty simulation to develop the non-technical skills medical students require for collaborative teamwork. *BMC Medical Education, 16,* 83. https://doi.org/10.1186/s12909-016-0588-2

Krain, M., & Lantis, J.S. (2006). Building knowledge? Evaluating the effectiveness of the Global Problems Summit simulation. *International Studies Perspectives, 7*(4), 395–407. https://doi.org/10.1111/j.1528-3585.2006.00261.x

Levine, A.I., DeMaria, S., Jr., Schwartz, A.D., & Sims, A.J. (Eds.). (2014). *The comprehensive textbook of healthcare simulation.* New York: Springer.

Littlejohn, A., & Pegler, C. (2007). *Preparing for blended e-learning.* New York: Routledge.

Murdoch, N.L., Bottorff, J.L., & McCullough, D. (2014). Simulation education approaches to enhance collaborative healthcare: A best practices review. *International Journal of Nursing Education Scholarship, 10*(1), 307–321. https://doi.org/10.1515/ijnes-2013-0027

Murray, C., Grant, M.J., Howarth, M.L., & Leigh, J. (2008). The use of simulation as a teaching and learning approach to support practice learning. *Nurse Education in Practice, 8*(1), 5–8. https://doi.org/10.1016/j.nepr.2007.08.001

Nestel, D., Kelly, M., Jolly, B., & Watson, M. (Eds.). (2018). *Healthcare simulation education: Evidence, theory and practice.* Hoboken, NJ: Wiley-Blackwell.

Palangas, J.C., Maxworthy, J.C., Epps, C.A., & Mancini, M.E. (Eds.). (2014). *Defining excellence in simulation programs.* Philadelphia, PA: Wolters Kluwer.

Paschall, M., &Wüstenhagen, R. (2012). More than a game: Learning about climate change through role play. *Journal of Management Education, 36*(4), 510–543. https://doi.org/10.1177/1052562911411156

Prinsen, G., & Overton, J. (2011). Policy, personalities and pedagogy: The use of simulation games to teach and learn about development policy. *Journal of Geography in Higher Education, 35*(2), 281–297. https://doi.org/10.1080/03098265.2010.548508

Raymond, C., & Usherwood, S. (2013). Assessment in simulations. *Journal of Political Science Education, 9*(2), 1–11. https://doi.org/10.1080/15512169.2013.770984

Rivera, S.W., & Simons, J.T. (2008). Engaging students through extended simulations. *Journal of Political Science Education, 4*(3), 298–316. https://doi.org/10.1080/15512160802202805

Russ, T., & Drury-Grogan, M. (2013). Assessing the impact of a business communication simulation on students' self-perceptions. *Communication Quarterly, 61*(5), 584–595. https://doi.org/10.1080/01463373.2013.822404

Schedlbauer, J.L., Nadolny, L., & Woolfrey, J. (2016). Practising conservation biology in a virtual rainforest world. *Journal of Biological Education, 50*(3), 320–328. https://doi.org/10.1080/00219266.2015.1117510

Schnurr, M.A., De Santo, E., & Craig, R. (2013). Using a blended learning approach to simulate the negotiation of a multilateral environmental agreement. *International Studies Perspectives, 14*(2), 109–120. https://doi.org/10.1111/j.1528-3585.2012.00470.x

Schnurr, M.A., De Santo, E., & Green, A. (2014). What do students learn from a role-play simulation of an international negotiation? *Journal of Geography in Higher Education, 38*(3), 401–414. https://doi.org/10.1080/03098265.2014.933789

Schnurr, M.A., De Santo, E., Green, A. & Taylor, A. (2015). Investigating student perceptions of learning within a role-play simulation of the Convention on Biological Diversity. *Journal of Geography, 114*(3), 94–107. https://doi.org/10.1080/00221341.2014.937738

Serby, T. (2011). Willing suspension of disbelief: A study in online learning through simulation, and its potential for deeper learning in education. *Liverpool Law Review, 32*, 181–195. https://doi.org/10.1007/s10991-011-9095-z

Shellman, S.M., & Turan, K. (2006). Do simulations enhance student learning? An empirical evaluation of an IR simulation. *Journal of Political Science Education, 2*(1), 19–32. https://doi.org/10.1080/15512160500484168

Smolinski, R., & Kesting, P. (2012). Transcending the classroom: A practical guide to remote role plays in teaching international negotiation. *Negotiation Journal, 28*(4), 489–502. https://doi.org/10.1111/j.1571-9979.2012.00353.x

Tawalbeh, L.I., & Tubaishat, A. (2014). Effect of simulation on knowledge of advanced cardiac life support, knowledge retention, and confidence of nursing students in Jordan. *Journal of Nursing Education, 53*(1), 38–44. https://doi.org/10.3928/01484834-20131218-01

Tivener, K.A., & Gloe, D.S. (2015). Designing simulations for athletic training students through interprofessional teaching collaboration. *Athletic Training Education Journal, 10*(3), 249–255. https://doi.org/10.4085/1003249

Watson, C.E., & Hagood, T.C. (Eds.). (2018). *Playing to learn with Reacting to the Past: Research on high impact, active learning practices.* New York: Palgrave Macmillan.

Willhaus, J. (2010). Interdepartmental simulation collaboration in America: Exploring partnerships with other disciplines. *Clinical Simulation in Nursing, 6*(6), e231–e232. https://doi.org/10.1016/j.ecns.2010.02.011

Wright, A., Moss, P., Dennis, D., Harrold, M., Levy, S., Furness, A., & Reubenson, A. (2018). The influence of a full-time, immersive simulation-based clinical placement on physiotherapy student confidence during the transition to clinical practice. *Advances in Simulation, 3*(1), 3. https://doi.org/10.1186/s41077-018-0062-9

Youde, J. (2008). Crushing their dreams? Simulations and student idealism. *International Studies Perspectives, 9*(3), 347–355. https://doi.org/10.1111/j.1528-3585.2008.00340.x

SECTION ONE

Social Sciences

1 Framing Chapter: The Utility of Simulations in the Social Sciences

CHAD RAYMOND

Simulations were first employed in the social sciences as a means of understanding complex processes that did not lend themselves to experimental testing, and their use soon expanded in scope to include the teaching of social science disciplines themselves. Simulations have numerous benefits as social science teaching tools. First and foremost, they place students in a model of reality that allows them to directly experience unfamiliar phenomena that are frequently studied in the social sciences, such as the exchange of economic goods, the choices of bureaucratic actors, and the effects of cultural norms. This experiential environment allows students to gain comprehension through continuous empirical observation of behaviour (Enterline & Jepsen, 2009). In a simulation, there is little to no separation between observing an event, formulating a hypothesis about that event, and being able to test that hypothesis. This allows simulation participants to more deeply engage with and reflect upon the world that actually surrounds them. Traditional pedagogies, in contrast, require that students passively receive information from the instructor, work to understand it, and then, after some delay, attempt to apply it. When such a delay exists, the content being learned becomes less relevant to students, resulting in decreased interest and a diminished acquisition of content knowledge and skills (Dorn, 1989). Simulations can also improve students' motivation to learn by exposing them to information in a way that heightens their interest in understanding it. The presence of challenging but achievable goals, uncertain outcomes, and prompt feedback in simulations can lead to feelings of autonomy and accomplishment (Giovanello, Kirk, & Kromer, 2013; Shellman & Turan, 2006; Sørebø & Hæhre, 2012).

Simulations embody several broad principles that are inherent to the social sciences. The first of these is the notion that the world can be modelled. In simulations, small sets of relatively simple rules encapsulate the fundamentals of given phenomena that cannot be reduced to a laboratory experiment. Rules might take the form of a decision-making architecture, institutional arrangements, or even random events, but they do not have to mirror every possible aspect of the concept being studied, just those that are needed to bring the concept to life in a manner that makes it easier for students to understand (Asal, Raymond, & Usherwood, 2015).

The ability of simulations to manifest the abstract as lived experience also facilitates teaching students that human interactions, especially at a mass scale, are frequently ambiguous, complex, and non-linear (Asal, Raymond, & Usherwood, 2015). Although a simulation is a stripped-down representation of reality bound by explicit rules, its outcomes can vary from participant to participant and from iteration to iteration. Simulations often demonstrate how the behaviour of groups can differ from that of individuals and that theoretical predictions based on statistical probabilities will never achieve complete certainty. These are important lessons for social science students to learn.

But perhaps most importantly for social science instructors, simulations can serve as vehicles for integrating different forms of learning. Research, preparation, rhetoric, and consensus-building become understood by students as vital to the lives they create both within and outside of simulated events. Students become better equipped to discuss, debate, and analyse, and the purposive interaction with others that occurs in simulations can generate a sense for them of what life is like for people whose norms, socio-economic statuses, or political attitudes are very different from their own (Adcock, 2010; Cuhadar & Kampf, 2014).

The starting point for incorporating any simulation into one's teaching is to identify the learning process that the simulation is supposed to generate. The worst mistake an instructor can make in this regard is to use a simulation without having specific reasons for doing so. The reason might be for students to understand something as specific as "Why did Hitler invade Poland?" or as general as "Do people make rational economic decisions?" but if learning outcomes do not drive the use of simulations, they become little more than diversions, without substantial pedagogic value.

Learning outcomes commonly associated with simulations in the social sciences typically fall into three categories: the acquisition of domain knowledge; the development of negotiation, research, writing, and other skills; and emotional or attitudinal self-awareness (Raymond & Usherwood, 2013). The overlapping nature of these outcomes makes it all the more important to clarify for students why they will be participating in a simulation. Simulations are unusual events for most students, who can find them to be, especially in their initial phases, confusing, awkward, and emotionally overwhelming. While some might be eager to participate, others will hesitate or even resist. Instructors should recognize a simulation's potentially disruptive effects and communicate to students that their meta-cognitive interpretations of their experience matter more than who might "win" or "lose." Transparency about how participation in a simulation will be assessed, as well as bracketing the exercise with related assignments, can help to minimize these tensions. Creating clarity about intended outcomes helps guide everyone involved and increases the probability that a simulation will achieve its desired learning objectives.

Simulations are often context dependent, and instructors should ensure that a simulation's design is compatible with desired learning outcomes. While some simulations have features that make them useful for teaching a wide variety of subject material, others have much more limited applicability (Kollars & Rosen, 2016). For example, a simulation in which students engage in negotiation might focus on imparting bargaining skills in an abstract environment, or it might be grounded in a public-policy-making scenario with the intent of teaching students about the formal rules and procedures of institutions. Similarly, the suitability of a simulation is often driven by the constraints of time, space, and technology. A simulation that plays out over a period of several weeks requires a far heavier investment than one that takes only a single class session. Some simulations require a limited number of participants, while others can be scaled upward or downward at will.

Just as learning outcomes need to be brought to the attention of students before a simulation begins, so too do the relationships between what happens in the simulation and methods of assessment (Raymond & Usherwood, 2013). The best forms of assessment act as components of a feedback loop that supplement the signals that students obtain from experiencing the simulation. Students' comprehension and recall are strengthened when they can communicate their conclusions to others and receive responses in return. Assessment mechanisms can also encourage students to engage in higher-order thinking about their experience. For example, a reflective exercise can enable a student to benchmark their memory of the simulation against both the scholarly literature on the subject and the actions of fellow students. Assessment can thus contribute to – and be informed by – a wide set of feedback processes, such as classroom debate, comparisons of theoretical premises with actual historical events, and debriefing discussions.

University faculty are increasingly expected to demonstrate that students achieve institutionally determined learning outcomes. It is therefore crucial for instructors to empirically validate whether a simulation was useful, and why. The gold standard for measuring the pedagogical effectiveness of simulations is, as in the social sciences generally, the use of treatment and control groups. A control group can be created by running a simulation in some rather than all sections of a course, or making a simulation an optional experience for some students in a single section. However, given the institutional settings that many university faculty operate in – small class enrolments, infrequent course rotations, and lack of institutional support – it is often difficult to engage in this type of experimental research. Even when the institutional environment permits it, the ethical dilemma of using different teaching methods, with potentially varying degrees of efficacy, on separate groups of students remains. Methods of measurement that can serve as an alternative to a randomized, controlled experiment include pre- and post-simulation comparisons of exam scores, analytical essays, and meta-cognitive assignments. An instrument used to gauge student learning in a course can be administered again in a subsequent semester after a simulation has been added. At minimum, the evaluation of whether simulations enable students to efficiently achieve desired learning outcomes should aim to extend beyond relying exclusively on student self-reports, given that people are remarkably bad at gauging what and how they have learned (Maznick & Zimmerman, 2009; Nestler & von Collani, 2008).

Once an instructor has aligned intended learning outcomes with assessment mechanisms, attention can turn to matters that are logistical in nature, such as the best number of simulation participants, time requirements, the availability of necessary physical space, and how a simulation will relate to students' course grades. While the most useful simulations are ones that can be deployed in a variety of circumstances, instructors should consider how a given context might fundamentally affect the students' experience and their ability to achieve desired outcomes. For example, a simulation that is intended to examine how norms of reciprocity are expressed by different cultures might work with just two players or as many as one hundred, but as its scale changes, so might each participant's range of actions. Likewise, longer simulations allow for deeper exploration of a topic, but they are also more likely to displace other, perhaps vitally important, content from a course. Online simulations offer the option of preserving classroom time for other activities while still being an effective tool for learning (Zappile, Beers, & Raymond, 2017). By including students enrolled in other academic programs or at other universities, online simulations can also present participants with a more nuanced and diverse experience than is sometimes possible in the physical classroom. Commercially available, off-the-shelf products – whether for use in face-to-face or online environments – can reduce the burdens of managing simulations for instructors.

Finally, the use of simulations does not have to be, and probably should not be, a solitary endeavour. There is probably a faculty member or instructional designer at your university who can help identify which features of a simulation best fit your needs or troubleshoot a simulation that did not perform as expected. And there are undoubtedly faculty in your discipline teaching elsewhere who can share their successes and failures with simulations. Communicating with others contributes to the development of better teaching practices, which can only increase students' understanding of the social sciences.

REFERENCES

Adcock, A.B., Duggan, M.H., Watson, G.S., & Belfore, L.A. (2010). The impact of content area focus on the effectiveness of a web-based simulation. *British Journal of Educational Technology, 41*(3), 388–402. https://doi.org/10.1111/j.1467-8535.2009.00947.x

Asal, V., Raymond, C., & Usherwood, S. (2015). War, peace and everything in between: Simulations in international relations. In J. Ishiyama, W. Miller, and E. Simon (Eds.), *Handbook of teaching and learning in political science and international relations* (pp. 304–314). Cheltenham, UK: Edward Elgar Publishing.

Cuhadar, E., & Kampf, R. (2014). Learning about conflict and negotiations through computer simulations: The case of PeaceMaker. *International Studies Perspectives, 15*(4), 509–524. https://doi.org/10.1111/insp.12076

Dorn, D.S. (1989). Simulation games: One more tool on the pedagogical shelf. *Teaching Sociology, 17*(1), 1–18. https://doi.org/10.2307/1317920

Enterline, A.J., & Jepsen, E.M. (2009). Chinazambia and Boliviafranca: A simulation of domestic politics and foreign policy. *International Studies Perspectives, 10*(1), 49–59. https://doi.org/10.1111/j.1528-3585.2008.00357.x

Giovanello, S.P., Kirk, J.A., & Kromer, M.K. (2013). Student perceptions of a role-playing simulation in an introductory international relations course. *Journal of Political Science Education, 9*(2), 197–208. https://doi.org/10.1080/15512169.2013.770989

Kollars, N., & Rosen, A. (2016). Bootstrapping and portability in simulation design. *International Studies Perspectives, 17*(2), 202–213. https://doi.org/10.1093/isp/ekv007

Maznick, A.M., & Zimmerman, C. (2009). Evaluating scientific research in the context of prior belief: Hindsight bias or confirmation bias? *Journal of Psychology of Science and Technology, 2*(1), 29–36. https://doi.org/10.1891/1939-7054.2.1.29

Nestler, S., & von Collani, G. (2008). Hindsight bias, conjunctive explanations, and causal attribution. *Social Cognition, 26*(4), 482–93. https://doi.org/10.1521/soco.2008.26.4.482

Raymond, C., & Usherwood, S. (2013). Assessment in simulations. *Journal of Political Science Education, 9*(2), 1–11. https://doi.org/10.1080/15512169.2013.770984

Shellman, S.M., & Turan, K. (2006). Do simulations enhance student learning? An empirical evaluation of an IR simulation. *Journal of Political Science Education, 2*(1), 19–32. https://doi.org/10.1080/15512160500484168

Sørebø, Ø., & Hæhre, R. (2012). Investigating students' perceived discipline relevance subsequent to playing educational computer games: A personal interest and self-determination theory approach. *Scandinavian Journal of Educational Research, 56*(4), 345–362. https://doi.org/10.1080/00313831.2011.594609

Zappile, T., Beers, D., & Raymond, C. (2017). Promoting global empathy and engagement through real-time problem-based simulations: Outcomes from a policymaking simulation in post-earthquake Haiti. *International Studies Perspectives, 18*(2), 194–210. https://doi.org/10.1093/isp/ekv024

2 Gaming "Fog and Friction": How Simulations Enhance Student Understanding of Complex Policy Processes in Political Science

REX BRYNEN

Lectures and assigned readings can suggest to students that policy processes are like flow charts: neat, technocratic, and transparently rational. In practice, of course, policymaking is rather messier and much more uncertain than this. Information is always imperfect. Multiple interests and perspectives – some of them supportive, some opposing, and others only partially overlapping – are at play. Coalition-building involves compromises. Organizations engage in institutional rivalries, stove-piping, and other bureaucratic pathologies. Many public policy and planning issues are so-called "wicked problems" (Rittel & Weber, 1973, p. 155), which do not lend themselves to blindly applying cookie-cutter solutions and instead require much deeper analysis of the social complexity involved.

Carl von Clausewitz, the famous Prussian military theorist, argued that military operations are hampered by both imperfect information and the difficulties of moving and commanding large military institutions – elements that are often labelled "fog" and "friction," respectively. The interaction of these adds to risk and uncertainty. Strategy and tactics must be prepared to accommodate the unexpected. Much of my teaching is not about war, but rather insurgency, negotiations, complex peace operations, humanitarian assistance, politics, and development. However, Clausewitz's observations ring equally true here too.

In emphasizing this balance of skill, risk, and uncertainty, Clausewitz pointed to a gaming analogy, noting that "in the whole range of human endeavours, war most resembles a game of cards" (Clausewitz, 1984, p. 86). Indeed, at around the same time that he was writing on military doctrine, the Prussian military itself was the first to adopt serious games as a major pedagogical (and, later, planning) tool. In 1811, Georg Leopold von Reiswitz invented the first modern wargaming (*kriegsspiel*) rules. These were subsequently further developed by his son, Georg Heinrich Rudolf von Reiswitz. Chief of the Prussian General Staff Karl von Mueffling, upon first playing *kriegsspiel*, enthusiastically commented, "It's not a game at all! It's training for war. I shall recommend it enthusiastically to the whole army" (Vego, 2012, p. 5).

Gaming techniques were thus introduced for Prussian professional military education, and some contemporary observers suggested that the skills and insights developed through wargaming played a significant role in Prussia's victory in the Franco-Prussian War (1870–71). Prussian military success, coupled with the introduction of more flexible, less cumbersome game procedures (*free kriegsspiel* relying on umpire adjudication, in contrast to rules-based *rigid kriegsspiel*), led to the widespread adoption of wargaming in armies around the world from the late nineteenth century onward (Perla, 1990) and up to the present day (Caffrey, 2018).

This chapter will explore the use of games and simulations to explore the "fog and friction" inherent in complex policy processes. It will draw heavily upon my own experience of teaching about peace and humanitarian operations to illustrate the value in such use. The key point to be made throughout concerns the value of immersive learning (whether in political science or other disciplines), in which students gain a better understanding of policy processes by dealing with them in a simulated environment – an environment characterized by some of the pressures and constraints that shape real-world decision-making.

Before going any further, however, a few words of caution are in order. The broader literature points to games-based learning as a moderately effective pedagogical tool. It is not, however, a silver bullet. Games that are badly designed, badly taught/facilitated, or badly integrated into course curriculum can have poor, even negative, effects on learning. This point was well illustrated by an extensive debate regarding the international relations simulation *Statecraft*, and whether "virtual worlds are dangerous" (Carvalho, 2014) or whether the poor educational outcomes that Carvalho reported should instead be attributed to suboptimal employment and curriculum integration rather than simulation design (Keller, 2014; Saiya, 2017). There is also an opportunity cost to time spent gaming in the classroom, in that this is lost to other forms of teaching such as lectures or class discussions. Games-based learning thus needs to justify its place on a usually crowded syllabus, rather than instructors assuming that "gamification" is always the way to go. The number of students, the amount of time available, and even the layout of the classroom or the availability of other resources are all important considerations.

Many justifications of using games and simulations for teaching point to differences in learning styles, and the value of experiential learning. Some of these, it must be said, rest on rather weak theoretical and methodical foundations, since is doubtful that the typologies of "learning styles" one so often sees cited in the literature on gaming actually exist (Coffield, Moseley, Hall, & Ecclestone, 2004; Pashler, McDaniel, Rohrer, & Bjork, 2008). However, it is the case that such techniques can provide a welcome break from the potential monotony of classroom lectures and engage participants in different kinds of ways – an "intellectual cross-training" of sorts. In the case of negotiations and policymaking, ample research shows that role-playing in games and simulations increases knowledge about issues and processes (Schnurr, De Santo, & Craig, 2013), improves the ability of participants to understand the motives and viewpoints of others (Green & Armstrong, 2011), and improves forecasting of conflict outcomes (Green, 2002). In my own classes, there is also considerable value in having students make the sort of mistakes – poor understanding of underlying cultural, political, and social dynamics; weak coordination; falling prey to organizational blinkers; failure to appreciate second- and third-order effects; and hubris – that can afflict real-life peacebuilding efforts (Aoi, de Coning, & Thakur, 2007; Autesserre, 2014; Brynen, 2014a).

Negotiation Simulations

The easiest form of classroom policy simulation is a negotiations exercise wherein students take the role of various contending stakeholders and try to reach agreement on an issue in dispute. At their simplest, such exercises require little more than briefing materials for each participant and team, and the time and mechanisms for negotiation and other interaction. They can be held within a single session or spread over multiple sessions through a term. In the history and the humanities, the very successful *Reacting to the Past* (RTTP) series provides pre-written resource guides for both instructors and students on more than a dozen topics, including the evolution of Athenian democracy, the Catholic Church trial of Galileo, and the independence of India – with even more in development (RTTP, 2018). Mark Carnes's excellent book *Minds on Fire* (2014) highlights the value and techniques of role-immersion of this sort in college classrooms, focusing on the RTTP series. In my own field, both Kumar (2009) and the United States Institute of Peace (2018) offer a series of ready-made negotiation simulations focusing on ethnic disputes, interstate conflict, peace negotiations, and similar topics.

Key Considerations

As simple as they are to prepare and conduct, negotiation simulations do present a number of challenges.

The first is whether to use real-life situations or create fictional issues for students to address. Using actual policy challenges allows one ready access to a large amount of background history and supporting data, and may make the simulation seem much more real and relevant to participants (Gill, 2015). On the other hand, participants may find it difficult to think outside of historical solutions or existing paradigms (McMahon & Miller, 2012). Inventing fictional scenarios makes it more difficult to provide supporting information, since all of this needs to be invented and may make the simulation seem rather artificial. On the other hand, it does allow an instructor to build a variety of desired elements into the simulation in order to best match the activity to learning objectives (Brynen, 2019), albeit at the cost of extra time and effort.

A second question is whether to hold sessions entirely face to face, use digital means (email, chat software, voice and video), or some combination of the two (Ben-Yehuda, Levin-Banchik, & Naveh, 2015). Simulation platforms are readily available to fully support digital communications between participants, with all text communications available for an instructor to view (ICONS Project, 2018). However, readily available course support software, email, chat, and video applications such as Skype can also be used. Using technology to enhance or support student interaction can add additional flexibility, allowing students to engage outside of the classroom and regular class hours. It provides useful insight into the importance of careful precision in formal written communications, especially during consultations and negotiation – something that is important for students to understand if they ever go on to future policy-relevant careers. It may also make it easier for shy or anxious students, who might be prone to "freeze up" if faced with public speaking before a group, to contribute more effectively.

A third issue is how to make sure that students reflect their social, political, and organizational perspectives accurately. If this is not done, they may treat the process as a purely technocratic problem-solving exercise, making concessions that would never be offered in real life and agreeing to "solutions" that would be deeply problematic. Tangible elements can be introduced into the simulation to provide constraints (e.g., regarding available material resources) or feedback mechanisms (e.g., some gauge of how popular their current negotiating position would be with their primary constituents). Initial player briefings can outline goals and constraints, although if this is done too stringently it risks limiting player creativity too much. Ideally, players should internalize their respective viewpoints, engaging in the simulation narrative because it seems authentic and sensible, not merely because of extrinsic limits and reward. Indeed, Perla and McGrady (2011) argue that serious games "work" precisely because of this sort of narrative immersion. Having students prepare their own background research prior to beginning the simulation can be useful in this regard, but it can also be very useful for the instructor to provide briefing materials that work to reinforce or amplify the different perspectives of players.

A final issue with negotiation simulations is how "clean" or "noisy" they should be. Should players be free to focus their full attention on the issue at hand, or should they be deliberately distracted with ongoing events and complications? Gill (2015) argues that distractions and injects during negotiation simulations inhibit learning by preventing participants from thoughtfully contemplating the issues at hand. Much depends, of course, on how the policy issue is addressed in the real world. Multilateral environmental negotiations and ceasefire negotiations during a civil war take place in rather different settings. If we are to accurately reflect fog and friction in situations such as the latter, however, it is important that participants are placed under pressure, find themselves affected by unexpected or exogenous events, and must deal with "two-level games" (Putnam, 1988) whereby they are seeking to maintain internal support against possible critics and rivals at the same time that they are engaged in negotiation with outside parties.

Structured Games: Digital and Manual Games

In negotiation simulations, the simulation is what the participants make of it. Although there may be briefings, an agenda, and schedule, the interaction between players and the offers and counter-offers they make are largely self-determined. Conversely, in a structured policy game (much like *rigid kriegsspiel*), the dynamics of policymaking must be built into formal rules and procedures. Such rules are themselves a model of policy (or other) dynamics – an exercise in embedded social science, as it were – and so formal rulesets can help students think through how different variables shape policy dynamics. Indeed, for that very reason, games-based training is used at the Central Intelligence Agency to help analysts better understand the key drivers of social, political, and military outcomes (Hall, 2017).

Ready-Made Games

In some cases, it may be possible to use or modify a pre-existing game. Digital games tend to require less player knowledge of the rules, because the software typically has players select their actions from a menu of permissible choices and thereby prevents them from violating the rules.

However, digital games are also very difficult to tweak for particular purposes. While their graphic presentations, potential complexity, and interface can be appealing, it may also be the case that the underlying causality and social model at work are relatively opaque to players, or even to the instructor. Such "black boxing" can stand in the way of effective learning. Finally, there can be issues of platform compatibility: no instructor wants to be bogged down troubleshooting computer issues when students have trouble running assigned software packages.

With regard to manual games, unless you are teaching military history (Sabin, 2012) or medicine (e.g., GridlockED, 2018) it is unlikely you will find many existing commercial games that address serious topics in a useful way. Some (Romano, 2014) have suggested using or modifying simple hobby games (such as *Diplomacy* or *Risk* in the field of international relations), but frequently these are very removed from the actual conduct of global affairs as to be potentially problematic – unless students are being asked to critique how they diverge from their real-life counterparts.

I have used a few pre-existing digital games in conjunction with teaching: *Stop Disasters!* (United Nations Office for Disaster and Risk Reduction, 2007), *Inside the Haiti Earthquake* (Inside Disaster, 2010), and *Mission Zhobia* (GCSP, UNITAR, ACCORD, USIP, & PeaceNexus Foundation, 2017). None of these offer much complexity, but rather focus on narrow aspects of humanitarian and development policy: resources scarcity and opportunity cost; stakeholder perceptions and the lived experience of disaster relief; and the challenges of negotiation and cross-cultural communication, respectively. However, because all three are relatively quick and simple online browser games that students can play from home, they are a fun and painless way to highlight a few issues that are more fully addressed elsewhere in the course. In other words, in making them part of the course curriculum, there is an implicit cost/benefit analysis at work: while they make only a modest contribution to learning, they also make only limited demands on students. Students are typically eager to try them out, and willingly discuss their lessons, strengths, and weaknesses afterwards in online class discussions.

I have also, at times, assigned "unrealistic" simulations – notably the "banana republic" developing-country game *Tropico* (various editions, 2001–18) – as a critical review assignment. In this case, students are asked to critique the game's shortcomings, and in so doing think about how it diverges for real-world processes (Brynen, 2012). Interestingly, while this was intended to offer a more innovative and interesting assignment than the usual paper or book review, the novelty of playing an entertainment game in an academic setting and thinking about it from a political science/development studies perspective was rather unsettling for some students. They preferred to complete a more traditional assignment instead, perceiving it to be the "safer" bet.

Designing Your Own

If existing commercial, off-the-shelf digital or tabletop games are not appropriate for classroom use, it may be possible to design a new game that addresses the topic at hand. Here, digital games are rarely an option: they either require considerable technical expertise to build or require an expensive outside developer to do so. Design and play-testing are also very time-consuming. Consequently, this option of purpose-built software is usually only practical for large organizations (such as the US military, currently the world's largest consumer of digital simulations and e-learning games).

Manual games are less costly to develop, since they require few resources beyond readily available game pieces, a word processor, and a printer. However, while simple games intended to quickly illustrate basic principles might be relatively quickly developed, more sophisticated games are rather more of a challenge. Game procedures and rules must be kept parsimonious and elegant so as to not confuse non-gamers. Moreover, the system must be rigorously playtested to expose shortcomings. Never underestimate the ability of a student to "break" your game system, losing sight of game objectives as they exploit aspects of the game system to achieve "victory" no matter how unrealistic their mode of play might be (Frank, 2011). On the other hand, students are (in my experience, at least) enthusiastic playtesters for games in development, and happy to contribute their own ideas on how a design can be improved.

The case of *AFTERSHOCK: A Humanitarian Crisis Game* provides an example. This board game was designed to teach both university students and professional audiences (entry-level aid workers, as well as military personnel and diplomats) about the major challenges of humanitarian assistance and disaster relief, with particular emphasis on needs assessment, logistics planning, and the challenges of inter-agency coordination. The game has been quite successful, used by various universities and the US Army, and to train humanitarian aid workers and peacekeepers. Our own surveys found that over 90% of both university students and trainee aid workers report that the game does a good or very good job of illustrating issues relating to coordination and humanitarian assistance, and a similar proportion thought it should be used in future courses (PAXsims, 2018). Smaller studies by the Canadian military (Dixson & Ma, 2018) and German medical students (Drees, Geffert, & Brynen, 2018.) found similar positive results.

Still, developing a "player-proof" design that would teach the intended lessons (and minimize unintended ones) within two hours of play was a considerable effort. Initial design followed consultation with both aid experts and fellow game designers as part of a "game lab" session at the 2012 Connections professional wargaming conference. Two years of development and playtesting then followed, followed by many months of graphic design of production-quality components. Moreover, as with most manual games, *AFTERSHOCK* still works best with an instructor or game facilitator running the sessions, both to clarify rules/procedures and to add commentary to the many teachable moments that arise during gameplay. This limits the number of participants it can be used with, requiring either multiple experienced players to facilitate several simultaneous games, a series of games spread over the term to accommodate all interested students, or other adaptations (Brynen, 2017a).

The "fog" of *AFTERSHOCK* is provided by random event cards, coupled with conditions that are not fully evident until needs assessments are undertaken. Some friction is also provided via the event cards, and much is also provided by the challenges of coordination among players. By trial and error, we have also found that not fully explaining all rules at the outset of the game both speeds gameplay (participants are not preoccupied with remembering everything) and replicates some of the confusion of a major natural disaster. We also usually play the game to a timer, deterring participants from over-studying their moves ("analysis paralysis"), and again adding to an immersive sense of emergency (Brynen, 2015). When it was used at the Centro Conjunto para Operaciones de Paz de Chile (Chilean Joint Peacekeeping Operations Centre) to train military and civilian personnel, instructors "add[ed] an extra layer of confusion to the game by deliberately triggering the building's earthquake alarm system one hour into play," whereupon players were "immediately evacuated by members of staff dressed as firemen and instructed to wait outside until the all-clear had been given" (Mac-namara & Blessley, 2015). However, context is everything. However valuable stress is in a game about a catastrophic earthquake, it would be rather inappropriate in a game examining urban public transport policy or wetland ecological diversity.

To go back to a point made earlier in this chapter, everything depends on educational objectives and practical constraints. It is certainly possible to design a more limited manual game with fewer dynamics at play with somewhat less effort, if the point is quick play and illustration of only a few key points. Nevertheless, a wise instructor will treat structured game design as an experiment. It will take a few classroom iterations before a purpose-designed game does exactly what is intended, in a way that students finding engaging and playable.

Hybrid Approaches

Hybrid gaming approaches, as the name suggests, couple the flexibility of negotiation simulations and *free kriegsspiel* adjudication with the structure of some more rigorous rules-based game systems.

One example of this is *The Impact of Colonial Incorporation into the Global Capitalist System on Pre-Colonial Subsistence Agriculture!*, a game that I ran for many years in an introductory-level course on developing countries (Brynen, 2014b). Because it was used in a large introductory class with six hundred students, the technique used was to have five student volunteers play the game on stage in front of their classmates during a 50-minute period. Because of this presentation format, and in order to maintain student attention, it was run like a game show, complete with *The Price Is Right* and *Jeopardy!* theme music, exaggerated presentation style, crowd applause, contestant interviews, and other appropriate gimmicks. Participants are free to negotiate arrangements among themselves, but the underlying game rules encourage a gradual concentration of landholdings and increased rural class stratification. While players play to the best of their ability, the game show host/ instructor is also able to both nudge the game in appropriate directions and draw out lessons for learning purposes. The event uses up only one classroom period, but provides material that is referenced in class lectures (and sometimes in the exam) for the remainder of the course.

While this hybrid game involves only a small number of actual players (with most of the class watching), other games make it possible to engage quite large groups as active participants. An example of this is the *Brynania* peacebuilding simulation, which has been conducted annually at McGill University since 1998 (Brynen, 2010). The simulation typically involves over one hundred participants, playing up to 12 hours a day, for a full week (during the regular term, no less) and has become perhaps the largest simulation of its kind outside of the military. This extraordinary student commitment of time and intellectual energy for what is a non-compulsory part of the course highlights the enthusiasm and engagement that games-based learning can generate. The basic approach is certainly viable with much smaller groups, however, and during much shorter periods of time.

The *Brynania* simulation explores seven or more months of an ongoing civil war and peace process in a fictional country. Students assume the roles of government officials, rebel and opposition groups, civil society activists, neighbouring countries, United Nations agencies, aid organizations, the media, and the international community. Much of the simulation consists of negotiations and other interaction, conducted face to face or via email, telephone, messaging, and/or video chats, as students prefer. When students wish to take an action, they simply inform Control what they want to do, and at that point (in classic *free kriegsspiel* style) the instructor makes an adjudication decision as to how long it might take, what additional resources it might take, and what effects the action might have. Military actions are a little more structured, in that the location and status of all units are tracked on a master map, and each has an appropriate offensive and defensive combat rating (the value of which is known to military players only in general terms). The humanitarian assistance component is the most rules-based part of the simulation; in order to calculate civilian losses from food insecurity and disease in more than two dozen different regions of the country, a spreadsheet and associated algorithms are used to track the destruction of social and economic infrastructure; access; population displacement; aid resources allocated; and organizational effectiveness (derived from the quality of student play). Gameplay is continuous during the day (when one hour of real time represents on day of simulation time) and turn-based overnight (the game clock is advanced to the next month, in preparation for another day of play).

The *Brynania* simulation is unabashedly filled to the brim with both fog and friction. The information provided to players is often only partial, skewed to the ideological viewpoint or organizational perspective of their role, and not always completely accurate. Additional information is scattered across an array of supporting materials, including from Wikipedia-type entries, simulation articles, and media coverage. Only Control is omniscient – players are told only what their actor might reasonably know. Of course, a great deal of imperfect information is generated by the players as the game goes on, whether through deliberate deceit, imperfect communication, failure to coordinate with or consult key stakeholders, or stress and a lack of time – all reflecting the sort of real-world challenges of this kind of policy environment. The information flow can be daunting. Simulation participants collectively send some 10–15,000 emails during the week, in addition to other methods of communication. Actors are forced to manage and prioritize information flows.

It is also the case that not everything functions with complete efficiency – Brynania, after all, is a less developed country in the grip of a debilitating civil war. Some of this inefficiency is introduced by Control, but again much of it occurs because of the large number of player interactions. Deployment of a (simulated) United Nations peacekeeping force, for example, typically requires multi-sided discussions with the various belligerents; initial assessment by the UN Department of Peacekeeping Operations of what is needed and feasible (not always the same thing); the negotiation and approval of a United Nations Security Council resolution (with all the inevitable politics involved); negotiations with troop-contributing countries; drawing up a concept of operations, rules of engagement, and deployment plan; securing specialist personnel (engineers, helicopter lift, and so forth); coordinating the transportation of peacekeeping personnel and their equipment, often in conjunction with third countries; and so forth. It can also involve complications arising from exogenous factors (weather, labour disruption, crises elsewhere). By encountering these many inevitable points of friction, most of them self-inflicted, students soon learn why it may take four months of more for a peacekeeping mission to deploy significant numbers of personnel to a conflict area and 10 months to reach peak deployment (Rappa, 2016). Similarly, implementing an aid program in the simulation might involve needs assessment, consultation with local actors, project design, finding a willing donor, securing local permissions, and physically accessing the site – all in an unstable political environment where personnel are at risk and violence can force a sudden rethink or suspension of operations.

As Table 2.1 shows, a post-simulation survey conducted in 2011 showed the exercise to be highly effective in conveying such real-world complications (Brynen, 2013). Students also showed some self-reported improvement in the skills that contribute to managing the fog and friction of complex policy process, such as time management, communications, empathy, and leadership.

An outside study of the simulation by Nowlan (2016) also reported very positive learning effects, arguing that the approach was well suited for teaching about other complex decision-making processes, such as business management.

Additional analysis of our own survey results suggested that gender had little or no impact on educational effectiveness, nor did most personality traits (such as introversion/extraversion) – with the exception of "need for closure." Not surprisingly, students who disliked ambiguity and preferred definitive outcomes found the fog and friction of the simulation disquieting. This was not necessarily a negative: to the

Table 2.1. Survey results from *Brynania* simulation

Question	Average response (7-point scale; 1 = "no, not at all," 4 = neutral, 7 = "yes, completely")
Did the simulation increase your understanding of the material covered in the class readings?	5.51
Did the simulation increase your understanding of organizational processes involved in politics?	5.80
Did the simulation increase your understanding of the bureaucracy involved in politics?	5.87
Did the simulation increase your understanding of the real-world constraints on peace operations?	6.20
Was the simulation more useful to you than a week of readings on the subject?	6.18
Was the simulation more useful to you than a week of lectures on the subject?	5.98

extent that the simulation accurately reflects the stress of work in conflict-affected countries, it is probably preferable that students who like a well-ordered work environment be shorn of any excessively romantic or idealized notions of what aid work and peacebuilding can be like before they make major career decisions. Other studies (Youde, 2008; Schnurr, De Santo, & Green, 2014) have also noted the value of simulations in addressing such student preconceptions.

Matrix Games

A rather simpler approach to hybrid gaming is provided by matrix gaming. In matrix games, there are few or no pre-established rules – instead, players simply declare what action they wish to take, what effect it will have, and why they believe the action will be successful. Other participants then weigh in with additional arguments. After a short period of discussion, the odds of success are assessed and the outcome is determined – typically, either by applying positive or negative modifiers to the roll of two dice (+1 for each solid pro argument, -1 for each con), or by aggregating the probability estimates offered by each player (Brynen, Mouat, & Fisher, 2017a; Curry, Engle, & Perla, 2018; Mouat, 2018). As simple as this process seems, it has been used in real-world settings as diverse as security planning for the Vancouver Olympics; professional military education in the US Army; diplomatic assessment by the UK Foreign Office; doctrine and capability analysis by the UK Ministry of Defence and Canadian Department of National Defence; multi-agency planning in Australia; and training analysts at the Central Intelligence Agency.

Matrix games intrinsically produce both a narrative and a highly analytical summary of variables that enable or impede success. They work well when addressing complex issues where multiple stakeholders have both complementary and competitive objectives. They are also surprisingly quick to design (less than a day, in some cases) and run (usually a game can be completed in three hours, or even played by email in distributed or asynchronous mode). I have used them in the classroom to teach students about the political-military campaign in Iraq against Daesh (the so-called "Islamic State") and about a possible future conflict between Israel and Hizbullah in Lebanon; to train human rights workers about mass atrocity prevention (Brynen, 2016); and to explore future diplomatic challenges in the South China Sea with Canadian diplomats (Brynen, 2017b). Indeed, such is their utility as a simple technique for eliciting innovation, crowdsourcing ideas, and structuring discussion that the UK Defence Science and Technology Laboratory asked Tom Mouat, Tom Fisher, and me to develop an introductory *Matrix Game Construction Kit* (See Brynen, Mouat, & Fisher, 2017a, 2017b) that could be used by the military, government agencies, and others wanting to try out the approach. Key to matrix games' success is the way the game system forces participants to think about causal relationships, both in terms of what effects actions might have, and identification of which variables might shape policy effectiveness – and does so in a way that is intuitive and easy to learn.

Some Final Thoughts

This chapter has made the argument that serious games and simulations can – when designed and used appropriately – be a helpful tool for teaching about the "fog and friction" of complex policy processes. It is important to note, however, that no game or simulation truly teaches by itself. Effective debriefing is essential (Crookall, 2010), both to reinforce the points that students should be learning and to make sure that they do not take away any incorrect lessons. Any game, after all, involves abstraction and simplification to be playable. Certain game dynamics are necessarily weak representations of the real world – and it is important that students are aware of this. In *AFTERSHOCK*, for example, the United Nations is played by a single player, rather than as the collection of sometimes semi-autonomous institutions and specialized agencies that it really is. In *Brynania*, players often come away with the view that face-to-face diplomacy is always the most effective, in part because the simulation cannot fully capture organizational complexity, bureaucratic inertia, and the importance of written statements and policies. The simulation might also lead them to overestimate the ease of policy communications – President Donald Trump's Twitter feed notwithstanding, most inter-agency or international communication requires more effort, process, and consultation than simply text messaging a classmate or posting a statement online. Because of this, it is important the debriefing be a two-way process: not only should the instructor underscore key lessons for students, but they should also use it as an opportunity to perceive the simulation from the players' perspectives, and thereby correct any shortcomings.

Second, when introducing simulations into or designing them for the classroom, start modestly and build from there. As noted earlier about playtesting, trial and error is your friend as you refine a game design. However, precisely because there will be inevitable shortcomings in initial iterations, it is important not to overreach. Prolific commercial and professional wargame designer James Dunnigan (2000) once laid down the two essential rules of effective game design: "keep it simple" and "plagiarize." It is important not to fall into the trap of adding complexity to the point that you lose or confuse your players. Established gaming techniques can be very useful when designing new games.

Finally, having students design their own games can also be a very effective educational tool. In doing so, student designers are required to think about key elements, drivers, and relationships in the process they are modelling (Sabin, 2012). Indeed, some research suggests that game design may have even greater positive educational impact than game playing (Druckman & Ebner, 2007). Having taught a course on simulation design, I can certainly attest to this: my students' designs have been insightful enough to attract interest from both commercial game publishers and professional wargamers. However, do not underestimate the amount of work this requires – it typically involves far more hands-on discussion time with students than is the case in the typical lecture or seminar course.

REFERENCES

Aoi, C., de Coning, C., & Thakur, R. (Eds). (2007). *Unintended consequences of peacekeeping operations*. Tokyo: United Nations University Press.

Autesserre, S. (2014). *Peaceland: Conflict resolution and the everyday politics of international intervention*. Cambridge: Cambridge University Press.

Ben-Yehuda, H., Levin-Banchik, L., & Naveh, C. (2015). *World politics simulations in a global information age*. Ann Arbor: University of Michigan Press.

Brynen, R. (2010). (Ending) civil war in the classroom: A peacebuilding simulation. *PS: Political Science and Politics*, *43*(1), 145–149. https://doi.org/10.1017/S1049096510990719

Brynen, R. (2012, April 29). A digital "banana republic" and teaching the political economy of development. *PAXsims*. Retrieved from https://paxsims.wordpress.com/2012/04/29/a-digital-banana-republic-and-teaching-the-political-economy-of-development/

Brynen, R. (2013, June 29). Assessing simulation effectiveness in *Brynania*. *PAXsims*. Retrieved from https://paxsims.wordpress.com/2013/06/29/assessing-simulation-effectiveness-in-brynania/

Brynen, R. (2014a). Teaching about peace operations. *International Peacekeeping*, *21*(4), 1–10. https://doi.org/10.1080/13533312.2014.946740

Brynen, R. (2014b, February 4). *The Impact of Colonial Incorporation into the Global Capitalist System on Pre-Colonial Subsistence Agriculture* (the game). *PAXsims*. Retrieved from https://paxsims.wordpress.com/2014/02/04/the-impact-of-colonial-incorporation-into-the-global-capitalist-system-on-pre-colonial-subsistence-agriculture-the-game/

Brynen, R. (2015, December 31). Facilitating *AFTERSHOCK*. *PAXsims*. Retrieved from https://paxsims.wordpress.com/2015/12/31/facilitating-aftershock/

Brynen, R. (2016, June 3). Exploring matrix games for mass atrocity prevention and response. *PAXsims*. Retrieved from https://paxsims.wordpress.com/2016/06/03/exploring-matrix-games-for-mass-atrocity-prevention-and-response/

Brynen, R. (2017a, March 18). McGill *AFTERSHOCK* tournament 2017. *PAXsims*. Retrieved from https://paxsims.wordpress.com/2017/03/18/mcgill-aftershock-tournament-2017/

Brynen, R. (2017b, October 10). Diplomatic challenges in the South China Sea. *PAXsims*. Retrieved from https://paxsims.wordpress.com/2017/10/10/diplomatic-challenges-in-the-south-china-sea/

Brynen, R. (2019). Crisis in Galasi: Simulating the urban dimensions of religious conflict. In M. Dumper (Ed.), *Contested holy cities: The urban dimensions of religious conflict*. London: Routledge.

Brynen, R., Mouat, T., & Fisher, T. (2017a). *MaGCK Matrix Game Construction Kit user guide*. Retrieved from https://www.thegamecrafter.com/games/pdf-only-magck-matrix-game-construction-kit-user-guide

Brynen, R., Mouat, T., & Fisher, T. (2017b). *Matrix Game Construction Kit*. Retrieved from https://www.thegamecrafter.com/games/magck-matrix-game-construction-kit

Caffrey, M. (2018). *On wargaming: How wargaming has shaped the past and could shape the future*. Annapolis: Naval War College Press.

Carnes, M. (2014). *Minds on fire: How role-immersion games transform college*. Cambridge, MA: Harvard University Press.

Carvalho, G. (2014). Virtual worlds can be dangerous: Using ready-made computer simulations for teaching international relations. *International Studies Perspectives, 15*(4), 538–57. https://doi.org/10.1111/insp.12053

Clausewitz, C. (1984). *On war*. Princeton, NJ: Princeton University Press.

Coffield, F., Moseley, D., Hall, E., & Ecclestone, K. (2004). *Learning styles and pedagogy in post 16 learning: A systematic and critical review*. London, UK: Learning and Skills Research Centre.

Crookall, D. (2010). Serious games, debriefing, and simulation/gaming as a discipline. *Simulation & Gaming, 41*(6), 898–920. https://doi.org/10.1177/1046878110390784

Curry, J., Engle, C., & Perla, P. (Eds.) (2018). *The Matrix Games Handbook: Professional applications from education to analysis and wargaming*. Retrieved from http://www.wargaming.co/professional/details/matrixgameshandbook.htm

Dixson, M., & Ma, F. (2018). *Investigation into wargaming methods to enhance capability based planning* [Report No. DRDC-RDDC-2017-D147]. Ottawa: Defence Research and Development Canada. Retrieved from http://cradpdf.drdc-rddc.gc.ca/PDFS/unc293/p806080_A1b.pdf

Drees, S., Geffert, K., & Brynen, R. (2018). Crisis on the game board – a novel approach to teach medical students about disaster medicine. *GMS Journal for Medical Education, 35*(4), 1–5. https://doi.org/10.3205/zma001192

Druckman, D., & Ebner, N. (2007). Onstage or behind the scenes? Relative learning benefits of simulation role-play and design. *Simulation & Gaming, 39*(4), 465–497. https://doi.org/10.1177/1046878107311377

Dunnigan, J. (2000). *Wargames handbook: How to play and design commercial and professional wargames* (3rd ed). iUniverse.

Frank, A. (2011). Gaming the game: A study of the gamer mode in educational wargaming. *Simulation & Gaming, 43*(1), 118–132. https://doi.org/10.1177/1046878111408796

GCSP, UNITAR, ACCORD, USIP, & PeaceNexus Foundation. (2017). *Mission Zhobia* [Computer simulation game]. Rotterdam: &ranj.

Gill, N. (2015). *Inside the box: Using integrative simulations to teach conflict, negotiation and mediation*. Retrieved from http://www.css.ethz.ch/content/dam/ethz/special-interest/gess/cis/center-for-securities-studies/pdfs/Inside_the_Box-Gill.pdf

Green, K. (2002). Forecasting decisions in conflict situations: A comparison of game theory, role-playing, and unaided judgement. *International Journal of Forecasting, 18*(3), 321–344. Https://doi.org/10.1016/S0169-2070(02)00025-0

Green, K., and Armstrong, J.S. (2011). Role thinking: Standing in other people's shoes to forecast decisions in conflicts. *International Journal of Forecasting, 27*(1), 69–80. https://doi.org/10.1016/j.ijforecast.2010.05.001

GridlockED. (2018). *Home*. Retrieved from https://www.gridlockedgame.com

Hall, C. (2017, June 22). The art and craft of making board games for the CIA. *Polygon*. Retrieved from https://www.polygon.com/2017/6/22/15730254/cia-board-game-volko-ruhnke-coin-series-gmt-games

ICONS Project. (2018). *ICONS Project*. Retrieved from https://www.icons.umd.edu.

Inside Disaster. (2010). Inside the Haiti earthquake. Retrieved from http://insidedisaster.com/haiti/experience

Keller, J. (2014). Misusing virtual worlds can be dangerous: A response to Carvalho. *International Studies Perspectives, 15*(4), 558–563. https://doi.org/10.1111/insp.12087

Kumar, R. (Ed.). (2009). *Negotiating peace in deeply divided societies*. Los Angeles: SAGE Publications.

Mac-namara, F., & Blessley, C. (2015, April 28). *AFTERSHOCK* at the Chilean Joint Peacekeeping Operations Center. *PAXsims*. Retrieved from https://paxsims.wordpress.com/2015/04/28/aftershock-at-the-chilean-joint-peacekeeping-operations-center/

McMahon, S., & Miller, C. (2012). Simulating the Camp David negotiations: A problem-solving tool in critical pedagogy. *Simulation & Gaming, 44*(1), 134–150. https://doi.org/10.1177/1046878112456252

Mouat, T. (2018, July 30). Adjudication in matrix games. *PAXsims*. Retrieved from https://paxsims.wordpress.com/2018/07/30/adjudication-in-matrix-games/

Nowlan, N. (2016). *From* Brynania *to business: Designing an evidence-based business education simulation from an exploration of a blended real-time model* [Doctoral dissertation]. Retrieved from Simon Fraser University Summit Institutional Repository (Identifier etd9811).

Pashler H., McDaniel M., Rohrer D., & Bjork R. (2008). Learning styles: Concepts and evidence. *Psychological Science in the Public Interest, 9*(3), 105–119. https://doi.org/10.1111/j.1539-6053.2009.01038.x

PAXsims. (2018). *AFTERSHOCK*. *PAXsims*. Retrieved from https://paxsims.wordpress.com/aftershock/

Perla, P. (1990). *The art of wargaming: A guide for professionals and hobbyists*. Annapolis: Naval Institute Press.

Perla, P., & McGrady, E. (2011). Why wargaming works. *Naval War College Review, 64*(3), article 8. Retrieved from https://digital-commons.usnwc.edu/nwc-review/vol64/iss3/8

Putnam, R. (1988). Diplomacy and domestic politics: The logic of two-level games. *International Organization, 42*(3), 427–460. https://doi.org/10.1017/s0020818300027697

Rappa, R. (2016, September 7). The challenges of full deployment on UN peace operations. *Global Peace Operations Review*. Retrieved from https://

peaceoperationsreview.org/thematic-essays/the-challenges-of-full
-deployment-on-un-peace-operations/

Reacting to the Past. (2018). *Published games*. Retrieved from https://reacting
.barnard.edu/games

Rittel, H., and Webber, M. (1973). Dilemmas in a general theory of planning.
Policy Sciences, 4(2), 155–169. https://doi.org/10.1007/BF01405730

Romano, D. (2014, September 7). Teaching international relations through
popular games, culture and simulations. *PAXsims*. Retrieved from https://
paxsims.wordpress.com/2014/09/07/teaching-international-relations
-through-popular-games-culture-and-simulations-part-1/

Sabin, P. (2012). *Simulating war: Studying conflict through simulation games*. London,
UK: Continuum Books.

Saiya, N. (2017). How dangerous are virtual worlds really? A research note
on the *Statecraft* simulation debate. *Social Science Computer Review, 35*(2),
287–296. https://doi.org/10.1177/0894439315607019

Schnurr, M.A., De Santo, E., & Craig, R. (2013). Using a blended learning
approach to simulate the negotiation of a multilateral environmental
agreement. *International Studies Perspectives, 14*(2), 109–120. https://doi.org
/10.1111/j.1528-3585.2012.00470.x

Schnurr, M.A., De Santo, E., & Green, A. (2014). What do students learn from
a role-play simulation of an international negotiation? *Journal of Geography
in Higher Education, 38*(3), 401–414. https://doi.org/10.1080/03098265.2014
.933789

United Nations Office for Disaster and Risk Reduction. (2007). *Stop disasters!*
[Computer simulation game]. Retrieved from http://www.stopdisastersgame
.org

United States Institute of Peace. (2018). *Simulations*. Retrieved from https://
www.usip.org/simulations.

Vego, M. (2012). German wargaming. *Naval War College Review, 65*(4), article
10. Retrieved from https://digital-commons.usnwc.edu/nwc-review
/vol65/iss4/10

Youde, J. (2008). Crushing their dreams? Simulations and student idealism.
International Studies Perspectives, 9(3), 348–356. https://doi.org/10.1111
/j.1528-3585.2008.00340.x

3 Simulation Learning in the Legal Academy

LAURA K. DONOHUE AND CRAIG FORCESE

Introduction

Law is a learned profession, the practice of which requires skill. It might reasonably follow that law schools should be attentive to both scholarly and applied legal training. Debates in North American legal education, however, are often heated on this topic, with the distinction between podium courses and clinical education often institutionally entrenched. There is more than a little bit of snobbery on both sides.[1]

Skills-training, in the minds of some scholars, conflates with trade school – something that law schools are not. Those supporting this position state that the purpose of legal education is to convey a deep theoretical foundation and to sharpen students' analytical skills. The normative objective is to cultivate the ability to think, to reason – and to educate the students about the difficult questions that permeate law. The actual practice of law can be learned on the job, once students go to a law firm.

This approach provokes eye-rolling among many clinicians, who well know the importance of being able to practise law. What good is theoretical or substantive knowledge if it cannot be applied? Yes, knowledge and theory matter, but the goal, they argue, is to produce good lawyers. And so we see increasing emphasis in both Canada and the United States on experiential learning as the new wave in clinical education.

No less disparaging is the profession itself, which often bemoans the inability of early law graduates to perform even the simplest technical functions. Squeezed by client pressures to reform a billable-hour form of legal practice, it imagines salvation if law schools would only produce "practice-ready lawyers" for law firms – that is, people firms do not need to train in the basic mechanics of legal practice. Many students, whose core preoccupation is entry into a competitive legal marketplace, share the clinicians' and profession's scepticism.[2]

Dissatisfied with the resulting pedagogical inertia reflected in these debates, each of us has reached for alternative forms of teaching responsive to the merits of both sides. Neither of us believes that law school pedagogy has reached a pinnacle of perfection, with its last meaningful reform being the case-based, Socratic method developed at Harvard Law School in the late 19th century.[3] Neither of us believes that law school is all about trade skills. Nor do we believe that law school is all about substantive data-dumping or pure theoretical enquiry. Both of us believe that some skills are eternal. Still, we think that in the substance/ skills debate, law schools can eat their cake and have it too. And to that end, both of us have reached for simulations in our own classrooms and jointly as an effective means to "put into practice" substantive principles, while also addressing practical skills that would be difficult to develop in conventional classrooms.

In this chapter, we describe what we have done and have learned. In part 1, Craig Forcese outlines how he has weaved micro-simulations into "flipped" large-format (sometimes 90-students plus) and smaller, seminar-style doctrinal courses. In part 2, Laura Donohue and Craig Forcese describe a course at Georgetown Law Centre, Washington, DC, built around a large-scale multi-day simulation in national security law. Both approaches blur the lines between podium and clinical teaching, giving students a more holistic approach to legal education, which will prepare them with the skills needed immediately upon graduation as well as generate a deeper understanding of the law.

Part 1: Flipping with a Purpose

A law school course is a congested activity. Modern society is complex, as are the laws that govern it. Gone is the era in which most laws applicable in lightly governed societies were generated in stately "common law" precedent, derived incrementally over time from judicial decisions. Yet even as the world becomes more complex, hours in the classroom have not increased in law degree programs.

The Challenge

There are still "training wheel" law courses – typically in the first year. Here, students might expend a full-year course learning to derive principles from case law in common-law-heavy courses, like contracts or torts. But for other subjects – the subjects we both teach – the volume of substantive material is a serious challenge, as is the increased level of abstraction (especially in constitutional law). The sedate pace of the case-based method would expose students to a tiny fraction of core materials in most modern law courses.

Meanwhile, the diversity of skills that a modern lawyer might reasonably expect to deploy has increased. Listening, writing, and communication skills are now no longer assumed – students need training to develop these essential skills. Surveys in the profession suggest that basic "talking to humans" skills are valued above all others, and rarer than one might assume (IAALS, 2018).[1] Likewise, students need to be trained in reflexive ethical practice. These are not skills that will ever stale-date. Students also should develop some ability to navigate the bureaucratic process of practising law. These processes are idiosyncratic and can vary with time, place, and area of speciality. They are not, therefore, quite as universal as the other skills noted above. The pedagogical emphasis here, therefore, should be training students on "how to figure out these processes." Indeed, figuring things out is the uber skill of any lawyer.

The "Flip" and "Micro-Simulations"

Reconciling these challenges led one of us (Forcese) to discard every one of his traditional lecture and conventional Socratic-heavy courses in favour of "flipped teaching." And even in more classic-discussion-based seminar courses, he has moved to a quasi-flip. (In the balance of this section, first-person pronouns refer to Forcese.)

With a colleague, I have discussed elsewhere the mechanics of "flipping" a law school course (Sankoff & Forcese, 2015). The "flip" boils down to this: a professor off-shores passive learning lecture material to pre-recorded lectures, reviewed in advance of class by students. Commentators debating flipped teaching often focus on this off-shoring process, which in my case is done mostly through a conventional podcast platform now supplemented in some classes by videos.[5] But this common preoccupation with the technology and mechanics of a flip is a mistake. The core purpose of the flip is to free up classroom time for active learning. The challenge (considerable in a large class) is to then use that repurposed classroom time usefully, in a manner that does not replicate the flipped material but rather enhances understanding of it through different pedagogical means. Repeating an off-shored lecture would be an invitation to declining class attendance, and purposeless.

Active learning in a flipped classroom may take various forms. After some trial and error, I chose to build active learning exercises around practical lawyering skills, creating a loose focus on "experiential education." One of us (Donohue) has proposed a spectrum of "experiential learning" techniques that are used in doctrinal law classes (i.e., classes focused on substantive rules of law): hypotheticals; doctrinal problems; single exercises; extended/continuing exercises; tabletop exercises; and simulations (Donohue, 2013).

By liberating 40 hours of teaching time per course once consumed by delivery of doctrinal materials, I have focused on variants of these techniques, blending together hypotheticals, doctrinal problems, single events, and extended exercises. However, in each of these exercises, I have included a simulation aspect. Having students role-play through "micro-simulations" has allowed me to professionalize the exercises in order to enhance their "real-world" significance for lawyers-in-training. The specific tools I have used are as follows:

- "Two-minute" simulations, or "slow-motion" Socratic: Classic law school Socratic-style instruction involves repeated questioning of students, who are often "cold called" without warning from a class list and usually asked to analyse some discrete component of a legal issue, concept, or case or respond to a hypothetical problem. It is not passive learning, in the sense that students are compelled to participate. Carefully questioned, they themselves pull "signal" from "noise" in the materials. But poorly done, it is an intimidating, alienating experience that leaves students scrambling to identify proverbial trees in the material but without guidance as to the scope of forests. It lacks, therefore, a narrative arc, with definitive expla-nations and overviews. That may work for a classic common law course like contracts. It does not, however, work if one wishes to understand, for example, the state's capacity to engage in intrusive surveillance.

  Still, if the narrative arc is off-shored to podcast lectures, Socratic teaching can supplement passive learning by testing students' absorption and understanding of materials covered in the pre-recorded lectures, even in doctrinally complex courses. And careful forethought can minimize the intimidation factor. Simulation-style role-playing aids these objectives. I have adopted two practices in Socratic-style teaching. First, I project onto the screen a short hypothetical fact problem, raising legal issues I wish to probe. Depending on its complexity, I then give students two to five minutes to react and discuss with their near fellows. They are motivated to do so, because they know I will then revert to the class list and call on this. This is, however, a "warm call." They have had time to digest and discuss – I am not measuring their reaction time. Moreover, since they have digested and discussed, they have higher confidence in their responses. But to further "professionalize" the discussion, I often ask students to role-play. In teaching public international law, for instance, I regularly ask one set of students to respond to the question as if they were advising the legal advisor at Global Affairs Canada. Other students will be asked to respond as if they were acting for another state. This micro-role-playing surfaces legal uncertainty, as each student is incentivized to contemplate weaknesses in legal argumentation from different perspectives. It also frees students from the prison of "there must be only one right answer," a source of considerable anxiety if they fear making a mistake. There are stronger and weaker arguments. My operating theory is that a student dealt a weak hand because their state is more clearly in the wrong is less likely to feel they are "wrong" in presenting those weaker arguments. This would be a more paralyzing prospect if students were participating in their personal capacity, and risked being judged by their peers as individuals rather than simulated representatives.

- "Ten-minute" simulations, or insta-research projects: In the active learning classroom, I also have space to walk students through how to solve technical, more bureaucratic issues in the practice of law, again using role-playing. These "10-minute simulations" are built into a larger storyline. For instance, in Administrative Law, I present students with two simulated client files at the outset of the course. The entire course is built around resolving these clients' administrative law problems. At one juncture, developments in the case oblige the filing of a federal access to information request – something to which most students have no exposure, and that in fact has not been covered anywhere else in the course. Playing "senior partner," I instruct my students (role-playing "articling students," a status they will have in their first year of practice): they are to explain to me, in exact detail, how they will file the access request for our client. They have 10 minutes of classroom time to prepare this oral briefing, which at the simulated billing rate costs the client $50. Again, they may work with their peers, after which I resort to my class list and call upon one or more students.
- Role-played legal writing projects: I continue the simulated client file in a third exercise, this time conducted as out-of-class writing assignments. Rather than simply obliging students to prepare an essay on a given legal topic, I ask them to address hypothetical legal issues in forms of legal writing requiring some specialized skill. These include a memorandum to me, the senior partner, and a draft notice of application for judicial review. The students must submit

the exercises in role – indeed, I have a "senior partner" Gmail account specifically for this purpose. And I respond with feedback, in role. That feedback focuses not just on substance but also on the technical form of the written materials. Moreover, because I am role-playing a senior partner whose reputation as a tyrant I have shared with students, they expect the comments to be blunt. Most appear to accept this critical feedback with more grace than might otherwise be the case because of the role-played nature of the exercise. (I also communicate that is it better to receive this feedback from a simulated senior partner now than the real thing a year from now. This creates, I believe, a sense of shared solidarity: that I am training them for "the real world.")

• Bundled role-played written and oral advocacy projects: In a smaller-format class, where I can lavish more attention on individual students, I have expanded simulated learning to include both out-of-class writing done in a simulated context and a follow-up simulated oral advocacy exercise. Oral advocacy, in law school, takes many forms. It is, however, often confined to specialized trial or appellate-style advocacy courses (many of which do involve simulations). I wished, however, to weave together this skills-training with substantive materials in a policy-heavy course in national security law. Because I have considerable experience appearing before parliamentary committees, I played to that experience and built simulated learning around "how to write effective parliamentary briefs" and "how to present in front of a parliamentary committee." Students assume the role of experts on a given legal policy issue, in a half-dozen "hearings" held during class time over the semester. With instruction, students prepare short briefs in advance, upon which I give feedback. The four or five students appearing as experts during any given "hearing" have five minutes (ruthlessly enforced) to present their testimony (all video recorded). Thereafter, the other students in the class, assembled as parliamentarians on the committee, ask questions of the witnesses. This converts a conventional discussion-based seminar into a format where every student is obliged to participate, again behind the cloak of a comforting, imagined role. And they learn a form of short-form writing and oral advocacy that transfers well to many other facets of professional life. For feedback, I narrate comments over the video of each student's testimony and share the video file with the student – most students have never seen how they present. (My view is that simulated learning must include reflective feedback, or will otherwise simply constitute a jumble of experiences in students' minds.)

Lessons from the Flip

Elsewhere, I have reflected on lessons learned from simulation-heavy flipped teaching (Sankoff & Forcese, 2015).[6] Drawing firm conclusions about its effectiveness is difficult to do. For one thing, other demands mean that I am not able to devote serious research time to this question. But even if I did have such time and resources, one of the challenges in pedagogical research is the absence of an adequate control group. Key methodological challenges include how to ensure the experimental and control classes and their students are truly sealed from one another to avoid cross-section collaboration; how to avoid selection bias in terms of students who opt to register in one class or another; and how to grapple with problems in sample size in which even large law group classes are still relatively small and thus overall outcomes may be heavily influenced by a handful of student-outcome outliers. I am also discomforted by ethical quandaries: Can I ethically commit to teaching a control group through a conventional teaching method I believe teaches less effectively?

I will say, however, that as an instructor, I feel much more is conveyed and much more learned. Enrolment data and teaching evaluations are positive, although the flipped course is indisputably more work for students than is a passive learning lecture course where students coast all the way to the exam. Moreover, while I have not run a controlled experiment, I have regularly juxtaposed student exam performance after a flipped class against their performance on substantively identical exams sat during my pre-flip period of teaching. Consistently, student averages are 5% (or a letter grade) higher now, post-flip, than they were pre-flip. Moreover, mark distributions are usually much better, in the sense that I have fewer students in a long tail of C+ or below grades.[7] The flip seems to produce a more normal grade distribution. This is not a scientifically rigorous analysis, but in the absence of a more plausible control group it supports the virtue of simulation-heavy flipped teaching, even in doctrinally dense law classes. How much of this difference can be attributed to the simulation component, rather than simply the availability of recorded off-shored lectures and in-class active learning, is unknowable.

A side benefit of the flip is the constant interaction and feedback orientation of the active learning component of the course. This means I gather intelligence on what works and what does not, in a way I did not with conventional teaching. This allows me to "circle back" and address matters with which students are struggling. I hypothesize that this approach has proved especially valuable to students who have struggled with more classic, lecture-based instruction. As I have used them, simulations are not a necessary ingredient of this diagnostic. Still, as I have suggested, they may facilitate deeper classroom engagement and make a role-playing student less risk averse in those discussions than might otherwise be the case. Moreover, they are a vessel for professionalization. Carefully designed micro-simulations can improve basic skill-learning and hone professional and ethical instincts. As noted above, I regard professionalization as an important objective, producing long-term benefits of a sort not necessarily reflected on an exam testing substantive knowledge.

Part 2: Full-Immersion Simulation

Experientially oriented micro-simulations, of the sort discussed in part 1, have several virtues from an instructor's perspective. First, they are difficult to prepare, but once done, they can generally be recycled across years. Second, while much more consuming of time and energy in the medium term than conventional, lecture-style teaching, they do not require complex choreography and logistics. They scale well, in other words, across years and most can be deployed in both small and large class formats. This manageability advantage is of considerable importance. A pedagogical technique that consumes vast amounts of professor time and energy is unsustainable. The risk of instructor burnout increases. The career consequences – in terms of foregone time and energy devoted to research – can be injurious.

Micro-simulations do, however, suffer from one shortcoming: they require simplicity. The legal and factual issues must be reasonably straightforward. They are a tool for addressing discrete areas, but they are neither deep nor wide. A micro-simulation is, in other words, a cookie-cutter simulation, of short duration with few dynamic variables. Moreover, the larger the class, the more micro the simulation must be. Law classes are taught by a single professor – teaching assistants are unknown. Micro-simulations work in this resource-constrained environment, where they replicate the question and answer format of traditional Socratic instruction without requiring complex orchestration of roles and factual injects.

In comparison, "immersive" simulations, drawing on many more resources, allow for much greater complexity. As we define the term, a total-immersion simulation follows a series of more traditional, doctrinal classes, giving students the opportunity to delve into critical substantive law and theoretical constructs that inform their understanding of the law. The simulation serves as a capstone in which students are expected to deploy this information to resolve difficult legal and factual dilemmas. One of us (Donohue) has designed and executed the to-tal-immersion simulation on national security law at Georgetown Law since 2010, building off a more basic tabletop simulation she conducted while at Stanford Law School in 2009. The other (Forcese) was invited to join in 2017, in a supportive role as the faculty instructor for a "Team Canada" group of Canadian law students and junior lawyers.

Pedagogical Goals for the Full-Immersion Simulation

National security law is distinguished by several attributes that are well suited to instruction through total-immersion simulations. These simulations have an additional advantage because security clearance requirements mean that clinical programs in national security law are not feasible – and so they may be the only way in which students can get hands-on experience in the field before joining a government entity. The Georgetown Law simulation has been designed to educate students in seven attributes critical to the practice of national security law.

First, upon entering the field, students must understand a signifi-cant amount of black-letter law and policy. It is not a narrow domain. National security, premised on global threats, involves international law, treaties, other countries' domestic law, constitutional law, and stat-utory and regulatory measures. Students also must master policy docu-ments that detail agencies' roles and responsibilities. As the law is often not settled across the board, students must be able to identify where the law is unclear, indicate the level of legal certainty where novel issues present, and make recommendations based on these judgments to their principal (the primary individual within the bureaucratic chain of com-mand to whom the lawyer reports). In clarifying the law, students must further be careful to separate law from policy and to make the demar-cation transparent to policymakers.

Second, it is not just the law as written that matters, but the law as it is applied. This means that students must have command of legal and political processes. Some of these relate to individual institutions, with lawyers needing to understand their role, authorities, and relationship to others. Others stem from the different roles of various institutions themselves, and the inter-agency process. Students must develop sophisticated decision-making algorithms to ensure that the right stakeholders are brought into the discussion. They must also be able to navigate meetings, learning how to set (and influence) agendas, partic-ipate in, run, and follow up from them. They also must construct both formal and informal networks with other role-players. Getting things done in this world, as in many others, is about building relationships of trust and cooperation. On top of this is the political overlay of national security events.

Third, national security lawyers must be able to exhibit exceptional information management skills. They must be able to track information accurately and efficiently. They also must be able to deal with factual chaos and uncertainty.

One of the most important challenges here is learning how to separate the wheat from the chaff – that is, figuring out which information is relevant to the issues and questions at hand. In a traditional law school class, and even in the mini-simulations, students are given the information they need to make a determination. But the danger of availability bias can have significant, detrimental effects in the realm of national security. So students also have to step back to figure out what information is available, what information is needed, and how to get that information, using legally and institutionally available channels. Once it is obtained, they must evaluate its relevance and determine who *else* needs the information. That data must be provided in a timely manner, even as the student properly navigates classification regimes.

In the context of national security, time is frequently at issue. So students additionally must learn *when* they have to make a decision, even when there is incomplete factual data. They must decide when to and when not to offer advice. And when they do give the advice to their principal, they must convey their confidence level in the data and make it clear which legal conclusions are dependent on which facts, so that, if the situation changes, the principal knows that the legal analysis may alter.

Fourth, in a classified world, students must be particularly attentive to decision-making. This means protecting against cognitive biases, such as due (or undue) reliance on early or accessible information; due (or undue) persistence in a particular course of action (e.g., commitment bias, confirmation bias, and path dependence); and an ability to appreciate different perspectives and interests (avoiding projection or mirroring biases). At the same time, students must be cognizant of group dynamics and work to ensure that the group functions well, avoiding ineffective conflict, groupthink, and ineffective information processing among the players. Students also must be able to analyse their judgment, to ensure that they are acting professionally in such an intense setting. This means, in part, learning how to work with ambiguity, identifying which issues are legal and which are non-legal, holding appropriate discussions with the stakeholders, and exhibiting respect in dealing with others.

Fifth, practice in this area requires non-traditional written and oral communications skills. In law school, legal briefs and motions in court are typically the norm. But almost none of what national security lawyers do will ever end up before a judge. Students need to learn how to write intra- and inter-agency memos, agendas, emails, short legal analyses, recommendations, agendas, and action items. Instead of arguing before a judge, they may have to brief both lawyers and non-lawyers, possibly translating difficult legal concepts to individuals not schooled in the law.

Sixth, leadership is especially important in national security law, where the stakes are high. Students will have to perform well in terms of how they (a) interact with their client, (b) perform their role, (c) synthesize information, (d) exercise judgment, (e) uphold standards of professional responsibility, and (f) act ethically. Leadership also means looking to the institution, and is measured by how well the student represents its interests, functions, and team. Leadership requires students at times to assume and at other times to delegate responsibility. It also requires the student to learn to develop, elicit, and select among alternatives for action. And it goes to the strength of the student's product, such as documents, advice, management, and decisions.

Seventh, relative to other areas, national security law is an insular and specialized area in which formal learning opportunities are sparse. Classification means that one's actions are often not visible to the person who might otherwise serve as a long-term mentor or supervisor. So students must acquire the ability to self-learn (see discussion in Donohue, 2013).

The Georgetown Law National Security Crisis Law Simulation

These pedagogical goals necessitate a complex simulation environment. In its present form, Professor Donohue's National Security Crisis Law Simulation course at Georgetown is an intensive substantive-law-heavy course that also teaches students the skills necessary to succeed in the field of national security law. It thus brings together theory, sharp analytical skills, black-letter law, and operational considerations, to provide students with a strong foundation.

The course begins with the doctrinal and theoretical portion, with emphasis placed on different slices of national security law – such as the law of armed conflict, surveillance provisions, and counterterrorist finance. Classroom instruction is primarily Socratic and lecture-based. One of us (Forcese) has experimented, in addition, with a "slow-motion" sim during this time, designed to habituate students to the role-playing dynamics of the immersive sim over the course of the semester. This amounts to short tabletop exercises where substantive problems are addressed, in role, driven by a dribble of factual injects. Donohue, meanwhile, is looking at ways to automate the slow-motion sim in a series of computer "games" that can be undertaken by the students, outside of class time.

While the doctrinal portion proceeds, students are assigned roles in national, provincial/state, and local government. Students research their roles and the legal authorities within which they, and their institutions, will be operating. They are then assigned mentors, who are often senior-level government officials and lawyers who have held positions either the same as or like the roles they have been given. Students prepare questions for their mentors, which are reviewed by the professors prior to their mentor meetings. The purpose of the meetings is to help the students answer questions that they may have about their position, the informal processes in place, and institutional relationships. After meeting with their mentors, students prepare a reflection paper with the answers to their mentor questions. They also write a 7- to 10-page paper detailing the legal authorities for which they are responsible, as well as the primary legal and policy documents that govern their institutions. These, too, are reviewed by the faculty to make sure the students are well prepared going into the simulation.

Following the doctrinal lectures, students have two hours of class time focused on the inter-agency process and four hours focused on decision-making and leadership. The course then moves into a week-long simulation, receiving factual "injects" for the first several days, and then assembling for the "live" simulation for the last 48 hours. The first part of the week and the first day of the 48-hour portion act as a formative assessment, with students being provided with immediate instructional feedback. The final 24 hours is a summative assessment, with the students not receiving a formal assessment until after the exercise has concluded.

This model has evolved over time from the tabletop exercise Donohue first conducted as part of the Constitution Center at Stanford Law School. Each year, alterations and input from the control team and colleagues have shaped the general form, allowing for significant experimentation.[8] For several years the course alternated between a Georgetown-only simulation and one where Donohue invited other schools to join the course and week-long exercise.

For two years, the Georgetown students were joined remotely via video conferencing software during the instructional portion of the course by "Team Canada," comprised mostly of law students from the University of Ottawa, but also several from other Canadian law schools. These students role-played Canadian officials in the simulation. During 2018, players from other US law schools, as well as players from Australia and the United Kingdom, also took part. In 2019, we had four US law schools, as well as teams from Canada. These students participated remotely during the doctrinal portion of the course. They were assigned roles and mentors and prepared papers. And then they all physically came to Georgetown Law for the in-person portion of the simulation.

During the simulation, the students are fed factual injects through (simulated) classified and unclassified emails accounts, as well as simulated news networks. These injects drive developments in multiple, complex storylines, which have been developed prior to the simulation. Each is based on real-world national security threats that have already emerged, with further thought given to how similar issues may present in the future. The storylines (many pages long and kept from students) constitute the script for unfolding national security dilemmas, while an hourly chart over the week-long period details precisely which information will be delivered to which roles and by what means (e.g., sim-AP wire, the sim VNN broadcast network, in person, via telephone, or through sim-NIPR or sim-SIPR email accounts).

As this suggests, the simulation is technology-heavy. Students communicate on dedicated classified and non-classified email accounts, assigned to each player, yielding up to 10,000 emails over a week-long period. (In one year, the resulting traffic load on the system prompted the university to shut it off, as it assumed a cyber-attack. Now the university IT people are notified in advance.) Classrooms, doubling as agency meeting rooms, are wired for video and sound, allowing the control group to monitor developments. A virtual news network is closed-cast to the participants over a special simulation website and on televisions all over the law school campus.

A premium is placed on authenticity. The storylines are assiduously researched, sourced, and validated to ensure plausibility. They are designed to address national security pedagogical goals. That is, they are written to raise not just hard substantive law dilemmas, but also questions of communications, ethics, judgment, leadership, cognitive bias, and the like. Storylines build in opportunities to test, for example, student ability to brief senior leaders, seek emergency warrants before role-playing judges, and draft responsive memos in short time frames. In the total-immersion simulation, students must also make difficult choices, factoring in time management, fatigue management, and nutrition.

Crafting these storylines involves a score of individuals. Managing the simulation over its two days and two nights requires *several* scores of individuals assembled as a control team in a campus classroom bearing every resemblance to a space-centre mission control: several screens are mounted across the front and sides of the room, with video and audio access to the student deliberations. The control team is made up of professors, lawyers from practice, and alumni from previous simulations, most of whom work in national security law. The control team plays all non-player characters (NPCs), allowing students to interact with countries, agencies, and individuals not otherwise represented in the simulation. It also runs the AP wire and a real-time broadcast network.

During play, students have two options: they can make requests for information (ROIs) from the control team, or they can make decisions, notifying the relevant players and the control team of their actions. In the latter capacity, the control team requires that the students provide the legal authority or pre-established policies in accordance with which they are acting. These interactions, as well as a series of pre-set "choke points," such as National Security Council meetings, principals' or deputies' Meetings, congressional hearings, or appearances before judges, provide key moments of learning.

With a high ratio of control group members to students, the storylines develop in real time. Student decisions in their roles, memorialized through communications over the simulation's email network, galvanize responses from not just the control team but the other players. Based on these interactions, and student achievement of specific pedagogical goals, the simulation director determines the pace of the storylines. Some are resolved successfully by the student players. Some are not. Failure and success are both teachers. At the close of the simulation, prominent lawyers from practice deliver their remarks, based on the student decision-making they witnessed.

Following the simulation – described by many students as the most intensive experience of their lives – students debrief in the final classroom sessions, present a 90-second presentation to their peers reflecting on lessons learned, and then author a longer, reflective "after-action," lesson-learned assignment.

Lessons from the Total-Immersion Simulation

A total-immersion simulation is not for the faint of heart, either for students or for professors. While the micro-simulations described in part 1 are more work than recycled lectures, that workload pales in comparison. A total-immersion simulation is the logistical equivalent to scripting and then mounting a one-production, cast-of-thousands stage play, every year. It depends on the enduring loyalty of members of the control team, who volunteer hundreds of hours to help bring up the next generation of national security lawyers. It also depends on deans and faculty administrators supportive of a resource-intensive process, a reality that requires careful management. It can be scaled to include large numbers of students (in the 200-student range), but only through an equivalent expenditure of resources – the control group to student ratio is just shy of 1:1.

Still, there is no doubt in either of our minds that the total-immersion National Security Crisis Law Simulation is the most robust pedagogical exercise that either of us has ever run. Practitioners participating in the control group have singled out some student performances as on par with their expectations of experienced practitioners working in the national security field. For their part, students report being stretched in ways nothing else in law school (and occasionally life) has stretched them. Moreover, because it departs from conventional pedagogy, the simulation enables students who struggle with conventional instruction to flourish. That is validating to those students, and from the perspective of maximizing student potential, is also validating to us.

The information-rich environment gives students an opportunity to continue learning well after the simulation has ended. The collection of papers that the students produce, a memo on their performance in light of the theoretical grounding for cognitive bias and leadership (prepared by our colleague Professor Mitt Regan), an individualized memo evaluating each student's performance throughout the course and simulation, the judges' remarks, and detailed control team feedback often give rise to further questions, the answers to which help to inform students about not just their successes and failures in the simulation, but *why* they succeeded or failed at different points. This, in turn, allows them to construct models going forward for how to avoid pitfalls and how to reinforce good decisions and practices.

A few years back, a generous grant from Georgetown University allowed Professor Donohue to analyse the considerable email traffic generated during the simulation to provide insight into how students managed both their formal and informal networks. The social network analysis provided students with a clear picture of why certain practices worked (or failed to work). Professor Donohue was able to show each student a dynamic model of their actions in navigating the social structures, calling attention to the relative power of the different nodes in the network – and how that power was wielded. In addition, the grant allowed for quick tracing of what happened to primary information injected into the simulation, which helped to elucidate how cognitive biases subtly shifted the nature of the data – and legal analysis of its relevance – as the simulation progressed. The technologies funded by the grant also visually depicted what occurred in each storyline, helping to put the elephant back together during the three classes following the exercise. By providing such a rich learning environment, the simulation allows these types of tools to be brought to bear to deepen students' learning.

An unexpected consequence has also emerged: the simulation steers students to consider a career in national security law – something that we had not previously contemplated. Based on conversations with members of the "Team Canada" participants over two years, roughly 50% of students had not originally contemplated a career in national security law, but they now wish actively to seek one out. Since both of us believe that principled and skilled national security lawyering is essential in democratic societies, this too constitutes a beneficial outcome from the total-immersion sim.

Conclusion

Simulations in law schools are our answer to the endless debate between "law school as trade school" and "law school as theoretical grounding." Carefully done, it is possible to reach for both objectives. Time is a constraint, and resources are not endless. But the real impediment to forward progress in rethinking legal pedagogy is often imagination.

To this end, simulations reflect how developments in the real world create opportunities to think about teaching in new and innovative ways. The coronavirus outbreak in spring 2020 proved no exception. From initial plans to run a high-tech in-person simulation, with a new model for the control team based on swarm intelligence, the exercise had to be suddenly moved to an intensive exchange online. Instead of running a series of different storylines set in the contemporary world, the exercise focused on developments clustered around a future US presidential election, with the assumption that technologies just now emerging (such as augmented reality, 5G networks, and fourth-generation social media) had become commonplace. Conducted in four modules that built on the prior fact patters, the new model had the advantage that students were on call the entire time, in common conversation with practising attorneys in the field. The exercise generated a transcript that could subsequently be analysed, and it allowed the students to take full advantage of the expertise of the lawyers on the control team, as each attorney could press each student on any question that arose.

Such information-rich environments give students opportunities to deepen their scholarly understanding of the law and the skills necessary to be a strong lawyer. Again and again, we have seen students rise to the challenge, surpassing even their own expectations. Simulations also provide an opportunity for students to learn from their mistakes – much as we do, as we continue to try to move the debate forward and craft a better legal pedagogy for the future.

NOTES

1 Not all law schools have such entrenched battle lines, nor, of course, do all faculty align with one side in this debate. This is a rough characterization of a debate that plays out in myriad contexts within the legal academy – an institution itself made up of individuals that come out of practice, as well as others who have remained within the scholarly realm. Legal education and its woes have been an active area of discussion, especially since the publication of *Educating Lawyers: Preparation for the Profession of Law* by Sullivan, Colby, Wegner, Bond, and Shulman (2007). In the Canadian context, see the Canadian Bar Association (2016). For examples of the public debate in the profession in Canada, see, e.g., Ferguson (2010); Pedersen (2014); Singer (2016).
2 For scholarship discussing some of these issues, see, e.g., Woolley (2014). For views in the profession on skills students should have, see, e.g., the Federation of Law Societies (2018). See also, e.g., Garcia (2017); Munro (2016).
3 There is a lengthy literature dedicated to debating the merits and demerits of the Socratic method. See, e.g., Madison (2008); Hawkins-Leon (1998).
4 The result has been discussion of legal education for the "whole lawyer." See the Canadian Association of Law Teachers (2016).
5 Most course materials in these flipped courses may be accessed via www .cforcese.ca.
6 See also Forcese's blog site, containing reflections of lessons learned on flipped teaching through 2015: http://craigforcese.squarespace.com/ bleaching-law/category/flipped-classroom.
7 See, e.g., the discussion in Craig Forcese (2015), "Flipping the First Year Mandatory Law Class: The Results": http://craigforcese.squarespace.com/bleaching -law/2015/12/29/flipping-a-first-year-mandatory-law-class-results.html.
8 I am grateful to my friends and colleagues Jocelyn Aqua, Leonard Bailey, Alan Cohn, Mary De Rosa, Rosemary Hart, David Kris, Mitt Regan, Dakota Rudesill, and Bill Treanor, as well as my former students (and now friends and colleagues) John Benton, Andrew Christie, Edward George, Kevin Jinks, Phil Lockwood, Thomas McSorley, Chris Morgan-Reiss, Sarah Mortazavi, Pete Pascucci, Katie Pasietta, Logan Perel, Alan Schuller, and Marc Sorel, who have spent countless hours helping to develop the simulation and to think outside the box for determining how best to prepare students for the future. (Donohue)

REFERENCES

Canadian Association of Law Teachers. (2016). *CALT/ACCLE conference 2017 call for participants*. Retrieved from https://www.acpd-calt.org/2017_call_for _participants

Canadian Bar Association. (2016). *Transforming legal education in Canada: A workshop to inspire change.* Retrieved from https://www.cba.org/CBA -Legal-Futures-Initiative/Events/Transforming-Legal-Education-in-Canada -A-Workshop

Donohue, L.K. (2013). National security pedagogy and the role of simulations. *Journal of National Security Law and Policy, 6*(2), 489–547. Retrieved from http://jnslp.com/2013/04/11/national-security-law-pedagogy-and-the -role-of-simulations/

Federation of Law Societies. (2018). *National requirement.* Retrieved from https://flsc.ca/wp-content/uploads/2018/01/National-Requirement-Jan -2018-FIN.pdf

Ferguson, D. (2010, October 6). It's time to debate the reform of legal education in Canada. *Canadian Lawyer.* Retrieved from https://www.canadianlawyermag .com/article/its-time-to-debate-the-reform-of-legal-education-in-canada-945/

Forcese, C. (2015, December 29). *Flipping the First Year Mandatory Law Class: The Results* [Blog post]. Retrieved from http://craigforcese.squarespace .com/bleaching-law/2015/12/29/flipping-a-first-year-mandatory-law-class -results.html

Garcia, F. (2017, October 16). Law school 2.0: What the next generation of lawyers needs to know. *Canadian Lawyer.* Retrieved from https://www .canadianlawyermag.com/author/fernando-garcia/law-school-20-what-the -next-generation-of-lawyers-needs-to-know-14786/

Hawkins-Leon, C.G. (1998). The Socratic method-problem method dichotomy: The Debate over teaching method continues. *BYT Education and Law Journal, 1998*(1), 1–18. Retrieved from http://digitalcommons.law.byu.edu/cgi /viewcontent.cgi?article=1082&context=elj;The

Institute for the Advancement of the American Legal System. (2018). *Foundations for practice.* Retrieved from http://iaals.du.edu/projects/foundations-practice /phase-one-survey-results

Madison, B.V. (2008). The elephant in the law school classrooms: Overuse of the Socratic method as an obstacle to teaching modern law students. *University of Detroit Mercy Law Review, 85*(3), 293–346. Retrieved from https://papers.ssrn .com/sol3/papers.cfm?abstract_id=1266869

Munro, S. (2016, 16 March). Helping new lawyers become practice-ready. *Slaw.* Retrieved from http://www.slaw.ca/2016/03/16/helping-new-lawyers -become-practice-ready/

Pedersen, Z. (2014, February 24). The evolution of legal education. *Canadian Lawyer.* Retrieved from https://www.canadianlawyermag.com/article/the -evolution-of-legal-education-2383/

Sankoff, P., and Forcese, C. (2015). The flipped law classroom: Retooling the classroom to support active teaching and learning. *Canadian Legal Education Annual Review,* 119. Retrieved from https://ssrn.com/abstract=2402379

Singer, L. (2016, Spring). Shaking up the academy. *CBA National*. Retrieved
    from http://nationalmagazine.ca/Articles/Spring-2016-Issue/Shaking-up
    -the-Academy.aspx?lang=EN&utm_source=cba&utm_medium=email
Sullivan, W.M., Colby, A., Wegner, J.W., Bond, L., & Shulman, L.S. (2007).
    Educating lawyers: Preparation for the profession of law. Princeton, NJ: The
    Carnegie Foundation for the Advancement of Teaching. Retrieved from
    http://archive.carnegiefoundation.org/pdfs/elibrary/elibrary_pdf_632.pdf
Woolley, A. (2014). Legal education reform and the good lawyer. *Alberta Law
    Review, 51*(4), 801–818. Retrieved from https://papers.ssrn.com/sol3/papers
    .cfm?abstract_id=2375480

4 The Use of Simulation in Teaching and Assessing Holistic Competence in Social Work Students

MARION BOGO

Introduction

Social work practice relies on strong interpersonal communication abilities on the part of the practitioner; these abilities are the essence of delivering an effective service. Traditionally social work students developed these competencies in their clinical internships. Resource constraints in social service and health organizations have resulted in less time for intensive supervision in these clinical settings. As a result, social work educators are eager to consider additional pedagogical approaches to promote student learning, particularly as it relates to professional best practice. Simulation-based education offers a unique approach to developing the core communication competencies necessary for social work practice. This chapter will present current developments in the way social work educators are using simulation to teach and assess holistic competence.

The Nature of Social Work Practice

Since its origins in Western societies over one hundred years ago, the purpose of social work has been to enhance the well-being of individuals, families, and communities, especially those affected by societal issues such as poverty, ill health, violence, marginalization, and oppression. The focus of the discipline is on both "private troubles of individuals ... and the public issues that surround them," and includes a commitment to social justice and human rights (Reamer, 1994, p. 2). A systemic framework guides the understanding of personal issues by recognizing that aspects of an individual's physical environment such as their housing, employment opportunities, financial income, and the presence or absence of nourishing and supportive relationships and social networks all have significant impacts on their functioning and well-being. Social workers intervene directly with those who seek services, while simultaneously addressing social and economic inequities, advocating for enhanced policy and programs for vulnerable populations, and administering a range of health and welfare programs. Such programs represent the basic Canadian values of fairness, equity, and sharing resources through universal coverage for medically necessary healthcare and a social safety net to mitigate hardships, meet urgent needs, and promote the development of human potential.

Social workers find employment in a wide range of services that assist individuals across the life course. For example, they work with children and families to ensure child safety and positive growth and development, in child protection agencies, children's health and mental clinics, and schools and community centres. As members of inter-professional teams, they work with adults in health, mental health, addictions, rehabilitation, and long-term care, as well as in correctional settings. Their role can involve providing counselling, advocacy, coordination of resources, and linkage between a team or service and the client. This form of practice is referred to as direct practice, micro practice, or clinical practice.[1] Since the literature and studies in social work have exclusively focused on direct practice, the focus in this chapter is on the use of simulation for teaching and assessing competence in this area.

Social work practice rests on some fundamental themes: collaboration with clients through building trusting, emotionally connected relationships; demonstrating acceptance of individuals, a non-judgmental attitude, respect, and positive regard; attention to clients' strengths; and building capacity for clients to address their own needs and to choose effective responses to the issues they face (Bogo, 2018). These skills, what have been termed "the soft skills" in related health professions, are the essence of social work practice and receive considerable support from empirical studies in social work and in related fields (Wampold & Budge, 2012). Social work students must master these competencies and use them intentionally and flexibly to forge and maintain relationships with diverse clients characteristic of contemporary Canadian society.

While students can understand the values, concepts, and empirical support for this type of interpersonal interaction, it is far more difficult to actually enact these complex behaviours. This is especially so in the case of situations that social workers confront, such as those in practice in child protection, intimate partner violence, abuse of older adults, and mental illness. They may experience client behaviours and attitudes that make it challenging to provide nourishing relationship qualities. Since learning with human simulation involves interacting with actors, students can develop the necessary skills and personal grounding through practice, feedback, and reflection. This learning occurs in situations that do not pose a threat to the safety of the client or the student.

Social Work Education Programs

The systemic perspective in social work results in presenting students with a highly complex framework for understanding and responding to the numerous dimensions in the situations presented by clients. For educators, the age-old task has been to find ways of presenting these multiple components in a way that highlights their interconnections and provides guidance for interventions. Historically, in an effort to legitimize social work as a profession, social work training in higher education emphasized the theoretical and empirical underpinnings of the discipline. Educational programs were divided into two separate domains that persist today (CSWE, 2015). In one domain, the university, courses provide substantive knowledge, research methods, and develop critical thinking; instructors are mainly tenure-stream faculty members, many of whom have not been engaged in the practice of the profession for many years. In the other domain, the field practicum (similar to a supervised clinical experience in health professions education), students spend half their time in organizations where they learn to use knowledge taught in courses through skilful application to client situations (Hunter, Moen, & Raskin, 2016). A field instructor, a social worker employed by the organization, guides, mentors, and supervises student practice – usually a front-line social worker with a minimum of three years of experience (Farber & Reitmeier, 2019). While organizations agree to have a student involved in their program, there is no reduced workload for the social worker who serves as the field instructor, and time for education is limited. To some extent an apprenticeship model of education prevails, with students shadowing their instructor and other experienced social workers (Gushwa & Harriman, 2019).

An empirically supported body of knowledge identifies effective processes for field learning: observing students' practice, debriefing with constructive feedback, and reflective discussions that provide conceptual frameworks to link theory and practice (Bogo, 2015; Fortune, McCarthy, & Abramson, 2001; Lee & Fortune, 2013a, 2013b). Field instructors work hard to carve out time for this type of instruction. In recent years, however, social work educators have identified a crisis in field education. Ayala et al. (2018) studied the experiences of field coordinators in Canadian schools, those responsible for procuring quality placements and assignment of students. Using an online survey and focus groups,

34 participants (out of a possible 39) representing eight of ten Canadian provinces and all five regions responded to a range of questions. The researchers found that "field placement scarcity abounds in Canada ... As many social workers grapple with increasing caseloads and fewer resources, taking on the responsibility of supervising a practicum student in addition to their demanding workload is increasingly considered unfeasible" (p. 2). In the United States, a field summit was convened in 2014 to address the crisis in locating field sites. Over one hundred participants were unanimous in reporting "increasing difficulty in finding sufficient numbers of quality placements ... due to economic constraints in agencies, insurance regulations, and competition between programs" (CSWE, 2015, p. 7). A recommendation from this meeting was to think creatively to replace and expand placement opportunities. Four years later the problem persists, as Gushwa and Harriman (2018) describe "an over-taxed voluntary workforce of field supervisors, and overextended programs and agencies" (p. 1). Similar concerns have been expressed regarding practicum sites in Australia (Gursansky & Le Sueur, 2011). Traditionally, social service and health organizations voluntarily committed time for front-line social workers to provide field education for students. Since this arrangement is currently being challenged, field education is struggling to provide sufficient systematic teaching to develop the necessary competencies in all students.

Assessment of student competence is also of concern. Students' field instructors primarily assess their practice according to dimensions provided by the university program (Bogo, Regehr, Hughes, Power, & Globerman, 2002). Studies have shown that students' actual practice is not regularly observed; instead, assessment is largely based on verbal and written reports (Maidment, 2000; Saltzburg, Greene, & Drew, 2010). In studies, instructors have discussed their reluctance to give negative ratings or to fail students, hence creating a leniency bias (Bogo, Regehr, Power, & Regehr, 2007; Finch & Taylor, 2013; Vinton & Wilke, 2011). This research has found that the intense nature of the student–field instructor relationship renders it difficult for instructors to provide objective assessment.

Simulation-Based Education and Assessment for Social Work Practice

Social work educators concerned with the importance of preparing students for practice have used role-play between student peers as a way of illustrating concepts in action and providing students with opportunities to practise. Role-play is used extensively in generic and specialized practice courses and seen as an adjunct to field learning. These role-plays involve peer student pairs enacting client roles in situations similar to those encountered in real-world social work (Doekler & Bedics, 1987). Role-plays are limited, though, as students often do not have the lived experience to authentically portray situations presented by clients, may present a superficial enactment, and help their peers out when emotional material becomes challenging (Badger & MacNeil, 1998, 2002; Petracchi & Collins, 2006). A recent Canadian study found that students had mixed reactions to role-plays; on the one hand, working with friendly and helpful peers was not anxiety provoking, especially when colleagues gave each other material to help the progress of the interview. On the other hand, role-plays did not feel authentic and hence were not approached as a serious learning experience. Furthermore, some students felt judged by peers, and this later affected the relationships in the classroom (Tufford, Asakura, & Bogo, 2018).

In an attempt to strengthen education and assessment of students' social work practice competence, our research team created a simulation-based teaching program at the Factor-Inwentash Faculty of Social Work, University of Toronto, that relied on trained actors as an additional pedagogical method. Initial work was influenced by the use of simulation in health professions education, following the definition provided by Gaba (2007) as a method "to replace or amplify real experiences with guided experiences, often immersive in nature, that evoke or replicate substantial aspects of the real world in a fully safe, instructive and interactive fashion" (p. 136). In Factor-Inwentash's master of social work (MSW) graduate program, students spend only the first semester in academic courses and enter a three-day-a-week field practicum in the second semester. This structure enables the use of simulation, specifically human simulation with trained actors, to provide students with foundation competencies to use when subsequently engaged in learning in the field. Two companion courses required in the first semester of the MSW program are offered to approximately 140 students. These courses provide the foundation for social work practice, and focus on integrating the teaching of theoretical concepts, related empirical support, and processes and skills for practice. In small classes of 18, students work intensively in full-day sessions, with each student having the chance to interview a simulated client. All students observe and participate in the debriefing of each other's interviews. The course instructor is able to clearly articulate and demonstrate the ways in which concepts apply to practice and provide constructive feedback to each student. An enhancement, known as Practice Fridays, was recently added to offer additional experiences for students to practise with simulated clients, engage in debriefing, and receive feedback (Kourgiantakis, Bogo, & Sewell, 2019). Our studies have found that students report that the authenticity presented by the live actor, the immediacy of focused feedback, and the opportunity for reflection result in simulation as a powerful learning approach (Kourgiantakis, Bogo, & Sewell, 2018).

At the end of the semester, the final assessment of student competence is conducted using an objective structured clinical examination (OSCE) adapted for social work (Bogo et al., 2011). This involves each student interviewing a trained actor who is portraying a client situation typical of those seen in social work practice. The actor plays the client in a consistent manner for each student, hence providing a standardized portrayal and a fair examination. The interviews are generally 15 minutes in length and are observed and rated by a course instructor using a standardized rating scale. The rating scale has been tested in our initial studies and found to be reliable and valid (Bogo et al., 2011; 2012). As noted above, studies found that the relationship between students and field instructor raters interferes with instructors' ability to provide an objective assessment of students' performance (Bogo et al., 2007; Finch & Taylor, 2013; Vinton & Wilke, 2011). Since this is a multi-section course, the rater in the OSCE is a course instructor other than the student's. In the OSCE adapted for social work, the interview with the simulated client is immediately followed by a reflective exercise aimed to access dimensions of competence that are not observable. These dimensions are discussed later in this chapter. For over a decade we have conducted a series of studies, funded by the Social Science and Humanities Research Council, on this approach to using simulation in teaching and in assessing practice competence, providing evidence that this is a value-added approach for social work education (Bogo et al., 2011; 2012; 2013; 2017; Katz et al., 2014; Logie et al., 2015; Tufford et al., 2015).

While simulation-based education (SBE) developed out of course instructors' desire to teach not only *about* social work, but how to *do* social work, an additional impetus for the increased use of simulation for teaching and assessment was to prepare students with foundation competencies. With the recognition that field education was changing, that field instructors had less time to teach core competencies, the use of simulation in these courses provided an opportunity to supplement what students would gain in agency practice. The hope was that when students went into their field settings they would already have basic competencies that would facilitate engagement in field learning with actual clients. As educational theorist Michael Eraut (2004) noted, when teaching professional practice in contexts such as classrooms, which are different from the workplace, educators cannot assume students will automatically transfer learning into the field setting. Mechanisms need to bridge learning through simulation with learning in the field. We used a detailed assessment of students' learning on competency categories that parallel those used to guide and assess students' learning in the field setting to accomplish this. At the end of the first-semester courses, instructors provide a detailed written assessment drawing on all of the student's practice in the courses, including in simulated interviews and in the OSCE. The assessment specifies areas of strength and areas for further learning, providing an outline of specific goals for the field practicum. When students begin the practicum, they must bring this assessment to their field instructor to review and build upon it in developing individual goals and a learning plan. Learning plans are submitted to the liaison from the program, assigned to each student–field instructor pair. Liaisons review the plan to ensure that recommendations based on simulated learning have been incorporated.

Field instructors benefited from orientation to this new approach. They were better able to assist students in transforming their course-based knowledge in a manner relevant to clients. A number of mechanisms were used to convey information about learning from simulations to field instructors. A video-recorded lecture was developed, with written educational material to inform field instructors. A fact sheet was also provided for all students and field instructors that provided a summary of the various components of SBE. Through email communication field instructors were made aware of these resources one month prior to the beginning of the field practicum, and again one month after it had begun.

Field instructors were interviewed to elicit their reactions to this new approach. They reported that information provided about learning through simulation served as a useful baseline assessment and a foundation to identify issues for transfer of learning (Bogo, Lee, McKee, Ramjattan, & Baird, 2017). Additionally, they stated that students' ability to discuss their experiences in learning to practise, their reactions to participating in the simulations and in the OSCE, and their responses to constructive feedback provided the impetus for relatively quick and open engagement in the student–supervisor relationship. Field instructors valued students who were critically reflective about their gains and learning needs.

Empirical Support for Using Simulation in Social Work Education

An increasing number of studies in social work using simulation-based education appear to demonstrate that it is an approach worthy of further investigation. Our research team undertook a critical appraisal of studies using standardized clients, examining 18 studies conducted between 1997 and 2011 (Logie, Bogo, Regehr, & Regehr, 2013). Due to insufficient data and methodological issues in the studies reviewed, we were unable to draw useful conclusions. However, all studies found that learning generated from simulated-based learning had high satisfaction ratings from students and instructors.[2]

Since that review there have been a number of well-executed studies reporting increases in students' knowledge and skills, and higher self-confidence. These studies were conducted in areas of specialization such as motivational interviewing skills in child welfare (Pecukonis et al., 2016), assessing the presence of depression in older adults (Gellis & Kim, 2017), and substance use screening, brief intervention, and referral to treatment, known as SBIRT (Sacco et al., 2017). More recently the OSCE method has been used with adaptations of the scales developed by the University of Toronto research team (Bogo, Rawlings, Katz, & Logie, 2014; Bogo et al., 2011). One large study involved the evaluation of performance of social workers trained in a unique graduate fast-track program, Frontline in England, in comparison to social workers trained in a traditional curriculum (Scourfield et al., 2017). In the United States the scales were adapted for an OSCE to evaluate the development of integrated behavioural health skills for work with lesbian, gay, bisexual, and transgender youths in primary care health settings (Sampson, Parrish, & Washburn, 2018). Both studies found that the OSCE method and scales captured variability across students. These researchers conclude that using simulation in teaching and in OSCE for assessment has benefits for social work education. Scourfield et al. (2017) note that it "provides an enhanced and more objective method of assessment which has the unique ability to develop and assess not just the skills needed to apply knowledge practically but also interpersonal skills and self-awareness; giving it a distinct advantage over traditional teaching and assessment methods" (p. 10). Sampson et al. (2018) conclude that "the noninflated ratings highlight a strength of this method in comparison to potentially more biased approaches (e.g. field evaluation or course grades) that typically yield higher ratings of practice skill" (p. 294).

In summary, it appears that a growing community of scholars and researchers on the use of simulation in social work education are arriving at similar conclusions. It is an effective method to teach generic and specialized competencies, and it is also a more robust and objective method to assess students' development of social work competence.

Developing Simulation-Based Scenarios for Social Work Education

The emerging empirical data from social work education research suggest that SBE and assessment are an extremely useful method for social work education. At the University of Toronto this method originated in teaching and assessing core foundation competencies for social work (Bogo et al., 2011). It has also been adopted in a wide range of specialized social work courses and modules. The following iterative process to develop simulation-based educational experiences has proven useful in teaching about particular populations, issues, and intervention techniques. Some examples are reported in teaching about the following: clients struggling to "come out" (Logie, Bogo, & Katz, 2015); social work practice in acute care health settings (Craig, McInroy, Bogo, & Thompson, 2017); potential child neglect situations (Tufford, Bogo, & Asakura, 2015); practice with ethnically diverse clients (Asakura, Bogo, Good, & Power, 2018); and mental health, addictions, and suicide risk assessment (Kourgiantakis et al., 2019). As well we have found that teaching with simulation is particularly well suited for courses teaching social work with families and with adolescent clients, and where there is intimate partner violence or custody battles in high-conflict situations.

Conceptualization of Holistic Competence in Social Work

In each course that plans to use simulation, the first step is to identify the dimensions of competence to focus on. A holistic model of competence for generic social work practice was developed through a multi-project program of research (Bogo, 2018; Bogo et al., 2013; 2006). The model depicted in Figure 4.1 has proven to be a robust, useful, and applicable framework for guiding the articulation of competencies in specialized areas.

The holistic model recognizes that social workers are involved in complex practices or practice behaviours such as forming the type of collaborative relationship described earlier, conducting assessments that lead to joint goal setting with clients, and planning and implementing interventions to achieve those goals. These processes are carried out through the use of interpersonal skills informed by the value and knowledge base of the profession. Sources of knowledge include generic concepts and empirical findings and are supplemented with specialist knowledge related to populations, substantive areas, and

Figure 4.1. A model of holistic competence in social work.

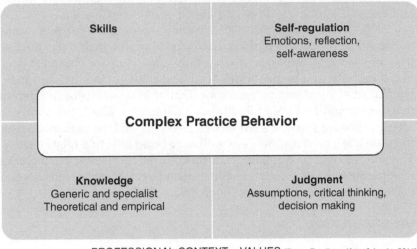

ORGANIZATION AND COMMUNITY CONTEXT

Skills	Self-regulation Emotions, reflection, self-awareness
Complex Practice Behavior	
Knowledge Generic and specialist Theoretical and empirical	Judgment Assumptions, critical thinking, decision making

PROFESSIONAL CONTEXT – VALUES (Bogo, Rawlings, Katz, & Logie, 2014)

Reprinted with permission of the Council on Social Work Education. From Bogo, Rawlings, Katz, & Logie (2014), *Using simulation in assessment and teaching: OSCE adapted for social work*, Alexandria, VI: Council on Social Work Education.

particular interventions. Social workers generally work in organizations whose mission and mandate define the nature of their roles.

From its earliest inception, professional leaders in social work recognized the impact of the personal self of the social worker in the professional role (Brandell, 2011). They acknowledged the powerful, often out-of-awareness role of practitioners' own implicit biases, norms, and expectations about human behaviour, function and dysfunction, and change. These dimensions operate in professional encounters, influencing practitioners' emotional reactions to the client and the situation. These reactions will, in turn, affect and be affected by their cognitive processes. Hence, a long-standing, important tradition is self-regulation achieved through reflection, self-awareness, and the development of effective strategies to remain intentional and client-centred. This view of holistic competence renders it as highly complex with intricate interactions between numerous dimensions.

Put another way, this view of effective practice concerns the ability to carry out two interrelated types of competencies: meta-competencies and procedural competencies (Bogo et al., 2006, 2013; Katz, Tufford, Bogo, & Regehr, 2014). As other scholars of the professions have noted, meta-competencies are higher-order, overarching qualities, abilities, and capacities of a cognitive and affective nature (Cheetham & Chivers, 2005; Deist & Winterton, 2005). In common with the concept of meta-cognition, practitioners think about the way in which they think so that they come to understand what they know and are able to engage in critical reflection in the service of clinical analysis and decision-making. Affective meta-competencies are similar to what has been referred to as emotional and social intelligence (Goleman, 2006): the ability to identify emotions in one's self as well as others and use that awareness to guide one's own responses as well as to build effective relationships. The second type of competencies, procedural competencies, includes the operational, behavioural techniques and performance skills needed to carry out professional tasks (Bogo et al., 2014).

Use of Reflection

The view of holistic competence presented in this chapter involves both procedural competencies, that which can be observed, and meta-competencies, that which is internal to the student and influences their understanding of the situation and triggers their professional response. In order to be effective in both teaching and assessing competence, an educational method needs to capture both of these interrelated components. A two-part process was created that entails students conducting a 15-minute interview with a simulated client followed immediately by a reflective activity (Bogo et al., 2011). Students respond to a series of standardized questions on targeted dimensions of meta-competence. In our initial study, reflection involved a structured dialogue with the rater. When a reflective activity is used in teaching and in assessing performance with the entire student body, students write responses to the same questions used in the original study. Questions access students' understanding of the scenario, their use of knowledge to explain dynamics in the situation and in the interview, and their cognitive and affective processing.

The initial purpose of gathering reflections was to evaluate students' integration of the dimensions in our competence model. Since the written information provided rich data, numerous qualitative analyses were conducted that led to further insights about concepts related to meta-competence and to the substantive areas we were targeting. For example, an analysis of reflections revealed competencies with a similar structure, along a continuum from in-depth, rich, textured discussions to those that were more superficial, scant, and concrete (Bogo et al., 2013). As well, some students' reflections demonstrated a degree of emotional dysregulation that had rendered them unable to use the knowledge learned from the courses in their interviews. These themes were also found in a later study where similar reactions were reported by some experienced social workers and students in the mental health field (Bogo, Regehr, Baird, Paterson, & LeBlanc, 2017).

In general, analysis of the reflections assisted the teaching team in detecting topics that students had not fully mastered, as well as student-perceived gaps in learning. Further teaching and curriculum enhancement ensued, especially more regular articulation of the links between theory, research support, and actual practice behaviours. Regarding issues in learning, an analysis of reflections on affective states and emotional reactions to the interview situation revealed many students describing levels of anxiety that impeded attunement to and engagement with the simulated client (Katz, Tufford, Bogo, & Regehr, 2014). The teaching team incorporated new strategies throughout the courses to address this issue, including relaxation techniques and the practice of mindfulness.

In our recent study of students' descriptions of the value they receive from learning through simulation, a major theme that emerged was the importance of reflection, both while observing peers' interviews and thinking back on their own performance after their interview and responding to reflective questions (Kourgiantakis et al., 2018). The importance of reflection is similar to Schon's (1987) discussion of reflection-in-action and reflection-on-action. After each student's interview in the classroom, both the student who conducted the interview and those who observed engaged in debriefing. This included peers and the instructor providing feedback that focused on particular procedural competencies and the instructor helping students link the practice behaviours to the conceptual frameworks studied in the course.

Designing Authentic Scenarios

In common with all educators using simulation, the challenge in social work is to develop scenarios that are authentic and that provide rich information and the complexity reflective of the real-life practice of the profession. However, given time constraints, scenarios cannot be overly complicated. The aim is to have students not only gather pertinent information but also engage the client in exploring their goals for meeting with a social worker. If the scenario is too complex, students spend most of the time in gathering information. The method used in producing social work scenarios works back and forth from examining the competency framework to identifying the basic information students need in order to demonstrate the particular behaviour. Drawing from the instructor's professional experience, and involving expert social workers in the particular area, a preliminary case situation is developed. In the United Kingdom service users and carers are required by law to be involved in all social work programs, and they contribute to simulations by drawing on their own lived experience (Robinson & Webber, 2012). Social work scenarios typically describe the following: the simulated client's identifying information, psychosocial history, and family; the social systems relevant to them; and their diverse characteristics and emotional state. Included alongside are the presenting problem, the organization and its services, the social worker's role, and tasks and goals for the meeting.

Pilot testing the scenario with a standardized client is crucial, as the actor will help identify missing information, elaborate on the range and type of emotion to be displayed, and, if in an OSCE, develop verbatim statements with appropriate emotions to be offered at particular intervals in the interview to every student. Since social work students' ability to engage with difficult emotions is an important competence, such statements add to the uniformity of the examination. Another advantage of pilot testing is to determine whether the actor and scenario provide sufficient material to facilitate students' learning. When used for assessment purposes, the client material and scenario need to provide enough content so that students can demonstrate the procedural competencies and stimulate self-reflection regarding cognitive and affective dimensions of meta-competence. Pilot testing has also helped instructors identify additional competencies to be developed and further specify behavioural indicators.

Conclusion

Social work education has primarily relied on clinical field instructors to teach the behaviours and competencies necessary for professional practice. Increasingly, educators are using and studying SBE and an adaptation of the OSCE, developed in medicine, to assess student competence. Instructors who use simulation must have expertise in social work practice as well as knowledge of how to execute a meaningful simulation experience. This may present challenges for faculty members who have primarily focused their academic programs of research on areas that contribute important knowledge to the discipline but are not directly connected to practice interventions. Doctoral programs in social work can influence the next generation of social work educators through involving them in the design and delivery of simulation-based education and in research studies that accompany these projects. Recent graduates of our doctoral program are now leading their own simulation centres and conducting externally funded studies, which is in turn helping to increase the profile of this pedagogical tool across Canada.

NOTES

1 Community organization, community development, social policy analysis, and social change activities are undertaken on behalf of and, in some instances, with groups of people concerned about a similar issue. The aim is to provide or enhance current policies and programs to meet a wide range of needs. Social workers also provide leadership through social administration of agencies and government programs. These forms of practice are referred to as mezzo or macro practice. Increasingly, educators are interested in using simulation for mezzo-and macro-level roles; however, to date a scholarly literature has not developed.
2 Methodological limitations included incomplete reporting of participant characteristics and few studies reporting reliability for scales used. Most studies that assessed student performance with standardized clients did not report scores or results.

REFERENCES

Asakura, K., Bogo, M., Good, B., & Power, R. (2018). Social work serial: Using video-recorded simulated client sessions to teach social work practice. *Journal of Social Work Education, 54*(2), 397–404. https://doi.org/10.1080 /10437797.2017.1404525

Ayala, J., Drolet, J., Fulton, A., Hewson, J., Letkemann, L., Baynton, M., ... Schweizer, E. (2018). Field education in crisis: Experiences of field education coordinators in Canada. *Social Work Education, 37*(3), 281–293. https://doi .org/10.1080/02615479.2017.1397109

Badger, L.W., & MacNeil, G. (1998). Rationale for utilizing standardized clients in the training and evaluation of social work students. *Journal of Teaching in Social Work, 16*(1/2), 203–218. https://doi.org/10.1300/J067v16n01_13

Badger, L.W., & MacNeil, G. (2002). Standardized clients in the classroom: A novel instructional technique for social work educators. *Research on Social Work Practice, 12*(3), 364–374. https://doi.org/10.1177/1049731502012003002

Bogo, M. (2015). Field education for clinical social work practice: Best practices and contemporary challenges. *Clinical Social Work Journal, 43*(3), 317–324. https://doi.org/10.1007/s10615-015-0526-5

Bogo, M. (2018). *Social work practice: Integrating concepts, processes, and skills.* New York, NY: Columbia University Press.

Bogo, M., Katz, E., Regehr, C., Logie, C., Mylopoulos, M., & Tufford, L. (2013). Toward understanding meta-competence: An analysis of students' reflections on their simulated interviews. *Social Work Education, 32*(2), 259–273. https://doi.org/10.1080/02615479.2012.738662

Bogo, M., Lee, B., McKee, E., Ramjattan, R., & Baird, S.L. (2017). Bridging class and field: Field instructors' and liaisons' reactions to information about students' baseline performance derived from simulated interviews. *Journal of Social Work Education, 53*(4), 580–594. https://doi.org/10.1080/10437797 .2017.1283269

Bogo, M., Rawlings, M., Katz, E., & Logie, C. (2014). *Using simulation in assessment and teaching: OSCE adapted for social work.* Alexandria, VA: Council on Social Work Education.

Bogo, M., Regehr, C., Baird, S., Paterson, J., & LeBlanc, V.R. (2017). Cognitive and affective elements of practice confidence in social work students and practitioners. *British Journal of Social Work, 47*(3), 701–718. https://doi.org /10.1093/bjsw/bcw026

Bogo, M., Regehr, C., Hughes, J., Power, R., & Globerman, J. (2002). Evaluating a measure of student field performance in direct service: Testing reliability and validity of explicit criteria. *Journal of Social Work Education, 38*(3), 385–401. https://doi.org/10.1080/10437797.2002.10779106

Bogo, M., Regehr, C., Katz, E., Logie, C., Tufford, L., & Litvack, A. (2012). Evaluating the use of an objective structured clinical examination (OSCE) adapted for social work. *Research in Social Work Practice, 22*(4), 428–436. https://doi.org/1049731512437557

Bogo, M., Regehr, C., Logie, C., Katz, E., Mylopoulos, M., & Regehr, G. (2011). Adapting objective structured clinical examinations to assess social work students' performance and reflections. *Journal of Social Work Education, 47*(1), 5–18. https://doi.org/10.5175/JSWE.2011.200900036

Bogo, M., Regehr, C., Power, P., & Regehr, G. (2007). When values collide: Field instructors' experiences of providing feedback and evaluating competence. *The Clinical Supervisor, 26*(1/2), 99–117. https://doi.org/10.1300/J001v26n01_08

Bogo, M., Regehr, C., Woodford, M., Hughes, J., Power, R., & Regehr, G. (2006). Beyond competencies: Field instructors' descriptions of student performance. *Journal of Social Work Education, 42*(3), 191–205. https://doi.org /10.5175/JSWE.2006.200404145

Brandell, J. (Ed.). (2011). *Theory and practice in clinical social work* (2nd ed.). Thousand Oaks, CA: Sage.

Cheetham, G., & Chivers, G. (2005). *Professions, competence and informal learning.* Cheltenham, UK: Edward Elgar.

Craig, S.L., McInroy, L.B., Bogo, M., & Thompson, M. (2017). Enhancing competence in health social work education through simulation-based learning: Strategies from a case study of a family session. *Journal of Social Work Education, 53*(Suppl. 1), S47–S58. https://doi.org/10.1080/10437797.2017.1288597

Council on Social Work Education (CSWE). (2015). *Report of the CSWE Summit on Field Education 2014.* Alexandria, VA: Council on Social Work Education.

Deist, F.D.L., & Winterton, J. (2005). What is competence? *Human Resource Development International, 8*(1), 27–46. https://doi.org/10.1080/1367886042000338227

Doekler, R., & Bedics, B.C. (1987). Differential use of role-play in social work education. *Arete, 12*(3), 53–60.

Eraut, M. (2004). Transfer of knowledge between education and workplace settings. In H. Rainbird, A. Fuller, & A. Munro (Eds.), *Workplace learning in context,* pp. 201–221. London, UK, and New York, NY: Routledge.

Farber, N., & Reitmeier, M.C. (2019). (Re) Capturing the wisdom of our tradition: The importance of Reynolds and Towle in contemporary social work education. *Clinical Social Work Journal, 47,* 5–16. https://doi.org/10.1007/s10615-018-0666-5

Finch, J., & Taylor, I. (2013). Failure to fail? Practice educators' emotional experiences of assessing failing social work students. *Social Work Education, 32*(2), 244–258. https://doi.org/10.1080/02615479.2012.720250

Fortune, A.E., McCarthy, M., & Abramson, J.S. (2001). Student learning processes in field education: Relationship of learning activities to quality of field instruction, satisfaction, and performance among MSW students. *Journal of Social Work Education, 37*(1), 111–124. https://doi.org/10.1080/10437797.2001.10779040

Gaba, D.M. (2007). The future vision of simulaton in healthcare. *Simulation in Healthcare, 2*(2), 126–135. https://doi.org/10.1097/01.SIH.0000258411.38212.32

Gellis, Z.D., & Kim, E.G. (2017). Training social work students to recognize later-life depression: Is standardized patient simulation effective? *Gerontology and Geriatrics Education, 38*(4), 1–13. https://doi.org/10.1080/02701960.2017.1311882

Goleman, D. (2006). *Social intelligence: The new science of human relationships.* New York, NY: Random House.

Gursansky, D., & Le Sueur, E. (2011). Conceptualizing field education in the twenty-first century: Contradictions, challenges and opportunities. *Social Work Education, 31*(7), 914–931. https://doi.org/10.1080/02615479.2011.595784

Gushwa, M., & Harriman, K. (2019). Paddling against the tide: Contemporary challenges in field education. *Clinical Social Work Journal, 47,* 17–22. https://doi.org/10.1007/s10615-018-0668-3

Hunter, C.A., Moen, J.K., & Raskin, M.S. (Eds.). (2015). *Social work field directors: Foundations for excellence.* Chicago, Il: Lyceum Books.

Katz, E., Tufford, L., Bogo, M., & Regehr, C. (2014). Illuminating students' pre-practicum conceptual and emotional states: Implications for field education. *Journal of Teaching in Social Work, 34*(1), 96–108. https://doi.org/10.1080/08841233.2013.868391

Kourgiantakis, T., Sewell, K.M., & Bogo, M. (2018). The importance of feedback in preparing social work students for field education. *Clinical Social Work Journal, 47*, 124–133. https://doi.org/10.1007/s10615-018-0671-8

Kourgiantakis, T., Bogo, M., & Sewell, K.M. (2019). Practice Fridays: Using simulation to develop holistic competence. *Journal of Social Work Education, 55*(3), 551–564. https://doi.org/10.1080/10437797.2018.1548989

Kourgiantakis, T., Sewell, K.M., Lee, E., Adamson, K., McCormick, M., Kuehl, D., & Bogo, M. (2019). Enhancing social work education in mental health, addictions, and suicide risk assessment: A teaching note. *Journal of Social Work Education.* https://doi.org/10.1080/10437797.2019.1656590

Lee, M., & Fortune, A.E. (2013a). Do we need more "doing" activities or "thinking" activities in the field practicum? *Journal of Social Work Education, 49*(4), 646–660. https://doi.org/10.1080/10437797.2013.812851

Lee, M., & Fortune, A.E. (2013b). Patterns of field learning activities and their relation to learning outcome. *Journal of Social Work Education, 49*(3), 420–438. https://doi.org/10.1080/10437797.2013.796786

Logie, C., Bogo, M., & Katz, E. (2015). "I didn't feel equipped": Social work students' reflections on a simulated client "coming out." *Journal of Social Work Education, 51*(2), 315–328. https://doi.org/10.1080/10437797.2015.1012946

Logie, C., Bogo, M., Regehr, C., & Regehr, G. (2013). A critical appraisal of the use of standardized client simulations in social work education. *Journal of Social Work Education, 49*(1), 66–80. https://doi.org/10.1080/10437797.2013.755377

Maidment, J. (2000). Methods used to teach social work students in the field: A research report from New Zealand. *Social Work Education, 19*(2), 145–154. https://doi.org/10.1080/02615470050003520

Pecukonis, E., Greeno, E., Hodorowicz, M., Park, H., Ting, L., Moyers, T., ... Wirt, C. (2016). Teaching motivational interviewing to child welfare social work students using live supervision and standardized clients: A randomized controlled trial. *Journal of the Society for Social Work and Research, 7*(3), 479–505. https://doi.org/10.1086/688064

Petracchi, H.E., & Collins, K.S. (2006). Utilizing actors to simulate clients in social work student role plays: Does this approach have a place in social work education? *Journal of Teaching in Social Work, 26*(1/2), 223–233. https://doi.org/10.1300/J067v26n01_13

Reamer, F.G. (Ed.). (1994). *The foundations of social work knowledge*. New York, NY: Columbia University Press.

Robinson, K., & Webber, M. (2012). Models and effectiveness of service user and carer involvement in social work education: A literature review. *British Journal of Social Work, 43*(5), 925–944. https://doi.org/10.1093/bjsw/bcs025

Sacco, P., Ting, L., Crouch, T.B., Emery, L., Moreland, M., Bright, C., & DiClemente, C. (2017). SBIRT training in social work education: Evaluating change using standardized patient simulation. *Journal of Social Work Practice in the Addictions, 17*(1–2), 150–168. https://doi.org/1080/1533256X.2017.1302886

Saltzburg, S., Greene, G.J., & Drew, H. (2010). Using live supervision in field education: Preparing social work students for clinical practice. *Families in Society, 91*(3), 293–299. https://doi.org/10.1606/1044-3894.4008

Sampson, M., Parrish, D.E., & Washburn, M. (2018). Assessing MSW students' integrated behavioral health skills using an objective structured clinical examination. *Journal of Social Work Education, 54*(2), 287–299. https://doi.org/10.1080/10437797.2017.1299064

Schon, D. (1987). *Educating the reflective practitioner*. San Francisco: Jossey-Bass.

Scourfield, J., Maxwell, N., Zhang, M.L., de Villiers, T., Pithous, A., Kinnersley, P., ... Tayyaba, S. (2017). Evaluation of a fast-track postgraduate social work program in England using simulated practice. *Research on Social Work Practice, 29*(4). https://doi.org/10.1177/1049731517735575

Tufford, L., Bogo, M., & Asakura, K. (2015). How do social workers respond to potential child neglect? *Social Work Education, 34*(2), 229–243. https://doi.org/10.1080/02615479.2014.958985

Tufford, L., Asakura, K., & Bogo, M. (2018). Simulation versus role-play: Perceptions of pre-practicum BSW students. *Journal of Baccalaureate Social Work, 23*(1), 249–267. https://doi.org/10.18084/1084-7219.23.1.249

Vinton, L., & Wilke, D.J. (2011). Leniency bias in evaluating clinical social work student interns. *Clinical Social Work Journal, 39*, 288–295. https://doi.org/10.1007/s10615-009-0221-5

Wampold, B., & Budge, S. (2012). The 2011 Leona Tyler Award Address: The relationship–and its relationship to the common and specific factors of psychotherapy. *The Counseling Psychologist, 40*(4), 601–623. https://doi.org/10.1177/0011000011432709

5 Role-Play Simulation: Using Cases to Teach Business Concepts

BINOD SUNDARARAJAN

Introduction

Business education involves the use of group work and case-based learning approaches as tools to help students appreciate the myriad organizational scenarios that shape real-world outcomes. Students in their early undergraduate years and first-year direct-entry MBA degree programs often struggle to grasp the complexity of business problems, mainly because these students have not yet gained any significant experience within the workforce (Benjamin & O'Reilly, 2011). When these students sit in business classes and are exposed to theories and concepts in finance, strategy, marketing, or management, they often struggle to understand how course concepts are directly applicable to business problems. Many business schools have adopted the use of experiential learning approaches to have their students engaged in the learning processes and better retain the concepts as they are applied to the business world.

David Kolb proposed the experiential learning model (ELM) in 1984. In this model, a learner (1) receives information about a concept (abstract conceptualization), (2) proceeds to experiment with that concept (active experimentation), (3) gains experience from the experimentation process (gaining experience), and (4) reflects on that experience (reflective observation), gaining knowledge about the concept through this iterative process. Kolb (1984) states that knowledge is continuously gained through both personal and environmental experiences and that for a learner to gain real knowledge from an experience, the learner must have four abilities: (1) they should be willing to be actively involved in the experience; (2) they should be able to reflect on the experience; (3) they should possess analytical skills and use them to conceptualize the experience; and (4) they should possess decision-making and problem-solving skills in order to use the new ideas gained from the experience.

These very same skills are at the root of most education programs, particularly so in business education. Moore, Boyd, and Dooley (2010) found that experiential learning teaching approaches tied to each of the four stages of the experiential learning cycle, with a required reflective writing component (journaling), helped students learn in a deep manner. Students were enrolled in a leadership development course, and the purpose of the study was to gauge undergraduate students' perception of learning in this course, which emphasized experiential learning methods. The experiential components of the course involved lectures and assignments (abstract conceptualizations); the use of case studies and group projects participation in leadership learning communities (active experimentation); films, games, and activities (concrete experiences); and journaling, rhetorical questions, and discussions (reflective observations). Students received abstracts concepts and theories around leadership and were able to experience these by participating in leadership learning communities and experimenting with the ideas they had received. They were then tasked to reflect on these observations and learnings in a personal, reflective journal and repeat the process as the course progressed, ending in a reflective paper to test deeper understanding of the course material.

Bevan and Kipka (2012), writing about a series of articles on the role of experiential learning in management education, describe experiential learning as an interdisciplinary approach based in management education and psychology. They further state that its connection to management education is powerful: "It is perceived to be effective in the support of training and education in fields as diverse as talent management, leadership performance, competence development, change management, community involvement, volunteering, cross-cultural training, and entrepreneurship" (p. 193). Often it is hard to describe the various complexities that people can face at the workplace, and using simulations and experiential learning can prepare managers to be immersed in complex workplace situations involving conflict negotiation, workplace harassment, performance evaluation, et cetera, and provide them with complex experiential learning (CEL). Bevan and Kipka discuss papers that present a need for experiential learning in management training because simulations and experiential learning approaches can help managers and leaders be better prepared to deal with the physio-psychological needs of themselves and their direct reports and to use corporate theatre and drama techniques as a change management tool. Using balanced experiential enquiry can help managers to develop sustained moral performance and managers and leaders to be prepared to respond to the challenges and opportunities around sustainable business operations.

Experiential learning constitutes a spectrum that contains several options within it that allow for differing types of student/learner engagement. These options range from apprenticeships, job shadowing, and practicum to case-based learning, simulations/role-playing, and internships and work-integrated learning opportunities. Early in the students' stay at an undergraduate degree program, possibly in the first year of college/university, students need to be eased into the concept of experiential learning by being provided with increasingly complex workplace scenarios. These scenarios or mini cases describe workplace situations involving minor decisions around the textbook concepts that the students are currently learning and require the students to determine what concepts tie into specific workplace behaviours.

As students begin to attend advanced courses in subject areas of their interest (or majors), case-based learning begins to take on more importance. These cases are often on more involved organizational situations, requiring greater levels of thinking, analysis, and integration of course-based concepts into finding suitable recommendations for the organizational issues discussed in the case. Many of these case-based learning approaches, as adopted and used currently in business schools, require or task students to look at the organizational issues in the cases from an outside-looking-in perspective. These are good approaches as they provide outside perspectives, but are limited because they do not give students an inward, contextual perspective.

This is where simulations and role-play are particularly beneficial: they allow students to gain inside-looking-in and inside-looking-out perspectives as organizational contexts become clearer; that is, they allow them to understand the ground realities of being in a role in an organization before going on to actual internships or work-integrated learning experiences at real jobs. Students can then be prepared to work with organizations for their capstone strategy courses – a recent trend in business schools where partner organizations provide real projects for student teams to work on in order to provide actionable recommendations to the organizations to implement (Sanyal, 2004; Inamdar & Roldan, 2013).

The case for running simulations in the social sciences is quite strong, and researchers have pointed to multiple layers of student benefits. Schnurr et al. (2015) have reported that role-play simulations have been shown to accelerate knowledge acquisition, as have Sheakley et al. (2016). Chasek (2005) and Martinez Munoz et al. (2013) found that using role-play simulations in their classrooms stimulated interest in the course material. Other researchers have found that students are able to apply course concepts in a real-world situation (Asal & Blake 2006; Shellman & Turan 2006) and that simulation hones skill development

(Schroedl et al. 2012). While the above scholarship is drawn from various social science disciplines, the purpose of this chapter is to (1) highlight the shortage of research or other works describing the use of role-play and simulations in management and business school education; and (2) describe ways in which role-play simulations can be integrated in management education and add to this body of literature.

Each department or program needs to choose the best experiential learning approaches for their students and their contexts. Choosing the experiential learning approach most suitable for the level of the students is extremely important, as each approach comes with its own sets of challenges, constraints, and opportunities. First-year management students need to be eased into experiential learning approaches by using small business scenarios and having them work through the scenarios in the classroom. Immersing them into complex role-play simulations, while stimulating and challenging, can also serve to overwhelm them. However, as they prepare to enter the workforce in their second year, in internships or co-op work placements, using mock interviews is an excellent way to get them ready for job interviews.

Additionally, for second- and third-year students in an undergraduate business degree program, adding complexities in stages can further enhance student engagement and learning. Baranowski (2006), Schnurr et al. (2014), and Homer et al. (2012) have found that using role-play simulations can deepen student understanding of the complexity of achieving real-world outcomes. Computer-based workplace simulations, such as those on customer relationship management concepts and strategies, and effective ways to employ data analytics and mine business intelligence, can be taught this way. Students working in teams representing functional areas in an organization, like finance, marketing/sales, distribution, human resources (HR), et cetera, can learn to simulate real-life workplace problems and tackle them as a group. The peer-learning approach, based on social constructivism (Vygotsky, 1978), is a way to have learner peers engage in deliberation and dialogue, gain perspectives different from their own, and seek to reach an agreement or consensus about their individual understanding of complex constructs and contexts. Additionally, when student teams are switched about during a course, students will interact with more and different members of their class, and the multiplicity of perspectives becomes a mainstay in their learning behaviours.

As students move into their final year (the fourth year of an undergraduate program), business schools begin to use a fair amount of complex business cases, computer simulations, and gaming to have students experience retail sales management and distribution, customer relationship management, payroll and HR, and enterprise resource planning (ERP). They partner with industry leaders like SAP (ERPsim), IBM (Cognos Business Analytics), Microsoft (Microsoft Dynamics), Oracle (ERP Cloud), PeopleSoft, et cetera and train students to engage in various management information systems so that they can become familiar with business scorecards and business intelligence dashboards and become better at business decision-making. Many business schools have partnerships with industries to help create live projects for student teams to work on, giving students the flavour of working with real-world problems.

Role-Play Simulations with Business Cases in Management Education

In the rest of the paper, we showcase examples of how to use role-play simulations in business teaching. These approaches are designed to (1) give students a glimpse of organizational contexts and complexities; (2) enable students to work in different groups during the semester to gain multiple perspectives; and (3) gain an inside-looking-out perspective and contextual awareness as they role-play stakeholders dealing with current organizational scenarios. Using examples from both undergraduate and graduate courses, we will lay out the process for effectively using these simulations in a business school curriculum.

Using Role-Play Simulations in Business Courses

We present below two case-based role-play simulation assignments, one designed for the fourth year of an undergraduate business degree program and the second a simulation that takes place in a graduate-level MBA course.

Case Study #1: Role-Play Simulation in a Fourth-Year BComm Course – Corporate Communication

This simulation takes places in a fourth-year undergraduate bachelor of commerce (BComm) course that is required for students in the Organizational Behaviour or Managing People & Organizations majors. It is an elective for other majors in the BComm degree program offered by the business school. There are typically between 25 and 30 students in the class. This course is designed to be a capstone course that allows students to use their business communication skills in writing incident reports and analytical reports, and where necessary include marketing, financial, and accounting knowledge to provide support for their arguments, all in the context of organizational crises.

In this course, student teams work on three cases that each take place in three-week intervals. As a pedagogical approach, the teams are changed for each case, allowing students to work with many classmates during the semester and appreciate all the associated complexities of the given case. When an organization is undergoing a crisis, there are financial implications that the finance department is focused on and corporate branding implications that the marketing/sales department is focused on. The senior leadership is focused on external corporate image and reputation, while keeping an eye on the possible impact on stock prices and shareholder concerns if it is a publicly traded organization. When student teams don these roles in the various functional units of this organization under crisis, their world views are often limited to the direct impact on their unit's primary stakeholders (internal or external), and this inside-looking-out perspective is crucial to the students' understanding of the organizational ground realities. This cross-pollination of roles, perspectives, and contexts will begin to provide glimpses of the big picture and the minutiae surrounding organizational practices and strategies.

The purpose of the simulation is to help students devise a viable communication and post-incident marketing strategy to help restore the reputation of the brand and the image of the organization. Student teams create a portfolio for a stakeholder involved in the case. The portfolio contains an overall strategy for pursuable courses of action, an incident report, a post-incident organizational strategy, an accounting/financial implication assessment where applicable, and a statement on legal issues: potential lawsuits and other legal implications like amended contracts, revisions of terms, et cetera. Finally, the student teams make a presentation of their report to the targeted audience (e.g., shareholders who might sometimes be hostile).

Two examples from a recent delivery of this course are the cases of Starbucks and Tim Hortons. The following sections describe how to structure the assignment, the concepts addressed in each case, how the teams in each case are divided, what the evaluation criteria are, and how the debriefing occurs.

STARBUCKS

The Starbucks case occurred a few years ago and involved two decisions the organization made that went against their own corporate values statements. The first involved Starbucks actively lobbying the US Patents Office to prevent Ethiopia from patenting their homegrown coffee beans in order to maintain Starbucks' exclusive sourcing arrangement. The second issue involved legal tax avoidance in the UK.

Student teams adopt the roles of Starbucks senior management, Ethiopia, and the NGO Oxfam. If all student teams have only the Starbucks case as the primary assignment, additional stakeholder groups include employees, Starbucks' customers, the public, and the media. Students within each team adopt specific roles in each of these stakeholder groups and build a persuasive argument about the stated positions of their adopted stakeholder. In these adopted roles, students produce internal memos, letters to external stakeholders, press releases, legal briefs, an overall public relations/corporate communication portfolio, and a post-incident marketing campaign strategy. In the case of customers or the public, such forms of communication do not exist, so students in the roles of either customers or the public form fictitious customer/public groups (such as societies, fan clubs, etc., as relevant to the case under discussion). Finally, the student teams present their positions to the rest of the class, who serve as the most important stakeholder that each team has identified; for example, the senior management group can present internally to their employees or externally to the organization's board of directors, the HR group can present to senior management or to employees, et cetera. For this, the students use the stakeholder salience model (Mitchell, Agle, & Wood, 1997) to sort the organizational stakeholders according to their power to influence the organization, the legitimacy of the stakeholders' relationship with the organization, and the urgency of the stakeholders' claim on the organization. Using this approach to identify the organization's stakeholders for the crisis or organizational problem under discussion, student teams, staying in their assigned organizational roles, respond to specific questions posed to them with these identified stakeholders as the target audience.

TIM HORTONS

The Tim Hortons case is more recent and involved issues stemming from the minimum wage increase in Ontario, Canada. Some franchisees raised coffee prices, while others cut benefits, resulting in a public relations crisis for the brand. While these two cases were about coffee companies, their crises were different; however, they involved similar actors. The interesting thing about the Tim Hortons case was that it was an ongoing, live case that developed rapidly as the semester progressed. Students had an idea about what had happened with Starbucks, and they had to extrapolate on what could happen to Tim Hortons' brand, image, and reputation as the issue dragged on on the public stage and everyone played the blame game. Live cases allow students to test whether textbook concepts can be applied and see them play out in real time.

The stakeholder groups that each student team adopts in this case are Tim Hortons' senior management, franchisees, and the Durham Region Labour Council (the NGO in this case). If all the teams work on only the Tim Hortons case, then additional stakeholder groups are franchisee employees, the media, the public, and the Ontario government. Within each adopted stakeholder group, students again take on specific individual roles (CEO, corporate communication officer, country leader, president of the franchisees' union or labour official, etc.). This allows for both individual and group work. As individuals, students in these adopted roles are tasked with producing specific communication pieces (memos, letters, press releases, legal statements), and as a team, they must produce the analytical reports and marketing campaign strategies, all the while using course concepts that were imparted earlier in the semester.

Each team gets 15–20 minutes to complete their role-play presentation. Other student teams are present in the audience in the roles of their adopted stakeholders and ask questions in these roles. This situation simulates real-life press conferences, internal organizational meetings/town halls, and public discourse, and staying in their roles allows students to defend their stakeholder's position to the key constituencies.

Debrief and Evaluation of Learning Objectives

The verbal debrief occurs after the last team presents. Initially during the debrief, students stay in their adopted roles. As the debrief progresses, students drop out of their adopted roles and become learners in the class. Student teams are asked what they would have done differently, now that they had witnessed other groups present the same case from the perspectives of the different stakeholders involved in the case. During the debrief period, students can openly discuss what assumptions they had made for the positions their adopted stakeholder(s) took. This results in several visual and audible "aha" moments from students as they see the different perspectives and approaches. Their learning of corporate communication strategies and related concepts gets directly applied to their interpretation of the case and how it unfolded in the past or, if it is a live case, how it could possibly continue to unfold. In this course, some of the key concepts revolve around corporate branding, corporate image, and corporate reputation and what organizations do (or do not do) to safeguard these in the face of a public relations crisis. The students can study the actual messages delivered by organizations in response to a current crisis and note whether there was an attempt made to employ good strategies to restore lost image and reputation. Thus, during this verbal debrief, students' questions to one another revolve around why a strategy was recommended and how well that strategy can go to repair any damage to the organization's image and reputation.

Student comments from the recent delivery of the course are given below, which reflect the level of engagement students had with the material and the approach.

Student comment 1: "[The instructor's] content is interesting. I liked that he used cases that were ongoing during the semester – added interest!"

Student comment 2: "I also really liked that the groups for the case assignments were switched every time. It was interesting to get to know more people in the class and experience working with new people each project."

Student comment 3: "The way the group work was conducted really pushed us to work with people we had not, and ended up being a great learning experience. The open communication and interest in our ideas motivated me to work hard on assignments and projects."

Student comment 4: "[The instructor] used a lot of real-world application in class lectures, and allowed us to work on our group projects in class. This helped us with our communication and time management."

Student comment 5: "[The instructor] used real world applications to teach us, and repetitive assignments to drive every point home. It was very helpful!"

Student comments 1, 4, and 5, highlight the value of real, live cases as students can see what the organizations are doing, what their press releases look like, which organizational stakeholders they are addressing, and how the crisis is unfolding. Student comments 2 and 3 speak directly to the value of switching group membership for each case.

Another important takeaway from these comments is that the students gain multiple perspectives when they adopt stakeholders both internal and external to the organization facing the crisis. Going through three different cases, each time in a different organizational role, allows students to gain an agility around the most important thing related to solving business cases – understanding the problem, as well as understanding, from the perspective of a specific department in an organization, how it impacts that department specifically and the organization in general. This from-the-inside-looking-out perspective adds an additional dimension to the "aha" moment. Students must act, produce documentation, and speak as representatives of their adopted stakeholders, as opposed to just hired consultants providing recommendations for future courses of actions. While the latter is the default approach in many business school courses using case-based learning, it relies exclusively on an outside-looking-in perspective, which is limited in terms of actual insights that the students can gain from the exercise. Students will get those experiences and insights when they enter the workplace for their internships, co-op work term placements, and full-time jobs. According to Harvard Business School, a leading publisher of business cases for educational purposes, "the case method is a profound educational innovation that presents the greatest challenges confronting leading companies, nonprofits, and government organizations – complete with the constraints and incomplete information found in real business issues – and places the student in the role of the decision maker. There are no simple solutions; yet through the dynamic process of exchanging perspectives, countering and defending points, and building on each other's ideas, students become adept at analyzing issues, exercising judgment, and making difficult decisions – the hallmarks of skillful leadership" (HBS, n.d.). But until students get to the workplace, a role-play simulation involving student teams solving these business cases and gaining the perspectives of organizational stakeholders serves this purpose quite well.

Of course, not all the feedback received was glowing. There were a few comments that gave us pause to think and will help us change things as required.

Student comment 6: "Please, give us at least ONE individual assignment. I felt so much pressure working in a group, no one had anything done on time and it made me so anxious! In the commerce program we have over forty group projects in total. We don't need 3 more – 1 or 2 maybe!"

Comment 6 above indicates a certain level of fatigue; some students felt that three cases was too much in a single semester. The burden placed on students in courses such as these is rather heavy, particularly because many of these case scenarios do not have a clear right or wrong answer. The pedagogical rationale for completing three cases is the need for imparting rigour so that students can learn about how complexities in businesses can grow exponentially. When students get to their workplace, they are more likely to recognize the business problem in that context and take relevant and timely action. What the student commented is true, in that business schools use a lot of case-based teaching. But as instructors, we base our teaching/pedagogical decisions on the complexity of the course material, what we need to impart to students in terms of knowledge, and how much rigour is required for students to acquire the ability to understand a problem from an inside-looking-out perspective, analyse how the problem came to be, explore viable solutions, and recommend the optimal course of action. These decisions thus directly relate to the learning objectives for the course.

Case Study #2: Role-Play Simulations in a Graduate MBA Course – Managing People

The second case study takes place in a first-year MBA course that serves as an introduction to organizational theory and organizational behaviour concepts. The students in the MBA program are direct entrants from their undergraduate programs and typically do not have a business or commerce background. This course provides them a high-level overview of various organizational theory and organizational behaviour concepts, like organizational structure, organizational culture, managing employee/co-worker behaviours, and leadership, and HR issues like selection, recruitment, and performance evaluations.

Learning objectives for this course require students to demonstrate competence in devising an organizational strategy that considers how organizational structure, culture, and leadership play a role in determining the fate and growth or demise of an organization. There are typically 35–40 students in the class. Students are in their second semester of their MBA studies and are expected to shortly enter their eight-month corporate residencies, during which time they work (for pay) in an organization and usually in the roles the students saw themselves in upon graduation. Such a class size yields about 8–10 student teams. As the instructor for the course, I assign each student to a group and also reassign them to a different group for each of the three cases that students are expected to work on during the course. This way, each student gets to work with different students throughout the semester (at least 8–10 other classmates), and this cross-pollination of ideas and perspectives is an added dimension in their learning process. Students within each team then select individual roles in their stakeholder group by themselves. This is definitely manageable and allows for constant communication among students both within their own groups, as well as across groups.

We will take the example of the final case assignment in a recently concluded semester. The case revolved around issues related to leadership, organizational culture, and human resource challenges in the Weinstein

Company (TWC). In this assignment the student teams adopted the roles of internal and external stakeholders of the Weinstein Company.

This case was chosen as the final team case, mainly because it sheds a light on the crucial role that HR departments play within a well-functioning organization. Course concepts detailed how the HR department and the leadership of a company need to work to protect the employees and provide a safe, respectful, and healthy work environment for them. In this case, it was revealed that both the leadership and the HR department of the Weinstein Company were negligent in their duties to protect the employees from sexual harassment and abuse from CEO Harvey Weinstein and created a work environment that was both hostile and fearful. The key takeaways for students were how bad leadership, bad organizational culture, and bad HR practices can combine to undermine an organization.

Student teams adopt stakeholders internal and external to TWC, such as HR, board of directors, employees, and senior management (all internal stakeholders) and the media, the Motion Picture Association of America (MPAA), the public, and investors/sponsors (all external stakeholders). Having eight teams required us to look for cases where there are multiple stakeholders and where these stakeholders interact with one another and actions by one group impact the fate and actions of the other groups.

Within each stakeholder group, students adopt a specific organizational role. For example, CEOs generally worry about profitability and growth, but in the face of an organizational crisis, they need to focus on how these things are affected by the specific context of the crisis. For example, when a building in which the organization has its offices catches fire, the organization needs to immediately focus on the direct implications of the fire on its business operations, the safety of its employees, insurance and liability claims, workflow, et cetera. The focus therefore shifts from regular business-related concerns to helping the organization and its employees in the crisis created by the fire in the building. A media outlet reporter may report on many things, but in this case's context, they will be reporting on the developments surrounding the TWC case and the start of the #MeToo movement. Student teams get to respond to one another during the Q&A period and during the debrief period. When they ask the questions, they ask them as representatives of their adopted stakeholders.

On the day of the final presentations, student teams present from the perspective of their adopted stakeholders and the individual roles within these stakeholder groups. The CEO and/or senior management, department managers, and employees all present to their internal or external audiences. The media group (in this case the team played the roles of the anchor and guests on *Anderson Cooper 360*, a CNN news program) presents the crisis as breaking news. To recreate a TV scenario, students dress up as TV anchors and converse with field reporters and guests. The reason for this approach is that each stakeholder group needs to decide who they need to address first to mitigate the fallout from the crisis. The senior leadership needs to answer to the board of directors; this is simulated as a closed-door meeting of senior leadership presenting to and answering questions from the board of directors. The HR department needs to address the senior leadership or a TV reporter, appearing as guests on a TV news program, while key organizational spokespersons need to present an organizational response, possibly to external stakeholders.

The student team representing the MPAA wrote and presented communication pieces and reports that took a firm stand on not screening films produced by TWC, instituting clear policies on what would not be tolerated in the film industry, and endorsed the growing #MeToo movement. The student team representing the public had a range of options on how to respond to the crisis. The #MeToo movement began to gain momentum in real life and in real time, and the student team representing the public launched campaigns at the grassroots and national levels to bring awareness to sexual harassment and assault, not only in the movie industry, but in workplaces everywhere.

The student team playing the HR department had the most challenging position, as they were vilified along with Harvey Weinstein. The team had to prepare statements that defended their inaction against the wanton behaviour of senior leaders in the organization. Their response was to revise their policies and institute new one, if the organization continued to exist. Their audiences were both internal and external to the organization.

All student teams stayed in role and character during all the presentations and only came out of character during the debrief. In this assignment, students understood that the discussion centred on how and why the leadership and HR of TWC let down their employees; this formed the crux of the learning. Using a live case – any news story that is ripped from the headlines and is currently unfolding in the news media – allows students to research the company themselves and make assumptions about how things could develop. Students find this approach to learning about organizational behaviour a great way to drive home many of the key concepts in the course. Many of the details of the TWC case were not available as it was a live and ongoing case being discussed in media outlets and other organizations, by the public, and in classrooms; these details were probably being kept confidential, as happens in ongoing investigations. So it was necessary for students to base their findings on research from credible sources that discussed these issues, like the Associated Press, Reuters, CNN, and the MPAA.

Debrief and Evaluation of Learning Outcomes

Once all team presentations are completed, the verbal debrief happens, either at the end of the class period, if time permits, or at the beginning of the next class. This sets up a vigorous discussion in the class as students have had an opportunity to witness other perspectives and the "aha" moments kick in. The discussion involves both course concepts and the current developments around the case. The debrief in this situation works best as group debriefing, as this allows students to come out of their adopted roles and see how others explained their decisions and positions when they were presenting in character. These are team decisions and team positions, and the group-level debrief allows others in the class to get a glimpse of the thought processes of the other teams in their approach to the case.

Some student comments are presented below.

Student comment 1: "Learned a lot analyzing the cases, creating the reports, and doing the presentations as a group. Definitely continue that in the future!"

Student comment 2: "The cases were helpful in applying learned content."

Student comment 3: "We were able to apply course content to cases, which was really beneficial to my learning."

The student comments in this course were rather general, but they do highlight that the use of cases and how the students went about analysing them were beneficial to their learning. There were far fewer comments from students in this course. This is possibly due to our university having moved to an online instructor evaluation system in recent years, which has probably improved the integrity of the data, but has resulted in lower response rates. That said, the comments reveal that when students are given techniques to directly and immediately apply course concepts in real-world situations, they begin to see the value of learning these concepts. Being in the simulations gives them the extra view needed to help drive home these concepts.

Conclusion

The inherent challenge of running role-play simulations with cases is that this approach can be confusing to students, particularly when they are not accustomed to certain organizational roles but are required to adopt the roles as part of the role-play simulations. As a result, most business school courses have case-based learning for students in their later years, that is, the third and fourth years of their undergraduate degree programs, and only smaller-business scenarios in the early years. Using immersive role-play simulations can also be challenging for introductory first-year courses with large student numbers (250–300). Breaking them into groups can work, but the preferred simulations in these courses tend to be the computer-based simulation programs like ERPsim, Microsoft Dynamics, and PeopleSoft's application-based HR simulations. Instructors also tend to shy away from trying new things because it can tend to lower their teaching evaluations, particularly if the role-play simulations are not executed properly or if the students do not take to them at all.

Having clear pedagogical reasons for running the role-play simulations and stressing why this approach is relevant to students can help get the message across. The graduate MBA course was taught to the students before they left for their eight-month corporate internships, but it would have served them better if it had been delivered after they returned from their internships or maybe delivered online during their internships. So the timing of role-play simulations is critical to students getting the appropriate perspectives around workplace issues and business challenges. (That said, role-play simulations in online courses can be tricky because there are fewer options to conduct group presentations, and where available, the courses can be logistically challenging to organize and conduct as students are probably geographically dispersed and in different time zones.) Such tweaks could become part of the ongoing course correction and improvement for many courses (with the caveat that they provide sound pedagogical benefits), particularly those where role-play simulations are an important component to have the students engage with the course material and be motivated to learn.

Students gain insights when they pivot into roles they would not normally adopt and gain the contextual perspective of someone in that organizational role, and these insights are best provided when students take part in role-play simulations coupled with case-based learning. This quasi-immersive experience allows even those with work experience to see the viewpoints of other professionals and enhances their learning and participation. To this point, the author recently received an email from a current MBA student in a course on sustainable leadership, and this is presented below as a sign that, for the most part, this approach is extremely effective.

> I am enjoying the course material and group assignments thus far. An interesting thing to point out: I have worked in two groups for the Case Assignments. Both groups have approached the case in completely different (yet I believe equally efficient) ways. The nice part of the course is seeing how professionals from diverse backgrounds work. I have learned a lot from the group work and have already applied some strategies and methods to my own workplace.

These are a different set of MBA students. They are all working professionals with 5–15 years of work experience and take courses as part of a blended MBA program. Their approach to case-based learning is different from that of direct-entry MBA students and undergraduates. These blended MBA students are much more engaged with the case-based role-play simulation approach, are active on the course discussion boards, and bring real-world insights to their opinions and views.

Wright (2017), writing in his blog about experiential learning versus simulations, states, "Experiential learning sits in the middle of this spectrum. It has the high-energy, engaging feel of activities, but it also has the teeth and value of a simulation, which mimics real-world scenarios exactly." Simulations, when done well, can really help move students to greater levels of understanding of course concepts and how these can be applied to real-world situations, business or otherwise. However, before students get to actual workplaces (for jobs or internships), simulations can serve as an excellent pedagogical tool to help them understand the various levels of complexity in real-world situations and be better prepared when they encounter these situations at work. Thus, this role-play simulations with case-based learning approach to management and business teaching and learning has three real positives: (1) it allows students to get glimpses of complex business scenarios, particularly before heading out on co-op work term assignments, internships, or corporate residencies; (2) working with different students in the class across two to three organizational cases can provide learners with different ways of looking at organizational problems; and (3) the inside-looking-out perspective gained while playing an organizational role can increase the contextual awareness of the students as they prepare to enter the workforce.

REFERENCES

Asal, V., and Blake, E. (2006). Creating simulations for political science education. *Journal of Political Science Education, 2*(1), 1–18. https://doi.org/10.1080/15512160500484119

Baranowski, M. (2007). Single session simulations: The effectiveness of short congressional simulations in introductory American government classes. *Journal of Political Science Education, 2*(1), 33–49. https://doi.org/10.1080/15512160500484135

Benjamin, B., and O'Reilly, C. (2011). Becoming a leader: Early career challenges faced by MBA graduates. *Academy of Management Learning and Education, 10*(3), 452–472. http://dx.doi.org/10.5465/amle.2011.0002

Bevan, D., and Kipka, C. (2012). Experiential learning and management education. *Journal of Management Development, 31*(3), 193–197. https://doi.org/10.1108/02621711211208943

Chasek, P.S. (2005). Power politics, diplomacy and role playing: Simulating the UN Security Council's response to terrorism. *International Studies Perspectives, 6*(1), 1–19. https://doi.org/10.1111/j.1528-3577.2005.00190.x

HBS (n.d.). *The HBS case method.* Retrieved from https://www.hbs.edu/mba/academic-experience/Pages/the-hbs-case-method.aspx

Homer, B.D., Hayward, E.O., Frye, J., & Plass, J.L. (2012). Gender and player characteristics in video game play of preadolescents. *Computers in Human Behavior, 28*, 1782–1789. https://doi.org/10.1016/j.chb.2012.04.018

Inamdar, S.N., & Roldan, M. (2013). The MBA capstone course: Building theoretical, practical, applied, and reflective skills. *Journal of Management Education, 37*(6), 747–770. http://dx.doi.org/10.1177/1052562912474895

Kolb, D. (1984). *Experiential learning: Experience as the source of learning and development.* Englewood Cliffs, NJ: Prentice-Hall.

Lateef, F. (2010). Simulation-based learning: Just like the real thing. *Journal of Emergencies, Trauma, and Shock, 3*(4), 348–352. https://doi.org/10.4103/0974-2700.70743

Martínez Muñoz, M., Jiménez Rodríguez, M.L., & Gutiérrez de Mesa, J.A. (2013). Electrical storm simulation to improve the learning physics process. *Informatics in Education, 12*(2), 191–206. https://doi.org/10.1136/jamia.2001.0080570

Mitchell, R., Agle, B., & Wood, D. (1997). Toward a theory of stakeholder identification and salience: Defining the principle of who and what really counts. *The Academy of Management Review, 22*(4), 853–886. https://doi.org/10.5465/amr.1997.9711022105

Moore, C., Boyd, B.L., and Dooley, K.E. (2010). The effects of experiential learning with an emphasis on reflective writing on deep-level processing of

leadership students. *Journal of Leadership Education, 9* (1), 36–52. https://doi
.org/10.12806/v9/i1/rf3

Sanyal, R.N. (2004). The capstone course in business programs. *Journal of Teaching
in International Business, 15*(2), 53–64. https://doi.org/10.1300/J066v15n02_04

Schnurr, M.A., De Santo, E., & Green, A. (2014). What do students learn from
a role-play simulation of an international negotiation? *Journal of Geography
in Higher Education, 38*(3), 401–414. https://doi.org/10.1080/03098265.2014
.933789

Schnurr, M.A., De Santo, E., Green, A. & Taylor, A. (2015). Investigating
student perceptions of learning within a role-play simulation of the
Convention on Biological Diversity. *Journal of Geography, 114*(3), 94–107.
https://doi.org/10.1080/00221341.2014.937738

Schroedl, C.J., Corbridge, T.C., Cohen, E.R., Fakhran, S.S., Schimmel, D.,
McGaghie, W.C., & Wayne, D.B. (2012). Use of simulation- based education
to improve resident learning and patient care in the medical intensive
care unit: A randomized trial. *Journal of Critical Care, 27*(2), 219.e7–219.e13.
https://doi.org/10.1016/j.jcrc.2011.08.006

Sheakley, M.L., Gilbert, G.E., Leighton, K., Hall, M., Callender, D., & Pederson,
D. (2016). A brief simulation intervention increasing basic science and
clinical knowledge. *Medical Education, 21*(1). https://doi.org/10.3402/meo
.v21.30744

Shellman, S.M., & Turan, K. (2006) Do simulations enhance student learning?
An empirical evaluation of an IR simulation. *Journal of Political Science
Education, 2*(1), 19–32. https://doi.org/10.1080/15512160500484168

Wright, J. (2017, February 15). *Experiential learning vs. simulation: What's the
difference?* [Blog post]. Retrieved from https://www.eaglesflight.com/blog
/experiential-learning-vs.-simulation-whats-the-difference

Vygotsky, L.S. (1978). *Mind in society: The development of higher psychological
processes.* Cambridge, MA: Harvard University Press.

SECTION TWO

Natural Sciences

6 Framing Chapter: Three Lenses through Which to Reflect on Simulations for Science Education

DAVID YARON

Simulations allow students to interact with and visualize the complex phenomena of STEM domains in new ways that can help build their intuition and understanding. This chapter begins by considering the affordances of simulations that position them to substantially improve learning in the natural sciences. We then consider three lenses through which to view their design and use. Our use of lenses, as opposed to design principles, recognizes that designing new modes of interaction with domain content is a formidable challenge at the intersection of the STEM domains and learning science. Design principles, such as those for multimedia learning (Mayer, 2009), tend to focus on finer-grained issues related to implementation of a learning activity. What is more urgently needed at this stage in the development and adoption of educational STEM simulations are creative ideas for using simulations to transform instruction. Our lenses are intended to help with the generation of such ideas by providing different perspectives through which to evaluate and refine the design of learning activities built around computer simulations. The lenses consider the degree to which a simulation (1) targets aspects of learning that research reveals as especially problematic in current instruction, (2) engages students in practices, such as experimental design and drawing connections across representations, that are otherwise difficult to support, and (3) allows students to focus on one aspect of a complex phenomenon while keeping all aspects visible.

Although the use of simulations in STEM education is not new, they do not figure prominently in higher education. This is in contrast to the rapidly growing adoption of other technologies such as course management systems (CMSs) and online homework systems. The early adoption of these latter technologies is not surprising since they integrate smoothly into existing instruction and provide immediate and tangible benefits. For example, CMSs help keep a course organized and enhance communication among instructors and learners through email lists, file shares, discussion boards, and online grade books. Online homework systems help instructors regularly assign graded homework and help scaffold student learning through hints and immediate feedback on responses. While these are valuable ways to improve the delivery of current instruction, simulations have the potential to more fundamentally alter instruction by using visualization and manipulation of simulated phenomena to motivate, contextualize, and provide practice with the key conceptual and analytical tools of the STEM domains.

Simulations allow learners to interact with and gain intuitions about phenomena that are complex and outside the realm of everyday experience. Complexity may arise when expertise requires simultaneous understanding of a set of rules, the phenomena that emerge from those rules, and how changes to the rules influence the emergent phenomena. Examples include the emergence of elliptical orbits from Newton's laws, chemical equilibrium from balancing of chemical reaction rates, and observable properties of materials from interactions between molecules. Computer simulations allow learners to explore how alterations to the rules, such as changes in the mass of a planet or changes in the forces between molecules, alter the emergent properties, such as the size of an orbit or the boiling point of a substance. In some cases, the emergent behaviour can be counterintuitive. Consider, for example, how the directional flow in diffusion or heat conduction emerges from the undirected random motion of particles (Chi, Roscoe, Slotta, Roy, & Chase, 2012). By allowing students to visualize the flow of mass and energy in systems with large numbers of particles undergoing random motion, simulations can help make the emergence of directional flow more intuitive. Simulations can also allow students to gain experience with phenomena that occur at scales that are outside those of everyday experience. These include spatial scales that range from the molecular up through the astrophysical, and time scales that range from the vibrational period of a molecule up through the life cycle of a star.

In most STEM courses, especially introductory courses, students interact with the domain through a set of paper-and-pencil activities that have evolved over decades and have been canonized in textbooks and standard exams. It is natural that the first widely adopted uses of technology will treat mastery of the problems found in these long-standing activities as the end goal of instruction. For example, in most online homework systems, the problems are nearly identical to the problems that have been at the end of textbook chapters for decades. Although these activities were developed and refined by communities of instructors, their design was constrained by the restrictions imposed by paper and pencil.

Simulations relieve these constraints and enable interactions that would be difficult, if not impossible, to achieve without a computer. The need to re-envision the way students engage with STEM content is spurred by research on learning that suggests that, in many cases, students may perform well on assessments tied to the canonical activities, yet fail to gain the understanding of the domain that those activities were designed to instil (National Research Council, 2012). This is causing many educators to step back and consider new ways to help students develop a coherent understanding of the central ideas in their domains (Freire, Talanquer, & Amaral, 2019). These central ideas are often connected to phenomena with which students have little direct experience. Simulations can provide this experience and help students develop intuitive knowledge. Learning activities can then use this intuition as a base on which to build formal knowledge by showing how the conceptual tools of the domain are used to characterize, explain, and control the phenomena.

Although simulations have the potential to fundamentally transform the way that learners engage with content in STEM domains, considerable work remains in order for simulations to realize this transformative power. This especially includes generating creative ideas for simulations that can help students move along the pathway from novices to experts. The following three lenses are intended to help with generating and refining such ideas.

Lens 1: Research-Based Design

Moving students along the pathway from novices to experts is a complex human process. Fortunately, the discipline-based education research (DBER) literature is a rich source of information on this pathway, including what makes the transition to expert reasoning particularly difficult for novices; the preconceptions that instruction can build upon; and the common misconceptions that simulations can help combat (National Research Council, 2012). Use of research data is especially important to avoid expert blind spots whereby "knowledge in a content area can lead to notions about learning that are in conflict with students' actual developmental processes" (Nathan, Koedinger, & Alibali, 2001, p. 644). For example, when middle school teachers were given math problems to rank by difficulty, their rankings agreed with student data much better than those from high school teachers. In designing simulations, experts must be careful not to assume that novices will view and interact with a simulation in the same way that they do.

Blind spots can also manifest when knowledge is held so innately by experts that they fail to recognize the need to make that knowledge explicit in the instruction. For example, in chemistry, traditional instruction assumed novices were envisioning the effects of a chemical reaction on collections of molecules in an expert manner. The instruction emphasized limiting reagent problems, a mathematical procedure related to this phenomenon. Because, for experts, this procedure is closely connected to reasoning about collections of particles, instructors assumed that mastery of this mathematical procedure implied conceptual understanding. Instruction that made the connection between the mathematical procedure and conceptual reasoning more explicit led to substantial improvements in learning (Davenport et al., 2014).

Through the following questions, the first lens focuses attention on what is known about the pathways from novice to expert and on finding ways to navigate around expert blind spots.

Does the simulation address an aspect of expert reasoning that is both difficult to learn and powerful once mastered? It is natural that initial ideas for simulations will be driven by technical considerations, such as what can be simulated and what looks visually compelling. But design decisions should also emphasize aspects of a domain that are particularly difficult to learn and that, once learned, bring substantial power to reasoning. For example, in the molecular sciences, a primary source of difficulty is the need to simultaneously consider a number of different representations that are summarized by the Johnstone triangle (Taber, 2013). The corners of this triangle correspond to the *macroscopic* representations that we directly see and manipulate in the laboratory or other environments, the *particulate* representations of molecules and their interactions, and the *symbolic* representations that experts have developed to concisely describe and model molecular phenomena. Although experts can flexibly use each of these representations and fluidly move between them as needed, novices struggle with understanding each representation and, even more, with making connections between them. Traditional instruction has emphasized the symbolic domain, with the bulk of student practice time being dedicated to learning how to carry out calculations or manipulate chemical structures. However, many students who are able to successfully carry out chemical computations are not able to answer questions that test their ability to connect those computations to what is occurring in the laboratory or at the particulate level (Nakhleh & Mitchell, 1993). Simulations can couple visualizations at the molecular scale with numerical and symbolic representations, and with manipulations of chemical substances. This allows for design of learning activities that provide practice with connecting representations and that thereby help address a well-known challenge in the teaching and learning of molecular science.

Does the simulation gather data that can be used to better understand and support the transition from novice to expert reasoning? In addition to using past DBER results, design of simulations may require advancing this research. Because simulations enable new modes of interaction with domain content, we may have little past data on how novices will engage within these new modes. Fortunately, simulations make it possible to gather detailed data on the ways that students interact with the simulation and other learning materials. Such data can help designers identify and remediate flaws in the instruction. For example, our addition of explicit instruction regarding the effects of reactions on collections of particles was motivated by analysis of log files detailing student interactions with a virtual laboratory simulation (Yaron, Karabinos, Lange, Greeno, & Leinhardt, 2010). Such log data can reveal unanticipated novice behaviours and shed light on expert blind spots, especially when the simulation is flexible and the activities are open ended. This information can then be used to drive iterative improvements in the learning activities.

Lens 2: Science Practices

This lens focuses on the specific ways in which a simulation allows students to engage with the domain content. Recent reform efforts in science education have developed lists of science practices that attempt to capture the ways that experts use domain knowledge. The science practices enumerated by the redesigned Advanced Placement (AP) science courses include *construction and use of representations, design and interpretation of experiments, argumentation,* and *drawing connections between concepts and across length and time scales* (Posthuma-Adams, 2014). A similar list of practices is present in the Next Generation Science Standards (NGSS) as one of the three dimensions in NGSS's three-dimensional learning (National Research Council, 2014). An underlying assumption of these reform efforts is that learning can be improved by coupling domain content with a diverse set of science practices.

Does the simulation couple the domain content to new science practices? In some cases, the limitations of paper-and-pencil activities have caused traditional instruction to pair content with a narrow list of practices. For example, paper-and-pencil activities based on science experiments often simply present students with experimental data and ask them to interpret the data. Although an ideal situation may be to have students design and carry out experiments in a physical laboratory, this is largely impractical due to economic and safety constraints. Simulations can function as virtual laboratories that allow students to design experiments and generate their own data. Simulations can also support science practices that involve drawing connections between concepts, representations, and length/time scales. This can be done by simulating phenomena that involve concepts from across the domain and by providing multiple representations of the phenomena.

Are the new science practices supported by the simulation likely to improve learning? Finding ways to engage students in science practices that reflect those of experts is a reasonable general strategy for improving learning. But having more specific hypotheses on the means through which engagement with science practices improves learning can lead to more effective simulation designs. As an example, consider the following possible mechanism through which generating experimental data may help improve learning. For many students, a first-year course in physics equips them to carry out relatively complex mathematical procedures based on Newton's laws, but does little to improve their performance on the Force Concept Inventory, an assessment of qualitative understanding of physical motion (Savinainen & Scott, 2002). Many instructors are surprised by this result because they assume that students are connecting the mathematical procedures covered in their class to the physical motions the mathematics was designed to model. Although experts innately connect the symbolic notations to physical observables, this is not the case for the majority of students. One reason students may be able to develop proficiency in mathematical computations without developing conceptual understanding is that they are using a shallow problem-solving method such as means-ends analysis (Larkin, McDermott, Simon, & Simon, 1980). In means-end analysis, algebraic relations are used to transform the quantities given in the problem statement to the quantities requested by the problem. Because the problem-solving process is purely algebraic, and divorced from the phenomena being modelled, the student does not get practice with connecting the algebra to the phenomena of interest. Simulation activities that require experimental design and interpretation can redress this by requiring students to engage with the phenomena as they generate the data needed for their computations. This more detailed view of how the science practice of *experimental design* improves learning may help curriculum developers design more effective simulations.

Lens 3: Component Skills within the Broader Context

This lens considers the ways in which a simulation can allow students to interact with a specific aspect of a complex phenomenon while keeping the overall context visible. Instruction can begin by isolating each of the individual components and can later assemble these into the broader context. However, students may have difficulty learning the individual concepts and skills when they are isolated from the whole. In addition, the knowledge gathered in such isolation may be inert and difficult to assemble and utilize in the broader context (National Research Council, 2000). An alternative approach is to situate the learning of the individual knowledge components in the broader context of use, but designing such instruction can be difficult in practice. Simulations can help make such instruction practical by allowing the student to interact with one aspect of the phenomena while the remainder are present but handled by the computer simulation.

Does the simulation allow students to focus on individual aspects of a complex phenomenon? Consider a phenomenon that involves multiple interacting physical or chemical components, such as the dissolution of salt or sugar in a solution (Moore, Chamberlain, Parson, & Perkins, 2014). Students' attention can first be focused on the distinct behaviours of salt versus sugar on a particulate level. Attention can then shift to the conductivity of the solution and how this varies between substances. Activities that focus on individual aspects of the phenomena can be created using control panels that allow students to alter only those simulation parameters associated with the aspect of current interest. The simulation keeps the entire system visible and so helps situate the learning in the overall context. Simulations can also allow students to focus on specific representations while keeping other representations visible. For example, a virtual chemistry laboratory can couple a workbench that displays macroscopically observable features, such as the colour and volume of a mixture, with information panels that display symbolic information, such as concentrations and other quantities that are not directly visible in an actual laboratory (Yaron et al., 2010).

Concluding Comments

Simulations are poised to play a transformative role in STEM education by enabling students to engage with content in new ways, and by gathering the rich data on student interactions needed to inform iterative improvements in the learning activities. Achieving this transformative potential will require creative ideas at the intersection of the STEM domains and the learning sciences. The lenses described above provide three complementary perspectives on simulations, each based on a different aspect of learning science. Our hope is that these lenses will help curriculum developers generate and refine ideas for effective simulations, and will help instructors envision ways to use simulations to improve their students' learning.

NOTE

This material is based upon work supported by the National Science Foundation under Grant No. 1726856.

REFERENCES

Chi, M.T.H., Roscoe, R.D., Slotta, J.D., Roy, M., & Chase, C.C. (2012). Misconceived causal explanations for emergent processes. *Cognitive Science, 36*(1), 1–61. https://doi.org/10.1111/j.1551-6709.2011.01207.x

Davenport, J.L., Leinhardt, G., Greeno, J., Koedinger, K., Klahr, D., Karabinos, M., & Yaron, D.J. (2014). Evidence-based approaches to improving chemical equilibrium instruction. *Journal of Chemical Education, 91*(10), 1517–1525. https://doi.org/10.1021/ed5002009

Freire, M., Talanquer, V., & Amaral, E. (2019). Conceptual profile of chemistry: A framework for enriching thinking and action in chemistry education. *International Journal of Science Education, 41*(5), 674–692. https://doi.org/10.1080/09500693.2019.1578001

Larkin, J., McDermott, J., Simon, D.P., & Simon, H.A. (1980). Expert and novice performance in solving physics problems. *Science, 208*(4450), 1335–1342. https://doi.org/10.1126/science.208.4450.1335

Mayer, R.E. (2009). *Multimedia learning*. Cambridge, UK: Cambridge University Press.

Moore, E.B., Chamberlain, J.M., Parson, R., & Perkins, K.K. (2014). PhET Interactive Simulations: Transformative tools for teaching chemistry. *Journal of Chemical Education, 91*(8), 1191–1197. https://doi.org/10.1021/ed4005084

Nakhleh, M.B., & Mitchell, R.C. (1993). Concept learning versus problem solving: There is a difference. *Journal of Chemical Education, 70*(3), 190. https://doi.org/10.1021/ed070p190

Nathan, M.J., Koedinger, K.R., & Alibali, M.W. (2001). Expert blind spot: When content knowledge eclipses pedagogical content knowledge. In *Proceedings of the Third International Conference of Cognitive Science* (pp. 644–648). Beijing: University of Science and Technology of China Press.

National Research Council. (2000). *How people learn: Brain, mind, experience, and school* (Expanded ed.). Washington, DC: The National Academies Press.

National Research Council. (2012). *Discipline-based education research: Understanding and improving learning in undergraduate science and engineering*. Washington, DC: The National Academies Press.

National Research Council. (2014). *Developing assessments for the Next Generation Science Standards*. Washington, DC: The National Academies Press.

Posthuma-Adams, E. (2014). How the chemistry modeling curriculum engages students in seven science practices outlined by the College Board. *Journal of Chemical Education, 91*(9), 1284–1290. https://doi.org/10.1021/ed400911a

Savinainen, A., & Scott, P. (2002). The Force Concept Inventory: A tool for monitoring student learning. *Physics Education, 37*(1), 45. https://doi.org/10.1088/0031-9120/37/1/306

Taber, K. S. (2013). Revisiting the chemistry triplet: Drawing upon the nature of chemical knowledge and the psychology of learning to inform chemistry education. *Chemical Education Research and Practice, 14*(2), 156–168. https://doi.org/10.1039/C3RP00012E

Yaron, D., Karabinos, M., Lange, D., Greeno, J.G., & Leinhardt, G. (2010). The ChemCollective – virtual labs for introductory chemistry courses. *Science, 328*(5978), 584–585. https://doi.org/10.1126/science.1182435

7 Teaching General Chemistry with Interactive Simulations

JULIA M. CHAMBERLAIN

Introduction

The dynamic, often invisible nature of molecules, atoms, and electrons makes learning chemistry challenging for many students, who must use their mental models from macroscopic experiences to construct an understanding of molecular-level processes and properties (Johnstone, 1993). Dynamic visualization tools, such as animations and simulations, can illustrate important chemical concepts, animate reaction mechanisms, and provide a platform for virtual experiments around topics central to chemistry (National Research Council, 2011; Suits & Sanger, 2013; Angelo, Rutstein, Harris, Bernard, Borokhovski, & Haertel, 2014).

As scientists began using computational models for research in the latter half of the 20th century, it was natural for them to apply these tools to chemistry teaching. Research software was adapted for educational activities (e.g., Shusterman & Shusterman, 1997), and scientists with programming knowledge developed education-specific simulations to fulfil their teaching needs. Interactive simulations provide chemistry students and instructors with models that expert chemists use to explain and predict chemical properties and reactions. Simulations include dynamic visualizations, adjustable settings, and controls that enable students' exploration of causal relationships (Angelo, Rutstein, Harris, Bernard, Borokhovski, & Haertel, 2014; Suits & Sanger, 2013). Once built, many of these simulations were shared on the internet, and over decades, educational simulation projects grew in use and funding. Today, several collections of free educational chemistry simulations have been developed for public use (ChemCollective, n.d.; Chemical Thinking Interactives, n.d.; The Concord Consortium, 2013; PhET Interactive Simulations, 2019; ChemDemos, 2012). Each suite of simulations offers a slightly different design philosophy and set of features – for example, the Molecular

Workbench offers tools for users to build their own simulations – and some collections include simulations in disciplines outside of chemistry (PhET Interactive Simulations, Molecular Workbench).

In this chapter, I first describe what an interactive simulation is by discussing the designs of two different simulations that are available online. I then present a range of implementation strategies for teaching with simulations, as well as design-based best practices for engaging students and integrating simulations into the curriculum. Finally, I present examples from a one-semester large general chemistry course where many simulations were used in a variety of implementations. I describe the outcomes of this project in terms of student reception, instructor observations, and lessons learned from integrating simulations throughout the first-semester general chemistry curriculum.

Simulation Design for General Chemistry

The simulations used to teach at this level have specific qualities:

1 Abstract mathematical models are presented through ready-made, intuitive representations for the student to manipulate and explore.
2 Multiple representations help students visualize atomic and molecular behaviour and interactions.
3 An interactive interface allows students to engage with the chemistry content in a mode that is different from reading a text, solving equations, or memorizing facts.
4 Students who may be learning chemistry for the first time can easily use the simulations.
5 The scope of the learning objectives is limited, with constraints to guide student exploration. These qualities are distinct from those of simulations used for teaching advanced topics in upper-division courses, where chemistry students are introduced to research-level programming tools and may begin to program their own models and generate their own representations and visualizations.

Chemistry education simulations employ a range of designs and design features based on the audience and the content of the simulation. Two examples – one from Chemical Thinking Interactives, and one from PhET Interactive Simulations – demonstrate the general design principles of chemistry simulations, and illustrate some of the ways in which simulations can help students interactively explore quantitative and conceptual relationships that may not be visible or intuitive to students by examining an equation or table of information alone.

Interactive Simulation Example 1: Chemical Kinetics

Chemical Thinking Interactives (Chemical Thinking Interactives, n.d.) are a collection of free, interactive simulations designed to complement the Chemical Thinking curriculum (Talanquer & Pollard, 2010; Sevian & Talanquer, 2014; Talanquer & Pollard, 2017). For example, in the Chemical Thinking simulation *Kinetics: Activation and Rate*,[1] a user can explore the cause-and-effect relationships between reaction rate and temperature, volume, activation energy, and number of particles in the system using the controls in the top-right quadrant of the screen. Each variable increases or decreases the rate of reaction, and as the user changes variables, the multiple representations provide feedback on the atomic interactions, reaction pathway, and extent of the reaction's progress to help students construct a mental model of molecular behaviour. The *Kinetics: Activation and Rate* simulation gives students an interface to explore their ideas, ask and answer questions, and communicate phenomena graphically. When students use the simulation, they are given the opportunity to take ownership of exploring the relationship in the model, and can compare the cause-and-effect relationships in the simulation to their understanding and expectations for molecular behaviour. *Kinetics: Activation and Rate* can be used flexibly – in lecture or outside of class, by students or as an instructor-led demo – based on the instructor's preference, time constraints, and technological capabilities.

Interactive Simulation Example 2: Molecule Geometry

Molecule Shapes,[2] from PhET Interactive Simulations, has an interactive, intuitive interface (Lancaster, Moore, Parson, & Perkins, 2013; Moore, Chamberlain, Parson, & Perkins, 2014; PhET Interactive Simulations, 2019). It presents a molecule that, using a mouse or touch-screen interface, a user can "grab," rotate in three dimensions, and change by adding or removing atoms. The sim provides dynamic feedback when bonds or lone pairs are added through the controls on the right side of the screen by changing the geometry and reorienting the molecule. The geometry labels update for each new molecule shape the user creates.

Like the previous example, *Molecule Shapes* offers multiple representations, in this case via the hide/show checkboxes for lone pairs and bond angles. Showing and hiding the lone pairs are particularly important for correlating electron geometry and molecule geometry. *Molecule Shapes* provides a three-dimensional visualization of molecules, and allows pedagogically useful actions through tools for comparing geometries, while limiting the number of electron groups (bonds or electron lone pairs) to six – the highest number of groups typically discussed in first-year chemistry. The design of *Molecule Shapes* guides the user, without explicit instructions, to specific learning objectives. In the first screen, the set of actions a user can take (adding bonds and lone pairs) and the feedback provided (changing geometry names and bond angles) prompt the user to connect the resulting geometries to the number and type of electron domains. The simulation's feedback conveys the underlying model of VSEPR theory, that electron groups repel one another in space to the largest set of bond angles possible. The second screen builds on the model by presenting differences between the bond angles in the model and in real molecules, challenging students to identify and resolve the discrepancies. The design of each screen offers tools that enable students to explore these concepts.

These two simulations, *Kinetics: Activation and Rate* and *Molecule Shapes*, show how simulations express important relationships and molecular-level representations. The design focuses students on conceptual learning objectives and cause-and-effect relationships, and gives students control of the model so that they can test their ideas and answer their own questions, in addition to questions posed by the instructor.

Using Simulations in Chemistry Classrooms

With the growing availability of student-owned laptops, tablets, and cellphones in the classroom, simulations are more easily included in large lectures, small group activities, and laboratory settings (Moore, Chamberlain, Parson, & Perkins, 2014). Students can access simulations on school computers or through their own devices, via a link provided by the instructor or by doing a simple internet search for keywords (e.g., "PhET Molecule Shapes").

Different simulation designs may cue different educational implementations (Norman, 2002). For example, simulations with detailed controls or difficult-to-navigate interfaces may prompt instructors to write explicit step-by-step directions for students to follow as they work through exercises with the simulation. In contrast, intuitive controls enable greater focus on the chemistry content of the simulation and the scientific practice of investigation, by reducing the users' cognitive load related to operating the software (Sweller, van Merrienboer, & Paas, 1998; Lee, Plass, & Homer, 2006; Chamberlain, Lancaster, Parson, & Perkins, 2014). Students can develop conceptual understanding by answering their own questions using the simulation when those questions arise – using the simulation model as a "just in time" answering tool (Robinson, 2000; Rutten, van Joolingen, & van der Veen, 2012; Moore, Herzog & Perkins, 2013; Moore, Chamberlain, Parson, & Perkins, 2014; Carpenter, Moore, & Perkins, 2016). However, since even the most intuitively designed simulations cannot provide all of the guidance needed for students to address the desired learning objectives, most simulation use in chemistry education is accompanied by instructor guidance. Instructors can guide students' learning either by controlling the simulation, such as in a lecture demonstration, or by soliciting students' investigation of specific concepts. For example, instructors can use a series of questions addressed by the simulation as part of a learning progression. These questions can be introduced as a worksheet or as clicker questions, to guide students' simulation use toward examining important relationships in the underlying model (Chamberlain, Lancaster, Parson, & Perkins, 2014).

In addition to teaching chemistry topics, simulations can catalyze and advance enquiry-based approaches to science instruction, particularly when the simulations are in the hands of students. Interactive simulation activities can address multiple goals in chemistry education, including science process skills, understanding the nature of science, skills in scientific discourse and argumentation, and students' identification with science and science learning (National Research Council, 2011). Several decades of research indicate that simulations help learners experience excitement, interest, and motivation to learn about phenomena in the natural and physical world (Clark, Nelson, Sengupta, & D'Angelo, 2009). Including simulations in curricula can motivate learners by providing authentic, interesting tasks and contexts (Adams, Reid, LeMaster, McKagan, Perkins, Dubson, & Wieman, 2008a, 2008b; Edelson, Gordin, & Pea, 1999; Angelo, Rutstein, Harris, Bernard, Borokhovski, & Haertel, 2014; Clark & Chamberlain, 2014). Instructor guidance and framing determine the way simulations are used, their level of integration in chemistry curricula, how simulation-based education is assessed, and the extent to which students are prompted to reflect on their learning.

Teaching First-Semester General Chemistry with PhET Sims

In this section, I present examples from a full-semester multi-modal integration of simulations in a general chemistry course, and outcomes from that project. In 2013, another instructor and I aligned 23 PhET Interactive Simulations (PhET Interactive Simulations, 2019) to the curriculum of a large-lecture first-semester general chemistry course.[3] The course used a standard textbook for the Atoms First curriculum

(Esterling & Bartels, 2013), and was taught the same way to two large lectures with enrolments of 200 and 350 students, respectively.

The instructors' goals were to

- increase student engagement in learning chemistry with interactive course materials in an otherwise traditional lecture room setting;
- leverage the advantages that simulations offer for communicating chemistry, including dynamic visualization of the particulate nature of matter; and
- support students' development of scientific practices through enquiry, using the implicit scaffolding in the simulation designs, and supporting activities.

PhET sims were chosen because they offered content relevant to the first semester of general chemistry, a user-friendly design for instructors and students, and ease of use: because PhET sims are free on the internet, students were able to use them at no cost (PhET Interactive Simulations, 2019).

The presentation of the outcomes here includes instructor reflections on teaching with simulations across the curriculum, and student affect and simulation use in the course.[4] Student affect was measured through an online survey given in week 12 of the semester. The survey was administered using a protocol that had been approved by the Institutional Review Board. Eighty-four per cent of students in the course completed the survey and gave informed consent.

Curriculum Alignment

The instructors aligned 23 PhET sims to the course curriculum. Such a large number of simulations were used for two reasons: the general chemistry curriculum is topic dense, and each simulation addressed a different aspect of the learning outcomes for the course. Additionally, the instructor team wanted to embed simulations within the course resources for the full semester to convey their value to students; these learning tools were to be considered a major part of the curriculum – not optional or supplemental material. By using many simulations from the same suite, students became familiar with software requirements for running PhET sims, which reduced the logistical barriers to using simulations throughout the semester.

The simulations were introduced in seven different instructional modes (Table 7.1), based on the importance of the topic within the general chemistry curriculum and the design features provided by each

Table 7.1. Simulation use modes and the number of PhET sims used in each context during the semester

Category	Mode of Simulation Use	# of Sims
Instructor-led demonstrations	1. Demonstration by the instructor	6
	2. Interactive demonstration with clicker questions	13
Homework	3. Review outside of lecture with clicker questions	2
	4. Written activity for enrichment outside of lecture	2
	5. Prelab questions for laboratory course	1
Exam questions	6. Exam questions based on sims	3
Student use in class	7. Student use in lecture with clicker questions	5

Note: The category column reflects the groupings for this chapter's discussions of different uses.

PhET sim. Further examples of chemistry teaching with simulations are described by Moore, Chamberlain, Parson, and Perkins (2014).

Instructor-Led Demonstrations Using PhET Sims

1. Demonstration by the instructor. The two most-used simulation modes consisted of the instructor manipulating the simulation during class to illustrate or communicate part of the lecture. Lectures were presented as slides on a large screen at the front of the lecture hall, and the instructor conducted a demo by projecting the simulation from the lecture computer and manipulating it while discussing their actions. This mode of simulation-based education was convenient and time efficient, as the instructor stayed in control of the simulation and the audience's attention. It also enabled using simulations in specific ways and in small groupings of several related simulations. For example, the PhET sim *Vector Addition* is not a chemistry-specific sim, but was used to connect foundational mathematics concepts (vector sums) to the chemical concept of molecule polarity. Prior work involving PhET sim demos has been presented and published (Barbera & Kowalski-Carlson, 2009; Finkelstein, Adams, Keller, Perkins, & Wieman, 2006; Wieman, Adams, Loeblein, & Perkins, 2010). It is worth noting that a simulation demo during class retains the interactive quality that differentiates simulations from animations, since the instructor can adapt their in-class demo to ask and answer questions, or revisit a concept during class discussion in order to address a specific concept or student question.

2. Interactive demonstration with clicker questions. Interactive lecture demos with PhET sims were an extension of the traditional demo that included one or more clicker questions (Woelk, 2008) on aspects of the simulation topic. Clickers were used each day throughout the course and were incorporated as a complementary pedagogy to simulations. Clicker questions enabled prediction questions and concept understanding checks for the simulation demos, providing feedback to the instructor on students' interpretation of the simulation model in the large-lecture classroom.

Homework

3. Review outside of lecture with clicker questions. A small number of simulations were assigned to students to use on their own outside of class. PhET sims such as *Balancing Chemical Equations* and *Reactants Products and Leftovers* include games for practising balancing reactions as part of the simulation design, and the instructors thought that repetitive practice balancing reactions could help students gain mastery of this skill. To motivate simulation use, a clicker question, taken from the simulation game, was given at the beginning of the next lecture as part of students' clicker score. However, surveys showed that 17% or fewer respondents reported using these simulations outside of class. This low participation may have been because students had already mastered the topic to their satisfaction, or preferred to practise this skill through online homework in a separate platform rather than with the simulation. The instructors were not concerned by these numbers, but found them helpful in understanding how much use a simulation got when assigned for review and practice outside of class, without a corresponding graded component.

4. Written activity for enrichment outside of lecture. Toward the end of the term, the instructors developed an optional guided enquiry worksheet to support students' exploration of the relationships in the ideal gas law and the assumptions of kinetic molecular theory, to supplement the lecture curriculum.[5] This mode was not pursued further with the large-lecture course because few students were willing to complete optional work when required work for course credit was already assigned. This view is supported by the number of students who reported using the simulation for review and practice.

5. Prelab questions for laboratory course. The most successful implementation of PhET sims outside of class was a for-credit pre-laboratory activity included in the lab grade. In this assignment, students used the *Beer's Law Lab* PhET sim on their own and recorded their responses in their lab notebook before a related laboratory exercise. The goal of the activity was to provide students with background in the theory underlying the analytical method of spectrophotometry, and provide tools to explore their own questions more freely – which is often not allowed in the general chemistry laboratory owing to safety concerns.[6] I suspect that because the activity was included as part of the prelab assignment score, more students were motivated to complete it; 54% of student respondents reported that they used the *Beer's Law Lab* sim. These results underline the importance of assessment in student uptake of simulations: assigning grades that correspond with work undertaken greatly increases the likelihood of student participation.

6. **Exam questions based on sims.** While many exam questions were written on the topics that were taught using sims, the exam questions themselves were typically presented without using simulations. For a few questions, screen images from the PhET sims used in class were included as a reference point to help cue student thinking around that topic, but were not explicitly needed to answer the question. For two questions on the topic of atomic structure – which was taught using student-led activities with *Models of the Hydrogen Atom* in lecture (described in the next section) – the model in a complementary sim (*Neon Lights and Other Discharge Lamps*) was used to generate images for exam questions. These questions evaluated students' ability to apply their learning of atomic theory rather than simply memorize the hydrogen system presented in class. Using the simulation enabled the construction of pedagogically useful assessment questions and gave the instructors confidence that the model and spectra for the exam question were physically correct and consistent with theory. This application stemmed from the instructors' desire to integrate simulations into assessment for the course, to make the exam questions consistent with the model behind atomic theory, and to convey to students the importance of the chemistry presented in these resources.

Student Use in Class

7. **Student-led simulation use in lecture with clicker questions.** The most innovative instructional mode was student-led simulation use during lecture. Simulations were used for multiple lectures during two (non-consecutive) weeks of the semester. In both weeks, students were asked to bring their laptops with sims pre-loaded and ready to run in lecture. In the first unit, students used simulations relating to atomic structure: *Blackbody Spectrum*, *Neon Lights and Other Discharge Lamps*, and *Models of the Hydrogen Atom*. *Models of the Hydrogen Atom* is rich in content and conceptually challenging, and students used this sim in class during two consecutive lectures. The instructors used their

experience in the first lecture (which was also their first time using sims in a large lecture hall) to tailor the second lecture with *Models of the Hydrogen Atom* to address student questions and group discussions they observed during the first day. The simulation was used to make scaffolded clicker questions, where challenging concepts were broken down into smaller units. Scaffolded questions can help students identify the aspects of a larger concept that they do not yet understand, and provide feedback to instructors to target those areas for clarifying explanations.

In the second unit of student-led sim use in lecture, students used *Molecule Shapes* (Example 2 from the introduction) and *Molecule Polarity*, which were used in consecutive lectures to scaffold students' learning of how to determine the properties of molecules based on structure and charge distribution.

During student-led sim activities, the instructors presented a series of questions for students to investigate and answer, and allowed time for students to work with the sims before facilitating a whole-class discussion. The discussion addressed the activity questions provided by the instructors, and addressed student questions and discussion points that the instructors heard while students were working in groups on their laptops. The activity and discussions were interspersed with clicker questions to assess student progress and to build on the learning from the simulations. For example, in a clicker question after the initial sim exploration and whole-class discussion with *Molecule Shapes*, students responded 98% correct when identifying the number of electron domains for a molecule, and were 60% correct on the molecular geometry. The instructor then used the simulation to demonstrate and discuss the effect of adding lone pairs on the geometry.

During student-led simulation activities in lecture, the instructors observed students engaging in rich discussions with their peers. These discussions yielded thoughtful student questions and helped reveal some common student misconceptions. For example, in the simulation lecture where students used the *Molecule Polarity* PhET sim, a student asked, "If the electronegativity for the atoms is the same, will the molecule always be non-polar?" This question was then written on the lecture slide as an impromptu clicker question, and students were given a few minutes to explore the answer using the simulation before answering with clickers. The instructor then explained the answer. PhET sims proved to be a useful communication tool, being used by instructors and students to ask and answer questions for each other.

Not all students participated with simulations in the in-class activities. The student survey showed that 53% of students brought a laptop to class to use sims, and 44% were able to run them. While there were enough laptops for groups of two to three students, students were reluctant to change seats to work with a group when they did not have a laptop, even when directed by the instructor. Students closer to the laptop were able to participate more actively in controlling the sim and in discussions, while students sitting farther away observed the actions of others. Passive observation can be useful for learning, but was not the instructors' intent for the student-led sim activities. In future implementations of simulation activities in lecture, student participation could be increased by addressing two issues:

1 Access to technology. While an approximately 2:1 ratio of students to laptops was observed, students did not all have access to the sim because of their unwillingness to move seats. Simulation accessibility has made progress since the time of this teaching project, as many more simulations will run on any device, including tablets and phones. At the time of this project, these simulations could run only on laptops or desktop computers.
2 Student engagement. Engaging students can be a challenge for any active learning course. Strategies for increasing student engagement include using interactive simulations in class, assigning course credit for in-class simulation participation (e.g., through clickers or quizzes), the inclusion of undergraduate peer leaders or learning assistants in large lectures, and the redesign of classroom spaces to support group work. While clickers were used in this course, they were assigned a very small number of extra credit points, rather than required participation points in the course grade. Ultimately, engagement hinges strongly on classroom norms and the culture and expectations around learning set by faculty and students.

Students survey responses were sorted based on whether students reported using simulations themselves (as opposed to observing instructors or peers), and an interesting correlation emerged. Students who reported using simulations themselves found the PhET sims to be more useful and more enjoyable than the students who did not use sims (Fig. 7.1). Since these groups were not randomly assigned, one must consider that some of the students who chose to not use the sims themselves did so because they did not think the sims would be helpful to their learning. While this may seem obvious, two things are worth noting. First, more than a third of students who did *not* report using the simulations themselves still reported that they found the simulations enjoyable and useful for their learning. I hypothesize that this

Figure 7.1. *Student perceptions of simulation usefulness for their learning. The graphs show combined average Likert responses for the three PhET sims students most reported using:* Molecule Shapes, Molecule Polarity, *and* Beer's Law Lab (n = *303).*

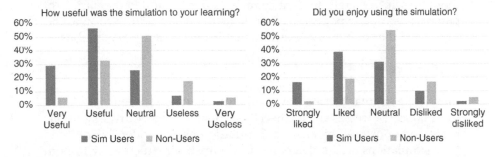

population of "non-user" students includes those who sat next to a laptop in class and participated fully in the group discussion and learning, without physically controlling the simulation themselves. Second, this demonstrates that the context for simulation use influences whether students use them, which determines students' affective response. This should be taken into consideration in studies evaluating students' perceptions of their learning with simulations, because students who only observe will hold differing opinions – shaped by experience – than peers who engaged with the simulation. The average of these two groups' affective responses may not accurately portray student perceptions of simulations' utility for learning. This discrepancy might be resolved by asking student pairs to take turns operating the simulation, but in the lectures described here, the instructors observed only some groups doing this when prompted. Since students brought their own laptops, other students may have hesitated to use another's personal property.

Quotes from the survey show that students' reception of active learning in a large-lecture course also contributed to their perspectives on sims in this context. One student wrote about *Molecule Shapes,* saying, "[The sim was] extremely helpful, used it inside and outside of class and [it] has helped me further visualize and understand geometry or molecules." Another student identified an advantage of in-class simulation activities: "It was really cool to fiddle with the dials and see what happened, and [it] was informative when coupled with [the instructor's] explanation." Some of the reasons students opted to not use sims were confirmed by their comments: "[I] didn't use it 'cause it makes sense on its own." And "I haven't used them because they haven't been for a grade." Finally, some students voiced their preference for direct instruction instead of active learning pedagogies: "I personally don't really think the sims are very helpful. I would just rather have my professor explain it to me in class using the sim rather than trying to use them myself." Overall, student comments demonstrated the variety of perspectives and experiences of students in a large-lecture course, and illustrated the complexity of factors that influence these perceptions.

Conclusion

Interactive simulations are powerful tools that help students to visualize chemical processes and connect their mental imagery to the symbolic representations used by experts. Simulation designs offer flexibility in how simulations are implemented in chemistry instruction, with both students and instructors operating the software and guiding its use. In this chapter, I have described how 23 PhET sims were used in a variety of modes in the first semester of General Chemistry, and discussed instructor and student perspectives on the use of simulations in this course. The instructors observed increased student engagement during the simulation activities in lecture, and students demonstrated their learning from these activities through scaffolded clicker questions. Students reported that they enjoyed using the simulations and that simulations supported their learning of chemistry. A major challenge that emerged was low student engagement with simulations for ungraded work outside of class. Engagement was substantially increased by making simulation activities part of graded homework, and I conclude that building simulation activities into graded assignments or online quizzes is a successful strategy for increasing student engagement with these powerful teaching tools. I further conclude that instructor framing and presentation of classroom expectations and norms are a crucial piece of any active learning pedagogy, including student-led interactive simulations in class.

For instructors interested in using simulations in large-lecture classrooms, I recommend articulating clear learning goals for the lecture period, adjusting the balance of student-led exploration and instructor-provided guidance based on the complexity of the simulation design, scaffolding activity prompts to build students conceptual knowledge from the simulation, and finally, asking students to access and run simulations before class on the device they plan to bring, to reduce logistical issues with technology.

As technology advances, particularly with the popularity of tablets and Chromebooks, some chemistry simulations are no longer supported on newer devices, rendering them inaccessible for instructional use. Popular programming languages for simulations such as Java and Flash are being replaced with web-based programming languages such as HTML5. This change offers advantages for teaching with simulations, such as greater accessibility on student-owned tablets and phones without a download. However, the conversion process for old programs to current software is costly and time intensive. Groups such as the Greenebowe Chemistry Education Research Group (ChemDemos, 2012), PhET Interactive Simulations (PhET Interactive Simulations, 2019), and others are working to convert existing chemistry simulations to HTML5, so that the designs and accompanying supporting activities can continue to be used for chemistry instruction with simulations.

Acknowledgments

Thanks to Oliver Nix for assistance with surveys; Robert Parson for thoughtful edits; the University of Colorado Boulder Department of Chemistry and Biochemistry for their support; and the PhET team for making these, and many other, terrific sims. This work was funded in part by the Hewlett Foundation and the National Science Foundation DUE #1226321 and #0817582.

NOTES

1 *Kinetics: Activation and Rate* can be viewed online: https://sites.google .com/site/ctinteractives/kinetics
2 *Molecule Shapes* can be viewed online: https://phet.colorado.edu/en /simulation/molecule-shapes
3 A full-year alignment of PhET sims to general chemistry topics is available on the web at https://phet.colorado.edu/en/contributions/view/3871
4 Student learning outcomes from simulations are not presented in this chapter, and generally speaking were not evaluated for this course. Numerous course resources (e.g., textbook readings, online homework, laboratory, etc.) were accessed asynchronously by students each week, making it difficult to discern which had contributed significantly to learning. Subsequent research on simulation-based learning outcomes may be conducted in more carefully controlled educational settings.
5 The Gas Properties activity is posted online in the PhET Activity Database at http://phet.colorado.edu/en/contributions/view/3687 (PhET Interactive Simulations).

6 The Beer's Law Warm-Up activity is posted online in the PhET Activity Database at https://phet.colorado.edu/en/contributions/view/3661 (PhET Interactive Simulations).

REFERENCES

Adams, W.K., Reid, S., LeMaster, R., McKagan, S.B., Perkins, K.K., Dubson, M., & Wieman, C.E. (2008a). A study of educational simulations part I – engagement and learning. *Journal of Interactive Learning Research, 19*(3), 397–419. Retrieved from: https://www.learntechlib.org/p/24230/

Adams, W.K., Reid, S., LeMaster, R., McKagan, S.B., Perkins, K.K., Dubson, M., & Wieman, C.E. (2008b). A study of educational simulations part II – interface design. *Journal of Interactive Learning Research, 19*(4), 551–577. Retrieved from https://www.learntechlib.org/p/24364/

Angelo, C., Rutstein, D., Harris, C., Bernard, R., Borokhovski, E., & Haertel, G. (2014, March). *Simulations for STEM learning: Systematic review and meta-analysis (Executive summary)*. Menlo Park, CA: SRI International. Retrieved from https://www.sri.com/

Barbera, J., & Kowalski-Carlson, L.M. (2009, March 22–26). *Use of an interactive simulation in the presentation of gas properties: The effect on students' conceptual learning*. Presented at the 237th ACS National Meeting, Salt Lake City, UT.

Carpenter, Y., Moore, E.B., & Perkins, K.K. (2016). ConfChem Conference on interactive visualizations for chemistry teaching and learning: Using an interactive simulation to support development of expert practices for balancing chemical equations. *Journal of Chemical Education, 93*(6), 1150–1151. https://doi.org/10.1021/acs.jchemed.5b00546

Chamberlain, J.M., Lancaster, K., Parson, R., & Perkins, K.K. (2014). How guidance affects student engagement with an interactive simulation. *Chemistry Education Research and Practice, 15*(4), 628–638. https://doi.org/10.1039/C8RP00251G

ChemCollective. (n.d.). *Resources for teaching and learning chemistry*. Retrieved from http://www.chemcollective.org

ChemDemos. (2012). Retrieved from https://chemdemos.uoregon.edu

Chemical Thinking Interactives. (n.d.). *Welcome!* Retrieved from https://sites.google.com/site/ctinteractives/

Clark, D., Nelson, B., Sengupta, P., & D'Angelo, C. (2009, October 6–7). *Rethinking science tearning through digital games and simulations: Genres, examples, and evidence*. Paper commissioned for the National Research Council Workshop on Gaming and Simulations, Washington, DC. Available at http://sites.nationalacademies.org/dbasse/bose/dbasse_080136

Clark, T.M., & Chamberlain, J.M. (2014). Use of a PhET Interactive Simulation in general chemistry laboratory: *Models of the Hydrogen Atom. Journal of Chemical Education, 91*(8), 1198–1202. https://doi.org/10.1021/ed400454p

Edelson, D.C., Gordin, D.N., & Pea, R.D. (1999). Addressing the challenges of inquiry-based learning through technology and curriculum design. *Journal of the Learning Sciences, 8*(3/4), 391–450. https://doi.org/10.1080/10508406.1999.9672075

Esterling, K.M., & Bartels, L. (2013) Atoms-first curriculum: A comparison of student success in general chemistry. *Journal of Chemical Education, 90*(11), 1433–1436. https://doi.org/10.1021/ed300725m

Finkelstein, N.D., Adams, W.K., Keller, C., Perkins, K.K. & Wieman, C. (2006). High-tech tools for teaching physics: The Physics Education Technology project. *Journal of Online Learning and Teaching, 2*(3), 110–121. Available at: http://jolt.merlot.org/Vol2_No3.htm

Johnstone, A.H. (1993). The development of chemistry teaching: A changing response to changing demand. *Journal of Chemical Education, 70*(9), 701–704. https://doi.org/10.1021/ed070p701

Lancaster, K.V., Moore, E.B., Parson, R., & Perkins, K. (2013). Insights from using PhET's design principles for interactive chemistry simulations. In *ACS Symposium Series, Washington DC, 1142,* 97–126.

Lee, H., Plass, J.L., & Homer, B.D. (2006). Optimizing cognitive load for learning from computer-based science simulations. *Journal of Educational Psychology, 98*(4), 902–913. https://doi.org/10.1037/0022-0663.98.4.902

Moore, E.B., Chamberlain, J.M., Parson, R., & Perkins, K.K. (2014). PhET Interactive Simulations: Transformative tools for teaching chemistry. *Journal of Chemical Education, 91*(8), 1191–1197. https://doi.org/10.1021/ed4005084

Moore, E.B., Herzog, T.A., & Perkins, K.K. (2013). Interactive simulations as implicit support for guided-inquiry. *Chemistry Education Research and Practice, 14*(3), 257–268. https://doi.org/10.1039/C3RP20157K

National Research Council. (2011). *Learning science through computer games and simulations.* Washington, DC: The National Academies Press.

Norman, D. (2002) *The design of everyday things.* New York, NY: Basic Books.

PhET Interactive Simulations. (2019). Retrieved from https://phet.colorado.edu

Robinson, W.R. (2000). A view of the science education research literature: Scientific discovery learning with computer simulations. *Journal of Chemical Education, 77*(1), 17–18. https://doi.org/10.1021/ed077p17

Rutten, N., van Joolingen, W.R., & van der Veen, J.T. (2012). The learning effects of computer simulations in science education. *Computers & Education, 58*(1), 136–153. https://doi.org/10.1016/j.compedu.2011.07.017

Sevian, H., & Talanquer, V. (2014). Rethinking chemistry: A learning progression on chemical thinking. *Chemistry Education Research and Practice, 15*(1), 10–23. https://doi.org/10.1039/C3RP00111C

Shusterman, G.P., & Shusterman, A.J. (1997). Teaching chemistry with electron density models. *Journal of Chemical Education, 74*(7), 771–776. https://doi.org/10.1021/ed074p771

Sweller, J., van Merrienboer, J.J.G., & Paas, F.G.W.C. (1998). Cognitive architecture and instructional design. *Educational Psychology Review, 10*(3), 251–296. https://doi.org/10.1023/A:1022193728205

Suits, J.P., & Sanger, M.J. (2013). Dynamic visualizations in chemistry courses. In *ACS Symposium Series, Washington DC, 1142,* 1–13.

Talanquer, V., & Pollard, J. (2010). Let's teach how we think instead of what we know. *Chemistry Education Research and Practice, 11*(2), 74–83. https://doi.org/10.1039/C005349J

Talanquer, V., & Pollard, J. (2017). Reforming a large foundational course: Successes and challenges. *Journal of Chemical Education, 94*(12), 1844–1851. https://doi.org/10.1021/acs.jchemed.7b00397

The Concord Consortium. (2013). *Molecular Workbench.* Retrieved from http://mw.concord.org/modeler/

Wieman, C.E., Adams, W.K., Loeblein, P., & Perkins, K.K. (2010). Teaching physics using PhET simulations. *The Physics Teacher, 48,* 225–227. https://doi.org/10.1119/1.3361987

Woelk, K. (2008). Optimizing the use of personal response devices (clickers) in large-enrollment introductory courses. *Journal of Chemical Education, 85*(10), 1400–1405. https://doi.org/10.1021/ed085p1400

Alternatively, students can write computer programs related to course content. Some practising materials engineers develop computer code to create simulations, import data files, make two-dimensional plots, analyse datasets, and automate tasks using computer scripts. In my course on rate processes of materials, students use MATLAB, a popular programming software and development environment, to perform tasks similar to those executed by professionals. Below I describe a set of modules that entails using MATLAB to predict or analyse changes in a material over time.

Case Study: Simulating Rate Processes in Materials Science and Engineering

This case study presents computer simulation activities used in an upper-division engineering course on materials kinetics during the Winter 2018 term. The MSE course teaches how materials change over time, focusing on a material's structure on the atomic and microscopic length scales. In class, students learn about the rate of chemical reactions and the movement (diffusion) of atoms. These foundational topics are then extended for students to understand more complicated changes that occur in a material's microscopic structure. Prior to the course, students have taken a required course on materials thermodynamics. Many have also taken a programming course. The course includes three hours of lecture and one hour of discussion section per week.

Integrating computer simulations with traditional instructional modes is linked to increased student learning (Smetana & Bell, 2012). In my class, students complete traditional assignments, including in-class exams and weekly homework problems, that emphasize derivations and calculations. Additionally, I require students to complete programming assignments for which they write computer code that simulates physical behaviour that is taught in class. The learning goals of these Kinetics Simulations are articulated in the course-level learning objectives and engineering student outcomes listed below. The engineering student outcomes provide a broad set of learning goals for all ABET-accredited engineering degree programs; items (a), (b), and (g) refer to specific ABET student outcomes (ABET, 2015).

Course learning objectives:

1 Chemical reaction kinetics: Predict the change in concentration over time for a chemical reaction.
2 Chemical diffusion: Use physical laws to calculate changes in chemical concentration over time due to the movement of atoms.

3 Microstructural evolution: Characterize a given microscopic-level material structure (microstructure) and identify the mechanisms that dominate changes to this structure over time.
4 Simulations in MSE:

   (a) Develop programming code that uses computational methods to simulate materials phenomena.
   (b) Evaluate the accuracy of simulation results.

Engineering (ABET) student outcomes:

   (a) an ability to apply knowledge of mathematics, science, and engineering
   (b) an ability to design and conduct experiments, as well as to analyse and interpret data
   (c) an ability to communicate effectively

   To support student learning, I designed the Kinetics Simulations as a set of computer programming assignments that simulate materials phenomena and increase in complexity throughout the term. The Kinetics Simulations have two initial skill-building exercises (Skill Modules) that are designed to develop programming skills and knowledge of computational methods. The subsequent Scenario Modules require students to apply their programming skills to problems in MSE and report their findings in a written technical document. The topics of the Scenarios are listed in Table 8.1 and are selected so that they are distributed chronologically throughout the term and align with existing computer-based simulations. A summary of the activities, student handouts, and grading rubrics are available online (Gentry, 2018).

Execution of the Simulations

The Kinetics Simulations, homework problems, and exams are complementary learning activities in the course. Table 8.1 maps these activities to the course learning objectives and engineering student outcomes. Each of the three Scenarios provides additional opportunities for learning one of the MSE-specific course learning objectives (LO1, 2, and 3), as each of these are addressed in homework problems, exams, and one Scenario. Additionally, the Kinetic Simulations develop students' professional skills, as they must write and verify computer simulations, analyse data, and communicate effectively (LO4a and 4b and SO [b] and [g]).

   This chapter presents programming modules and assessment results from the Winter 2018 term, though the curricular development process spanned several years before that. For example, the only computer

Table 8.1. Matrix of course assessments mapped to select course learning objectives and engineering student outcomes

| | Course Learning Objectives | | | | | Engineering Student Outcomes | | |
| | LO1 | LO2 | LO3 | LO4a | LO4b | SO (a) | SO (b) | SO (g) |
	Reaction kinetics	Diffusion	Microstructural evolution	Simulate MSE phenomena	Verify simulation results	Apply knowledge	Analyse data	Communicate effectively
Homework Problems	X	X	X			X		
Exams	X	X	X			X		
Skill Module 1: Introduction to MATLAB				P				
Skill Module 2: Simulations Using the Finite Difference Method				P	X			
Scenario 1: Simulating Chemical Reactions Using the Finite Difference Method	X			X		X	X	X
Scenario 2A: Simulating Diffusion Using the Finite Difference Method		X		X		X	X	X
Scenario 2B: Analysing Microstructural Data Using MATLAB			X	X		X	X	X

Note: P indicates a module that prepares students to achieve student learning objectives and outcomes, and X indicates an activity where students demonstrate their achievement of the learning objective or student outcome.

module in 2016 required students to create a MATLAB program that predicted changes in chemical concentration over time. This task was similar to Scenario 2A and performed outside of class without additional supports. In 2017 a set of preparatory activities was created that guided students through increasingly complex tasks, similar to those in Skill Modules 1 and 2 and Scenarios 1 and 2A. In 2018 the Kinetics Simulations were refined by creating scenarios for the MSE-specific tasks and adding a data-analysis module (Scenario 2B). The Kinetics Simulations were also refined during an ongoing term. At the start of the Winter 2018 term, I

planned on having students complete three Scenarios, but this requirement was reduced to two during the term. Instead, all students completed Scenario 1 and selected between the final two Scenarios, which are
now denoted as Scenarios 2A and 2B. It will be shown that this iterative
model of course delivery helps support student learning as the instructor
identifies knowledge gaps and understands students' motivation.

Skill Modules

The Skill Modules are designed to equalize students' programming abilities and teach them the computational method that will be needed to
complete the ensuing Scenarios. In previous iterations I found that some
students struggled to complete basic tasks that others found trivial, even
though nearly all students had completed a prior programming course.
During office hours, it was apparent that the struggling students did not
understand the fundamentals of the computational method and could
not complete basic programming tasks. Furthermore, these students
experienced cognitive overload and felt overwhelmed as they tried to
integrate programming skills alongside content-specific tasks.

The Skill Modules support students based on pedagogical principles
presented in the book *How Learning Works* by Ambrose et al. (2010). Mastery of an area requires that students learn basic principles, integrate
concepts, and apply their knowledge to new problems, but this can be
difficult for students to do all at once. Through scaffolding, students are
given support structures that help guide them through the integration
and transfer of knowledge. Early in a course, learning modules should
target students' prior knowledge of relevant skills and concepts, ensuring
that this knowledge is "sufficient," "appropriate," "accurate," and "activated" (students can apply the knowledge) (p. 14). If any of these four
descriptors are missing, then new learning is impeded. For instance, a
prerequisite course may provide sufficient prior knowledge, but this may
not be activated if students cannot apply the information. Prior knowledge and scaffolding are foundational to the design of my course, as the
learning modules first reinforce prior skills, then students are taught new
information that they later apply to realistic Scenario Modules.

Skill Module 1 (Gentry, 2018) focuses on developing students' abilities to program in MATLAB, the software and language used for the
course programming assignments. As review, students complete several sections of an interactive MATLAB tutorial (MathWorks, n.d.) and
an open-note quiz. Finally, they write a short program to analyse data
in a file, such as the 2017 daily high temperature in Davis, California.
The tasks in Skill Module 1 require students to review and apply their

programming skills, ensuring that students have the requisite skills to complete future tasks.

Skill Module 2 scaffolds learning of the finite difference method (FDM) and a method for code verification, preparing students for the Scenario Modules. Specifically, this component (Gentry, 2018) requires students to predict the motion of a block that has been tossed in the air, using both the forward Euler method (a type of FDM) and the equation of motion for the block. The abridged prompt is as follows:

> *A 2.5 cm x 2.5 cm x 2.5 cm cube of tungsten is thrown straight up into the air with an initial velocity of 4.3 km/hr. The cube is released from a height of 1 m above the ground. How long does it take for the cube to hit the ground? Assume gravity is the only force acting on the block ...*
>
> 1 *Solve this problem using the forward Euler method ...*
> 2 *Solve this problem using the known solution from equations of motion.*
> 3 *Verify your code ... Create one plot of height vs time, containing the solutions from both the known equation (from Question 2) and the simulation (Question 1).*

To solve Question 1, students use MATLAB to develop a computer model that simulates the movement of the block, as opposed to using the equation of motion or performing an experiment where a block is thrown. Students verify their simulation code by visually comparing plots of the solution from their two methods. For a correct simulation, such as the one shown in Figure 8.1(a), there is good agreement between the simulation results (open circles) and known equation (solid line). Figure 8.1(b) shows an incorrect simulation; the misaligned results indicate an error, such as a typo in the code or a conceptual misunderstanding. This comparison provides students with a checkpoint for their knowledge and also teaches them a method of identifying coding errors. The Skill Modules train students on the FDM and MATLAB programming, which are required to complete the technical analyses in the Scenario Modules.

Scenario Modules

The Kinetics Simulations culminate with Scenario Modules that challenge students to complete realistic, multifaceted tasks based on a supervisor who needs a computer simulation performed to solve an engineering problem. The topics are selected to be similar to tasks that an engineer might encounter, with the scope of the projects constrained

Figure 8.1. Comparison of solutions for the simulation and known equation, indicated by open circles and solid lines, respectively. (a) The correct solution. (b) An example of a simulation with an error.

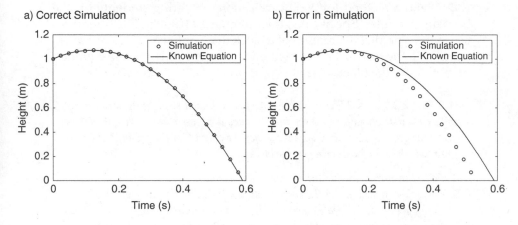

to match the course and students' abilities. Students take on the role of a practising engineer, individually completing the analysis and reporting their results in a written technical memo to their supervisor.

Scenarios are used to enhance students' motivation to learn. In previous iterations, the context and rationale for the computer-based simulations were not provided. Students expressed confusion about how these assignments would inform their professional experience after graduation. Students indicated that there was low task (or utility) value, which is one subset of motivation described by expectancy-value theory (Wigfield & Eccles, 2000). This theory posits that students' motivation is linked to the importance they perceive in mastering specific knowledge, such as whether the information or skills are needed for future courses or their career choice. The Scenarios "provide authentic, real-world tasks" (Ambrose et al., 2010, p. 83), which is a suggested method for enhancing task value. The three Scenarios are detailed below:

Scenario 1: Chemical reaction. Scenario 1 requires students to apply their knowledge of the FDM (Skill Module 2) to a specific materials engineering problem. The scenario is presented as follows:

You are working as a process engineer at a company that researches organic nitriles that undergo thermal decomposition ... Your boss would like you to develop a MATLAB program that will numerically determine how long the high-concentration solution will take to reach the concentration of the original solution. This information should be reported back to her in a technical memo by [the due date and time] ... The MATLAB program should use the finite difference method with the appropriate rate law to predict the changes in concentration over time.

In addition to the prompt, students are provided with the concentration of the chemical compound at different points in time and other technical parameters. Students achieve Learning Objective 1 through an analysis that determines the reaction rate law and constants and predicts the decrease in concentration over time.

Scenario 2A: Diffusion couple. The first option for Scenario 2 has students simulate the movement of atoms within a material through the process of diffusion:

> *You are working as a process engineer at a company that manufactures aerospace components. [The company runs large simulations of chemical diffusion to calculate processing times.] Your supervisor needs you to obtain information and validation for inputs of the larger simulation. She did a quick Google search and found an article by Boettinger et al. (2017) that seems promising.*
>
> *In MATLAB, you need to conduct a one-dimensional simulation of a diffusion couple using the finite different method. This simulation should serve as a benchmark for the larger simulation, so the MATLAB results should be compared to those in the paper. As a part of your work, you need to provide a summary of the key points of the paper, since your manager has other responsibilities preventing her from reading all the literature.*
>
> *This information should be reported back to your boss in a technical memo.*

Students must write a program that simulates diffusion utilizing the FDM, critically read the assigned paper, and compare their simulation results to those from literature.

Scenario 2B: Microstructural analysis. The final option introduces students to computer-based tasks that might be performed on large datasets. In this case, students analyse a dataset consisting of three-dimensional microstructures, which are the microscopic-level structures or organization within a material. Students are given several microstructures and are tasked with creating an automated analysis of the large dataset (Gentry, 2018):

> *You are working as a process engineer at a company that is interested in the three-dimensional structure of materials on a microscopic level. You recently sent samples out for data analysis. While you wait for your samples to return, your manager wants to begin preparing and verifying your data analysis using trial datasets. These research-quality data files are complex, so she has provided you with supplemental information on the file structure and MATLAB files that you may use in your analysis.*

Your manager requests that you consider what other quantitative information about the microstructure might be useful, and create a second analysis of your choosing. Your results should be framed in comparison to those measured in a paper by M. Syha et al. (2012). As a part of your work, you need to provide a summary of the key points of the paper, since your memo may be forwarded to others in the company who are unfamiliar with the literature.

All students complete Scenario 1. They are then given the option to select between two potential tasks for the last module. Scenario 2A (chemical diffusion) dictates that students use the FDM as their analysis method, extending the FDM code from Scenario 1 to a more complicated problem. In contrast, Scenario 2B (microstructure evolution) is more open-ended, with students developing their own analysis from provided materials data files. The use of project selection arose from course improvements within the 2018 term. Initially, I planned to require three Scenario Modules (now denoted 1, 2A, and 2B) for all students, since the modules supported different course learning objectives as given in Table 8.1. During the term I adjusted the course so that students completed only two Scenarios. Since I had already selected three modules with distinct learning goals, I allowed students to choose between Scenarios 2A and 2B. To decide between the topics, students were provided with both modules and their topics. It was also explained that the analyses for Scenarios 2A and 2B were constrained and open-ended, respectively. Project selection was used in the course because self-determination theory posits that motivation is enhanced when a learner perceives that their actions have an effect on a learning outcome (Deci, 1985; Ryan & Deci, 2000). Enabling students to choose between two potential assignments serves to increase student autonomy and their corresponding intrinsic motivation.

These Scenarios are used as holistic graded assessments of students' development of skills and knowledge. The graded Scenarios emphasize students' proficiency at career skills rather than test-taking abilities. To successfully complete the assignments, students must integrate their content knowledge (Learning Objectives 1–3) with skills development (Learning Objectives 4[a] and 4[b]) while achieving program-level competencies specified by the engineering student outcomes.

Assessment of Student Learning

The four components of the Kinetics Simulations accounted for 30% of students' course grades. The preparatory Skill Modules and intensive Scenario Modules comprised 10% and 20% of the final grade, respectively. The relative weight of each module increased over the term as the assignments became more complex. The unequal weighting allowed students to improve their grades if they performed poorly on early assignments and incentivized students to meet the course learning objectives through their performance on the Scenario Modules.

Grading rubrics were used to assign points for each of the modules. All modules assigned points for the submitted MATLAB code, judging both the correctness of the code and the use of standard programming practices (e.g., the use of comments and clear variable names). Skill Modules 1 and 2 required students to answer several questions and submit their code. Grades were assigned based on the correctness of the answers and the MATLAB code. However, Scenarios 1 and 2 emphasized written analysis, not just the correctness of the results. Thus, the grading rubric allotted points for synthesizing the results, discussing sources of error, and clearly presenting all information through words and figures, in addition to grading the correctness of the simulation and MATLAB code.

Feedback Methods

Throughout the term I obtained feedback on the Kinetics Simulations using four methods, selecting ones that aided students' development as self-directed learners and/or were informative to the instructor. This section describes the feedback methods and gives a timeline of the Kinetics Simulations in Figure 8.2; the following section will discuss how the results were used to guide course development.

1 *Weekly reflection.* Each week students self-reported their time on task for homework problems, Kinetics Simulations, and other aspects of the class (e.g., studying, reading), which informed the instructor about the workload of each component of the course. Students also answered two reflection questions, which rotated through topics such as identifying a "muddiest point" (an unclear part of the class) (Angelo & Cross, 1993, p. 154–158) or finding a connection between the course content and other classes. These reflection questions spurred students to think about their learning and extend their knowledge beyond the classroom instruction.
2 *Module reflection.* After completing the Skill Modules and Scenario 1, students reflected on their learning and work on the Kinetics Simulations. They identified areas of achievement and difficulty, and were prompted to consider their approach to struggles and to identify future changes. This was presented as a private meta-cognitive

144 Susan P. Gentry

Figure 8.2. Timeline of the Kinetics Simulations and feedback methods in the course, ordered by lecture number for the term. Kinetics Simulations are indicated above the timeline, with feedback methods indicated below the timeline.

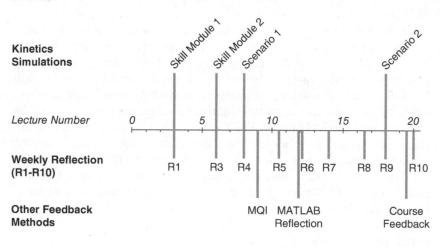

reflection on the Kinetics Simulations, in contrast to the course-level weekly reflections, which were not anonymous.

3 *Mid-quarter inquiry (MQI)*. The MQI is an optional guided course feedback process conducted by a campus educational consultant. Students provided their opinions on the aspects of the course and/ or instructor that enhanced or hindered student learning, generating suggestions for improvement. The results of the MQI were then shared with the instructor.

4 *Course feedback.* Finally, students completed the university-mandated course evaluation online during the last week of the quarter, answering multiple choice and short answer questions about the course and instructor.

Analysis of Feedback on the Kinetics Simulations

The various feedback mechanisms confirmed that a disparity of prior knowledge remained a major challenge for the simulations, even though all students had taken a previous course requiring programming in MATLAB. The MQI revealed that the class was split over the desired level of support, with 44% of students wanting more introductory MATLAB material. In contrast, 13% and 44% of students disagreed or had no opinion, respectively, citing that this information was already provided in Skill Module 1. This was supported by the module reflection. One student wrote, "To be honest, the programming assignments ... are pretty easy when compared to [introductory programming courses] ... They take me around 15 to 30 minutes to complete." However, another student noted, "I did encounter a struggle when it came to using [MATLAB syntax]. To deal with this struggle I read a complimentary [*sic*] book on Matlab, completed the [assigned] tutorial, and practiced using Matlab." Skill Module 1 was a checkpoint for students' prior knowledge; it was quickly completed by more capable students but also provided optional support (such as online tutorials) for students with less background knowledge.

Scaffolding the Skill Modules supported students' efforts on the more complex Scenarios. Although learning gains were not measured, feedback suggested that the scaffolding increased student confidence in these tasks. On the module reflection, one student wrote, "I struggled with skill 2 but felt that I had a better understanding for the [Scenario 1] code and I was able to find a solution." This was echoed in an anonymous course evaluation: "I found the MATLAB projects to be very helpful in growing confident with the program. Having the 2 small skills, and the 2 [Scenarios] seemed like a fair amount of workload. Enough to make one struggle to learn, but breaks to catch up with other classes." The short Skill Modules prepared students to complete Scenarios where they demonstrated their proficiency in course-level learning outcomes.

Finally, frequent feedback helped me dynamically adjust my course during the middle of the Winter 2018 term. The MQI suggested that two of the top four aspects of the course that hindered student learning were MATLAB issues (e.g., it taking too long, student inexperience) and the course workload (homework problems and MATLAB). A review of the students' self-reported workload from the week of Scenario 1 (Weekly Reflection 4) indicated that students spent a median of 10 hours on my class outside of the designated class times. While this matched the expected workload of 8–12 hours per week for my four-unit course, I was concerned since the Kinetics Simulations increased in complexity over the term. As a result, I changed my requirements so that students completed only two Scenario Modules, rather than the three that were initially planned. This allowed students to distribute their time among all aspects of the class: homework problems, Kinetics Simulations, and other coursework (e.g., reading, studying). When students' workload was averaged over the term, I found that the median student spent 9.6 hours on the course per week, which was reasonable given the number of units.

Anecdotally, I also believe that these in-quarter adjustments helped with student motivation and buy-in. Students saw that I was concerned about their learning and workload and was receptive to their feedback on the MQI and course reflections. At the end of the term, two of the anonymous course evaluations noted that the instructor was "very accommodating" and "takes all of our suggestions during the middle of the quarter so any issues we had she already addressed." I am of the opinion that adjusting the course based on student feedback promoted a supportive learning environment.

Finally, the set of four feedback mechanisms provided rich information about students' learning processes. For instance, on the module reflection one student wrote, "I struggled with conceptualizing the problem in terms of programming. I understood the steps to solve the problem but it took me a while to figure out the forward Euler method." From the reflection I found that several students had difficulty translating word problems into a series of steps that could be taken by a computer. This feedback could be used to further revise the modules, such as adding a Skill Module that guides students through starting a simulation assignment. The feedback also gave me a glimpse into students' personal accomplishments. One student noted, "It isn't fully pride, more of just satisfaction of things clicking into place. When the concept of the material and the coding of the mathematics click together to create understanding, not just knowledge, I feel great satisfaction." Some students advanced their programming skills, such as the student who noted, "I was most proud of getting code that ran and executed correct answers. I was glad to actually code again since I had not done it for two whole years." As an instructor, I find that feedback helps me continually refine my teaching to support and motivate students.

Summary and Reflections

This chapter presented a case study of computer-based simulations that were integrated into a materials science and engineering kinetics course. The Winter 2018 iteration of the Kinetics Simulations consisted of two Skill Modules that reviewed programming skills and taught students the computer-based simulation method that was required for later assignments. Students then completed two Scenario Modules centred on analyses that were needed by an employer. These modules used computer-based simulations to help students meet course learning objectives.

The Scenarios challenged students to combine technical knowledge with programming and communication skills to solve tasks they might encounter in their professional career. Incorporating realistic scenarios and computer-based simulations into fundamental engineering courses prompts students to think deeply about the course topics. When students write a computer program to simulate scientific phenomena, they must apply and evaluate the scientific basis of the relevant equations. In contrast, students studying for an exam or completing homework problems may only recall and plug numbers into those equations. Using scenarios for computer-based activities can help prepare students for their professional careers as they demonstrate proficiency on computer tasks across the discipline.

As faculty, it is important that we adjust our teaching in order to effectively prepare students for a modern workforce that is constantly evolving. This chapter described how the Kinetics Simulations evolved into their current form with two Skill Modules and two Scenario Modules. Student feedback provided the instructor with data that were used to adjust assignments within a term and over subsequent terms. For instance, the two Skill Modules were created to increase confidence in students with weaker prior knowledge; realistic scenarios and topic selection were used to increase student motivation. Course flexibility and nimbleness are key components of my instructional design, so that assignments and supporting material can be adjusted – both within and between terms. Future iterations of the course will continue to be refined based on student feedback and updated with modern topics.

Creating Scenario Modules can be a challenging but worthwhile task for the instructor. Scenarios can be difficult to develop since many realistic problems are complex and require knowledge that students have not yet learned. These tasks must be simplified to students' level while maintaining the realism provided by a scenario. For instance, Scenario 2A restricted the scope of the problem, whereas Scenario 2B provided supplemental resources, including MATLAB files used to open the data. Finally, these modules have been shared among the educational community to facilitate other faculty in using pedagogically based teaching tools (Gentry, 2018).

REFERENCES

ABET. (2015). *Criteria for accrediting engineering programs.* Retrieved from https://www.abet.org/

Ambrose, S.A., Bridges, M.W., DiPietro, M., Lovett, M.C., Norman, M.K., & Mayer, R. E. (2010). *How learning works: Seven research-based principles for smart teaching.* San Francisco, CA: Jossey-Bass Publishers.

Angelo, T.A., & Cross, K.P. (1993). *Classroom assessment techniques: A handbook for college teachers* (2nd ed.). San Francisco, CA: Jossey-Bass Publishers.

Boettinger, W.J., Williams, M.E., Moon, K.-W., McFadden, G.B., Patrone, P.N., & Perepezko, J.H. (2017). Interdiffusion in the Ni-Re system: Evaluation of uncertainties. *Journal of Phase Equilibria and Diffusion, 38*(5), 750–763. https://doi.org/10.1007/s11669-017-0562-7

Cyberlearning and Workforce Development Task Force. (2011). *A report of the National Science Foundation Advisory Committee for Cyberinfrastructure.* Alexandria, VA: National Science Foundation.

Deci, E.L. (1985). *Intrinsic motivation and self-determination in human behavior.* New York, NY: Plenum.

Enrique, R.A., Asta, M., & Thornton, K. (2018). Computational materials science and engineering education: An updated survey of trends and needs. *JOM, 70*(9), 1644–1651. https://doi.org/10.1007/s11837-018-2989-7

Gentry, S.P. (2018). *Scaffolding simulations in a rate processes of materials course.* Retrieved from https://nanohub.org/resources/28793

LeSar, R. (2013). *Introduction to computational materials science: Fundamentals to applications.* Cambridge, UK: Cambridge University Press.

Li, L. (2016). Integrating computational modeling modules into undergraduate materials science and engineering education. *Proceedings from the 2016 American Society for Engineering Education Annual Conference & Exposition, New Orleans.*

Magana, A.J., Falk, M.L., & Reese, M.J., Jr. (2013). Introducing discipline-based computing in undergraduate engineering education. *ACM Transactions on Computing Education, 13*(4), 1–22. https://doi.org/10.1145/2534971

Mason, P., Thornton, K., & Aagesen, L.K. (2018). Computational thermodynamics module. *Summer School for Integrated Computational Materials Education.* Retrieved from https://icmed.engin.umich.edu /downloads

MathWorks. (n.d.). *MATLAB onramp.* Retrieved from https://www .mathworks.com/training-schedule/matlab-onramp.html

National Research Council. (2008). *Integrated computational materials engineering: A transformational discipline for improved competitiveness and national security.* Washington, DC: The National Academies Press.

Reeve, S., Chow, C., Sakano, M.N., Tang, S., Belessiotis, A., Wood, M.A., ... Strachan, A. (2015). Nanomaterial mechanics explorer. *nanoHUB.org.* Retrieved from https://nanohub.org/resources/nanomatmech

Ryan, R.M., & Deci, E.L. (2000). Self-determination theory and the facilitation of intrinsic motivation, social development, and well-being. *American Psychologist, 55*(1), 68–78. https://doi.org/10.1037/0003-066X.55.1.68

Smetana, L.K., & Bell, R.L. (2012). Computer simulations to support science instruction and learning: A critical review of the literature. *International*

Journal of Science Education, 34(9), 1337–1370. https://doi.org/10.1080/09500693 .2011.605182

Syha, M., Rheinheimer, W., Bäurer, M., Lauridsen, E.M., Ludwig, W., Weygand, D., & Gumbsch, P. (2012). Three-dimensional grain structure of sintered bulk strontium titanate from X-ray diffraction contrast tomography. *Scripta Materialia, 66*(1), 1–4. https://doi.org/10.1016/j.scriptamat.2011 .08.005

Thornton, K., Nola, S., Garcia, R.E., Asta, M., & Olson, G.B. (2009). Computational materials science and engineering education: A survey of trends and needs. *JOM, 61*(10), 12. https://doi.org/10.1007/s11837 -009-0142-3

Wigfield, A., & Eccles, J.S. (2000). Expectancy–value theory of achievement motivation. *Contemporary Educational Psychology, 25*(1), 68–81. https://doi .org/10.1006/ceps.1999.1015

9 Physics Simulations: From Design to Discovery

MARK PAETKAU

A Brief History of ... Simulations

Simulations have long been a part of physics research. As mathematics is the language of physics, attempts to understand the physical word invariably lead to mathematical models in the form of differential equations. Generally speaking, the solutions to these equations are not analytically solvable, but require some numerical approach, or simulation, to compare theory with experiment. Numerical approaches to solving differential equations have been around since the earliest days of calculus (Newton's method, c. 1700; Euler's method, c. 1800; the Runge-Kutta method, c. 1900). Newton's contribution went beyond mere simulation, as he (and others) showed the stars and planets were subject to the terrestrial laws – that is, he revealed the universe was "mechanical." Arguably, the first simulations were created in the form of orreries, or mechanical models of the solar system, which used gears and chains to recreate the periodic motion of the planets.[1] The field of astronomy should also be credited with the first multimedia simulations in the form of the planetarium. With the advent of computer-based calculations, simulations of more accurate equations became possible, and the personal computer allowed physics undergraduates to simulate very complex equations (I recall using my first computer to simulate early space shuttle launches, including non-linear effects of air resistance, circa 1988). Multimedia simulations for teaching physics started to show up in textbooks in the mid-1990s. These discs included video, audio, and interactive animations allowing students to interactively engage with (i.e., simulate) physics concepts. The classic example is projectile motion – the user adjusts various parameters, such as launch velocity and angle, in an attempt to hit some target. This simplest of physics simulations most recently captured the world's whimsy with the ubiquitous *Angry Birds* app. With the introduction of Web 2.0 tools, interactive simulations became straightforward to develop and share. Today, there are many open-access, professionally developed, research-based collections of simulations spanning all areas of physics.

For the purposes of this chapter, a simulation is considered "a [computer] program that contains a model of a system [natural or artificial; e.g., equipment] or a process" (de Jong & van Joolingen, 1998, p. 180). As this definition is broad enough to include the *Angry Birds* app, the scope of the discussion is limited to those computer programs developed specifically to aid student learning of particular concepts or processes within the discipline of physics. Simulations delivered online provide interactive opportunities such as drag and drop, buttons to select options, and slider bars to choose values. Since the heart of physics is investigating how the change in one variable affects another, such interactivity represents a significant advance in teaching physics as it allows students to explore the laws of physics through simulation.

Of course, with increased access to simulations comes the need to determine best practices in design and implementation, and testing their efficacy as learning tools. What are the design philosophies in a "good" simulation? What is the best way to incorporate simulations into a course? Can simulations help students meet learning outcomes? Do physics simulations enhance learning, either by making students more efficient (learn faster) or perhaps helping students move toward expert-like behaviours? The rest of the chapter seeks to answer these questions as it examines best practices in the design, implementation, and testing of physics simulations.

The Elegant ... Simulation

There is an interesting dilemma faced by simulation designers: before the physics can be learned, the computer program must be learned. While the goal of physics simulations is to assist students in learning certain physics concepts, students using the simulation are required to also learn the simulation software or the interface itself. This concern is often expressed in terms of cognitive load (Sweller, 1988) on the learner. Keeping the cognitive load manageable is important in learning due to its connection to working memory, and working memory's connection to long-term memory (Sweller, 1988). As more and more information is presented, working memory is taxed, which can lead to slower cognition or task abandonment (Sweller, 1988).

Cognitive load has been extensively studied in computer-delivered multimedia content (Mayer & Moreno, 2003), and many of these findings are applicable to physics simulations. The core insights can be distilled into three design factors, each contributing to cognitive load: too many choices, too much ambiguity, and too much processing power required. It's instructive to look at each of these three aspects within the framework of an actual simulation, in this case a simulation of direct current (DC) circuits (University of Colorado, Boulder, 2018). Simple DC circuits are as straightforward as physics simulations get, with three variables related by a proportional relationship, $\Delta V = IR$, where ΔV is the voltage drop across the resistor, R, and the resulting current, I. In the DC circuit simulation, choice is limited to five options (wire, resistor, battery, light bulb, switch). Furthermore, ambiguity is reduced by using pictorial representations of each element. Finally, processing power is reduced by a single prompt, "Grab a wire," which conveys drag-and-drop interactivity, and from there it is a small logical step to infer similar drag-and-drop behaviour for the other elements. By keeping their cognitive load low, students can begin to create circuits almost immediately and move quickly toward more sophisticated learning outcomes.

Managing cognitive load does not mean limiting the complexity of a simulation, but rather that complexity should be introduced selectively or layered in. In the example of DC circuits presented above, students can selectively increase complexity by introducing measurement devices (voltmeters, ammeters) as a checkbox action. This action is user driven. Right-clicking on elements such as the battery or resistor allows the user to change the voltage or resistance, respectively. But this option shows up only when an object is active in the circuit and has been selected by the user, thus keeping the scope of choices manageable. As the user explores the simulation, more layers are uncovered, increasing complexity but at an appropriate, student-driven rate. The current trend in simulation design is toward exploration as opposed to explanation, which leads to a certain amount of built-in ambiguity in the sense that simulations do not contain explicit directions (Adams, 2007). As the complexity of the simulation increases, avoiding explicit instructions is challenging, especially if students are unfamiliar with elements of the simulation. Such instructions can be added as pop-up screens, or as an extra set of help pages (Kohnle, 2018).

The cognitive load framework discussed above is very general and may be applied to many aspects of online delivery, but is a useful aid to design or evaluate computer simulations. It is important to realize each introduced simulation effectively presents a new environment to students, so managing cognitive load promotes success. The three design factors contributing to cognitive load (choices, ambiguity, and processing power) act as guidelines for simulation selection and development. In a suite of simulations, the look and feel of each individual simulation should also be the same, to reduce any cognitive load associated with adjusting to a new environment.

Most importantly, a well-designed simulation is never achieved on the first iteration. Simulations need to be user-tested to continually improve quality. The term "research-based" implies simulations follow design guidelines for reducing cognitive load, are user-tested for design issues, and should also have had some measure of successful implementation in achieving learning outcomes. The rest of this chapter will look at ways to incorporate simulations into a physics course and methods to evaluate a simulation's ability to achieve learning outcomes.

Five Brief Lessons on Physics Simulations

Incorporating physics simulations can help students achieve a number of learning outcomes. Physics enjoys a uniquely interesting position as a science – students come in with years of experimental data (throwing/catching/dropping objects, driving vehicles, heating/cooling substances, etc.), and these personal experiences need to be reconciled with physical laws. Physical laws are governed by mathematics, which often requires abstractions, including numerical (a table of experimental data), graphical (quantity versus time), pictorial (microscopic elements), and algebraic (an equation) representations. In physics, an overarching learning outcome is for students to attain "representational fluency," which can be defined as the ability to make use of multiple representations and to move between them. Well-designed simulations can incorporate multiple representations and help show the connection between the real world and the abstraction. Less grand, but equally important learning outcomes can also be achieved with simulations, such as introducing new laboratory equipment or procedures. In the end, simulation use should be guided by targeting specific learning outcomes.

There are many opportunities to use simulations successfully in a typical physics course, such as in-class discussion points, tutorial group activities, homework assignments, or lab activities (Perkins et al., 2006). This section examines a range of implementation strategies and assessment methods employed when using physics simulations. How should simulations be incorporated into a given physics course? Can simulations help students meet both grand overarching and specific learning outcomes? Do physics simulations enhance learning, either by making students more efficient (learn faster) or perhaps helping students to model expert-like behaviours? The section surveys popular types of simulation-based teaching in physics, paying particular attention to strategies for evaluating their effectiveness at achieving learning outcomes.

In-Class Activities

Physics is renowned for its accessibility to live demonstrations, or "demos." The benefits of demos in physics education are well documented, with some of the most common being to highlight the experimental approach to physics, introduce or reinforce physical concepts, illuminate complex concepts, and stimulate student interest in a large lecture (Robertson, 1949). There are drawbacks to demos, such as the cost associated with their purchase, creation, and maintenance, the time to set them up and take them down, and the difficulty to adequately share them in large lecture theatres.

In some cases, simulations can serve as a suitable replacement for demos. Simulations have many of the benefits of demos plus the added benefits of allowing students to explore the simulations outside of class, making the invisible (microscopic or abstract) visible, and providing multiple representations of a phenomenon (graphs, numbers, pictorials, etc.). One of the most common practices for incorporating simulations is using hypothesis testing to engage students (Perkins et al., 2006). In this case, a simulation is introduced to students, who are then asked to make a prediction and discuss with their peers. After a short discussion, students can make a final prediction, and then the simulation is run. The class discussion continues by looking at the key physical concepts contributing to the behaviour and addressing erroneous predictions. Variations on this approach include the use of clickers, smartphone feedback, and "snowball fight"[2] activities to poll the classroom before running the simulation. Recent studies suggest simulations are useful tools to help students understand multiple representations. In one study (Fan, Geelan, & Gillies, 2018) two teachers were given training in enquiry-based methods employing simulations. Each teacher taught a class using the enquiry method and a class using the teacher's conventional method. The Force Concept Inventory (FCI), a 30-question multiple choice exam based on Newtonian mechanics (Hestenes, Wells, & Swackhamer, 1992), was used in a pre/post-test protocol to compare learning outcomes. In this study the conventional (control) group saw FCI gains of about 10%, while the enquiry-based approach relying on simulation-based instruction produced FCI gains of around 20% (Hake, 1998).

Homework Activities

Simulations can also be assigned as homework activities, providing students with independent learning opportunities. In these cases, where face-to-face guidance is not available, scaffolding must be provided to students, either via materials external to the simulation or built into the simulation itself. One study set out to test how much guidance students require for learning to be optimized when simulations are assigned as homework (Adams, Paulson, & Wieman, 2009). In this study students were provided with four levels of guidance: Type A – no instruction; Type B – driving questions; Type C – gently guided; and Type D – strongly guided. Using thinking-out-loud interviews, researchers collected data that allowed them to track how much of the simulation was explored as well as to infer conceptual transfer. Type A and B resulted in "very impressive student learning," but these results tended to be highly dependent on the complexity of the simulation. Type C and Type D resulted in stunted exploration – students explored enough to answer a question, then went to the next question. Similarly, simulations overly complex and intimidating simulations (i.e., leading to high cognitive load) decreased exploration, regardless of the type of guidance offered. These results suggest the best practice for self-directed simulation-based education (SBE) is to set clear learning outcomes and provide just enough guidance to get students moving toward the outcomes, but not so much guidance students swap exploration and discovery for an "answer the question and move on" mentality.

Physics education is closely tied to numerical problem-solving, and a good portion of grades are attributed to student work on problem-solving skills. Homework assignments typically consist of problems whose complete solution requires utilization of multiple representations, such as diagrams, graphs, algebra, et cetera. The effectiveness of simulations to promote a systematic approach to problem-solving has been investigated (Ceberio, Almudí, & Franco, 2016). In this study students were divided into two groups; one group was taught "conventionally," and the other group was taught using simulations designed to foster a systematic approach to problem-solving. Students solved problems individually, and their solutions were analysed according to a semi-quantitative scale designed to mimic an expert problem-solving procedure. Study results indicate a majority of students using the simulation progressed to the expert-type approach to problem-solving by the end of the course – in other words, they had moved beyond equation-based solutions and were actively employing one or more of the skills promoted by the simulations. About 4.5% of students had not progressed above the first level (down from 15% at start of term), and the number who achieved full grades on the semi-quantitative scale increased from 14% to 20% over the duration of the experiment. Furthermore, students who used the simulation outperformed the control group on four common exam questions (the average was about 15% higher for the simulation group).

While many simulations are directed at lower levels of physics education, which tend to be larger classes, simulations can also be used to elucidate more complex ideas. Compared to classical physics, quantum systems offer different conceptual learning paradigms for students. The most important difference is in classical physics, at any given time, a particle exists in a well-defined single energy state, whereas in quantum physics, a particle can be described as existing in multiple energy states at the same time (superposition of states). In quantum mechanics the measurement of a particle in a superposition of states is probabilistic, which again is a deviation from classical descriptions of nature. Simulations were used as stand-alone homework assignments in a quantum physics course, and the effectiveness of a series of simulations of quantum systems was investigated (Kohnle, Baily, Campbell, Korolkova, & Paetkau, 2015). The simulations (Kohnle, 2018) were designed to be stand-alone and included a detailed written explanation of the core concepts, followed by a chance to experiment with the simulation (free exploration of presented ideas). The simulations finished with a set of built-in puzzles, or challenge questions, for students to complete. To test the effectiveness of the above progression (introduction, free exploration, challenge questions), students first attended lectures on material tangentially related to the simulation. A single question of the form "check all true statements" was used in a pre/post-test protocol. Tests were coded as being correct, partially correct (including right answers, but with one untrue statement), or incorrect. In addition, students were asked to gauge their certainty using a 4-point Likert scale. After the pre-test, the simulation was assigned as homework, and students were given one week to work through the simulation challenge questions. The post-test was taken in class on the due date. The pre-test resulted in about 80% incorrect responses, whereas the post-test had roughly 80% correct responses, supporting the use of simulations as stand-alone elements in a class to convey complex ideas.

Tutorials

Tutorial settings augment a lecture course, providing students time to work on problems (worksheets, assigned problems, textbook questions), seek assistance from teachers/learning assistance, and undertake or review quizzes. Tutorials are often smaller classes, and the work is on low-stakes activities and review. In this setting, simulations can be employed as small group activities. In such situations, "activities need to have well-defined learning goals, and be designed to guide ... student exploration" (Perkins et al., 2006, p. 21). As previously mentioned, guidance must be sagely provided: too much guidance and students stop exploring, not enough and students can't get started (Adams, Paulson, & Wieman, 2009). Many open-access simulations come with tested and reviewed activity modules, which are an excellent starting point. A study by Kohnle and Passante (2017) looked at how simulation-based tutorials impact students' representational fluency. In this study, students' ability to "work with and translate between representations" (p. 1) was measured using representational competence framework developed by Kozma and Russell (2005). The ability to translate between representations constitutes a key difference between novice and expert problem-solving (Dufrensne, Gerace, & Leonard, 1997). Students completed a post-test with two types of treatment: simulation then tutorial and a combined simulation/tutorial. The combined simulation/tutorial led to an increase in the number of representations employed by students by providing crucial scaffolding to help them make sense of these complex abstractions.

Laboratory Activities

Despite widespread availability and the success of simulations in promoting interactive-engagement learning environments, the use of simulations in physics laboratories still has not gained widespread acceptance. One interesting study replaced real lab equipment with a simulated environment (University of Colorado Boulder, 2018); hands-on and conceptual learning were compared (Finkelstein et al., 2005). This study used a post-test where students built a circuit consisting of a battery, series/parallel lights, and a switch. The students were asked to describe "what happens and why" when the switch is opened. Using a standardized rubric, the researchers compared two measures: the time it took for students to build the circuit and the results of overall correctness of the write-up section. Students using the simulation circuit tended to take less time to set up the post-test circuit (14 minutes versus 18 minutes, against the control of 27 minutes for students who had done no previous electronics lab) and scored better on the write-up (1.86 versus 1.64 on a 4-point rubric from 0–3). Three final exam questions were also considered, and again students who used the simulation tended to outperform students who had used real equipment by about 10%. The authors concluded,

> In this particular environment, a fairly traditional DC circuit laboratory with the explicit goals of developing students' understanding of simple circuits, as well as skills at manipulating these components and reasoning about their behaviour, the virtual equipment is more productive than real equipment. (p. 7)

In 2013 (eight years later), a review of 30 articles concerning real and virtual laboratories in science and engineering education appeared in *Science* (Jong, Linn, & Zacharia, 2013), and the authors offered up the following conclusion: "Combinations of virtual and physical laboratories offer advantages that neither one can fully achieve by itself" (p. 308). Part of this debate comes down to what the actual purpose of the laboratory portion of the course is. Furthermore, evidence has been put forward showing hands-on laboratories have no measurable impact on student course performance (Holmes & Wieman, 2018).

So, despite virtual labs showing better ability to help students understand concepts, and, in the case of electric circuits, equal ability to help them work with real equipment *and* no real impact on course performance, why aren't departments jumping to them? I would suggest three reasons for the reluctance to abandon hands-on activities. First, physics is an experimental science, and the history of experimental physics is dotted with constructing intricate lab equipment and taking measurements by hand – simulations represent a departure from this historical paradigm. Second, the real world is not perfect, and there is something to be gained by dealing with this material imperfection. In the case of DC circuits, for example, in real life wires fail, and the learned process of troubleshooting is a key advantage of hands-on measurements over simulations.[3] The third reason brings us full circle: an elegant simulation is designed to minimize cognitive load in order to highlight conceptual elements. While hands-on measurements provide some limiting structure, in general they require students to manage the cognitive load, and self-managing cognitive load is an important skill to acquire.

Pre-Lab Activities

Yet another use for simulations is as preparatory learning in advance of a physics laboratory (Paetkau, Bissonnette, & Taylor, 2013). In this study, the learning objective for the simulations was to prepare students for the data-taking aspect of first-year physics labs.[4] Simulations allowed students to practise lab measurements prior to attending the lab. For example, a lab based on Hooke's law let students place various masses on a spring and measure the extension. The spring–mass system could also be made to oscillate, and the period of oscillation measured. These simulations were used in combination with a short online quiz administered through the course management system and due before the lab. The quiz provided guidance for exploring the simulation (free exploration – "what is the smallest unit of the ruler?"), making actual measurements ("measure the spring extension when 200g is placed on the holder"), and finally estimating measurement uncertainties ("what is the uncertainty in the time for one oscillation?"). To test the effectiveness of the simulations, students were divided into two groups. In preparation for the lab, one group worked with the simulation and was asked to read the manual, while the control group was asked to just read the manual. At the start of the lab, all students were asked to write a four- to five-sentence description of the data-taking procedure. The handwritten student descriptions were then ranked on their understanding of the data-taking procedure by experienced lab instructors using a 3-point (0 = little or no evidence of preparedness; 1 = some evidence; 2 = clear evidence) level of preparedness scale. The incorporation of the simulation as a pre-lab exercise resulted in a shift in about 40% of the students; that is, a simple histogram comparing students who used the simulations to the control showed 20% fewer 0s (little or no evidence) and 20% more 2s (clear evidence) in student understanding of the data-taking procedure.

Pre-laboratory exercises are common for most physics labs, and incorporating a simulation as a pre-lab activity can function as "flipping" the lab. In this model of delivery, allowing students to complete the lab as a simulation before attending the lab may help students to manage cognitive load in the laboratory itself, freeing up time to complete the analysis and communication portions of the laboratory.

Simulations of the Future

Starting from our basic definition of a simulation as "a [computer] program that contains a model of a system [natural or artificial; e.g., equipment] or a process" (de Jong & van Joolingen, 1998), the last 20 years have seen an explosion in the creation and availability of open-access, high-quality computer simulations for physics education. Smartphones and other touch-based interfaces (e.g., smart boards) have made incorporation of these simulations into classroom settings much easier. Perhaps the next level of simulation to gain widespread use will be based on augmented (or full virtual) reality simulations (Buesing & Cook,

2013). In augmented reality simulations, users use handheld devices to recognize objects; then other images are overlaid onto those objects. Buesing and Cook describe the use of augmented reality to allow students to use their smartphones to explore magnetic fields in three dimensions. When the devices capture a particular image with their camera, a new image is overlaid – in this case a 3D image of a magnetic field. The promise of this technology lies in the "wow" factor produced by the melding together of real-world and virtual components.

In terms of testing simulations and understanding how students interact with them, eye-tracking technology is becoming more common and serves to add to the interview process. Eye-tracking involves hardware and software working in conjunction to acquire information on where a user is looking at any given moment. This data can be used to determine which elements of a simulation grab the visual attention of a user and can be used to identify distracting or ignored elements. Chiou et al. reviewed eye-tracking studies involving educational software to develop guidelines for design, such as placing related text and graphics in adjacent areas; using one verbal mode at a time; ensuring animations are clear to reduce cognitive loading; and providing time to allow students to familiarize themselves with each new environment (Chiou, Hsu, Lee, & Tsai, 2017). These recommendations align with cognitive loading issues in multimedia learning (Mayer & Moreno, 2003). Eye-tracking has been used in conjunction with other tools to examine student use of different representations of a problem (algebraic, pictorial, and numerical) (Hansen, Moore, & Gordon, 2015). In particular, the study focused on "understanding how students, particularly struggling students, engage with interactive chemistry visualizations [as the] key to designing effective interventions using these tools" (p. 1). The gaze patterns found by tracking eye movements showed distinct trends among students, some relying heavily on the numeric portion of the simulation, while others cycled between different representations. Work on eye-tracking has also compared novices to experts in various tasks, either simulations or problem-solving (Law, Atkins, Kirkpatrick, Lomax, & Mackenzie, 2004). As teaching is really about moving students from a novice state of understanding to an expert state, eye-tracking could provide quantitative measure of students' progression along this path.

The Principia

The explosion of physics educational simulations has been followed by significant efforts to measure the effectiveness of simulations as learning tools and to pioneer ways to utilize them effectively. This chapter has looked at harnessing the power of simulations as inter-active-engagement tools in the lecture, and as group learning tools in tutorial settings. While the replacement of hands-on labs with virtual labs seems to be supported by improved conceptual gains, as well as some practical laboratory skills (e.g., setting up circuits), the ma-jority of university physics departments continue to recognize only the benefits of hands-on measurements. Since a typical laboratory pe-riod is half of the face-to-face learning time, serious consideration of learning outcomes drives decisions on simulations versus hands-on physics labs. Simulations offer a controlled cognitive load environ-ment, which is known to promote deep conceptual learning, whereas hands-on measurements require students to practise actively manag-ing cognitive load, perhaps at the expense of deep conceptual learn-ing. Finally, due to the ability to exactly model physics phenomena, simulations can be very useful in helping students prepare for their laboratory period, whether the simulation is to help students visualize the data-taking procedure, to introduce an apparatus, or to present a microscopic model to help them understand the experimental data. Well-designed, research-based simulations can be incorporated into a standard physics course in various ways, and simulations can impact student conceptual understanding of the universe, develop students' ability to use abstract representations of real systems, promote more expert-like problem-solving approaches, and aid in the acquisition of practical lab skills.

NOTES

1 Orreries get their name from one presented to Charles Boyle, the 4th Earl of Orrery, in 1704. Although there is evidence of earlier, geocentric versions made circa 100 BC (https://en.wikipedia.org/wiki/Orrery).
2 Alternately, students can write their prediction on a sheet of loose leaf and crumple it up, and the class can have a giant "snowball fight." I have found this to be an energetic method to sample the classroom.
3 We could just make simulations with breakable wires! But human error comes into play as well, and it is difficult to predict all the actions students will take.
4 Preparing students in this way should show them the "big picture" of the measurements, which is revealed by placing successively larger masses on the spring and making measurements. Students should be able to complete the task more quickly, as they are freed from the step-by-step guidance.

REFERENCES

Adams, W.K. (2007). *Development of a problem solving evaluation instrument; untangling of specific problem solving skills.* Boulder: University of Colorado.

Adams, W.K., Paulson, A., & Wieman, C. (2009). What levels of guidance promote engaged exploration with interactive simulations? *Physics Education Research Conference Proceedings, Edmonton, 1064*(1), 59–62. https://doi.org/10.1063/1.3021273

Buesing, M., & Cook, M. (2013). Augmented reality comes to physics. *The Physics Teacher, 51*(4), 226–228. https://doi.org/10.1119/1.4795365

Ceberio, M., Almudí, J., & Franco, Á. (2016,). Design and application of interactive simulations in problem-solving in university-level physics education. *Journal of Science Education and Technology, 25*(4), 590–609. https://doi.org/10.1007/s10956-016-9615-7

Chiou, G.-L., Hsu, C.-Y., Lee, M.-H., & Tsai, M.-J. (2017). Learning physics by computer simulations: An eye-movement analysis of learners with different levels of expertise. *ESERA 2017 Conference, Dublin.* Retrieved from https://keynote.conference-services.net

de Jong, T., & van Joolingen, W. (1998). Scientific discovery learning with computer simulations of conceptual domains. *Review of Educational Research, 68*(2), 179–201. https://doi.org/10.3102/00346543068002179

de Jong, T., Linn, M.C., & Zacharia, Z.C. (2013). Physical and virtual laboratories in science and engineering education. *Science, 340*(6130), 305–308. https://doi.org/10.1126/science.1230579

Dufrensne, R.J., Gerace, W.J., & Leonard, W.J. (1997). Solving physics problems with multiple representations. *The Physics Teacher, 35*(5), 270–275. https://doi.org/10.1119/1.2344681

Fan, X., Geelan, D., & Gillies, R. (2018). Evaluating a novel instructional sequence for conceptual change in physics using interactive simulations. *Education Sciences, 18*(1), 29–48. https://doi.org/10.3390/educsci8010029

Finkelstein, N., Adams, W., Keller, C., Kohl, P., Perkins, K., Podolefsky, N., & Reid, S. (2005). When learning about the real world is better done virtually: A study of substituting computer simulations for laboratory equipment. *Physical Review Special Topics – Physics Education Research, 1*(1), 1–8. Retrieved from https://journals.aps.org/prper/pdf/10.1103/PhysRevSTPER.1.010103

Hake, R.R. (1998). Interactive-engagement versus traditional methods: A six-thousand-student survey of mechanics test data for introductory physics courses. *American Journal of Physics, 66*(1), 64–74. https://doi.org/10.1119/1.18809

Hansen, S., Moore, F., & Gordon, P. (2015, May 8). *A multimodal examination of visual problem solving.* Retrieved August 2018 from Committee on

Computers in Chemistry Education: https://confchem.ccce.divched
.org/2015SpringConfChemP3

Hestenes, D., Wells, M., & Swackhamer, G. (1992). Force Concept Inventory.
The Physics Teacher, 30(3), 141–158. https://doi.org/10.1119/1.2343497

Holmes, N., & Wieman, C. (2018). Introductory physics labs: We can do better.
Physics Today, 71(1), 38. https://doi.org/10.1063/PT.3.3816

Kohnle, A. (2018). *The Quantum Mechanics Visualisation Project*. Retrieved from
https://www.st-andrews.ac.uk/physics/quvis/

Kohnle, A., Baily, C., Campbell, A., Korolkova, N., & Paetkau, M. (2015).
Enhancing student learning of two-level quantum systems with interactive
simulations. *American Journal of Physics, 83*(6), 560–566. https://doi.org
/10.1119/1.4913786

Kohnle, A., & Passante, G. (2017). Characterizing representational learning:
A combined simulation and tutorial on pertubation theory. *Physical Review
Physics Education Research, 13*(2), 1–13. https://doi.org/10.1103
/physrevphyseducres.13.020131

Kozma, R., & Russell, J. (2005). Students becoming chemists: Developing
representational competence. In J. Gilbert (Ed.), *Visualization in science
education* (p. 121–145). Dordrecht: Springer.

Law, B., Atkins, M.S., Kirkpatrick, A., Lomax, A.J., & Mackenzie, C.L. (2004).
Eye gaze patterns differentiate novice and experts in a virtual laparoscopic
surgery training environment. *Proceedings of the 2004 symposium on Eye
Tracking Research Applications, San Antonio*, 41–48.

Mayer, R.E., & Moreno, R. (2003). Ways to reduce cognitive load: Nine ways to
reduce cognitive load in multimedia learning. *Educational Psychologist, 38*(1),
43–52. https://doi.org/10.1207/S15326985EP3801_6

Paetkau, M., Bissonnette, D., & Taylor, C. (2013). Measuring the effectiveness
of simulations in preparing students for the laboratory. *The Physics Teacher,
51*(2), 113–116. https://doi.org/10.1119/1.4775536

Perkins, K., Adams, W., Dubson, M., Finkelstein, N., Reid, S., Wieman, C., &
LeMaster, R. (2006). PhET: Interactive simulations for teaching and learning
physics. *The Physics Teacher, 44*(1), 18–23. https://doi.org/10.1119/1.2150754

Robertson, W. (1949). On class room demonstrations. *American Journal of
Physics, 17*(1), 19–21. https://doi.org/10.1119/1.1989488

Sweller, J. (1988). Cognitive load during problem solving: Effects on learning.
Cognitive Science, 12(2), 257–285. https://doi.org/10.1207/s15516709cog1202_4

University of Colorado Boulder. (2018, August). *PhET: Circuit Construction Kit,
DC* [Computer simulation]. Retrieved from https://phet.colorado.edu/en
/simulation/circuit-construction-kit-dc

10 When the Societal Meets the Scientific: Learning through Simulation in the Earth and Environmental Sciences

ANNE MARIE RYAN AND SUSAN GASS

Introduction

There is a call for university teaching to move from traditional modes of passive learning to more effective means of teaching through active learning techniques, and the science disciplines are no exception (Freeman et al., 2014). Traditional modes of teaching such as lecturing tend to present science as a body of already developed and absolute facts, rather than as a complex, evolving, and "socially and culturally constructed" knowledge system (Zeidler & Nichols, 2009, p. 53). Simulations are one of a myriad of techniques that can be used to engage students in active learning and higher-order thinking (Bonwell & Eison, 1991). Simulations, in our pedagogical context of earth and environmental science (EES), include those described by Schnurr, De Santo, Green, and Taylor (2014) where students act in various stakeholder roles, adopting varied perspectives as they negotiate their way through a fictionalized re-creation of a real-world scenario. Although they are not typically applied in science teaching, we believe simulations can be an effective means to deepen our students' understanding of science and its role in society.

Traditionally, teaching strategies in the sciences have resulted in the representation of science as "clean and rather sterile" (Pedretti, 2003, p. 220), in part the result of many science educators emphasizing science as a body of knowledge that students need to be told (Aikenhead, 1994; Hodson, 1998). Within this approach, the non-linear, messy nature of science, the politics involved, and the moral and ethical dimensions are at best de-emphasized, or at worst, ignored (Pedretti, 2003). Hurd (1998) refers to the concept of strategic research to describe the emphasis on the functional aspects of science in relation to social and economic considerations. As this trend evolves, the practice of science is evolving to include a more holistic approach that is often transdisciplinary in nature. Together, these considerations speak to the need in our learning environments for developing greater science literacy for all.

Zeidler, Sadler, Simmons and Howes (2005), and references therein, discuss the concept of socio-scientific issues (SSI) and the importance of approaching science teaching from this perspective, and define scientific literacy broadly to include "informed decision-making; the ability to analyze, synthesize, and evaluate information; dealing sensibly with moral reasoning and ethical issues; and understanding connections inherent among socioscientific issues (SSI)" (p. 358). They further argue that developing what they refer to as "a practical degree of scientific literacy" (Zeidler et al., 2005, p. 358) requires developing scientific habits of mind such as open-mindedness, scepticism, critical thinking, acknowledging ambiguity, identifying many ways enquiry might be evoked, and identifying and using data-driven knowledge and evidence (Zeidler et al., 2005). To develop scientific literacy within our undergraduate students, it is not only critical to build a solid understanding of disciplinary concepts; we must also go beyond this to teach our students how to apply this knowledge in the context of real-world issues (Sabel, Vo, Alred, Dauer, & Forbes, 2017; Zeidler & Nichols, 2009). Once in the workforce, our graduates will be faced with the variety of new socio-scientific issues arising from the growing pressures of humans on earth systems (Steiner & Laws, 2006; Sabel et al., 2017). Modern enquiry into science education increasingly acknowledges and incorporates the importance not only of scientific enquiry, but also of the very nature of science and the sociocultural and ethical dimensions involved (Zeidler et al., 2005): collectively, these are encompassed in the concept of SSI.

In EES, societal aspects are very clearly connected to the science itself. As EES is inherently interdisciplinary, students studying it must understand the physical and biological features of natural systems and the ways in which humans interact within them. The very nature of science, and scientific issues of all kinds, comes with uncertainty – a tricky concept for students who commonly carry the misconception that science is objective and universal. When faced with relevant policy decisions, we must contend with both the scientific understanding and its level of uncertainty, and the human dimension of the effects the decision will have across all sectors of society. Privileging uncertainty while being able to recognize and incorporate different perspectives on science-based issues and associated policy decisions will be critical to our graduates' success in this field. This broader evolving vision of science education provides fodder for creating opportunities for students to practise science in rich contexts that most closely mimic "real world" situations. Role-play simulations provide one such example of how such practice might unfold.

Simulations used in science teaching offer many opportunities for students to grapple with SSI. Similar to Allen, Duch, and Groh (1996), Saddler (2004) argues that scientific literacy specifically is enhanced when students are engaged in personally meaningful experiences (e.g., students' involvement in a future-work-related role-play) that require evidence-based reasoning and provide a social context for the science in question. In other words, simulations can reveal practical aspects of otherwise abstract theories and approaches (Belloni, 2008). Zeidler and Nichols (2009) further conclude that scientific literacy is enhanced when students have to grapple with more than one perspective and when they are required to more completely develop their own arguments. We contend that these facets arise organically when students are actively engaged in simulations in which they are required to take a stand from a variety of perspectives. Simulations force students to grapple with the complexity and uncertainty of science, and in this way can help to hone students' understanding of the very nature of science (Zeidler et al., 2005). Simulations also have the potential to expose value-laden considerations, thus engaging students in ethical decision-making approaches (Grose-Fifer, 2017). When students are involved in an interaction with multiple diverse stakeholders, they are required to think on their feet, an added bonus and practice for a work environment in which employees must often respond in the immediate.

There are broad pedagogically sound reasons for using simulations in the classroom, in addition to the benefits they can provide for building science literacy. Simulations are a form of active learning, and as noted by Freeman et al. (2014), evidence confirms that such strategies increase success in science courses, and together with their realistic or authentic nature, allow for deeper learning (Kilgour, Hinze, Petrie, Long, & de-Berg, 2015; Bransford, Franks, Vye, & Sherwood, 1989). In simulations, active learning takes place, as students no longer rely on the instructor to provide the information and directions for interpretation of such, but rather the students are actively engaged and seek answers themselves (Belloni, 2008). In this way, they move toward more dependence on each other, building collaborative approaches to science, and they can begin to function as practicing scientists do, where in recent years, up to 95% of research reports are multi-authored, in stark contrast to 5% multi-authored reports at the turn of the 20th century (Spiegel-Rosing & Price, 1977).

Simulations create motivation for learning, a key principle identified by Ambrose et al. (2010) in their principles of student learning, by offering a novel approach – a break from routine. Motivation also comes from real-world or close-to-real-world environments where students can practise work-related interactions, factors further known to enhance learning (Allen, Duch, & Groh, 1996), and where they can see greater relevance for their learning (Williams & Williams, 2011; Schnurr et al. 2014).

The National Centre for Case Study Teaching in Science (NCCSTS) case study database documents a growing body of simulations being used in undergraduate science curricula.[1] A search for role-playing cases reveals 126 cases studies. The majority of these are targeted at medical and bioethics examples. There are 40 cases focused on environmental issues, but none fall within the geosciences. A search of the literature does not reveal a plethora of simulations, but there are several previously documented examples where simulations have been effectively used in our disciplines, and specifically within the environmental realm. Among these are the example by Stokes and Selin (2016), in which students negotiate a global mercury treaty; Gervich et al.'s (2016) game about toxic release of hazardous pollution; Cowlishaw, Hunter, Coy, and Tessmer's (2007) Kyoto protocol simulation; the mock environmental summit adopted by Gautier and Rebich (2005); and a policy role-playing exercise in which the threat of rapid sea-level rise as a result of climate change is imminent for the Thames Estuary (Lonsdale et al., 2008). In the geosciences *senso stricto*, the number of simulation cases drop, with exceptions including a study by Dohaney, Brogt, Wilson, and Kennedy (2017), who detail a research study of several iterations of a simulated volcanic hazard activity, and Klauk and Mogk (2007), who describe a role-play involving consideration of development of a coal-bed methane mining project within the Crow Nation community in the US, a development with significant environmental, economic, and societal implications. Additionally, a number of geoscience-related case study possibilities for use in simulations are presented on the Science Education Resource Centre (SERC) website.[2]

Although there is great variation in both the topics and the structures of these simulations, each of these examples addresses a prominent issue in environmental sciences and requires students to do some background research so that they can realistically and more completely assume roles of various stakeholders. Each engages students in actively becoming participants in attempting to resolve a complex, socially impactful problem in which there are variable degrees of uncertainty. Whereas these all share a common environmental thread, a specific, in-depth geoscience background tends not to be required for students to engage effectively in these simulations.

Simulations can be an excellent way of enabling our students' competencies in all the above areas, when used at the right time and for the right purpose. This raises the question as to why and when we should consider using simulations over other learning opportunities. Perhaps importantly, simulations provide a number of pedagogically rich opportunities for students to actively engage in course material at a deeper level. In terms of location and timing, simulations, as we use them, provide the next best thing to realistic or authentic opportunities for students to engage with material when it is not possible to allow them to go to a location in person or participate in an actual event, due to constraints related to distance, timing, or student numbers.

Objectives: Simulations in the Earth and Environmental Sciences Classroom

Simulations can be fun activities. But unless they do more than create a fun experience, they fall short of their potential impact. Consequently, choosing when and what to use for a simulation, and setting it up effectively, taps into deeper and more lasting learning and takes some planning and a set of objectives to guide this planning. An important part of the plan is to allow enough time for reflection following the simulation, to provide for students to unpack the learning and explore the concepts a second time, to create an opportunity for assessment, both by the students themselves and by the instructor, and to provide a record for them of this learning. Smith and Boyer (1996) similarly conclude the importance of clearly stated goals both during development of the simulation and as a means to evaluate effectiveness of the learning. With this in mind, when we use simulations, we consider the following general objectives. In any given case, there may be additional or more specific objectives to those outlined below:

- To provide an opportunity for students to explore a contextualized real-world-type scenario that would be difficult to experience first-hand
- To provide an opportunity for students to directly experience alternate perspectives and consider others' points of view
- To provide an opportunity for students to learn new science material and intelligibly integrate this new knowledge with prior scientific knowledge around a topic that is particularly rich in societal connections

- To facilitate students developing skill at "thinking on the spot," creating and developing scientific argumentation that supports their thinking, highlighting biases and assumptions, and considering uncertainty and ambiguity in science, while always maintaining a respectful stance
- To help students develop an understanding of decision-making around complex issues and to consider the various stakeholders involved
- To develop students' own voices and help them to identify their biases, communicate effectively to varied audiences, and develop agency

Case Study Scenario

We introduce an example of a role-play simulation piloted in a capstone undergraduate environmental geoscience course that adds to the growing repertoire of simulations in the environmental education literature. Many geoscience graduates enter careers in the resource sector, so providing a simulation that is analogous to what they may encounter in their work environment affords a real-world learning opportunity. While the scenario we outline below is rooted in geoscience content, it offers a specific example from which many parallel examples can be created as the basis for building deeper scientific understanding around a discipline-specific topic. Such examples can be of a local nature (e.g., a local landfill, a new neighbourhood chemical plant or pulp mill, the installation of wind turbines, the planting of genetically modified organisms, etc.), regional (e.g., air pollution, acid rain), or global in scope (e.g., climate change, mass extinction, artificial intelligence). On the basis of this simulation, and the experience of one of the authors using a second simulation of a community confronted with genetically modified crops (Gass & Scriven, 2019), we present a framework for how such simulations can be created and used in an undergraduate earth and environmental science course where the instructor wishes to expose students to some of the real-world challenges they may face as future professionals.

Proposed Framework for Developing Socio-scientific Simulations

Our proposed framework provides a series of questions to pose when considering whether to adopt a simulation learning opportunity (Fig. 10.1). Of primary importance is the existence of a real-world problem that is scientifically significant, has societal implications, and

Figure 10.1. Proposed framework for deciding when to and how to develop a socio-scientific simulation.

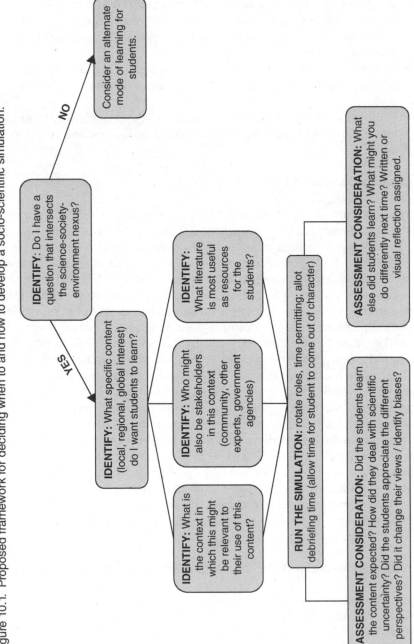

involves ethical dimensions. The steps outlined serve as aspects to think about prior to, and during the development of, a simulation, as not every class situation, or topic of discussion, lends itself to incorporation into learning through simulation.

In the simulation outlined below, priority considerations included when in the term this would be introduced, the size of the class, how well the class community had developed, and the prior knowledge students would bring to the activity. It was in this latter area that assumptions overestimated students' prior knowledge, so while there was definitely science learning that happened, it likely was not as great as hoped. In future renditions, the plan is to allow more time for students to integrate new scientific knowledge into their existing knowledge base in hopes of cultivating a richer exchange of ideas and deeper understanding of the particular scientific issues involved. Indeed, one positive outcome of this naivety was the recognition by the students themselves, as they constructed their arguments and rationale, of the need for such knowledge.

The scenario was planned with final-year undergraduates in mind. These students are about to transition from university to the workforce, where they will be commonly faced with new and varied challenges where their science training runs headlong into economic and societal influences that they may never have anticipated from their course-based experiences. Whereas simulations provide opportunities for learning at all levels in the undergraduate program, students in their fourth year can benefit particularly from opportunities to "practise" their science training in expanded settings, such as those afforded by role-play simulations. The course in which the simulation was adopted is an elective for geoscience majors, and typically has 15–20 students enrolled (this course was taught by AMR). The simulation takes place toward the end of the semester, and the seminar-style and issues-focused course ensures that at this point in the term there is a strong sense of community in which students know each other, are comfortable with engaging in the exchange of ideas, and are beginning to really come to terms with the complexity involved in environmentally related aspects of geoscience. The simulation offers students the opportunity to use their prior as well as newly learned geologic knowledge in a socio-environmental context, where analytic enquiry and societal, environmental, and ethical considerations are all factors. Zeidler and Nichols (2009) highlight the importance of making the science–society connection through interaction with such an SSI interface in the teaching and learning environment, and such simulations provide an excellent avenue for students to engage with societal issues while simultaneously building on their scientific knowledge. As a result, in addition to the objectives outlined in the introductory section, case-specific objectives were considered significant in this particular simulation:

- Students will build on their geologic knowledge related to rare earths and rare earth mining and their related environmental geology through developing geoscientific argumentation.
- Students will articulate the significance and importance of incorporating Indigenous issues and concerns into decision-making in the Canadian, and indeed, broader global contexts.

The scenario presented in the box below, while not verbatim the original material, represents the information given to students as an introduction to the simulation.

The Scenario Unfolds

A unique element of this particular simulation was that students rotated among the three stakeholders so that each group had a turn representing the role of the mining company, the community members, and the environmental experts. This meant that the exercise and debrief took close to three hours, but it was clear that students rapidly adapted to the different roles and immersed themselves in their respective roles thoroughly. Each group spent approximately 30 minutes in each of the different roles, essentially running until the conversation became repetitive or redundant. The rationale for doing this rotation included the hope that, through experiencing each of the roles, students would develop a more nuanced understanding of the impact on each of the stakeholder groups as well as a greater recognition of the complexity of the issues involved. Nestel and Tierney (2007) highlight the importance of role-play in creating opportunities for students to look at an issue from varied perspectives: rotating roles can help to solidify student considerations of these different viewpoints, which is a critical component of effective SSI (Zeidler & Nichols, 2009). In addition, rotating through the different stakeholder roles should provide an avenue for students to better understand the nuances of democratic group decision-making, as well as fostering basic human values and caring: aspects further considered critical within effective SSI (e.g., Berkowitz & Grych, 2000; Zeidler & Sadler, 2007). It was also expected that rotating roles could better facilitate development of critical thinking as outlined by Facione and Facione (2007).

The Scenario: Establishing a Rare Earth Mine in Canada's "Ring of Fire," Northern Ontario

A (fictional) mining company, Ring-of-Fire Inc., has uncovered significant evidence that there are enough rare earths found in the local area for it to be a viable and highly profitable mine. In reality, rare earths are not that rare, although they are not commonly found in high concentrations in many locations, and their extraction and separation from each other require a lot of energy. Rare earths have many properties in common; however, each also has a unique set of properties that make each element particularly useful for a specific purpose. Furthermore, they are commonly associated with thorium, which is a radioactive element. Despite all of these concerns, our modern needs rely on rare earth elements, from smartphones to electric cars and beyond.

The local area is home to a number of small communities, mostly of Indigenous populations. Canada's mining laws are stringent and require adequate corporate social responsibility, including consultation with potentially impacted local communities and other stakeholders, and compliance with Canada's environmental regulations. Issues around mining, the environment, and society are further complicated by various federal, provincial/territorial, and municipal responsibilities. In the case in question, Ring-of-Fire Inc. wants to proceed to the mining stage, at which point a more rigorous consultation and regulatory set of considerations come into play. As geoscience students, it is particularly important that you know and understand the nature of the rare earth distribution, the waterways and groundwater distribution, flow rates and direction, current background conditions, and the overall landscape features, as well as plans for dealing with mine waste and mitigating any spills, etc. Suggestions for readings about the geology of rare earths and their environmental implications will be given, as will be information bulletins related to mining, environment, and health for First Nations communities.

The question that the mining company and the communities need to resolve is: "Should the mine be allowed to go ahead or not?" During class next week, we will hold a town hall meeting or "open house," where the mining company gets to present its case, the community members get to ask questions and express their concerns, and the environmental experts clarify and answer any related questions that may arise. This "meeting" is to allow for an exchange of information and the development of positive relationships so that a middle ground can ultimately be reached, despite the complexity of the issues involved.

The class will be divided into three groups; each group must be willing and able to take on the role of any of the three stakeholder groups – the mining company, the community members, or the environmental experts – and be ready with your key points, questions, and counter-arguments. You should become familiar with all of the above aspects of the proposed mine using the sources given, and any additional sources you may find significant, to establish your credibility and make your case. Familiarize yourself with the given documentation around the environmental considerations, and with the information about the local communities. We aim for as authentic an experience as possible, so the better prepared you are, and the more you step into the role while also respecting the rights of others, the more authentic the experience.

Students were reminded that it was not sufficient to simply rehash previously stated arguments when switching roles. Despite this, there was, as might be expected, repetition of previously stated information and arguments. However, importantly, new information and insights were added, as students expanded on their explanations and input and built more solid arguments over time, allowing for deeper learning. Indeed, rather than creating redundancy, the repetition served to solidify the students in their new respective roles, highlight the critical issues involved, and create a launching pad for deeper engagement with the material. Significantly, in terms of course content, students came to realize the importance of being well informed and prepared as the mining company representation, a role that they may well come to play in their future work environment.

Throughout the exercise, the instructor served as a moderator, remaining present and ready to jump in if things got too heated, but otherwise was a passive observer, recording what remained to be addressed once the activity was finished, while also noting what would benefit from modification in subsequent iterations of the activity.

Wrapping It Up

There is no guarantee that deeper, more relevant and lasting learning will happen by simply exposing students to an active "learning" experience: students must grapple with the ideas and concepts (there must be a relevant problem or a question to address), use the concepts and the language in appropriate ways (effective practice), and importantly, reflect on this experience and what it means for their learning (evaluation). Consequently, this simulation was followed by an opportunity for debriefing and reflection by both the students and the instructor, a critical component of simulation learning, as identified by Fanning and Gaba (2007) and Palaganas, Fey, and Simon (2016). In the case of this pilot study, debriefing took the form of a group discussion following the final rotation. In future offerings of this simulation, a critical component for consideration in addition to a group debriefing would be the inclusion of a requirement for students to write a reflection on their experience. This reflection would include both content learning and address questions such as: In what way did the role-play format add or detract from their learning? Are there any changes you might suggest making to this, or similar, simulations in the future? (Belloni, 2008).

Discussion

For geoscience students, there are benefits to approaching a given issue and content through a simulation, and these become increasingly obvious as students migrate through a simulation. For example, in fieldwork, students may frequently encounter landowners or other members of the public, some of whom are distrustful of the very idea of mining. Such an encounter is more common for the average geoscientist who does fieldwork than for scientists who work in labs. Training young geoscientists for these interactions with non-scientists is best done through experiential learning, of which simulations form a core component. Simulation give students a "safe" place to practise their developing skills and knowledge, and to engage in aspects of life as a geoscientist that they may not have heretofore considered. Whereas we regularly teach our students how to read the maps and the GPS they use in the field, as well as teach them the relevant content and skills they need to effectively observe, record, and interpret what they are seeing in the rocks and landscape, learning about how to deal with various public interests as a professional scientist does not appear in the standard curriculum.

Lessons Learned

Below we evaluate some of the positive learning outcomes associated with this simulation.

1 *Students come to know self:* One positive learning outcome arises when we offer students opportunities to participate in a simulation in which interactions with otherness are key. Through such

experiences, they discover a number of heretofore hidden aspects of their chosen profession, and using this lens of self-reflection, begin to question more thoroughly who they are and their chosen values. This manifests itself as surprise at their own reactions to the conversations within the varied roles, and their acknowledgment that such conversations are not as simple as they might have imagined. Students have relayed these kinds of insights both immediately following their involvement in the simulation, but also at a later date, when they encounter something in a summer work situation where they are faced directly with some of the issues that arose in the simulation itself, such as the need for careful and full discussion or the value of using language that is accessible to all.

2 *Students realize the importance of having a sound scientific knowledge base:* When having to draw on the science on the spur of the moment, students learn just how important it is to have a sound understanding of the geoscience concepts in question. They come to realize that if they themselves do not understand the science involved, they will not be able to convey it effectively to others. Students have come to acknowledge this and expressed a wish to know and understand more about the geoscience involved in order to be better able to develop and defend their arguments. In this case study, the students themselves remarked – both immediately following their turn in the mining company role and in the final debriefing – that they would be better equipped to achieve their desired outcomes if they knew the geologic material in greater depth.

3 *Students realize that effective and appropriate communication is key:* There is always the very real concern that communicating specialized scientific knowledge to non-specialists can result in miscommunication. In a simulation, students can come to realize just how important it is to be able to communicate effectively with non-experts. Students may also come face to face with the idea that their specialized knowledge confers privilege and that with this privilege comes a responsibility to use this knowledge wisely, and not, as some within society fear, deliberately mislead or inadvertently overwhelm non-specialists with disciplinary jargon. Simulations provide an opportunity for students to practise effective communication, perhaps discovering for themselves the perils of ineffective communication in this practice environment.

4 *Students develop awareness of the importance of otherness:* As we teach students the science of a given issue, we often assume that they recognize the direct and important impact the science may have on humanity more broadly. Students may never have considered that many of the

people involved in situations akin to the simulation example above may hold different world views to themselves with strong emotional attachments to their land and to the environment, and therefore may not be readily responsive to a mining company's proposal. Further, there may be some within a community who see jobs and economic progress as the priority, so new divisions may arise that impact on how the geoscientist reacts and what they might do. Of course, geoscientists must retain respect and attempt to understand these alternate viewpoints, and in so doing, work to come to some kind of consensus or middle ground. Collectively, these facets are aspects that simulations can more readily reveal, through students actually experiencing them, than anything we might say (or more often might not say) when discussing scientific knowledge and skills in our classes.

In addition to the positives, there are a number of cautions and improvements that this pilot experience revealed and that serve as considerations to be incorporated in future iterations of the simulation.

5 *Preparation is key:* In a capstone course, adding simulations provides a rich avenue for students to integrate their previously learned geoscience material. However, where gaps arise, it is necessary to provide additional reliable and sufficient content knowledge, or point students in the direction of useful content. It is very easy for us to overestimate students' prior geologic or other content knowledge: we may well need to allow students more time and resources (in the form of primary literature, for example) than we initially imagine, in order to most effectively develop their geoscience knowledge. Students with only a superficial knowledge of the geologic conditions involved are limited somewhat in the learning, particularly in conveying and translating this scientific knowledge among the various stakeholders. Future iterations of this simulation plan to address this issue significantly, through greater scaffolding, particularly around including independent reading as well as incorporating this material more significantly into earlier course material. Perhaps this speaks most notably to the value of uncovering what students' prior knowledge and understanding about a given topic is, and in this way, identifying gaps prior to running the simulation so that these are addressed collectively before the activity.

6 *Student learning should be considered:* The primary purpose of this simulation was not assessment of student work, but more to provide an opportunity to expand the learning beyond traditional boundaries.

Because it was a pilot case, assessment of students' learning was downplayed. Assessment of student learning from the simulation is intended for inclusion in future iterations, building particularly on the debriefing process and student reflections of their learning, and connecting the specific objectives for the simulation more generally with evidence for student attainment of these objectives.

7 *A tighter structure and more systematic debriefing are needed:* Because this was the first attempt at this particular simulation, the choice was deliberately made to keep the structure somewhat loose and the debriefing fairly general. For example, strict time frames and development of briefing notes by students in advance would add to the scenario in question. However, we recommend a more formalized debriefing as the reflection that occurs during a debriefing is important for solidifying the learning.

8 Debriefing offers students the opportunity to articulate their learning, but also raise any emotional reactions they experienced as they moved through the simulation. As such, providing for students to debrief both in a whole-class setting and in an individual written reflection is beneficial, and again, future iterations of this simulation will incorporate both, to allow for the immediate response and an asynchronous, individual response. As always, grading of personal reflections must be done with sensitivity: it is important that students know their personal reactions and personal responses are not under grading consideration, but rather what is being assessed is the evidence they provide of their learning. Indeed, a rubric can be developed together with them so that they contribute to the process of assessment in this case.

Conclusion

The framework we present offers a systematic approach to exploring the use of simulations for student learning. This framework provides a roadmap for how to proceed, but also acknowledges that simulations might not be the optimal approach for a given situation. Not every "lesson" lends itself to a simulation, nor would we recommend a steady diet of simulations as a learning tool: there will always be students and specific content that do not "fit" with this model approach. However, based on our experience, we do conclude that simulations provide a rich learning opportunity for students to experience complex scientific situations in which a number of stakeholders are involved, and serve as a useful strategy for active and deep learning under such conditions. Short of actually living the working experience itself, there are few more impactful ways to introduce a topic in which socio-scientific complexity, the consideration of multiple perspectives, and the need for compromise are at the forefront.

NOTES

1 The database was accessed from http://sciencecases.lib.buffalo.edu/cs/ on 13 August 2018.
2 https://serc.carleton.edu/sp/library/simulations/index.html

REFERENCES

Aikenhead, G. (1994). What is STS science teaching. In J. Solomon & G. Aikenhead (Eds.), *STS education: International perspectives on reform* (47–59). New York, NY: Teachers College Press.

Allen, D.E., Duch, B.J., & Groh, S.E. (1996). The power of problem-based learning in teaching introductory science courses. *New directions for teaching and learning, 68*, 43–52. https://doi.org/10.1002/tl.37219966808

Ambrose, S.A., Bridges, M.W., DiPietro, M., Lovett, M.C., & Norman, M.K. (2010). *How learning works: Seven research-based principles for smart teaching.* San Francisco, CA: Jossey-Bass.

Belloni, R. (2008). Role-playing international intervention in conflict areas: Lessons from Bosnia for Northern Ireland education. *International Studies Perspectives, 9*(2), 220–234. https://doi.org/10.1111/j.1528-3585.2008.00328.x

Berkowitz, M.W., & Grych, J.H. (2000). Early character development and education. *Early Education and Development, 11*(1), 55–72. https://doi.org/10.1207/s15566935eed1101_4

Bonwell, C.C., & Eison, J.A. (1991). *Active learning: Creating excitement in the classroom* [ASHE-ERIC Higher Education Report No. 1]. Washington, DC: The George Washington University.

Bransford, J., Franks, J., Vye, N., & Sherwood, R. (1989). New approaches to instruction: Because wisdom can't be told. In S. Vosniadou & A. Ortony (Eds.), *Similarity and Analogical Reasoning* (pp. 470–497). Cambridge: Cambridge University Press.

Cowlishaw, R., Hunter, C., Coy, J., & Tessmer, M. (2007). The art of a deal: A Kyoto Protocol simulation. *Journal of College Science Teaching, 37*(1), 17–19. Retrieved from https://www.jstor.org/stable/i40116280

Dohaney, J., Brogt, E., Wilson, T.M., & Kennedy, B. (2017). Using role-play to Improve students' confidence and perceptions of communication in a simulated volcanic crisis. In C.J. Fearnley et al. (Eds.), *Observing the volcano world: Volcano crisis communication* (691–714). Cham: Springer International Publishing.

Facione, P.A., & Facione, N.C. (2007). Talking critical thinking. *Change: The Magazine of Higher Learning, 39*(2), 38–45. https://doi.org/10.3200/CHNG .39.2.38-45

Fanning, R.M., & Gaba, D.M. (2007). The role of debriefing in simulation-based learning. *Simulation in Healthcare: Journal of the Society for Simulation in Healthcare, 2*(2), 115. https://doi.org/10.1097/SIH.0b013e3180315539

Freeman, S., Eddy, S.L., McDonough, M., Smith, M.K., Okoroafor, N., Jordt, H., & Wenderoth, M.P. (2014). Active learning increases student performance in science, engineering, and mathematics. *Proceedings of the National Academy of Sciences of the United States of America, 111*(23), 8410–8415. https://doi.org /10.1073/pnas.1319030111

Gass, S., & Scriven, D. (2019). *The Canadian canola controversy: The role of genetically modified organisms in agriculture.* National Centre for Case Study Teaching in Science. Retrieved from https://sciencecases.lib.buffalo.edu/ collection/detail.html?case_id=1050&id=1050

Gautier, C., & Rebich, S. (2005). The use of a mock environment summit to support learning about global climate change. *Journal of Geoscience Education, 53*(1), 5–15. https://doi.org/10.5408/1089-9995-53.1.5

Gervich, C., Briere, C., Lopez, N., Eudene, J., Evans, C., Fonzone, J., ... Fernandez, A. (2016). Toxic release! The role of educational games in teaching and learning about hazardous pollution. *Journal of Environmental Studies and Sciences, 6*(3), 589–596. https://doi.org/10.1007/s13412-015-0270-8

Grose-Fifer, J. (2017). Using role play to enhance critical thinking about ethics in psychology. In R. Obeid, A.M. Schwartz, C. Shane-Simpson, & P.J. Brooks (Eds.), *How we teach now: The GSTA guide to student-centered teaching* (pp. 213–223). Washington, DC: Society for the Teaching of Psychology. Retrieved from http://teachpsych.org/resources/Documents/ebooks /gstaebook.pdf

Hodson, D. (1998). *Teaching and learning science: Towards a personalized approach.* Buckingham, UK: Open University Press.

Hurd, P.D. (1998). Scientific literacy: New minds for a changing world. *Science Education, 82*(3), 407–416. https://doi.org/10.1002/(SICI)1098-237X (199806)82:3<407::AID-SCE6>3.0.CO;2-G

Kilgour, P., Hinze, J., Petrie, K., Long, W., & deBerg, K. (2015). Role-playing: A smorgasbord of learning types. *International Journal of Innovative Interdisciplinary Research, 3*(1), 11–24. Retrieved from http://www.auamii .com/jiir/Vol-03/Issue%201/2Kilgour.pdf

Klauk, E., & Mogk, D. (2007). *Impacts of resources development on Native American lands.* Presentation at Indian Education for All Best Practices Conference, Bozeman, Montana.

Lonsdale, K., Downing, T., Nicholls, R., Parker, D., Vafeidis, A., Dawson, R., & Hall, J. (2008). Plausible responses to the threat of rapid sea-level rise in the Thames Estuary. *Climatic Change, 91*(1), 145–169. https://doi.org/10.1007/s10584-008-9483-0

Nestel, D., & Tierney, T. (2007). Role-play for medical students learning about communication: Guidelines for maximising benefits. *BMC Medical Education, 7*(1), 3. https://doi.org/10.1186/1472-6920-7-3

Palaganas, J.C., Fey, M., & Simon, R. (2016). Structured debriefing in simulation-based education. *AACN Advanced Critical Care, 27*(1), 78–85. https://doi.org/10.4037/aacnacc2016328

Pedretti, E. (2003). Teaching science, technology, society and environment (STSE) education. In D.L. Zeidler (Ed.), *The role of moral reasoning on socioscientific issues and discourse in science education* (pp. 219–239). Dordrecht: Springer.

Sabel, J.L., Vo, T., Alred, A., Dauer, J.M., & Forbes, C.T. (2017). Undergraduate students' scientifically informed decision making about socio-hydrological issues. *Journal of College Science Teaching, 46*(6), 71–79. https://doi.org/10.2505/4/jcst17_046_06_71

Sadler, T.D. (2004). Informal reasoning regarding socioscientific issues: A critical review of research. *Journal of Research in Science Teaching: The Official Journal of the National Association for Research in Science Teaching, 41*(5), 513–536. https://doi.org/10.1002/tea.20009

Schnurr, M.A., De Santo, E., Green, A., & Taylor, A. (2014). Investigating student perceptions of learning within a role-play simulation of the Convention on Biological Diversity. *Journal of Geography, 114*(3): 94–107. https://doi.org/10.1080/00221341.2014.937738

Smith, E.T., & Boyer, M.A. (1996). Designing in-class simulations 1. *PS: Political Science & Politics, 29*(4), 690–694. https://doi.org/10.2307/420794

Speigel-Rosing, I., & de Solla Price, D. (1977). *Science, technology and society: A cross-disciplinary perspective.* London and Beverly Hills: Sage Publications.

Steiner, G., & Laws, D. (2006). How appropriate are two established concepts from higher education for solving complex real-world problems? A comparison of the Harvard and the ETH case study approach. *International Journal of Sustainability in Higher Education, 7*(3), 322–340. https://doi.org/10.1108/14676370610677874

Stokes, L., & Selin, N. (2016). The mercury game: Evaluating a negotiation simulation that teaches students about science-policy interactions. *Journal of Environmental Studies and Sciences, 6*(3), 597–605. https://doi.org/10.1007/s13412-014-0183-y

Williams, K.C., & Williams, C.C. (2011). Five key ingredients for improving student motivation. *Research in Higher Education Journal, 12*, 1–23. Retrieved from http://www.aabri.com/manuscripts/11834.pdf

Zeidler, D.L., & Nichols, B.H. (2009). Socioscientific issues: Theory and practice. *Journal of Elementary Science Education, 21*(2), 49. https://doi.org/10.1007/BF0317368

Zeidler, D.L., & Sadler, T.D. (2007). The role of moral reasoning in argumentation: Conscience, character, and care. In S. Erduran & M.P. Jiménez-Aleixandre (Eds.), *Argumentation in science education* (pp. 201–216). Dordrecht: Springer.

Zeidler, D.L., Sadler, T.D., Simmons, M.L., & Howes, E.V. (2005). Beyond STS: A research-based framework for socioscientific issues education. *Science Education, 89*(3), 357–377. https://doi.org/10.1002/sce.20048

SECTION THREE

Health Sciences

11 Framing Chapter: Simulation-Based Education in the Health Professions

VICKI R. LEBLANC

In health sciences education, "simulation" refers to a multitude of modalities used to recreate some aspect of the clinical environment, for the purposes of education or assessment (LeBlanc, 2012). Simulation serves as a valuable complement to the traditional elements of health professional curricula, such as lectures, small group learning, and clinical rotations. By recreating some elements of the clinical world, simulation allows for the application of knowledge and the practice of skills/procedures in an environment that presents no risks to patients. Part-task trainers are used to teach basic technical skills such as intravenous insertion and intubation. Standardized patients are used to teach interpersonal and communication skills. Screen-based virtual patients are used to teach clinical reasoning. Full-body mannequins placed in recreated clinical environments or real clinical settings (in situ simulation) are used for team training and crisis management. In situations requiring a mix of skills, hybrid simulations are created by combining two or more of the modalities.

The use of simulation in health sciences education dates back more than 50 years. Programmed patients, now known as standardized patients (SPs), were introduced by Barrows and Abrahamson in 1964 (Barrows & Abrahamson, 1964). Defined as a "normal person who is trained to assume and present, on examination, the history and neurological findings of an actual patient in the manner of an actual patient" (p. 803), these individuals serve an important role in teaching interviewing skills, physical examination skills, and communication skills. By the mid-1990s, over 80% of North American medical schools reported using standardized patients in their curricula (May, Park, & Lee, 2009).

Despite the broad integration of SPs in health sciences education, the integration of other forms of simulation was protracted. As recently as the turn of the century, most forms of simulation-based education occurred at the periphery of core educational curricula: simulation centres were geographically separate from the mainstream education areas, and simulation activities occurred independently of the formal curricula, often by somewhat "rogue" champions. Educators were generally sceptical of a new teaching modality that consisted of practice on "dolls" or "plastic," that required significant resources, and that took learners away from where the true learning was thought to occur: in classrooms or with real patients.

Now, simulation-based education (SBE) has become an integral component of health sciences, and particularly health professions education across the spectrum. Students increasingly participate in boot camps to learn the procedures they'll need during their clinical rotations; they practise communication and interpersonal skills with SPs; technical skills such as intravenous injections and intubations are first performed on part-task trainers or full-body mannequins; orientation (Bittner, Gravlin, MacDonald, & Bourgeois, 2017) and foundational courses (e.g., Fundamentals of Laparoscopic Surgery; Okrainec, Soper, Swanstrom, & Fried, 2011) are required prior to learners and health professionals progressing to the clinical settings. There now exist large international simulation associations and conferences, peer-reviewed journals dedicated to simulation, simulation accreditation programs, and a plethora of courses and training programs aimed at teaching best practices to aspiring simulation educators.

Integral Role of Research

One of the factors leading to this significant change in attitudes toward – and usage of – simulation has been the wealth of research conducted around it. Partly because simulation came to maturity in the era of evidence-based medicine, and partly because of the sheer resources required to deliver good SBE, proponents of SBE were tasked with providing evidence that this new form of instruction added something more to the preparation of health professionals. As a result, significant research has been undertaken in the area of simulation-based education. It is one of the most investigated educational interventions in the health professions. Initial research efforts were aimed at providing justification evidence that learning with SBE provided a valuable and complementary method of instruction (Cook, Bordage, & Schmidt, 2008). This was followed by clarification research, to better understand the instructional design elements that could optimize SBE.

As with any educational innovation, the earliest literature regarding SBE tended to be descriptive. Early work, by champions such as

Amitai Ziv in Israel (Ziv, Wolpe, Small, & Glick, 2003), David Gaba in the United States (Gaba, 2004), and Richard Reznick in Canada (Reznick, Regehr, MacRae, Martin, & McCulloch, 1997), was focused on compelling arguments for the necessity of simulation-based training in the health professions in order to meet patient-safety goals. As argued by Ziv in 2003:

> the proper and careful development of SBME [simulation-based medical education] is an ethical imperative. While the actual contribution that SBME can make to improving skills awaits empirical study, there seems little question that, when used in a sophisticated manner, SBME has the potential to decrease the numbers and effects of medical errors, to facilitate open exchange in training situations, to enhance patient safety, and to decrease the reliance on vulnerable patients for training. Moreover, by adopting simulation as a standard of training and certification, health systems will be viewed as more accountable and ethical by the populations they serve. (p. 786)

In parallel with these advocacy-focused publications, there was significant justification research conducted in the 1990s and early 2000s. A review by Cook and colleagues (2011), which reviewed 604 empirical studies, found that when compared to no intervention, SBE leads to improvements in knowledge, skills, behaviours, and patient outcomes. When comparing SBE to other forms of instruction, Cook and colleagues (2012) found similar, albeit smaller, improvements in knowledge and skills. Well-designed SBE can translate to improved performance in the clinical setting for both technical tasks (Chandra, Savoldelli, Joo, Weiss, & Naik, 2008; Fried et al., 2004) and management of high-acuity events (Bruppacher et al., 2010; Draycott et al., 2006; Wayne et al., 2008).

Despite the large body of literature showing the benefits of SBE in the health sciences and health professions, it is important to note that the quality of the instructional design, rather than the simulation modalities themselves, appears to be responsible for improved knowledge and skills (Cook et al., 2012). While learning can be enhanced with simulation sessions, there are cases in which this does not occur. For example, Olympio, Whelan, Ford, and Saunders (2003) did not show improvement in anaesthesia residents' management of esophageal intubation following simulation-based training. Similarly, Borges et al. (2010) did not observe significant changes in practising anaesthesiologists' airway management of a "cannot intubate, cannot ventilate" scenario. In a review of SBE in nursing, Cant and Cooper (2010) observed that only half of the studies that compared simulation with a control group were able to show additional gains in knowledge, critical thinking, perceived clinical confidence, or satisfaction.

As such, it is not possible to draw conclusions as to whether simulation *itself* is or is not effective for learning. Rather, SBE can be delivered in a number of ways; those elements that lead to enhanced learning are not necessarily inherent to simulation itself. Thus, there are calls for a better understanding of the elements in SBE that facilitate learning, as well as how to optimize learning using this form of practice and instruction (Cook et al., 2012).

In 2005, Issenberg and colleagues (Issenberg, McGaghie, Petrusa, Gordon, & Scalese, 2005) undertook a review of the existing evidence regarding the value of SBE. They found that the features of simulation argued to optimize learning were as follows: (a) the provision of feedback/debriefing; (b) repetitive practice of skills; (c) the integration of simulation-based exercises into standard educational curriculum; (d) practice across a range of task difficulty levels; (e) the use of multiple learning strategies; (f) the presentation of a wide variety of clinical conditions; (g) learning in a controlled environment where learners can make, detect, and correct errors without adverse consequences; (h) the use of reproducible, standardized educational experiences where learners are active participants, not passive bystanders; (i) having clearly stated goals with tangible outcome measures, which allow mastery learning; and (j) use of simulation modalities that offer a high degree of realism in the approximation of the relevant clinical features.

In a recent systematic review and meta-analysis, Cook and colleagues (2013) found pooled support for the majority of the features listed in the above paragraph, namely: range of difficulty, repetitive practice, distributed practice, interactivity, multiple learning strategies, individualized learning, mastery learning, feedback, longer time spent training, and clinical variation.

Going beyond research that examines the presence or absence of the critical elements of simulation, there has been a growing interest in better understanding the mechanisms by which these elements optimize simulation-based education. For example, debriefing and feedback have been shown to be critical elements of improved performance following simulation-based education (Levett-Jones & Lapkin, 2014; Savoldelli et al., 2006). Considered essential elements of simulation, feedback and debriefing allow learners to reflect on their performance and identify performance gaps and their underlying reasons, as well as discuss possible solutions that can be applied in future real practice (Cheng et al., 2014). Feedback is defined as the one-way provision of information about performance to learners, with the intent to modify thinking and/or behaviour for learning and improved future performance. In contrast, debriefing is defined as interactive and bidirectional, involving some level of facilitation or guidance to assist in reflection (Sawyer, Eppich, Brett-Fleegler, Grant, & Cheng, 2016). There is significant interest in elucidating the best way to provide feedback and debriefing, and multiple approaches have been developed (Sawyer et al., 2016). However, little empirical support exists to favour one approach to debriefing over another (Cheng et al., 2014; Raemer at al., 2011).

As for feedback, research in this area has, at times, defied common expectations. For example, simulation educators have been curious as to the best timing for providing feedback during technical skills acquisition: concurrently (feedback provided *throughout* each practice trial) or terminally (feedback provided at the conclusion of each practice trial). In three studies that directly compared concurrent to terminal feedback during procedural skill acquisition (Chang, Chang, Chien, Chung, & Hsu, 2007; Walsh, Ling, Wang, & Carnahan, 2009; Xeroulis et al., 2007), there were no differences between concurrent and terminal feedback at either immediate or short-term post-tests (<1 week after intervention). However, on longer retention tests (1 month later – Xeroulis et al., 2007) and on delayed-transfer tasks (Walsh et al., 2009), terminal feedback resulted in superior skills performance. As such, terminal feedback is thought to lead to greater retention and performance on transfer tasks. These studies support the guidance hypothesis, in which conditions that lead to overreliance on feedback can lead to decrements of performance over the long term (Wulf and Shea, 2004).

Simulation for Interprofessional Education

While the majority of SBE tends to target the individual learner, there is growing use of simulation for interprofessional education. With the increased recognition of the importance of teamwork and collaboration, a larger emphasis has been placed on helping learners and clinicians effectively function in healthcare teams (Palaganas, Epps, & Raemer, 2014). One initiative that has been integral to the use of simulation for interprofessional education is crisis resource management (CRM; Gaba, Howard, Fish, Smith, & Sowb, 2001). Adapted from aviation, crisis resource management focuses on effective leadership, anticipation, and communication, as well as distributing the workload and effectively managing the available resources. Since CRM's introduction to the health professions, simulation is also increasingly viewed as a means through which to address socio-historical issues (e.g., gender, hierarchy, status, professional divisions) in interprofessional learning (Sydor et al., 2012; Pattni et al., 2017).

While the importance of simulation-based education for interprofessional education is widely recognized, system levels factors (such as scheduling of learners from different professions) are often barriers. As well, further study in needed to understand the impact of interprofessional SBE on quality and patient outcomes.

Conclusion

In summary, SBE has moved from the periphery of health professions education to being one of the core elements of health sciences curricula, at all levels of training and across multiple professions. The majority of health professions use SBE, from the undergraduate level to continuing professional education. Any skill, procedure, or communication interaction that takes place with the patient is increasingly likely to have been practised beforehand in a simulated setting. As SBE in health sciences has become a formalized approach to instruction, it is increasingly well resourced. Educators looking to integrate simulation into their education activities can easily access practical resources to guide them in the development and implementation of simulation-based education activities (e.g., Motola, Devine, Chung, Sullivan, & Issenberg, 2013; Sittner et al., 2015).

An important contributor in SBE's shift from the periphery to mainstream health sciences education has been research – aimed first at justifying its integration into curricula, and subsequently at better understanding the elements that optimize learning within this modality. As health sciences education increasingly moves toward competency-based education models and greater recognition of interprofessional teams in patient care, further developments and research are likely to focus on simulation for assessment (of individuals and teams). In addition, with the increasing fiscal pressures on Western healthcare systems, issues of resource optimization and costs are likely to be of greater concern.

REFERENCES

Barrows, H.S., & Abrahamson, S. (1964). The programmed patient: A technique for appraising student performance in clinical neurology. *Academic Medicine, 39*(8), 802–805. Retrieved from https://journals.lww.com /academicmedicine/

Bittner, N.P., Gravlin, G., MacDonald, C., & Bourgeois, D. (2017). A newly licensed nurse orientation program evaluation: Focus on outcomes. *The Journal of Continuing Education in Nursing, 48*(1), 22–28. https://doi.org/10.3928/00220124-20170110-07

Borges, B.C., Boet, S., Siu, L.W., Bruppacher, H.R., Naik, V.N., Riem, N., & Joo, H.S. (2010). Incomplete adherence to the ASA difficult airway algorithm is unchanged after a high-fidelity simulation session. *Canadian Journal of Anesthesia, 57*(7), 644–649. https://doi.org/10.1007/s12630-010-9322-4

Bruppacher, H.R., Alam, S.K., LeBlanc, V.R., Latter, D., Naik, V.N., Savoldelli, G.L., Mazer, C.D., Kurrek, M.M., & Joo, H.S. (2010). Simulation-based training improves physicians' performance in patient care in high-stakes clinical setting of cardiac surgery. *Anesthesiology, 112*, 985–92. https://doi.org/10.1097/ALN.0b013e3181d3e31c

Cant, R.P., & Cooper, S.J. (2010). Simulation-based learning in nurse education: Systematic review. *Journal of Advanced Nursing, 66*(1), 3–15. https://doi.org/10.1111/j.1365-2648.2009.05240.x

Chandra, D.B., Savoldelli, G.L., Joo, H.S., Weiss, I.D., & Naik, V.N. (2008). Fiberoptic oral intubation: The effect of model fidelity on training for transfer to patient care. *Anesthesiology, 109*, 1007–1013. https://doi.org/10.1097/ALN.0b013e31818d6c3c

Chang, J-Y., Chang, G-L., Chien, C-JC., Chung, K-C., & Hsu, A-T. (2007). Effectiveness of two forms of feedback on training of a joint mobilization skill by using a joint translation simulator. *Physical Therapy, 87*(4), 418–430. https://doi.org/10.2522/ptj.20060154

Cheng, A., Eppich, W., Grant, V., Sherbino, J., Zendejas, B., & Cook, D.A. (2014). Debriefing for technology-enhanced simulation: A systematic review and meta-analysis. *Medical Education, 48*(7), 657–666. https://doi.org/10.1111/medu.12432

Cook, D.A., Bordage, G., & Schmidt, H.G. (2008). Description, justification and clarification: A framework for classifying the purposes of research in medical education. *Medical Education, 42*(2), 128–133. https://doi.org/10.1111/j.1365-2923.2007.02974.x

Cook, D.A., Brydges, R., Hamstra, S.J., Zendejas, B., Szostek, J.H., Wang, A.T., Erwin, P.J., & Hatala, R. (2012). Comparative effectiveness of technology-enhanced simulation versus other instructional methods: A systematic review and meta-analysis. *Simulation in Healthcare, 7*(5), 308–320. https://doi.org/10.1097/SIH.0b013e3182614f95

Cook, D.A., Hamstra, S.J., Brydges, R., Zendejas, B., Szostek, J.H., Wang, A.T., Erwin, P.J., & Hatala, R. (2013). Comparative effectiveness of instructional design features in simulation-based education: Systematic review and meta-analysis. *Medical Teacher, 35*(1), e867–e898. https://doi.org/10.3109/0142159X.2012.714886

Cook, D.A., Hatala, R., Brydges, R., Zendejas, B., Szostek, J.H., Wang, A.T., Erwin, P.J., & Hamstra, S.J. (2011). Technology-enhanced simulation for health professions education: A systematic review and meta-analysis. *JAMA, 306*(9), 978–988. https://doi.org/10.1001/jama.2011.1234

Draycott, T., Sibanda, T., Owen, L., Akande, V., Winter, C., Reading, S., & Whitelaw, A. (2006). Does training in obstetric emergencies improve neonatal outcome? *British Journal of Obstetrics and Gynaecology, 113*(2), 177–82. https://doi.org/10.1111/j.1471-0528.2006.00800.x

Fried, G.M., Feldman, L.S., Vassiliou, M.C., Fraser, S.A., Stanbridge, D., Ghitulescu, G., & Andrew, C.G. (2004). Proving the value of simulation in laparoscopic surgery. *Annals of Surgery, 240*(3), 518–528. https://doi.org/10.1097/01.sla.0000136941.46529.56

Gaba, D.M., Howard, S.K., Fish, K.J., Smith, B.E., & Sowb, Y.A. (2001). Simulation-based training in anesthesia crisis resource management (ACRM): A decade of experience. *Simulation & Gaming, 32*(2), 175–193. https://doi.org/10.1177/104687810103200206

Gaba, D.M. (2004). The future vision of simulation in health care. *BMJ Quality & Safety, 13*(Suppl. 1), i2–i10. https://doi.org/10.1136/qshc.2004.009878

Issenberg, B.S., McGaghie, W.C., Petrusa, E.R., Gordon, D.L., & Scalese, R.J. (2005). Features and uses of high-fidelity medical simulations that lead to effective learning: A BEME systematic review. *Medical Teacher, 27*(1), 10–28. https://doi.org/10.1080/01421590500046924

LeBlanc, V.R. (2012). Simulation in anesthesia: State of the science and looking forward. *Canadian Journal of Anesthesia, 59*(2), 193–202. https://doi.org/10.1007/s12630-011-9638-8

Levett-Jones, T., & Lapkin, S. (2014). A systematic review of the effectiveness of simulation debriefing in health professional education. *Nurse Education Today, 34*(6), e58–e63. https://doi.org/10.1016/j.nedt.2013.09.020

May, W., Park, J.H., & Lee, J.P. (2009). A ten-year review of the literature on the use of standardized patients in teaching and learning: 1996–2005. *Medical Teacher, 31*(6), 487–492. https://doi.org/10.1080/01421590802530898

Motola, I., Devine, L.A., Chung, H.S., Sullivan, J.E., & Issenberg, S.B. (2013). Simulation in healthcare education: A best evidence practical guide. AMEE Guide No. 82. *Medical Teacher, 35*(10), e1511–e1530. https://doi.org/10.3109/0142159X.2013.818632

Okrainec, A., Soper, N.J., Swanstrom, L.L., & Fried, G.M. (2011). Trends and results of the first 5 years of Fundamentals of Laparoscopic Surgery (FLS) certification testing. *Surgical Endoscopy, 25*(4), 1192–1198. https://doi.org/10.1007/s00464-010-1343-0

Olympio, M.A., Whelan, R., Ford, R.P., & Saunders, I.C. (2003). Failure of simulation training to change residents' management of oesophageal intubation. *British Journal of Anaesthesia, 91*(3), 312–318. https://doi.org/10.1093/bja/aeg183

Palaganas, J.C., Epps, C., & Raemer, D.B. (2014). A history of simulation-enhanced interprofessional education. *Journal of Interprofessional Ccare, 28*(2), 110–115. https://doi.org/10.3109/13561820.2013.869198

Pattni, N., Bould, M.D., Hayter, M.A., McLuckie, D., Noble, L.M.K., Malavade, A., & Friedman, Z. (2017). Gender, power and leadership: The effect of a superior's gender on respiratory therapists' ability to challenge leadership during a life-threatening emergency. *BJA: British Journal of Anaesthesia, 119*(4), 697–702. https://doi.org/10.1093/bja/aex246

Raemer, D., Anderson, M., Cheng, A., Fanning, R., Nadkarni, V., & Savoldelli, G. (2011). Research regarding debriefing as part of the learning process. *Simulation in Healthcare, 6*(Suppl. 7), S52–S57. https://doi.org/10.1097/SIH.0b013e31822724d0

Reznick, R., Regehr, G., MacRae, H., Martin, J., & McCulloch, W. (1997). Testing technical skill via an innovative "bench station" examination. *The American Journal of Surgery 173*(3), 226–230.

Savoldelli, G.L., Naik, V.N., Joo, H.S., Houston, P.L., Graham, M., Yee, B., & Hamstra, S.J. (2006). Evaluation of patient simulator performance as an adjunct to the oral examination for senior anesthesia residents. *Anesthesiology, 104,* 475–481. Retrieved from: http://anesthesiology.pubs.asahq.org/article.aspx?articleid=1923161

Sawyer, T., Eppich, W., Brett-Fleegler, M., Grant, V., & Cheng, A. (2016). More than one way to debrief: A critical review of healthcare simulation debriefing methods. *Simulation in Healthcare, 11*(3), 209–217. https://doi.org/10.1097/SIH.0000000000000148

Sittner, B.J., Aebersold, M.L., Paige, J.B., Graham, L.L., Schram, A.P., Decker, S.I., & Lioce, L. (2015). INACSL standards of best practice for simulation: Past, present, and future. *Nursing Education Perspectives, 36*(5), 294–298. https://doi.org/10.5480/15-1670

Sydor, D.T., Bould, M.D., Naik, V.N., Burjorjee, J., Arzola, C., Hayter, M., & Friedman, Z. (2012). Challenging authority during a life-threatening crisis: the effect of operating theatre hierarchy. *British Journal of Aanaesthesia, 110*(3), 463–471. https://doi.org/10.1093/bja/aes396

Walsh, C.M., Ling, S.C., Wang, C.S., & Carnahan, H. (2009). Concurrent versus terminal feedback: It may be better to wait. *Academic Medicine, 84*(Suppl. 10), S54–S57. https://doi.org/10.1097/ACM.0b013e3181b38daf

Wayne, D.B., Didwania, A., Feinglass, J., Fudala, M.J., Barsuk, J.H., & McGaghie, W.C. (2008). Simulation-based education improves quality of care during cardiac arrest team responses at an academic teaching hospital: A case-control study. *Chest, 133*(1), 56–61. https://doi.org/10.1378/chest.07-0131

Wulf, G., & Shea, C. (2004). Understanding the role of augmented feedback: The good, the bad, and the ugly. In A. Williams & N. Hodges (Eds.), *Skill acquisition in sport: Research, theory and practice* (pp. 121–144). London: Routledge.

Xeroulis, G.J., Park, J., Moulton, C.A., Reznick, R.K., LeBlanc, V., & Dubrowski, A. (2007). Teaching suturing and knot-tying skills to medical students: A randomized controlled study comparing computer-based video instruction and (concurrent and summary) expert feedback. *Surgery, 141*(4), 442–449. https://doi.org/10.1016/j.surg.2006.09.012

Ziv, A., Wolpe, P.R., Small, S.D., & Glick, S. (2003). Simulation-based medical education: An ethical imperative. *Academic Medicine, 78*(8), 783–788. https://doi.org/10.1097/00001888-200308000-00006

12 The Natural History of Simulation Centres: Educational Support Systems or Expressions of Technology?

STANLEY J. HAMSTRA

Prologue

In this chapter, I have chosen to weave my personal reflections into a summary of relevant research to try to bring to life the experience of planning and managing a successful simulation centre. It is hoped that the reader will gain a deeper appreciation of some of the nuances involved, which are typically not communicated in the academic literature. In that light, I tie in research findings with my own personal reflections, which are based on years of experience, to provide "lessons from the field."

Introduction

As simulation centres become more popular in healthcare education programs, it is instructive to consider their typical course of development and whether any lessons can be learned from a broad overview of their history and establishment. Most simulation centres seem to evolve through three distinct phases of development: (1) establishment and stability of funding, (2) concerns with justification and accountability, and (3) a focus on systematic innovation and scholarship. An important factor in this process is the shift from a belief in technology as a solution to educational challenges to a recognition of its role as simply another educational tool. In this chapter, I will review studies that have used relatively simple training materials to produce gains in learner performance, and consider why these are effective.

Typical Course of Development: A Personal Story

What is the typical course of development (i.e., the "natural history") of a simulation centre? In my experience, it usually starts with the technology. A few "plugged-in" clinician-educators or enthusiastic champions of the latest technology approach hospital or university leadership to see if they can design a better way to train health professionals at various stages of their education and/or practice, whether they are junior residents, medical students, or sometimes, colleagues. A case in point is the rapid transition to laparoscopic surgery from "open" procedures in the field of general surgery in the 1980s. This approach involves small incisions to gain access to internal organs with special instruments. Traditional "open" surgery requires large incisions that provide a wide view and (relatively) easy access to abdominal organs that might require removal or repair. Laparoscopic surgery requires new skills and knowledge to manage the special instruments and techniques, including viewing the operative field on a TV monitor instead of directly. Unfortunately, many surgeons struggled with this new approach – even though they were operating on the same organs – and there were reports of increased complication rates (Deziel, Millikan, Economou, Doolas, Ko, & Airan, 1993). Why was it so difficult for some older surgeons to learn this new approach after they had been practising similar open procedures for years? That question is one of the reasons I was hired at the University of Toronto Department of Surgery back in 1997. I'm a visual neuroscientist by training. My specialized area of research was binocular stereoscopic depth perception. It became clear that my skills in understanding how people perceive depth in three dimensions from depictions in two dimensions (i.e., 3D from 2D) might be useful to understanding why some surgeons struggle with learning laparoscopic surgery and why others take to it quickly. Is it a matter of "innate ability"? I was asked. Does it have to do with visual perception? The answer to these questions is rather long and involved, but the point is that the surgeons at the University of Toronto really wanted to find a better way of assessing and teaching technical skills, and the emerging field of laparoscopic surgery was just the thing to present to stakeholders to justify building a simulation centre. The early laparoscopic surgery simulators were certainly cutting-edge at the time. They had haptic manual input devices, meaning a user was able to feel resistance and tension, and a virtual reality (VR) display that looked a lot like what you might see from the TV monitor in the operating room. What followed after my hiring was an educational adventure lasting two decades, leading to a deeper understanding of the rationale for simulation centre design.

Leadership in the University of Toronto Department of Surgery was interested in providing a dedicated space for junior surgery residents from a variety of specialties to learn all manner of procedural skills, including knot-tying, suturing, airway management, anastomosis, casting, skin grafting, bone fixation, and many other procedures that might be useful in any surgical specialty. When I was ultimately recruited to other centres (at the University of Michigan and then the University of Ottawa), I was asked to help design simulation centres and research programs in simulation. To do that properly, I decided to visit as many other simulation centres as I could, so from 2007–9 I toured around the US, Canada, and the UK to find out what the state of the art was in simulation-based medical education.

What I found during my travels was that most centres were limited to one specialty or a group of specialties (e.g., they might have a surgical simulation centre, plus one for anaesthesiology, another for internal medicine or pediatrics, another for nursing, etc.), were typically not large, and were usually located in a hospital department. There were a few exceptions: for example, the Val G. Hemming Simulation Centre at the Uniformed Services University of the Health Sciences in Silver Spring, Maryland, was one of the few designed to be comprehensive and inclusive, and included simulation training in trauma surgery, anaesthesia, critical care medicine, and interprofessional teamwork (Uniformed Services University of the Health Sciences Val G. Hemming Simulation Center, 2018). Unlike most other centres, this one was designed with specific training needs in mind, to allow the learner to gain practice in every aspect of care, from the battlefield, back to a stable urgent care facility, and through to rehabilitation planning and communication with family. Aside from centres like these, which took a comprehensive and inclusive approach to planning and design, I found that there was usually no attempt to coordinate with established resources that may already exist within the institution, such as programs that support objective structured clinical examinations (OSCEs) or standardized patients for training and testing. Another thing that became obvious during my tour was that each centre was most proud of its technology and infrastructure (i.e., the physical space and the high-tech simulator machines it had purchased). To give the reader a general idea of what these facilities look like, I have included some statistics and references for typical simulation centres in Table 12.1.

Another astonishing fact emerged during my travels. When I pressed a little further during each visit, I found that there were often high-tech simulators that were either underused or had broken down and not been repaired. This seemed to be either because of lack of structured time in the curriculum for learners to make use of the systems, or because of lack of sustainable maintenance funding for repair and replacement. Unfortunately for most of these centres, there was not a

Table 12.1. Typical cost and design characteristics for simulation centres

Item	Range (currency in USD)
Size	800 to 30,000 sq. ft.
Costs for Initial Design and Construction	$500,000 to $7,000,000
Annual Operating Costs	Up to $700k
Location	1. Within medical school, 2. dedicated space off-campus, or 3. within a hospital.
Layout for a Large Centre	• 2 fully functional operating theatres • 2 large procedural skills areas • 1 fully functional emergency room resuscitation/trauma area • 1 fully functional intensive care unit bed/area • 2 large conference rooms with teleconference capability • 6 clinical exam rooms

Note: Data for construction and operating costs are from Danzer et al. (2011), Kempenich et al. (2018), Kurrek & Devitt (1997), and Tsuda, Mohsin & Jones (2015). Data for cost per course are from Drosdeck et al. (2013), Henry, Clark & Sudan (2014), Rooney et al. (2010), and Schneider et al. (2017). Data for design considerations are from Friedell (2010) and Seropian & Lavey (2010). Uniformed Services University of the Health Sciences Val G. Hemming Simulation Center (2018) were sources for the design and elements of the table.

plan in place for ongoing financial maintenance. The business plan, if it existed at all, typically involved a vague notion to hold industry-sponsored continuing medical education events, for which the centre could charge overhead. Charging the medical school for training students was never really an option, and the residency programs usually had no extra money to spend on education.[1] All of this presented a problem when the leaders of respective simulation centres would return to their primary stakeholders seeking funds for maintenance or repair. The university dean (or hospital CEO) had typically not been involved in the detailed planning for establishment and management of the centre, and would ask sticky questions about what they were getting for the money they had already spent on the simulation centre. They would ask about the potential return on investment for any additional expense, and make statements such as "Oh by the way, our budget is about to be reduced, so we need to find places to decrease spending, not increase it." At this point, there was typically a transition in thinking, as the simulation leadership team would gather to strategize how they could raise funds to ensure the simulation centre was sustainable.

A Framework for Understanding This Evolution

It was in making these visits to other centres and living through similar experiences as a simulation centre leader in three different settings that I realized there was a pattern that seemed to be occurring everywhere. Most simulation centres seem to go through three distinct phases of evolution in their individual development. The first stage is usually concerned with marketing, promotion, and establishment. Most of the effort in this stage is to acquire models, mannequins, and equipment, with some limited effort at developing structured curricula, and usually no effort on developing systems to support program evaluation. It typically highlights a general motivation to "keep up" with other centres and to promote the brand or image of the local institution in the context of regional or national peer institutions, much like what is done in terms of the research enterprise. At this stage, there is generally minimal discussion related to issues of accountability or systematic approaches to program evaluation.

By contrast, the second stage of development is usually concerned with justification and accountability, as leaders begin to recognize the need for capturing metrics of impact and for tactics for responding to financial stakeholders. It is at this stage that leadership typically decides to bring in full-time educators or social scientists with expertise in program evaluation to examine approaches to curriculum development, and also to guide educational implementation. There is a recognition of the need to extend efforts beyond the time-consuming task of acquisition of space and equipment. At this stage, efforts are usually made to more carefully and fully articulate the purpose of the centre, often culminating in the development of detailed mission and vision statements, and specific work may begin on the development of metrics of impact or systems to support program evaluation. Although there is a rapidly expanding research literature on the effectiveness of simulation and evidence for successful transfer of skills into the clinical setting (Barsuk, McGaghie, Cohen, O'Leary, & Wayne, 2009; Cohen et al., 2010; Cook et al., 2011; McGaghie, Issenberg, Barsuk, & Wayne, 2014), by and large research is not seen as a priority at the majority of centres until this stage of development. During this second stage, there is considerable variation between centres on efforts to build an educational rationale that can be subject to measurement of outcomes.

The third stage of development is one that is rarely attained. This concerns the development of infrastructure, resources, and systems to support scholarship and the dissemination of innovations related to simulation-based pedagogy. Although research activity is highly

Table 12.2. Future directions for research in simulation-based health professions education

---

Theme 1: Major Categories of Study
- Effectiveness of simulators as training platforms: transfer to the clinical setting
- Retention of skills learned during simulation-based training
- Effectiveness of simulators as assessment platforms
- Use of simulation for remediation
- Trainee buy-in and motivation/engagement
- Cost-effectiveness
- Integration of simulation technology with simulated patients
- Where to situate simulators within curricula

Theme 2: Comparative Effectiveness of Instructional Design Features
- Group Composition: Compare different approaches to grouping learners (e.g., interdisciplinary vs. single discipline, single individual vs. group learning)
- Lesson Plan: Compare different design features to enhance instructional effectiveness (e.g., moderation of feedback, sequence of teaching, repetition schedules, task variability, etc.)
- Instructor: Compare different levels of instructor training or presence (e.g., instructor intensity, self-instruction, distance supervision, etc.)
- Modality: Evaluate the addition of one or more other modalities (e.g., lecture, computer-assisted instruction, or other simulation) to baseline simulation training
- Sensory Augmentation: Evaluate the addition of a feature or effect to enhance sensory experience (e.g., tactile/haptics, visual motion, 3D/VR, auditory, olfactory)
- Compare two technology-enhanced simulation modalities (e.g., VR vs. model, mannequin vs. cadaver, synthetic vs. animal products, etc.)

Note: Adapted from Hamstra (2012) and Cook et al. (2013).

valued in the healthcare professions, there has been limited success in supporting educational scholarship in these settings. Issues related to the support of such activity have been summarized recently by Varpio and colleagues (2017). Examples of successful scholarship in simulation have typically been narrowly focused (Barsuk et al., 2009; Naik et al., 2001; Savoldelli et al., 2006; Wanzel, Hamstra, Anastakis, Matsumoto, & Cusimano, 2002; Zendejas, Brydges, Hamstra, & Cook, 2013), and it is recognized that many fundamental questions remain to be addressed (Cook et al., 2013; Hamstra, 2012; Holmboe et al., 2011; also see Table 12.1). To be successful at this stage of development requires time and opportunity for critical reflection and discussion, and interaction with peers at other institutions. This is often at odds with other priorities and immediate concerns such as running the existing curriculum, or clinical work. If this conflict is realized, leaders of simulation centres at this stage tend to shift their concerns to the development of a feedback mechanism to improve their educational and administrative processes and reduce the likelihood of making the same mistakes they did in earlier stages of development. They also recognize the opportunity (and their responsibility) to disseminate their findings not only for academic credit and reputation, but also for the good of the public.

Spoiler Alert! Simulation Is Just Another Educational Tool

What occurred to me, and to other leaders of simulation centres as I met with them and discussed their journeys, was that *simulation is just another educational tool* ... albeit a very expensive and potentially powerful tool. In the end, just like any other educational tool, it needs to be strategically situated in a curriculum in order to clearly address specific educational needs. Once simulation leaders realize this, the typical response is to hire an educator or social scientist to develop curricula and plan for program evaluation. In many cases, this brings about a challenge in managing different cultures and expectations. This is because many of the social scientists brought in as educational resource experts often have little experience working in the healthcare field, or more importantly, with healthcare professionals. There is often a steep learning curve (but this is probably a topic for another treatise). One of the main challenges to this clash of cultures is manifest in the use of jargon. For example, many clinician educators speak of "validating" simulators, curricula, or simulation-based courses (Hung, Shah, Dalag, Shin, & Gill, 2015; Shepherd et al., 2014; Tsai et al., 2017). While there is some tradition of this usage of the term "validity" in the military, aviation, engineering, and some corners of medicine (Oberkampf, Trucano, & Hirsch, 2004), it makes little sense to someone trained in the psychology of psychometrics. For a psychologist or measurement scientist, "validity" is a property that refers exclusively to an assessment instrument or process, not an educational intervention like simulation-based medical education (Barnes & Konia, 2018).

Not surprisingly, the education specialist approaches their task based on their background, which in most cases results in the realization that they need to employ a scientific approach to the evaluation of the impact of the simulation centre. Sometimes they will hire a consultant to perform a thorough analysis of engagement and usage patterns by stakeholder groups, such as undergraduate medical education, graduate medical education, and continuing medical education, or by profession, such as nursing, anaesthesia, surgery, and medicine, or by technology, such as high-tech VR versus animal tissue versus cadaver, et cetera. Alternatively, they may employ a more quantitatively oriented approach that involves the establishment of randomized control trials comparing different modes of simulation-based education or different approaches to training – for example, mastery versus spaced-interval training (Brydges, Carnahan, Rose, & Dubrowski, 2010; Gauger et al., 2018; Verdaasdonk, Stassen, van Wijk, & Dankleman, 2007). Another approach often used is to examine all of the activities of the simulation centre in the context of the system in which it is situated – that is, from a program evaluation perspective. For some centres, educational researchers employ approaches that are often quite unfamiliar to their clinical colleagues, such as qualitative methods of research involving grounded theory, ethnography, and other such approaches. One of the lessons researchers have learned when trying to establish programs of educational research in the context of healthcare delivery and education is that "education research is easy to do, it's just not easy to do well" (Regehr, 2010; Scott, Caldwell, & Schuwirth, 2015).

How to Evaluate the Effectiveness of Simulation Centres: From Anecdotes to Research Evidence

There are many examples of obvious benefit to learners and patients that can be traced directly back to their experiences in a simulation centre. Anecdotes can be powerful and moving: one of the residents at our simulation centre in Ottawa sent an email to us one morning following a difficult case the night before, during which he saved a patient's life.[2] He had been in for a simulation session the previous week, which ended up being critical for both the patient and the resident:

> Because of simulation, I was able to react much more quickly in a critical situation in the emergency room. A code situation was recognized in a timely manner and return of spontaneous circulation was achieved rapidly. To top it off, this is the second case in my short career that has had improved patient outcome because of my experience in the simulator! (M. Doré, personal communication, 2010)

While unsolicited anecdotes like this can be very powerful, it is a different matter to demonstrate impact in a form that will appeal to a critical audience or stakeholder group; in that case, it is necessary to turn anecdotes like this one into scholarship.

There has been a great deal of literature published on simulation-based medical education in recent years, some of it based on deep and sophisticated research, while the bulk of the literature consists of opinion pieces and superficial studies that lack the kind of rigour that would help to establish the case for simulation as an effective educational tool.

Fortunately, there have been a number of excellent literature reviews (Issenberg, McGaghie, Petrusa, Lee, Gordon, & Scalese, 2005; McGhaghie, Issenberg, Petrusa, & Scalese, 2010; Lorello, Cook, Johnson, & Brydges, 2014; Tan & Sarker, 2011; Zendejas et al., 2013), which have spurred the field on to consider more difficult and broader questions, which are outlined in the sections below. The largest and most comprehensive review of the literature in simulation-based medical education has been conducted by Cook and colleagues; it involved an initial review of 10,903 studies as candidates for systematic meta-analysis, resulting in a thorough review of 985 studies involving some kind of rigorous comparison of approaches, covering the period 1966–2011 (Cook et al., 2011). These authors observed that while systematic research on the effects of simulation training on patient-related outcomes is still in its earliest stages, in general it has been found that simulation training produces large effects for outcomes of knowledge, skills, and behaviours, when compared with no intervention (e.g., effect sizes in the range of 0.79–1.20). One key takeaway point from this literature suggests that simulation-based medical education should be based on a structured approach involving specified goals and objectives (Gauger et al., 2010; Hamstra & Philibert, 2012; Maran & Glavin, 2003), consistent with principles espoused for effective education in general (Naik, Wong & Hamstra, 2012).

Major Directions for Research in Simulation-Based Medical Education

In spite of the large volume of literature on simulation-based medical education, there remains a need for focused research on a few broad questions that would be applicable to any form of educational intervention. Taken in this light, the major questions in this field are similar to those in other fields of education: (1) Is simulation effective? (2) How can we make it more effective? and (3) Is simulation cost-effective?

Is Simulation Effective?

It is clear that the overall effect of simulation-based training is very strong when compared to no alternative intervention (609 studies) (Cook et al., 2011), or interventions not based on simulation (92 studies) (Cook et al., 2012). In specific contexts, simulation-based training has been found to be effective enough to warrant changes in policy for education or quality improvement efforts (Buyske, 2010; The American Board of Surgery, 2008). With this picture of effectiveness in mind, it is helpful to reframe the question to focus on what type of simulation is effective for a given clinical skill.

How Can We Make Simulation More Effective?

In general, the literature shows that many instructional design features contribute to the effectiveness of simulation as an educational tool, including feedback, cognitive interactivity, repetitive practice, and exposure to a range of difficulty in procedural tasks (Issenberg et al., 2005). In their comprehensive review, Cook and colleagues (2013) found that it was necessary to divide the studies into those looking at different types of outcome. For studies looking only at skills acquisition as an outcome, their findings confirmed those of earlier reviews and highlighted the importance of additional instructional design features such as distributed practice, multiple learning strategies, individualized learning, mastery learning, longer time, and clinical variation. For different outcomes beyond skills acquisition, when compared with interventions involving alternate modes of simulation such as computer-based training, static mannequins and plastic models, live animals, inert animal products, and human cadavers (289 studies), technology-enhanced simulation appeared to be more effective for all types of outcomes measured, including knowledge acquisition, time taken to perform tasks, efficiency in process, product quality, behaviour in the clinical setting, and effects on patients (Cook et al., 2013). In general, these studies highlight the importance of specificity in the terms and approaches used in simulation-based training, as well as specificity in clearly identifying the outcomes of interest. For example, one simulation approach might work very well with a junior group of learners for immediate improvement in skills outcome, but this may not be the best approach for training transfer of skills to the clinical setting when looking at the more nuanced measurement of patient outcomes. These questions remain difficult to study given the complexity of both the training environment and the clinical context of application. In the meantime, it might be useful to consider in more detail how to make simulation-based medical education more efficient so that stakeholders continue to see the benefit of their investment.

Is Simulation Cost-Effective?

There have been very few studies examining cost outcomes related to simulation-based medical education. Perhaps the most dramatic example is the study by Cohen et al. (2010) on the effectiveness of a simulation-based intervention on reducing infection rates, showing that reduced costs in care greatly outweighed the cost of simulation-based training. Such studies are becoming more possible but are still much too rare, because of the difficulty in measuring and obtaining clinical outcomes data, as well as the inability to attribute clinical outcomes to specific educational interventions. While it may be that an individual practitioner might show improvement in a particular skill following simulation-based education, it is much harder to make a direct link to the context of clinical intervention, which most often involves a variety of players working together in a complex system. For example, healthcare delivery most often involves teamwork between doctor, nurse, technician, and other therapists (Boreham, 2004; Hawryluck, Espin, Garwood, Evans, & Lingard, 2002; Yardley & Dornan, 2012). Each member might contribute in significant ways, but it will most often be very difficult to determine whether clinical outcomes can be attributed to individual efforts. Thus, while simulation-based education is most often targeted to individual skill development, in practice healthcare is almost always delivered by more than one person.

For some time, there have been a number of thinly veiled critiques of costly high-technology systems in support of simulation-based healthcare education. Here, studies that have used relatively simple training materials have shown gains in learner performance when these materials are compared to complex training materials replicating anatomical and physiological features of a patient (Matsumoto, Hamstra, Radomski, Cusimano, 2002). This has led to a focus on understanding the essential principles underlying effective educational design (Hamstra, Brydges, Hatala, Zendejas, & Cook, 2014). One of the most basic questions that arises from such an analysis is related to cost. In other words, under what conditions can simulation-based training be effective in a context with limited resources? Is it necessary to employ highly sophisticated technology to train all skills? A study by Zendejas, Wang, Brydges, Hamstra, and Cook (2013) examined this question as part of a larger systematic review (Zendejas et al., 2013). It found that cost was almost never reported in studies of technology-enhanced simulation in medical education (i.e. only 6.1% of studies reported any cost elements), and if it was, the study almost always focused very narrowly on only the cost of hardware and training materials. This makes it very hard to make any kind of comparative judgment about whether simulation-based training is cost-effective. For now, we are left to make the assumption that simple technology is less expensive and examine the extent to which it might lead to measurable outcomes when compared with more sophisticated technology, and why this might be so. The evidence to date suggests that under certain conditions learners can attain the same extent of basic skill using simple bench models as they can with highly sophisticated mannequins and models (Anastakis et al., 1999; Chandra, Savoldelli, Joo, Weiss, & Naik, 2008; de Giovanni, Roberts, &

Norman, 2009; Friedman et al., 2009; Grober et al., 2004; Matsumoto et al., 2002; McDougall et al., 2009; Tan & Sarker, 2011). However, learners generally seem to prefer to use more sophisticated platforms (Grober et al., 2004). In spite of this, there is evidence that training on a simple model can be transferred to the clinical context (Anastakis et al., 1999), and learners acknowledge the educational value of simpler, low-cost platforms (Grober et al., 2004). So, we are left to ask why they acknowledge the value of these simpler platforms while preferring to practise on the more expensive ones. There may be a clue in one of the relatively early studies in surgical education involving the training of ureteroscopic skills using a coffee cup and drinking straws with senior medical students (Matsumoto et al., 2002). In this study, in designing the simple model, content experts were explicitly asked to focus on the learning objectives of the procedural skill and identify key *functional* parameters of the clinical task to be trained. It may be that learners focused so intently on details of the technical instruction that this over-rode any concern with such a simple physical platform and played the primary role in the success of learning this skill. Especially for junior learners, it may be that an emphasis on highly sophisticated technology causes an element of distraction from the task at hand, as this may cause increasing demands on the limited resources of working memory (Jones, Ross, Lynam, Perez, & Leitch, 2011; Sterman, 1994). A related explanation from cognitive science is that high structural fidelity might be best for promoting "near transfer" (i.e., transfer of specific skills to a similar context), while low structural fidelity is more effective for promoting "far transfer" (i.e., transfer of general principles to distant contexts) (Maran & Glavin, 2003; Munz, Kumar, Moorthy, Bann, & Darzi, 2004). It appears that an undue emphasis on sophisticated technology may have the effect of directing attention toward irrelevant aspects of the simulation platform while the primary objective is to train clinical skills. By asking "What are we going to teach?" rather than "How will we use this platform to teach this skill?" the instructor effectively shifts the focus toward the learner and allows them greater opportunity for engaging principles of active learning.

A Proposal for the Next Stage of Evolution of Simulation Centres

For simulation centres to truly evolve to realize their full potential, it is important that they demonstrate impact on healthcare outcomes. This is true of all aspects of health professions education, and it should be expected of simulation-based medical education as well. While this challenge has rarely been met by other promising initiatives in medical education (Colliver, 2000; Norman & Schmidt, 2001), there is an obvious and intuitive rational argument that can be made for medical education broadly, and simulation appears to address a gap in the current system of training. In addition, some corners of simulation-based medical education have shown strong evidence in outcomes, such as mastery-based learning in reducing procedure-based infections (Barsuk et al., 2009; McGaghie et al., 2014; Cohen et al., 2010).

What is required to move the field to the next level is an appropriate investment in educational resources, both in terms of equipment and personnel to staff simulation centres and an investment in the appropriate systems for program evaluation that can help to make the case for return on investment. Early examples exist, and they should be guided by methods and approaches that have been widely adopted by medical educators more broadly. One useful framework for assessing the impact of interventions in medical education comes from the field of human resources, and can be used as a model for developing outcome metrics for simulation-based medical education (Harden, Grant, Buckley, & Hart, 1999; Kirkpatrick, 1998). The Kirkpatrick hierarchy for evaluating outcomes of an educational intervention consists of four levels – reaction, learning, transfer to the workplace, and results (see Table 12.3). For example, at the lowest level (reaction), the intent is to determine the degree of learners' participation. At this level, one might ask questions about attendance, learner engagement, or subjective satisfaction with an educational intervention. At level 2 (learning), one could develop assessment instruments that measure changes in attitudes or improvements in knowledge or skills. At higher levels (transfer and results), one is interested in more lasting and deeper change that will result in the successful application of knowledge and/or skills in the clinical setting. At the highest level (results), one is concerned with the possibility for improvements in patient care, as measured objectively using complication rates, length of stay, or other indicators of change in morbidity. Generally speaking, health professions education scholars should attempt to develop outcome measures at the highest levels of the Kirkpatrick hierarchy, though this can often be quite difficult and should be attempted only after they have achieved some success with lower levels. Curriculum designers should also attend to the program-specific context of an educational intervention, as this will play a considerable role in determining desirable and feasible simulations.

The role of larger systemic or contextual issues in measuring outcomes of a healthcare team is an important consideration, and the Kirkpatrick framework can be used fruitfully to assess these effects. Using the Kirkpatrick hierarchy as a guide, we might first wish to address subtle

Table 12.3. Modified hierarchical version of the Kirkpatrick framework for assessing impact of educational intervention

---

Level 1 – Reaction
Level 1a – Participation
Level 1b – Satisfaction

Level 2 – Learning
Level 2a – Change in Attitudes/Confidence
Level 2b – Change in Knowledge/Skills

Level 3 – Transfer to the Workplace
Level 3a – Change in Clinical Practice
Level 3b – Successful Application of Learned Knowledge/Skills

Level 4 – Results
Level 4a – Improvements in Patient Satisfaction
Level 4b – Improvements in Patient Outcome

Note: Adapted from Hamstra (2012).

changes in outcome, such as whether each member of the team is partic-ipating appropriately in their role as a member of the team, or whether they have the appropriate attitude toward teamwork or patient-centred care. At an institutional level, one could measure participation rates or level of engagement in programs designed to enhance interprofes-sional work. Following this, one could measure attitude change toward teamwork, and knowledge change in the individual. In principle, the Kirkpatrick framework could be used to measure any changes in the system, such as whether learners notice that an educational program is in place to enhance teamwork and patient-centred care, for example, by examining transcripts from focus groups or interviews. This is an ideal context to employ qualitative research methods, including interviews, focus groups, surveys, or ethnographic field notes, to elicit and under-stand the perceptions of any of the parties involved (e.g., patients, fam-ilies, doctors, nurses, etc.).

This modified Kirkpatrick hierarchy has been taken up broadly in medical education and appears to have desirable benefits for helping to design outcome metrics for assessment instruments.

In addition to methods and approaches to framing evaluation for return on investment, it might be helpful to implement a simple struc-ture for management of the simulation centre that might lead more easily to the collection of data on impact. One idea that we began to im-plement at the University of Ottawa Skills and Simulation Centre was for course leaders to consider a number of basic educational criteria while planning their sessions. We developed a revised booking form, which was used to encourage simulation session instructors to more carefully plan each session, as well as to consider how they might systematically collect evidence for its effectiveness. The form was designed with the following four basic elements: (1) rationale: identify the outcomes or gaps in knowledge, skills, or attitudes for this session and how these were determined; (2) learning objectives: list the specific learning objectives of this session and how each addresses the gaps identified above, in (1); (3) lesson plan: provide details of the specific sequence of educational activities with a timeline for the session; and (4) evaluation plan: describe methods and tools for determining the impact of your session. With these elements in place for every session at the simulation centre, it would be possible in theory to capture enough data in a systematic way that stakeholders might begin to realize the impact of their investment, especially if analysed in an aggregate fashion according to particular stakeholder perspectives and interests.

The Need for a Theory-Based Approach to Assessing the Impact of Simulation

A final recommendation to help simulation centres demonstrate impact in a scholarly way is to adopt theory and methods from other disciplines. This seems especially important in simulation-based health professions education since it already crosses several traditional boundaries, and draws on contributions from aviation (crew-resource management), ergonomics (usability and standardization), kinesiology (challenge-point hypothesis), education (mastery learning), psychology (transfer of learning), engineering (materials and systems), and the military (closed-loop communication). This would help the field move past the first stage of evolution, where we are promoting the "wow" factor of sophisticated technology, to a systematic and scientific approach to honest and open exploration of what works, for whom and under what circumstances (Pawson, Greenhalgh, Harvey, & Walshe, 2005).

One example of this approach has to do with the concepts of "transfer" and "fidelity," both terms that are widely used in simulation, but poorly understood, as evidenced by the variation in use and application in the literature. Similarly to the concerns raised above about the term "validity," there is much confusion surrounding the term "fidelity," and a theory-based analysis might help to resolve some of this confusion. For example, in most cases it may be more productive from an educational standpoint if we consider the fidelity of the simulation scenario relative to clinical task demands (functional fidelity) rather than to the physical resemblance to the human patient (structural fidelity). We have seen that so-called "low-fidelity" simulation platforms can be as effective as "high-fidelity" systems (de Giovanni, Roberts, & Norman, 2009). A simple theoretical explanation from developmental psychology might help to explain this. Piaget first saw the power of extending the "Socratic" approach to abstract conceptual understanding in children, a theoretical framework that came to be known as constructivism (Piaget, 1954). In this framework, much like the Socratic method, the learner actively attempts to make the topic to be learned relevant to their experience in interacting with the world. When applied to the question of why "low-fidelity" models might be effective, we can see that the relevance of low structural fidelity depends on the goals of the learner (Boreham, 1985; Grober et al., 2004; Matsumoto et al., 2002; Paul & Nobel, 2005). An active learning framework helps to explain why low structural fidelity can be effective and, consequently, how fidelity is not a static attribute of the simulator or simulation. In simulation-based health professions education, close alignment between the clinical task and the simulation task (i.e., functional fidelity) is often more important than structural fidelity for achieving the educational goals. This highlights the benefits of *functional task alignment* (i.e., aligning the simulator's functional properties with the functional requirements of the clinical task), a new theoretical term that may help in understanding why simulation works for certain individuals under certain circumstances (Hamstra et al., 2014). The advantage of appealing to theory here lies in the ability to make recommendations for specific simulation-based curricular changes in order to address targeted learning objectives. Indeed, the key features of effective simulation identified earlier by Issenberg et al. (2005) and McGaghie et al. (2010) all have firm grounding in accepted theories of instructional design.

Summary and Conclusions

As simulation centres become more popular in health professions education programs across North America and around the world, it is instructive to consider their typical course of development and whether any lessons can be learned from this. In reflecting on my career to date in directing programs of research and helping to manage simulation centres, I have noticed a pattern of developmental processes at work. Most simulation centres seem to go through three distinct phases in terms of their "natural history," which may have broader implications for the collective evolution of the field. The first stage is usually concerned with establishment and stability of funding. The second stage of development is usually concerned with justification and accountability, as leaders begin to recognize the need for capturing metrics of impact and respond to their financial stakeholders. Lastly, the third stage of development concerns scholarship and the dissemination of ideas and innovations. While simulation can certainly assist in providing a highly structured framework for delivering curricula and providing for standardized assessment, it is, in the end, simply another educational tool and should be regarded as such. To continue to grow, we will need a continued emphasis on quality scholarship in our field, and efforts to advocate for the importance of educational scholarship in health professions education should continue to be made, both at the local and national levels.

NOTES

1 All of this changed later, when there was a push in some specialties to mandate simulation-based training for certain types of accreditation and certification, but that is another story, with its own literature base (see Buyske, 2010; Holmboe, Rizzolo, Sachdeva, Rosenberg, & Ziv, 2011; Kempenich, Willis, Campi, & Schenarts, 2018; The American Board of Surgery, 2008).
2 This anecdote was read aloud during a fund-raising dinner celebrating the acquisition of a new corporate sponsor at a black-tie event one evening.

REFERENCES

The American Board of Surgery. (2008). *ABS to require ACLS, ATLS and FLS for general surgery certification.* Retrieved from https://www.absurgery.org /default.jsp?news_newreqs

Anastakis, D.J., Regehr, G., Reznick, R.K., Cusimano, M., Murnaghan, J., Brown, M., & Hutchison, C. (1999). Assessment of technical skills transfer from the bench training model to the human model. *The American Journal of Surgery, 177*(2), 167–170. https://doi.org/10.1016/S0002-9610(98)00327-4

Barnes, J.J., III, & Konia, M.R. (2018). Exploring validation and verification: How they are different and what they mean to healthcare simulation. *Simulation in Healthcare, 13*(5), 356–362. https://doi.org/10.1097/SIH.0000000000000298

Barsuk, J.H., McGaghie, W.C., Cohen, E.R., O'Leary, K.J., & Wayne, D.B. (2009). Simulation-based mastery learning reduces complications during central venous catheter insertion in a medical intensive care unit. *Critical Care Medicine, 37*(10), 2697–2701. https://doi.org/10.1097/00003246 -200910000-00003

Boreham, N. (1985). Transfer of training in the generation of diagnostic hypotheses: The effect of lowering fidelity of simulation. *British Journal of*

Educational Psychology, 55(3), 213–223. https://doi.org/10.1111/j.2044-8279 .1985.tb02626.x

Boreham, N. (2004). A theory of collective competence: Challenging the neo-liberal individualisation of performance at work. *British Journal of Educational Studies, 52*(1), 5–17. https://doi.org/10.1111/j.1467-8527.2004 .00251.x

Buyske, J. (2010). The role of simulation in certification. *Surgical Clinics, 90*(3), 619–621. https://doi.org/10.1016/j.suc.2010.02.013

Brydges, R., Carnahan, H., Rose, D., & Dubrowski, A. (2010). Comparing self-guided learning and educator-guided learning formats for simulation-based clinical training. *Journal of Advanced Nursing, 66*(8), 1832–1844. https://doi .org/10.1111/j.1365-2648.2010.05338.x

Chandra, D.B., Savoldelli, G.L., Joo, H.S., Weiss, I.D., & Naik, V.N. (2008). Fiberoptic oral intubation: The effect of model fidelity on training for transfer to patient care. *Anesthesiology, 109*(6), 1007–1013. https://doi.org /10.1097/ALN.0b013e31818d6c3c

Cohen, E.R., Feinglass, J., Barsuk, J.H., Barnard, C., O'Donnell, A., McGaghie, W.C., & Wayne, D.B. (2010). Cost savings from reduced catheter-related bloodstream infection after simulation-based education for residents in a medical intensive care unit. *Simulation in Healthcare, 5*(2), 98–102. https:// doi.org/10.1097/SIH.0b013e3181bc8304

Colliver, J.A. (2000). Effectiveness of problem-based learning curricula: Research and theory. *Academic Medicine, 75*(3), 259–266. Retrieved from: https://doi.org /10.1097/00001888-200003000-00017

Cook, D.A., Brydges, R., Hamstra, S.J., Zendejas, B., Szostek, J.H., Wang, A.T., ... Hatala, R. (2012). Comparative effectiveness of technology-enhanced simulation vs. other instructional methods: A systematic review and meta-analysis. *Simulation in Healthcare, 7*(5), 308–320. https://doi.org/10.1097 /SIH.0b013e3182614f95

Cook, D.A., Hamstra, S.J., Brydges, R., Zendejas, B., Szostek, J.H., Wang, A.T., ... Hatala, R. (2013). Comparative effectiveness of instructional design features in simulation-based education: Systematic review and meta-analysis. *Medical Teacher, 35*(1), e867–e898. https://doi.org/10.3109 /0142159X.2012.714886

Cook, D.A., Hatala, R., Brydges, R., Zendejas, B., Szostek, J.H., Wang, A.T., ... Hamstra, S.J. (2011). Technology-enhanced simulation for health professions education: a systematic review and meta-analysis. *JAMA, 306*(9), 978–988. https://doi.org/10.1001/jama.2011.1234

Danzer, E., Dumon, K., Kolb, G., Pray, L., Selvan, B., Resnick, A.S., ...Williams, N.N. (2011). What is the cost associated with the implementation and maintenance of an ACS/APDS-based surgical skills curriculum? *Journal of Surgical Education, 68*(6), 519–525. https://doi.org/10.1016/j.jsurg.2011.06.004

de Giovanni, D., Roberts, T. & Norman, G. (2009). Relative effectiveness of high-versus low-fidelity simulation in learning heart sounds. *Medical Education, 43*(7), 661–668. https://doi.org/10.1111/j.1365-2923.2009 .03398.x

Deziel, D.J., Millikan, K.W., Economou, S.F., Doolas, A., Ko, S-T., & Airan, M.C. (1993). Complications of laparoscopic cholecystectomy: A national survey of 4,292 hospitals and an analysis of 77,604 cases. *The American Journal of Surgery,* 165(1), 9–14. https://doi.org/10.1016/S0002-9610(05)80397-6

Drosdeck, J., Carraro, E., Arnold, M., Perry, K., Harzman, A., Nagel, R., ... Muscarella, P. (2013). Porcine wet lab improves surgical skills in third year medical students. *Journal of Surgical Research, 184*(1), 19–25. https://doi.org /10.1016/j.jss.2013.06.009

Friedell, M.L. (2010). Starting a simulation and skills laboratory: What do I need and what do I want? *Journal of Surgical Education, 67*(2), 112–121.

Friedman, Z., Siddiqui, N., Katznelson, R., Devito, I., Bould, M.D., & Naik, V. (2009). Clinical impact of epidural anesthesia simulation on short-and long-term learning curve: High-versus low-fidelity model training. *Regional Anesthesia and Pain Medicine, 3*(4), 229–232. https://doi.org/10.1097/aap .0b013e3181a34345

Gauger, P.G., Hauge, L.S., Andreatta, P.B., Hamstra, S.J., Hillard, M.L., Arble, E.P., ... Minter, R.M. (2010). Laparoscopic simulation training with proficiency targets improves practice and performance of novice surgeons. *The American Journal of Surgery, 199*(1), 72–80. https://doi.org/10.1016 /j.amjsurg.2009.07.034

Grober, E.D., Hamstra, S.J., Wanzel, K.R., Reznick, R.K., Matsumoto, E.D., Sidhu, R.S., & Jarvi, K.A. (2004). The educational impact of bench model fidelity on the acquisition of technical skill: The use of clinically relevant outcome measures. *Annals of Surgery, 240*(2), 374–381. https://doi.org /10.1097/01.sla.0000133346.07434.30

Hamstra, S.J. (2012). Keynote address: The focus on competencies and individual learner assessment as emerging themes in medical education research. *Academic Emergency Medicine, 19*(12), 1336–1343. https://doi.org /10.1111/acem.12021

Hamstra, S.J., Brydges, R., Hatala, R., Zendejas, B., & Cook, D.A. (2014). Reconsidering fidelity in simulation-based training. *Academic Medicine, 89*(3), 387–392. https://doi.org/10.1097/ACM.0000000000000130

Hamstra, S., & Philibert, I. (2012). Simulation in graduate medical education: Understanding uses and maximizing benefits. *Journal of Graduate Medical Education, 4*(4), 539–540. https://doi.org/10.4300/JGME-D-12-00260.1

Harden, R.M., Grant, J., Buckley, G., & Hart, I.R. (1999). BEME Guide No. 1: Best evidence medical education. *Medical Teacher, 21*(6), 553–562. https:// doi.org/10.1080/01421599978960

Hawryluck, L.A., Espin, S.L., Garwood, K.C., Evans, C.A., & Lingard, L.A. (2002). Pulling together and pushing apart: Tides of tension in the ICU team. *Academic Medicine, 77*(10), S73–S76. https://doi.org/10.1097 /00001888-200210001-00024

Henry, B., Clark, P., & Sudan, R. (2014). Cost and logistics of implementing a tissue-based American College of Surgeons/Association of Program Directors in Surgery surgical skills curriculum for general surgery residents of all clinical years. *The American Journal of Surgery, 207*(2), 201–208. https:// doi.org/10.1016/j.amjsurg.2013.08.025

Holmboe, E., Rizzolo, M.A., Sachdeva, A.K., Rosenberg, M., & Ziv, A. (2011). Simulation-based assessment and the regulation of healthcare professionals. *Simulation in Healthcare, 6*(Suppl. 7), S58–S62. https://doi.org/10.1097/SIH .0b013e3182283bd7

Hung, A.J., Shah, S.H., Dalag, L., Shin, D., & Gill, I.S. (2015). Development and validation of a novel robotic procedure specific simulation platform: Partial nephrectomy. *Journal of Urology, 194*(2), 520–526. https://doi.org/10.1016 /j.juro.2015.02.2949

Issenberg, S.B., McGaghie, W.C., Petrusa, E.R., Lee Gordon, D., & Scalese, R.J. (2005). Features and uses of high-fidelity medical simulations that lead to effective learning: A BEME systematic review. *Medical Teacher, 27*(1), 10–28. https://doi.org/10.1080/01421590500046924

Jones, N.A., Ross, H., Lynam, T., Perez, P., & Leitch, A. (2011). Mental models: An interdisciplinary synthesis of theory and methods. *Ecology and Society, 16*(1): 46. https://doi.org/10.5751/es-03802-160146

Kempenich, J.W., Willis, R.E., Campi, H.D., & Schenarts, P.J. (2018). The cost of compliance: The financial burden of fulfilling Accreditation Council for Graduate Medical Education and American Board of Surgery requirements. *Journal of Surgical Education, 75*(6), e47–e53. https://doi.org/10.1016 /j.jsurg.2018.07.006

Kirkpatrick, D.L. (1998). *Evaluating training programs: The four levels.* San Francisco, CA: Berrett-Koehler Publishers.

Kurrek, M.M., & Devitt, J.H. (1997). The cost for construction and operation of a simulation centre. *Canadian Journal of Anaesthesia, 44*(11), 1191–1195. https://doi.org/10.1007/BF03013344

Lorello, G.R., Cook, D.A., Johnson, R.L., & Brydges, R. (2014). Simulation-based training in anaesthesiology: A systematic review and meta-analysis. *British Journal of Anaesthesia, 112*(2), 231–245. https://doi.org/10.1093/bja/aet414

Maran, N.J., & Glavin, R.J. (2003). Low-to high-fidelity simulation – a continuum of medical education? *Medical Education, 37*(Suppl. 1), 22–28. https://doi.org/10.1046/j.1365-2923.37.s1.9.x

Matsumoto, E.D., Hamstra, S.J., Radomski, S.B., & Cusimano, M.D. (2002). The effect of bench model fidelity on endourologic skills: A randomized controlled study. *Journal of Urology, 167*(3), 1243–1247. https://doi.org /10.1016/S0022-5347(05)65274-3

McDougall, E.M., Kolla, S.B., Santos, R.T., Gan, J.M., Box, G. N., Louie, M.K., ... Clayman, R.V. (2009). Preliminary study of virtual reality and model simulation for learning laparoscopic suturing skills. *The Journal of Urology, 182*(3), 1018–1025. https://doi.org/10.1016/j.juro.2009.05.016

McGaghie, W.C., Issenberg, S.B., Barsuk, J.H., & Wayne, D.B. (2014). A critical review of simulation-based mastery learning with translational outcomes. *Medical Education, 48*(4), 375–385. https://doi.org/10.1111/medu.12391

McGaghie, W.C., Issenberg, S.B., Petrusa, E.R., & Scalese, R.J. (2010). A critical review of simulation-based medical education research: 2003–2009. *Medical Education, 44*(1), 50–63. https://doi.org/10.1111/j.1365-2923.2009.03547.x

Munz, Y., Kumar, B.D., Moorthy, K., Bann, S., & Darzi, A. (2004). Laparoscopic virtual reality and box trainers: Is one superior to the other? *Surgical Endoscopy and Other Interventional Techniques, 18*(3), 485–494. https://doi.org /10.1007/s00464-003-9043-7

Naik, V., Matsumoto, E.D., Houston, P., Hamstra, S.J., Yeung, R., Mallon, J., & Martire, T.M. (2001). Fiberoptic orotracheal intubation on anesthetized patients: Do manipulation skills learned on a simple model transfer into the operating room? *Anesthesiology, 95*(2), 343–348. https://doi.org/10.1097 /00000542-200108000-00014

Naik, V.N., Wong, A., & Hamstra, S.J. (2012). Review article: Leading the future: Guiding two predominant paradigm shifts in medical education through scholarship. *Canadian Journal of Anesthesia, 59*(2), 213–223. https:// doi.org/10.1007/s12630-011-9640-1

Norman, G.R., & Schmidt, H.G. (2001). Effectiveness of problem-based learning curricula: Theory, practice and paper darts. *Medical Education, 34*(8), 721–728. https://doi.org/10.1046/j.1365-2923.2000.00749.x

Oberkampf, W.L., Trucano, T.G., & Hirsch, C. (2004). Verification, validation, and predictive capability in computational engineering and physics. *Applied Mechanics Review, 57*(5), 345–384. https://doi.org/10.1115/1.1767847

Paul, M., & Nobel, K. (2005). Papaya: A simulation model for training in uterine aspiration. *Innovations in Family Medicine Education, 37*(4), 242–244. Available at: https://www.ansirh.com

Pawson, R., Greenhalgh, T., Harvey, G., & Walshe, K. (2005). Realist review – a new method of systematic review designed for complex policy interventions. *Journal of Health Services Research and Policy, 10*(Suppl.1), 21–34. https://doi.org/10.1258/1355819054308530

Piaget, J. (1954). *The construction of reality in the child.* New York: Basic Books.

Regehr, G. (2010). It's NOT rocket science: Rethinking our metaphors for research in health professions education. *Medical Education, 44*(1), 31–39. https://doi.org/10.1111/j.1365-2923.2009.03418.x

Rooney, D., Pugh, C., Auyang, E., Hungess, E., & Da Rosa, D. (2010). Administrative considerations when implementing ACS/APDS skills curriculum. *Surgery, 147*(5), 614–621. https://doi.org/10.1016/j.surg.2009.10.067

Savoldelli, G.L., Naik, V.N., Joo, H.S., Houston, P.L., Graham, M., Yee, B., & Hamstra, S.J. (2006). Evaluation of patient simulator performance as an adjunct to oral examination for senior anesthesia residents. *Anesthesiology, 104*(3), 475–481. https://doi.org/10.1097/00000542-200603000-00014

Schneider, E., Schenarts, P.J., Shostrom, V., Schenarts, K.D., Evans, C.H. (2017). "I got it on Ebay!": Cost-effective approach to surgical skills laboratories. *Journal of Surgical Research, 207*, 190–197. https://doi.org/10.1016/j.jss.2016.08.017

Scott, K., Caldwell, P., & Schuwirth, L. (2015). Ten steps to conducting health professional education research. *The Clinical Teacher, 12*(4), 272–276. https://doi.org/10.1111/tct.12287

Shepherd, W., Arora, K.S., Abboudi, H., Shamim Khan, M., Dasgupta, P., & Ahmed, K. (2014). A review of the available urology skills training curricula and their validation. *Journal of Surgical Education, 71*(3), 289–296. https://doi.org/10.1016/j.jsurg.2013.09.005

Seropian, M., & Lavey, R. (2010). Design considerations for healthcare simulation facilities. *Simulation in Healthcare, 5*(6), 338–345. https://doi.org/10.1097/SIH.0b013e3181ec8f60

Sterman, J.D. (1994). Learning in and about complex-systems. *System Dynamics Review, 10*(2–3): 291–330. https://doi.org/10.1002/sdr.4260100214

Tan, S.S.Y., & Sarker, S.K. (2011). Simulation in surgery: A review. *Scottish Medical Journal, 56*(2), 104–109. https://doi.org/10.1258/smj.2011.011098

Tsai, A., Barnewolt, C.E., Prahbu, S.P., Yonekura, R., Hosmer, A., Schulz, N.E., & Weinstock, P.H. (2017). Creation and validation of a simulator for neonatal brain ultrasonography: A pilot study. *Academic Radiology, 24*(1), 76–83. https://doi.org/10.1016/j.acra.2016.09.007

Tsuda, S., Mohsin, A., & Jones, D. (2015). Financing a simulation center. *Surgical Clinics, 95*(4), 791–800. https://doi.org/10.1016/j.suc.2015.03.002

Uniformed Services University of the Health Sciences Val G. Hemming Simulation Center. (2018). *Facility*. Retrieved from https://simcen.usuhs.edu/site/facility/Pages/default.aspx

Varpio, L., O'Brien, B., Hu, W., ten Cate, O., Durning, S.J., van der Vleuten, C., ... Hamstra, S.J. (2017). Exploring the institutional logics of health professions education scholarship units. *Medical Education, 51*(7), 755–767. https://doi.org/10.1111/medu.13334

Verdaasdonk, E.G., Stassen, L.P., van Wijk, R.P., & Dankelman, J. (2007). The influence of different training schedules on the learning of psychomotor

skills for endoscopic surgery. *Surgical Endoscopy, 21*(2), 214–219. https://doi
.org/10.1007/s00464-005-0852-8

Wanzel, K.R., Hamstra, S.J., Anastakis, D.J., Matsumoto, E.D., & Cusimano,
M.D. (2002). Effect of visual-spatial ability on learning of spatially-complex
surgical skills. *The Lancet, 359*(9302), 230–231. https://doi.org/10.1016
/S0140-6736(02)07441-X

Yardley, S., & Dornan, T. (2012). Kirkpatrick's levels and education "evidence."
Medical Education, 46(1), 97–106. https://doi.org/10.1111/j.1365-2923
.2011.04076.x

Zendejas, B., Brydges, R., Hamstra, S.J., & Cook, D.A. (2013). State of the
evidence on simulation-based training for laparoscopic surgery: A systematic
review. *Annals of Surgery, 257*(4), 586–593. https://doi.org/10.1097
/sla.0b013e318288c40b

Zendejas, B., Wang, A.T., Brydges, R., Hamstra, S.J., & Cook, D.A. (2013). Cost:
The missing outcome in simulation-based education research: A systematic
review. *Surgery, 153*(2), 160–176. https://doi.org/10.1016/j.surg.2012.06.025

13 Simulated Participant Methodology in Health Professions Education: Theoretical Considerations in Design and Practice

NANCY MCNAUGHTON AND DEBRA NESTEL

Introduction

Simulation can be viewed broadly as a technique for use when learning to apply skills and knowledge in professional settings, as an assessment method, and as a pedagogical approach supported by an array of educational theories. Although we position this chapter in health professions education, we invite readers to consider applications in their own contexts of the natural sciences and social sciences. Simulated participant (SP) methodology is concerned with how individuals trained to take on specific roles can contribute to the development of health professional students and practitioners. Our use of the abbreviation SP should not be confused with "standardized patient," which is used frequently in North American settings where there has been interest and investment in the idea of reliability for large-scale health professions performance assessments known as objective structured clinical examinations (OSCEs). National licensing exams such as the Medical Council of Canada Qualifying Examination Part II (MCCQE Part II), the United States Medical Licensing Examination (USMLE Step 2), the Pharmacy Examining Board of Canada (PEBC) licensing examination, and Canadian Alliance of Physiotherapy Regulators (CAPR) certification, occur across geographical sites and time zones. Standardized patients are carefully trained to portray their role within the parameters of an assessment so that each candidate entering an exam encounter has the same opportunity to demonstrate their skills and gain marks to the best of their ability. In some instances, as in the United States, standardized patients are also trained to participate in assessment by completing evaluative checklists about the candidate they have just seen. This responsibility leads to an even greater necessity for SPs as raters to be standardized, not only in their role portrayal but also in their judgments about candidates' performance. While these ratings can cover experience from a patient perspective, they may also include judgements that would usually be considered within the realm of clinician rather than patient expertise (e.g., complete history-taking, depth of palpation, etc.). Different contexts, such as performance assessment, require different kinds of SP activities. Exams require standardization, while learning sessions as a rule do not place the same emphasis on standardized experiences. This is important to be clear about as we begin exploring the role of SPs as simulated participants in learning settings. An interest in standardization is not necessarily shared by educators working outside of healthcare or those who are more interested in the rich learning opportunities that live simulation experiences can provide. We challenge the language of describing patients as "standardized," preferring to refer to simulated patients who can standardize their portrayal for high-stakes assessments. We have previously argued that the language of "standardization" to describe patients is in tension with notions of patient-centredness and individuality (Nestel et al., 2018).

Originally, SP methodology focused only on patients, but it has now extended to include relatives, bystanders, students, and clinicians, and hence the expansive term "participants" rather than "patients." However, in this chapter, we focus on the SP participant as *patient*. Typically, SP-based encounters comprise an SP in a scenario in a simulated or real clinical environment (see the appendix to this chapter). We use the term "live simulation" to refer to SP-based scenarios.

Uptake of SP-based educational initiatives in training and assessment is expanding in scope but also in breadth methodologically, accompanied by a commitment within the field to ensure a high quality of practice standards. This commitment informs educational and curriculum design, as well as SP recruitment and training for role portrayals and for both verbal and written feedback.

Feedback is one of the hallmarks of live simulation because SPs are uniquely positioned within encounters to not only observe their interlocutors' behaviours but also teach-in-role through their "in the moment" responses. Following the simulation, these teaching moments can be addressed and possibly revisited in order to provide learners with an opportunity to experience a transformative success and reflect on their learning. The potential success may be experienced during the revisited interaction in the form of a different response from the SP, or at a later time in their practice. Feedback is also a helpful tool to reinforce positive learner behaviours (Bokken, Linssen, Scherpbier, Van Der Vleuten, & Rethans, 2009; Cleland, Abe, & Rethans, 2009). How we think about the contributions that SPs make in health professional activities is changing. SPs are no longer simply models for others to "use." Through their participation as co-teachers, they have also helped to develop a methodology that informs the larger field of simulation as well as health professional education more broadly (McNaughton, 2016). Several authors have noted the unhelpful objectification of SPs and a shift toward language that positions SPs as teachers, co-teachers, and educational allies (McNaughton & Anderson, 2017; McNaughton, 2016; Nestel, 2015; Nestel & Bearman, 2015; Nestel et al., 2011). SPs are beginning to be valued for their ability to contribute more formally to scenario development, especially those in which emotional presentation and intensity are of central consideration. Their involvement potentially ensures that learners are given access to appropriate challenges, which simulation as a methodology so effectively provides. Together with faculty, SPs are able to promote educational coherence and environmental and semantic "fidelity" in order to support students' understanding and skill development experientially (Dieckmann, Gaba, & Rall, 2007).

The Contested Notion of Fidelity

Fidelity is a multifaceted and contested concept within health professions simulation that threads through discussions about the merit and shortcomings of different modalities and pedagogical methods. A contentious term within the simulation field, "fidelity" can be employed to mean different things in different contexts, with important implications for access to resources such as investment in new technology or the design of simulation centres.

As a concept, fidelity attends to the realism of the model or mannequin itself (the feel of the skin, facial expression, etc.), to the realism of the environment, and, also, to the quality of the experience for the learner. The latter concern invites us to look beyond traditional instrumentalist notions of technology as neutral to one in which technology can be seen to "generate new forms of emotional experience and identity formation" (Zemblyas, 2005, p. 193). For example, SPs are referred to as both "high" and "low fidelity" in health professional simulations. SPs are considered high fidelity when they contribute to the emotional and affective realism of a clinical situation or when their bodies can be "used" for practising different non-invasive procedures, such as mocked-up wound dressings for injuries or physical exam practice for appendicitis. It has been suggested that the "experience of interacting with an actual living person makes them 'more real' and better suited for helping students to develop (and instructors to assess) clinical skills, especially communication skills" (Taylor, 2011, p. 137). There is also an advantage to the idea that they are not the "real thing" and that they therefore cannot be hurt. Indeed, some in the SP field group human actors (the so-called "wetware") "together with computer simulators, virtual reality devices, and high-tech 'realistic' computerized mannequins" (Taylor, 2011, p. 137). SPs are also sometimes considered low fidelity because as living people they are unable to fake certain clinical findings or be involved in invasive procedures. Therefore, where a label of low fidelity might be positive when referring to inert materials adapted for innovative and cost-effective use, it is a negative when attached to living bodies that are unable to enact more complex physical findings or take part in invasive clinical procedures (McNaughton, 2016).

Another term in the literature, "semantic fidelity," refers to the relationship between the learning goals and the design of the session. The goal is to create an illusion that is adequate to allow learners to suspend disbelief. Does it make sense that a person would be acting the way they are for the overarching goal of the learning? If the simulation "works," then participants experience the simulation scenario as relevant to the goal of the session and they are able to make semantical sense of the scenario (Hamstra, Brydges, Hatala, Zendejas, & Cook, 2014). Hamstra and colleagues critique fidelity as a concept although still agree with the importance of what they call "functional" fidelity, or the close alignment between the clinical task and the simulation task, described as *functional task alignment* (Hamstra et al., 2014). They argue that *learner engagement* is a more meaningful concept than the contested notion of *fidelity*.

In summary, fidelity in live simulations is not simply about the realism of a portrayal. It is achieved through the interaction between many different elements of educational design, such as alignment between learning objectives, scenario considerations, setting, equipment, SP portrayal, and level of learner. More recently, calls to "let go of the question of realism and narrowly defined effectiveness that have shaped much simulation literature [are encouraging shifts in thinking about] what forms of material set up and intelligibility are required to produce pedagogically rich performances and experiences for students" (Hopwood, Rooney, Boud, & Kelley, 2016, p. 175).

Historical Influences on SP Methodology

Simulation as a modality can be traced back centuries, with models of various sophistication being employed for educational purposes (McNaughton, 2016). Today, our engagement in simulation reflects yet another cycle in this very old drive to provide professional education through experiential methodologies (Owen, 2016). Harry Owen (2016) argues that we have had to rediscover the benefits of simulation as an educational method during the second half of the 20th century. Specifically, SPs have been on the front lines of health professional education as a living educational resource since the middle of the 1960s and represent a key innovation in the field of health professions training.

Professionalism

Some of the social forces credited for the growth of live simulation in health professions education today and for the work of SPs can be attributed to a focus on professionalism in the latter part of the 20th century, a shift in ideas about competence, an increased societal demand, globally, for accountability, and a resulting rationale that puts patients at the centre of healthcare practice and training (Hodges, 2009). When SPs are positioned as proxies for patients (Nestel & Kelly, 2018), they are integral to the dissemination of collective attitudes and beliefs about what it means to be a health professional through their roles, portrayals, and feedback. Professional identities are shaped in part by how others see us, and SPs have a critical role in explicitly shaping how healthcare students and professionals are seen/experienced. SPs often work closely with health professionals in designing simulation scenarios in order to make sure that the scenario and portrayal represent challenges for the clinical learner that require a professional response. Professional values, attitudes, clinical knowledge, and skills are experienced and reinforced through the interaction and SP responses. SPs do not represent patients so much as they are helpful resources in bringing to light desired patient-centred clinical responses. In this way SPs become the vehicles for transmission and reproduction of professional values, attitudes, clinical knowledge, and skills (McNaughton, 2016).

Patient Safety and Medical Error Reduction

Simulation offers an important route to safer care for patients and needs to be fully integrated into the health service.

Sir Liam Donaldson (2009, from Nestel & Kelly, 2018)

Patient safety and medical error reduction are widely recognized as important motivators for engaging in live simulation. Beginning with the aeronautics industry, the military, and the nuclear power industry, safety enhancement and error reduction have been key justifications for the development and investment in medical simulation technology.

What these industries "have in common is that for each of them, training or systems testing in the 'real' world would be too costly or too dangerous to undertake" (Bradley, 2006, p. 254–255). Similarly, the notion of patient and public safety is at the heart of health professions education, as reflected in Sir Liam Donaldson's quote above. He emphasized "the role of simulation in rehearsal for emergency situations, for team work and for learning psychomotor skills in settings and at times that do not put patients at risk" (Nestel & Kelly, 2018). Two important reports, *To Err Is Human* (Kohn, Corrigan, & Donaldson, 2000) and *An Organization with a Memory* (Department of Health, 2000), were also seminal in advancing a rationale for an institutional approach and agenda on patient safety. Both publications provided a systematic overview and list of recommendations that justified the increased activity in simulation as a valued training approach. Through sufficient access to simulation, learners are able to practise and make mistakes before they are faced with the real event.

Although it became an increasingly important motivator institutionally, the idea that live simulation could contribute meaningful learning on how to improve patient safety was not the original inspiration but a fruitful by-product of an educational need to provide learners with opportunities to rehearse and be observed in clinical practice. In the 1960s Howard Barrows, a neurologist and clinical teacher, initiated what is now known as SP methodology and the development of the first "programmed patient" (Barrows & Abrahamson, 1964, p. 802). Barrows framed his development of simulation "as a response to the lack of observation and feedback that was endemic in medical education in the 1960's" (Barrows & Abrahamson, 1964, p. 802).

Competence

It was at this time in the 1960s that clinical competence expanded from being thought about as what one "knew" to being about what one could "do" with acquired knowledge, leading to a drive for new methods of teaching and testing clinical skills performance (Miller, 1990). George Miller, the main architect of this shift, argued that it was imperative that medical education move away from the assessment of knowledge ("knows") to newer methods that could assess students' actual performance of clinical skills ("shows how"). He created a pyramid of competencies that powerfully crystallized the idea that performance was the "central" competence (McNaughton & Hodges, 2015).

The four-layered categorization of competency begins at the base of the pyramid with "knows." Competency at this level is represented as factual recognition without context and is most usually assessed through multiple choice or written reports or oral exams. At the next level, "knows how," learners are expected to demonstrate "the ability to apply biomedical information to the analysis and resolution of problems presented in written cases and simulations based on real-life patient care situations" (Albino et al., 2008, p. 1416). At the "shows how" level, "students are expected to demonstrate the capacity to apply patient care skills in laboratories and simulations that approximate clinical facilities and the dynamics of provider-patient interactions" (Albino et al., 2008, p. 1416). This level is where simulation as both a pedagogical and assessment approach is most relevant. As the step before going out into practice, at the top level, representing "does," learners are expected to demonstrate problem-solving, clinical decision-making, and their ability to apply their knowledge and skills under controlled, well-supervised conditions:

> At the ultimate "does" level, the student is expected to execute the core tasks and responsibilities of a health care provider in "real" or very realistic working conditions with limited instructor support over an extended period of time; the aim is to determine whether the student has mastered the fundamental competencies necessary for unsupervised practice and can reproduce these skills with a consistent level of performance over several weeks to several months. (Albino et al., 2008, p. 1416)

This shift in thinking about performance as essential to health professional education created a desire for more interactive and experiential formats for learning and assessment. SP-based simulation as a pedagogical and assessment methodology served to support the new skills-based competencies through practice and observation and paved the way for laypersons' presence as SPs in the medical classroom (Bearman, Nestel, & McNaughton, 2017).

Newer methods for defining and determining characteristics of competency have been developed since Miller, with competency-based education leading the way with different rubrics for assessing competency in practice (Royal College of Physicians and Surgeons of Canada, 2018). SP methodology as a practice has continued to remain relevant perhaps increasingly so now as a reminder of our humanity amid an increasingly technological world, and is supported by many different theoretical approaches. In the following section, we briefly describe some of the most referenced theories and conclude with a look at recent contributions to the field.

Theories Informing Simulation Practice

The broad *meso*-level category of adult learning theories has met the needs of many simulation educators since the early years. Operating from a constructivist approach to learning, experiential learning theory, the theory of deliberate practice, and situated learning theories, to name a few, have helped simulation educators in their approaches to design and implementation of simulation activities. Within a constructivist paradigm (Bryman, 2012; Schwandt, 2007; Schwandt, 1994), learning is an active process in which learners develop (construct) new ideas or concepts from their current (experiential) or past (pre-constructed) knowledge. The learner chooses and modifies (transforms) through their experiences.

Experiential Learning Theory

Experiential learning has been with us long before John Dewey (1852–1959). However, he is identified as a seminal contributor, along with Malcolm Knowles (1913–97), to the idea that there is an intimate connection between the processes of actual experience and education. Knowles's work was a significant factor in reorienting adult educators from "educating people" to "helping them learn" (Knowles, 1950). Both Dewey and Knowles are important to SP-based education because of their focus on learner experience and the acts of doing as crucial to learning. The more direct evidence of their contributions can be seen in the work of David Kolb.

Kolb's Learning Cycle

One of the most influential and most cited of the learning theories informing live-simulation-based education is Kolb's learning cycle theory. Derived from work in social psychology, Kolb's adaptation of the learning cycle offers simulation educators a systematic framework through which to think about learning processes and outcomes.

As formulated by Kolb (Fry & Kolb, 1979), experiential learning theory depicts learning as a four-stage cycle. In the first phase of the cycle, immediate concrete experience is the basis for observation and reflection. For example, an interview with an angry simulated participant can be reflected on for the successes and challenges encountered. In the second phase, the learner's reflection about how their approach to the event can be improved may be deepened by feedback from the SP, as well as observations from clinical faculty and other learners. In the third phase, these observations and reflections can be assimilated into an idea or theory from which new ideas about an approach can be tried out in the active experimentation of phase four. For example, the idea that using the patient's words is an effective way to de-escalate anger is something that the learner can take away from the experience and try out in practice. These new ideas then serve as guides in creating new experiences. According to Kolb,

> an effective learner needs four different abilities – concrete experience skills, reflective observation skills, abstract conceptualization skills, and active experimentation skills. That is, he or she must be able to get involved fully, openly, and without bias in new experiences [concrete experience], to reflect upon and interpret these experiences from different perspectives [reflection, observation], to create concepts that integrate these observations in logically sound theories [abstract conceptualization], and to use these theories to make decisions and solve problems [active experimentation] leading to new experiences. (Fry & Kolb, 1979, p. 81)

Deliberate Practice

The theory of deliberate practice was developed by psychologist K. Anders Ericsson, a professor of psychology at Florida State University in the 1990s. It describes how experts become highly skilled, particularly at psychomotor and intellectual tasks. This theory has more to do with the quality of learners' practice than simply with how many times they perform or repeat a task. According to Ericsson, "people believe that because expert performance is qualitatively different from normal performance the expert performer must be endowed with characteristics qualitatively different from those of normal adults" (1996, p. 399). However, proponents of deliberate practice do not believe that people have immutable skills that make them inherently better at something than others but rather argue that the differences between expert performers and normal adults reflect a lifelong period of deliberate effort to improve performance in a specific domain (Ericsson, 1996).

This theory is evident in educational design of learning in which formative feedback and debriefing methods are more central to achieving desired outcomes than are summative – or outcomes-focused – assessments. It is also apparent in strategies educators use to motivate learners and to encourage them to set goals as they engage in education and practice.

Donald Schön: Reflection-in-Action, Reflection-on-Action

More recently, Kolb's experiential learning theory is recognizable in Donald Schön's writing in the area of learning and the role of reflection (Schön, 1983). His concepts of reflection-in-action (immediate "thinking on your feet") and reflection-on-action (later analysis of actions in light of outcome, prior experience, and new knowledge) characterize ways in which practitioners react to unexpected experiences in their work. In live simulation, reflection-on-action following a learning event is most often facilitated by clinicians, teachers, or peers. Reflection-in-action is uniquely suited to live simulation, which provides immediate learning-in-action through an SP's response. Learner reflection-in-action is supported through "time-outs" or "pause and discuss," which provide valuable opportunities to refigure an approach and try again. These pauses enable access to learners' thoughts and feelings through discussion and then application of their proposed actions following their return to the scenario at signal of "time-in." As in Kolb's model, the learner has the opportunity to act immediately on what has been experienced (Bearman & Nestel, 2015). Using the example of an angry patient portrayal, the clinical teacher is able to implement both *in*- and *on*-action reflective discussions with the learner, allowing for focused experimentation with changes in the moment. Please see the appendix to this chapter for examples of other theories supporting SP methodology.

More recent theoretical contributions to literature in the field of SP-based education recognize that simulation with SPs is not simply a method for honing clinical skills through practice or reflection but is also a social activity through which values, beliefs, and ideas about what it means to be a professional are being learned. A group of theories that falls under the broad category of socio-materiality – that is, theories that reflect the complexity of the environments in which health professionals practise and students learn – is directing simulation educators' attention to the space between simulation education and the social and material worlds of work.

Tara Fenwick (2015) suggests socio-material theories as an approach to shedding light on the dynamic, emergent, and uncertain nature of health professional practice and the ways in which our education can better prepare learners. With respect to simulation-based education, she suggests that complexity theory is one of many within this umbrella of theories that offers educators ways to address the embodied, relational, and situational aspects of practice using ideas such as emergence, attunement, disturbance, and experimentation (Fenwick & Dahlgren, 2015). This theoretical lens helps us think differently about our day-to-day practices and recognizes that "learning ... emerges through the myriad intersecting webs of relationships that form among things including both social and material things, such as bodies, instruments desires, politics, settings and protocols" (Fenwick & Dahlgren, 2015, p. 360).

For example, when looking at SPs, we can see that they are not solitary agents, but rather working within a nested system of curriculum, scenarios, simulated clinical environments, and simulation tools. An illustration of this complexity was evident during a psychiatry OSCE for third-year clinical clerks. The incident was observed and reported on by the examiner and the SP taking part in the station. A student put an SP into a headlock during a station in this assessment setting in order to stop him from leaving the room. The station had been designed for the SP, who was portraying a patient with disorganized schizophrenia, to become more agitated over the course of nine minutes and leave the room quickly. The goal was to test the student's knowledge and problem-solving skills and to provide time for the examiner to ask the student about their plan. Needless to say, a headlock was not the expected or desired response. The situation reflects the different levels of reality that need to be negotiated by both student and SP in their exchange. The student needed to be attuned to the exam context, which required him to be aware of timing and clinical content while also performing clinical decision-making about what to do with this patient (or what he thought he was supposed to do to pass the exam). The SP was unhurt, but surprised and perplexed about how he should have responded, not having anticipated or planned for this action. Was he too real for the student and the situation? Was he not a "good" SP who was expected only to provide a fair and standardized opportunity for the student to gain marks in the station? He was aware that he was representing the student's opportunity to demonstrate his skill for a passing grade and felt quite guilty. Despite the assessment context, with examiners, bells, and whistles, and multiple stations at 10-minute intervals, the experience for the student seemed real enough to respond "as if" it was a real situation (Dieckmann, Gaba, & Rall, 2007). These questions have implications for the clinical work to which students will be progressing. Untangling intentional and unintentional consequences of learning through simulation is aided by a socio-material lens. Live simulation is complex and requires greater understanding about the myriad networks that are nested together, not to simplify but to be intentional about the messiness of learning and how best to engage learners The growth of in situ simulation reflects the value that simulation educators place on the socio-material aspects of clinical work.

Alexis Battista follows this thread, suggesting in her article on activity theory in scenario-based simulations that learner participation during engagement in a simulation exercise is part of a dynamic multi-modal system that incorporates other learners as well as equipment, tools, and active participants such as SPs (Battista & Nestel, 2019). For both Fenwick and Battista, the materiality of a practice environment, and a learner's negotiation of various relationships and activities within it, contributes to the formation of a professional identity as well as skills and knowledge. In this perspective, then, SP scenarios and portrayals can be viewed as interactional vehicles for the transmission and reproduction of professional values, attitudes, clinical knowledge, and skills (McNaughton, 2016). Learning through engagement in live simulation is experiential, providing opportunities for deep learning that is linked to learners' lives beyond the cognitive aspects of knowledge and skills acquisition.

There is an inherent tension within live scenario-based simulation, between the dynamic and responsive nature of many of the interactions and the deliberate planning that is required to provide such opportunities. This tension is part of an SP-based methodology that informs design decisions from the inception of any educational project. Traditionally, SPs are brought into an educational activity only after all the decisions have been made, and they are asked to "be" the patient. However, newer design thinking approaches suggest that if SPs are included from the beginning of a development process, the knowledge and unique location that they hold within any simulation activity can augment educational thinking about learning objectives and the feasibility of learners achieving them (Gottlieb, Wagner, Wagner, & Chan, 2017).

Other contributions that have been made to the field of live simulation include the work of Rosamund Snow (2015), who described how as a patient with diabetes, she was granted "trust" and associated "power" to determine the learning goals (as she saw them from her patient perspective) for junior medical staff who were attending the learning session. This became a fascinating mix of real and SP co-produced practice. Other examples of real patient involvement in SP methodology include development of scenarios that are based on real patients' experiences and reporting of procedural skills (Nestel et al., 2008) and of encounters in general practice (Nestel, Tierney, & Kubacki, 2008), on HIV-positive patients' clinical interactions (Jaworsky et al., 2014), and on composite roles constructed from patients' stories of a surgical procedure (Black et al., 2006).

We need to understand the power relations that shape SP involvement in professional education contexts. In the health professions, patients own their stories and the outcomes of their experiences in a very different way than SPs. Although SPs can be affected by the roles they portray (Bokken, Van Dalen, & Rethans, 2006; McNaughton & Tiberius, 1999), their relationships with health professionals are informed by educational, not clinical, need. Despite these differences, there is much to be shared between these two groups that can be helpful in developing a robust experiential pedagogy.

Education is ideally an ethical undertaking and as such requires conversations across multiple perspectives. Live simulation is an educational approach that is coming to recognize the effects of its practices as materially implicated in real bodies and lives (McNaughton, 2016). Common themes that connect socio-material (complexity and activity) perspectives to the issues of patient inclusion and power dynamics point to live simulation as a collaborative, complex, and socially situated educational methodology. In the case of health professions education, the patient or client is no longer the object to be constructed in scenarios by professionals but rather a key contributor to shaping educational experiences. Beyond health professions education, simulation that is informed theoretically stands to contribute to learning as an embodied practice "anchored to metaphors of emergence and multiplicity" (Hopwood et al., 2016, p. 176). There is growing appreciation for the collective and nested networks that inform simulation as an educational approach in professions outside of healthcare.

Establishing Standards of Practice

Today, effective practices suggest that SPs be engaged collaboratively in the whole of the educational activities in which they participate. This aligns with the recommendations found in the publication of the Association of Standardized Patient Educators (ASPE) Standards of Best Practice (SOBP) (Lewis et al., 2017). This living document is directed at those who support the work of SPs (rather than SPs themselves) and is underpinned by five values – (1) safety, (2) quality, (3) professionalism, (4) accountability, and (5) collaboration. Curiously, the only SP contributions in the standards were mediated through SP faculty who were once themselves SPs (Nestel, Roche, & Battista, 2017). However, recognizing that SPs are allied educationally with faculty in the development and design of simulation brings a valuable intentionality to the learning. By including SPs during the educational design of simulations, learning objectives can be tested and brought to life. A description of a role on paper will always change once an SP inhabits the part. Early involvement eliminates later changes and confusion (McNaughton, 2016).

Conclusion

In this chapter, we have sought to share historical and contemporary perspectives on SP methodology in the health professions. We have considered drivers for its evolution, which have varied over time. SP-based education has been influenced by social movements such as the patient safety movement, by patient-centred approaches to care, and by changes to ideas about competency in the health professions. We have also discussed the articulation of some newer theories that inform SP-based education from design to evaluation. We anticipate that SP methodology, with the current sensitivity to shifts in power between faculty, real patients, and SP, will adopt more real and SP co-produced *methodology practices*. Live simulation as an educational methodology and powerful experiential pedagogy is poised to become of greater relevance to professions outside of healthcare due to its ability to put relevant tenets of competency into action.

Appendix

Examples of SP-based encounters in health professions education

- A student nurse meets an SP at the bedside and is expected to check that the patient has understood discharge instructions after their brief stay in hospital for an acute episode of illness.
- A medical student enters a consultation room and is expected to undertake a full patient history from an SP with a complex set of medical and social problems.
- A physiotherapy student is in a simulated clinical environment and is expected to teach an SP exercises to restore strength and function after hip surgery.
- A trainee surgeon is asked to undertake a consent for surgery interview in a simulated setting with an SP who is reluctant to have the surgical procedure.
- A pharmacist intern is working in a real clinical setting and will be assessed by an SP for professionalism and information sharing.
- A doctor is developing skills to work with an interpreter and is assessed with an SP and translator in a simulated consultation setting.

Examples of theories supporting SP methodology

- Cognitive load theory (Sweller, 2011) directs simulation designers to tailor scenarios and learning objectives to the level of learning in

order to support and not overload working memory with tasks that
are too difficult or complex.
- The situated learning theory of Lave and Wenger (1991) argues that
learning is a social process whereby knowledge is co-constructed
and situated in a specific context and embedded within a particular
social and physical environment.
- Activity theory (Battista & Nestel, 2019) is akin to situated learning;
however, it extends the idea, suggesting that learning is inseparable
from doing or practice. Participants' goal-directed activity, the arte-
facts they use, and the objects they create during participation are
all conceptualized as learning through practice.

REFERENCES

Albino, J., Young, S.K., Neumann, L., Kramer, G.A, Andrieu, S.C., Henson,
L. ... Hendricson, W.D. (2008). Assessing dental students' competence: Best
practice recommendations in the performance assessment literature and
investigation of current practices in predoctoral dental education. *Journal of
Dental Education, 72*(12), 1405–1435. Retrieved from: http://www.jdentaled.
org/content/72/12/1405.short
Barrows, H.S., & Abrahamson, S. (1964). The programmed patient: A technique
for appraising student performance in clinical neurology. *Journal of Medical
Education, 39* (8), 802–805. Retrieved from https://journals.lww.com/
Battista, A., & Nestel, D. (2019). Simulation in medical education. In T.
Sanwick, K. Forrest, & B.C. O'Brien (Eds.), *Understanding medical education:
Evidence, theory and practice* (pp. 151–162). West Sussex: Wiley-Blackwell.
Bearman, M., & Nestel, D. (2015). Learning theories and simulated patient
methodology. In D. Nestel & M. Bearman (Eds.), *Simulated patient methodology:
Theory, evidence and practice* (pp. 33–38). West Sussex: Wiley-Blackwell.
Bearman, M., Nestel, D., & McNaughton, N. (2017). Theories informing
healthcare simulation practice. In D. Nestel, M. Kelly, B. Jolly, & M. Watson
(Eds.), *Healthcare simulation education: Evidence, theory & practice* (pp. 9–15).
West Sussex: Wiley-Blackwell.
Black, S.A., Nestel, D., Horrocks, E., Harrison, R.H., Norma, J., Wetzel, C., ...
Darzi, A. (2006). Evaluation of a framework for case development and
simulated patient training for complex procedures. *Simulation in Healthcare,
1*(2), 66–71. https://doi.org/10.1097/01.SIH.0000244446.13047.3f
Bokken, L., Linssen, T., Scherpbier, A., Van Der Vleuten, C., & Rethans,
J-J. (2009). Feedback by simulated patients in undergraduate medical
education: A systematic review of the literature. *Medical Education, 43*(3),
202–210. https://doi.org/10.1111/j.1365-2923.2008.03268.x

Bokken, L., Van Dalen, J., & Rethans, J.J. (2006). The impact of simulation on people who act as simulated patients: A focus group study. *Medical Education, 40*(8), 781–786. https://doi.org/10.1111/j.1365-2929.2006.02529.x

Bradley, P. (2006). The history of simulation in medical education and possible future directions. *Medical Education, 40*(3), 254–262. https://doi.org/10.1111/j.1365-2929.2006.02394.x

Bryman, A. (2012). *Social research methods* (4th ed.). New York, NY: Oxford Press.

Cleland, J.A., Abe, K., & Rethans, J.J. (2009). The use of simulated patients in medical education: AMEE Guide No 42. *Medical Teacher, 31*(6), 477–486. https://doi.org/10.1080/01421590903002821

Department of Health. (2000). *An organisation with a memory*. London: The Stationery Office.

Dieckmann, P., Gaba, D., & Rall, M. (2007). Deepening the theoretical foundations of patient simulation as social practice. *Simulation in Healthcare, 2*(3), 183–193. https://doi.org/10.1097/SIH.0b013e3180f637f5

Ericsson, K.A. (1996). *The road to excellence: The acquisition of expert performance in the arts and sciences, sports and games.* New Jersey: Lawrence Erlbaum Associates.

Fenwick, T., & Dahlgren, M.A. (2015). Towards socio-material approaches in simulation-based education: Lessons from complexity theory. *Medical Education, 49*(4), 359–367. https://doi.org/10.1111/medu.12638

Fry, R., & Kolb, D. (1979). Experiential learning theory and learning experiences in liberal arts education. *New Directions for Experiential Learning, 6*(19), 79–91. Retrieved from https://digitalcommons.unomaha.edu

Gottlieb, M., Wagner, E., Wagner, A., & Chan, T. (2017). Applying design thinking principles to curricular development in medical education. *AEM Education and Training, 1*(1), 21–26. https://doi.org/10.1002/aet2.10003

Hamstra, S.J., Brydges, R., Hatala, R., Zendejas, B., & Cook, D.A. (2014). Reconsidering fidelity in simulation-based training. *Academic Medicine, 89*(3), 387–392. https://doi.org/10.1097/ACM.0000000000000130

Hodges, B.D. (2009). *The objective structured clinical examination: A socio-history.* Koln, Germany: LAP Press.

Hopwood N., Rooney, D., Boud, D., & Kelley, M. (2016). Simulation in higher education: A sociomaterial view. *Educational Philosophy and Theory, 48*(2), 165–178. https://doi.org/10.1080/00131857.2014.971403

Jaworsky, D., Chew, D., Thorne, J., Morin, C., McNaughton, N., Downer, G., ... Rachlis, A. (2014). People living with HIV as instructors for medical students: A pilot study in HIV counseling and testing. *Journal of Therapy and Management in HIV Infection, 2*(1), 10–15. https://doi.org/10.12970/2309-0529.2014.02.01.1

Knowles, M.S. (1950). *Informal adult education: A guide for administrators, leaders, and teachers.* New York: Association Press.

Kohn, L.T., Corrigan, J.M., & Donaldson, M.S. (Eds.). (2000). *To err is human: Building a safer health system.* Washington, DC: Institute of Medicine, National Academies Press.

Lave, J., and Wenger, E. (1991). *Situated learning: Legitimate peripheral participation.* Cambridge, UK: Cambridge University Press.

Lewis, K.L., Bohnert, C.A., Gammon, W.L., Hölzer, H., Lyman, L., Smith, C., ... Gliva-McConvey, G. (2017).The Association of Standardized Patient Educators (ASPE) Standards of Best Practice (SOBP). *Advances in Simulation,* 2(10). https://doi.org/10.1186/s41077-017-0043-4

McNaughton, N. (2016). *The role of emotion in the work of standardized patients: A critical theoretical analysis.* Berlin: LAP Press.

McNaughton, N., & Anderson, M. (2017). Standardized patients: It's all in the words. *Clinical Simulation in Nursing, 13*(7), 293–294. https://doi.org/10.1016/j.ecns.2017.05.014

McNaughton, N., & Hodges, B. (2015). Foundational frameworks. In D. Nestel & M. Bearman (Eds.), *Simulated patient methodology: Theory, evidence and practice* (pp. 5–6). West Sussex: Wiley-Blackwell.

McNaughton, N., & Tiberius, R. (1999). The effects of portraying psychologically and emotionally complex standardized patient roles. *Teaching and Learning in Medicine, 11*(3),135–141. https://doi.org/10.1207/s15328015tl110303

Miller, G. (1990). The assessment of clinical skills/competence/performance. *Academic Medicine, 65*(9), S63–S67. https://doi.org/10.1097/00001888 -199009000-00045

Nestel, D. (2015). Expert's corner: Standardized (simulated) patients in health professions education: A proxy for real patients? In J.C. Palangas, J.C. Maxworthy, C.A. Epps, & M.E. Mancini (Eds.), *Defining excellence in simulation programs* (p. 394). Philadelphia: Wolters Kluwer.

Nestel, D., & Bearman, M. (2015). Introduction to simulated patient methodology. In D. Nestel & M. Bearman (Eds.), *Simulated patient methodology: Theory, evidence and practice* (pp. 1–4). West Sussex: Wiley-Blackwell.

Nestel, D., Burn, C.L., Pritchard, S.A., Glastonbury, R., & Tabak, D. (2011). The use of simulated patients in medical education: Guide Supplement 42.1 – Viewpoint. *Medical Teacher, 33*(12), 1027–1029. https://doi.org/10.3109/0142 159X.2011.596590

Nestel, D., Cecchini, M., Calandrini, M., Chang, L., Dutta, R., Tierney, T., ... Kneebone, R. (2008). Real patient involvement in role development evaluating patient focused resources for clinical procedural skills. *Medical Teacher, 30*(5), 795–801. https://doi.org/10.1080/01421590802047232

Nestel, D., & Kelly, M. (2018). An introduction to healthcare simulation. In D. Nestel, M. Kelly, B. Jolly, & M. Watson (Eds.), *Healthcare simulation education: Evidence, theory & practice* (pp. 1–6). West Sussex: Wiley-Blackwell.

Nestel, D., McNaughton N., Smith C., Schlegel C., & Tierney T. (2018). Values and valuing in simulated participant methodology: A global perspective on contemporary practice. *Medical Teacher*, 40(7), 697–702. https://doi.org/10.1080/0142159x.2018.1472755

Nestel, D., Roche, J. & Battista, A. (2017). Creating a quality improvement culture in standardized/simulated patient methodology: The role of professional societies. *Advances in Simulation*, 2(18). https://doi.org/10.1186/s41077-017-0051-4

Nestel, D., Tierney, T., and Kubacki, A. (2008). Creating authentic simulated patient roles: Working with volunteers. *Medical Education*, 42(11), 1122–1122. https://doi.org/10.1111/j.1365-2923.2008.03196.x

Owen, H. (2016) *Simulation in healthcare education: An extensive history*. Basel, Switzerland: Springer.

Royal College of Physicians and Surgeons of Canada. (2018). *Competence by design*. Retrieved from http://www.royalcollege.ca/rcsite/cbd/competence-by-design-cbd-e

Schwandt, T.A. (1994). Constructivist, interpretivist approaches to human inquiry. In N.K. Denzin & Y.S. Licoln (Eds.) *The landscape of qualitative research: Theories and issues* (pp. 221–259). Thousand Oaks, CA:Sage Publications.

Schwandt, T.A. (2007). *The SAGE dictionary of qualitative inquiry* (3rd ed.). Thousand Oaks, CA: Sage Publications

Schön, D. (1983). *Educating the reflective practitioner: Toward a new design for teaching and learning in the professions*. New York: Jossey-Bass.

Snow, R. (2015). Real patient participation in simulations. In D. Nestel & M. Bearman (Eds.), *Simulated patient methodology: Theory, evidence and practice* (pp. 105–109). West Sussex: Wiley-Blackwell.

Sweller J. (2011). Cognitive load theory. In J.P. Mestre & B.H. Ross (Eds.), *Psychology of learning and motivation* (Vol. 55, pp. 37–76). Amsterdam: Elsevier Science.

Taylor, J. (2011). The moral aesthetics of simulated suffering in standardized patient performances. *Culture, Medicine and Psychiatry*, 35(2), 134–162. https://doi.org/10.1007/s11013-011-9211-5

Zembylas, M. (2005). *Teaching with emotion: A postmodern enactment*. Greenwich, CT: Information Age Publishing.

14 Does Interactive Simulation Lead to Students Simply Performing? Exploring the Context of Simulation-Based Education in Medical Students' Development of Patient-Centredness

LEANNE PICKETTS AND ANNA MACLEOD

Introduction

Interactive simulation offers the opportunity for medical students to practise patient-centred communication, clinical, and procedural skills in a safe environment. However, the context within which learning takes place may influence student learning and behaviour. In a simulation-based education (SBE) context, the focus is on teaching, learning, and practice; in a work-based learning context, such as a hospital or clinical setting, the focus shifts to patient care. Introducing assessment into an SBE context might have the inadvertent effect of changing students' motivation from practising with and focusing on the patient to demonstrating competency and mastery of the curriculum. When students are assessed within an SBE context, they may "perform to the test" in order to overtly demonstrate their proficiency (Hanna & Fins, 2006; Mitchell et al., 2009; Wear & Varley, 2008). In other words, simulation may inadvertently teach students to behave artificially, and may encourage students to highlight and construct certain behaviours that display specific competencies that meet the expectations of the curriculum, rather than those that focus on the patient.

In this chapter, we describe our recent research exploring an educational intervention, the interview framework known by the acronym FIFE. FIFE was designed to help students develop and practise patient-centred communication. We were curious about how and why students decide to implement FIFE in practice, as we had anecdotally witnessed it being used both in a meaningful and inauthentic way. We explore the complexities of learning patient-centredness using FIFE in both simulated and clinical environments herein.

Patient-Centredness and FIFE

While there are many ways to define patient-centredness, in this chapter we define it as therapeutic and interpersonal communication skills that promote a collaborative understanding of the illness of the patient as a separate individual, where the healthcare provider takes into account the patient's inner experiences, perspectives, preferences, concerns, emotions, and social context. For many medical students, their first exposure to patient-centred communication is via FIFE. FIFE is a behaviourally anchored interview framework to guide students toward the development of patient-centred competence in patient encounters. It helps students move beyond clinical exploration into trying to understand how an illness affects a patient holistically. FIFE is designed to help students explore the four dimensions of a patient's illness experience: "(1) patient's feelings, especially their fears about their problems; (2) their ideas about what is wrong; (3) the effect of the illness on their functioning; and (4) their expectations of their clinician" (Stewart et al., 2014, p. 39).

Implementing FIFE during a medical interview aims to provide students with a framework to explore the patient's perceptions of their health and illness with the goal of discovering the patient perspective, empowering the patient, and providing essential patient-centred care (Stewart et al., 2014). FIFE encourages students to explore the different components of biomedical diagnosis, patient health, and the patient's illness experience to enable an integrated understanding of the patient as a person and their illness narrative.

Putting FIFE into Practice: Simulated Patients

In simulated clinical contexts, students are able to practise, develop, and refine how they use FIFE and explore patient-centredness. There are varying modes of simulation in healthcare, from low fidelity (low realism) to high fidelity (highly realistic). Some examples of simulators in health profession education include isolated body parts that are used as task trainers for medical procedures, high-fidelity full-body manikin simulators, and face-to-face human interaction with simulated patients (SPs). As real people, SPs are of the highest fidelity. SPs are healthy people who are trained to simulate the gestalt of a real patient – the patient's history, physical findings, body language, and emotional and personality characteristics (Barrows, 1987; McNaughton & Nestel, this volume).

SPs allow learners to engage in face-to-face role-play, which is recognized as the most effective approach to teaching patient-centred communication skills (Berkhof, van Rijssen, Schellart, Anema, & van der Beek, 2011). This pedagogical approach is particularly effective when the scenarios portrayed by SPs represent an authentic patient voice (i.e., SPs demonstrate feelings, ideas, or concerns) (Nestel & Bearman, 2015). Thus, in addition to clinical representations, psychosocial components are included as part of each SP scenario. Psychosocial factors are psychological and social influences that exist beyond a patient's disease and illness, and might include the patients' perspective, preferences, emotions, feelings, fears, ideas, function, and expectations, and social contexts such as a job, support system, relationships, and personal life (Beach & Inui, 2006; King & Hoppe, 2013). Building psychosocial factors into SP scenarios enables a representation of patients as unique individuals and allows students the opportunity to practise using behaviourally anchored interview frameworks, in our context FIFE, as part of the formal medical school curriculum.

In the undergraduate medical education program we explored, simulation is used as an experiential learning method where medical students interact with SPs in a simulated clinical environment to learn the foundational skills of clinical practice, including taking a history and performing a physical exam. FIFE is taught to students in the first week of the undergraduate curriculum, and SP scenarios highlighting psychosocial factors are consistently integrated into concrete face-to-face SP interactions throughout students' four-year undergraduate education. Implementing FIFE into students' work with SPs provides students with iterative opportunities to develop patient-centred communication, history-taking, and physical examination skills, in order to prepare students for interacting with real patients in a hospital or clinical setting.

Exploring FIFE and SP Methodology

Through one author's (LP) experiences as both an SP and an SP educator, we became interested in exploring how students incorporate FIFE into authentic practice. We had anecdotal evidence of FIFE as a formalized procedure, a ritualized performance, and a set of acting techniques (e.g., "I FIFE'd the patient!"), and we wondered about the effect of the interview framework on developing patient-centredness. We decided to investigate students' perceptions of working with SPs and using FIFE as a patient-centred interview framework – how the students interpret and value FIFE, and whether FIFE perpetuates performative elements in patient interactions.

We used institutional ethnography to better understand the relationship between FIFE and patient-centredness, which is an approach that focuses on how "textual systems coordinate work and social relations" (Smith, 2005, p. xii). Institutional ethnography emphasizes the subjective exploration of institutional knowledge, primarily through texts or documents; in this context, the FIFE framework is a text that the medical school has elevated into the curriculum. Institutional ethnography considers how textual systems impact social relations and organization, and how they govern our knowledge and actions (Campbell & Gregor, 2008; Mayan, 2009).

From this perspective, texts like FIFE exist outside the individual as objectified social facts in society, and have power to control and coordinate social action. In the context of our research, the FIFE framework was considered *institutional knowledge*; its inclusion in the curriculum directly impacts the social doctor–patient interaction by placing value on patient-centredness within the culture of medicine. FIFE act as a lens through which a learner might interact with a patient, and therefore it is important to consider how it might influence the student–patient interaction and student behaviour.

Using an institutional ethnographic framework, we set out to explore how using FIFE in simulated clinical environments might structure and regulate student behaviour. Because we believe texts are never neutral, we also believed they could have a positive or negative power over student behaviour. We wanted to explore whether FIFE provides a guiding template that is rigidly formulaic, potentially leading to social interactions that dismiss natural cues provided by the patient. This outcome could prove problematic; FIFE is meant to elicit the patient's point of view, but if it is used formulaically in a rigid step-by-step manner, students may be so focused on moving through the template that they don't actually listen to the patient's response.

Our research study received institutional ethics approval. Methods of enquiry included (1) a critical document analysis of FIFE to set an overarching framework and to explore patient-centredness within the curriculum; (2) observation of students interacting with SPs to see how FIFE translated into practice; and (3) semi-structured interviews to further explore students' perceptions and experiences with the patient-centred pedagogy. A combination of observation of and semi-structured interviews with six second-year undergraduate medical students allowed for an open-ended exploration of the relationship between students' demonstrated patient-centredness and their perceptions of and experiences with the formal curriculum.

Second-year students were purposefully selected because of where they are situated in their degree program. At their point of inclusion in the study, students had been introduced didactically to the concept of patient-centredness and FIFE, and had participated in experiential learning sessions in both simulated and clinical/hospital environments where they had seen both simulated and real patients (under supervision). The experiential learning sessions throughout first and second year provided an opportunity to use FIFE in practice. Six participants allowed us to arrive at the point at which "no new data emerge, when all leads have been followed, when negative cases have been checked, and when the story or theory is complete" (Mayan, 2009, p.63). This approach is consistent with an iterative qualitative analysis, where "the number of participants depends upon the number required to inform fully all important elements of the phenomenon being studied" (Sargeant, 2012, p.1). For Green and Thorogood (2014), a researcher is satisfied that there is a complete story to tell when there is a dense account of the topic and an understanding of the phenomenon of interest. In this study, six students enabled rich data, consistent with a focused ethnography.

LP conducted the interviews. As a simulated patient educator, her role at the medical school may have influenced the students' willingness to speak frankly. However, she had no supervisory or evaluative relationship with any of the participants and worked diligently to create a comfortable environment, ensuring participants that their participation was completely voluntary and confidential.

The combination of document analysis, observation, and interviews enabled an in-depth exploration of students' experiences of FIFE and working with SPs. The rest of this chapter will focus on insights garnered through the interview component of our work. We found that medical students felt that the particular context within which they were learning (i.e., the simulated versus clinical environment) affected their practice of patient-centredness. In a simulated environment, students described their use of FIFE to be ritualistic, performative, and verbatim. They noted formative and summative assessment as the key drivers of their behaviour. In contrast, when given the opportunity to work in an actual clinical or hospital environment with real patients, students incorporated FIFE based on the specific context and implemented it flexibly, with each individual patient's needs taken into consideration. In other words, using FIFE seemed more genuine in the clinical environment.

FIFE: Ritualistically Performed in Simulated Contexts

Institutional ethnography considers how textual systems govern our knowledge and actions. FIFE is a text that the medical school has elevated into the curriculum as a way to explore patient-centredness, and texts produced within the medical curriculum teach students what is institutionally and socially important and accepted. It has been argued that "we take this kind of textual coordination for granted, too often looking 'through' texts without noticing their power or using them, too unreflectively, as straightforward reports about social life" (Devault, 2006, p. 294). It is important to consider the organizing power of curricular texts, the values and messages being created by such texts, and how they influence students' behaviour.

Our participants viewed FIFE as a way to practise patient-centredness. They defined FIFE "as a tool toward patient-centered care," as "pillars if you will, or cornerstones of the medical interview that are supposed to promote patient-centered history-taking." These comments reinforce the position that texts have power and influence over social interactions, as outlined by Smith (2005), Prior (2008), and other institutional ethnographers. However, while some students saw value in FIFE, they also noted disadvantages and unintended consequences associated with its use. Students reported that FIFE was often enacted formulaically and word for word within a simulated environment, and that their use of the text sometimes felt like a performance or a set of pre-scripted lines that must be said aloud. Using FIFE formulaically might sound like: *What are your feelings or fears about your illness? What are your ideas about what is happening? How is this affecting your daily function? What are your expectations of today's visit?* This challenge has been echoed in the literature: "Behavioural objectives produce actors not doctors or thinkers" (Marinker, 1997, p. 294).

FIFE as ritual might be attributed to the fact that the interview framework is taught as a component of the formal curriculum and is therefore imbued with power; its inclusion in patient interactions becomes mandatory in the eyes of the students because it exists as a formalized text in the curriculum. When it is considered through an institutional ethnographic framework, we can see a documentary reality: documents like FIFE organize and structure individual behaviour and focus, and specific behaviours become real because documents exist.

In addition, medical students are often assessed in a simulated environment, whether formatively or summatively, and students may "perform to the test." In the simulated environment, students felt they had an obligation to use FIFE clearly and verbatim, almost as a script, as their classmates (who observed the simulation) or the SP often provided constructive feedback if they did not – yet they still recognized the inauthenticity of this patient-centred behaviour:

> But FIFE ... you know that your partner is going to be like: You didn't use the "E" or you didn't do the second bit. So that part I think I always do play back in my mind when I'm closing out the session, I kind of try and

make sure I hit them all. But do I think it sounds authentic when you try and use that terminology? No, I don't think so. Because the language is so different than what I would typically use with a patient that I think that it sounds like a kind of canned question.

When these questions are asked verbatim within a doctor–patient interview, anecdotal and research evidence from SPs suggests FIFE may be experienced as insincere, hollow, artificial, formal, or forced (Laughey, Sangvik Grandal, & Finn, 2018). This perception of the tool has been recognized by its creators, who acknowledged:

"FIFEing" the patient, as we have heard students remark, becomes just another interviewing technique or an additional step in their review of systems and does not reflect a genuine interest in and concern about the patient's unique illness experience and does not encourage attentive listening. (Stewart et al., 2014)

This may speak to the power of text, as it might ritualize, routinize, and constrain behaviour and compassion – the opposite of its intended effect. FIFE might actually increase students' cynicism toward patient-centredness, an unintended consequence of the curriculum.
   This concern was acknowledged by students:

It's super disingenuous sometimes ... it's like the person saying it is like a robot, just programmed to say it. And I don't know if the patients interpret it that way or not, but when you see it all the time it becomes very, like, a ritual.

Another student had a similar perception of FIFE seeming ritualized and artificial, and possibly impeding a real connection with the patient when it is too rehearsed:

FIFE, sometimes I feel like it's a little bit formal and forced, asking the four questions and trying to get them all out ... you can sometimes see it in the SP or the patient you're working with, they feel that it's artificial ... the FIFE questions [can] come across as not empathetic anymore.

These quotes demonstrate the potential to reduce patient-centredness, when taught in simulated contexts, to a mere set of four questions that need to be asked in every interaction, rather than viewing each patient as a separate individual with perspectives, preferences, concerns, and emotions. One medical student acknowledged that this disadvantage was due to using the acronym quite literally – that having a predetermined set of questions caused a "communication barrier to having conversations with patients ... a barrier to the natural flow of conversation." In other words, FIFE might dictate the interview and possibly impede the flow of attention to the patient's response. If the text is used without listening to the patient, it ironically subverts the power the text intends to give to the patient in the first place. Instead of exploring the patient as an individual person on the basis of empathy and caring, the questions are forced and performed, negating true and authentic aspects of humanism and caring. This theme has been acknowledged by Campbell and Gregor (2008): "While it may not be comfortable for those involved, it is important to recognize that well-intentioned work may be part of oppressive relations of ruling" (p. 39), and working within a textual framework may be at odds with patient-centred intentions.

This inauthentic performance seemed to be more pervasive during objective structured clinical exams (OSCEs), a method of assessment using SP methodology that measures clinical competency through performance of predetermined behaviours identified on a checklist. When asked about using FIFE in patient interactions, one medical student said, "Certainly for obvious reasons [*laughs*]: you want to get those OSCE checkmarks!" Another student recognized that FIFE is a necessary performance component of a patient interview during an OSCE:

> If I don't ask it exactly one way, then sometimes it's not apparent we're doing it. I think a lot of people worry about that relative to OSCE. Because sometimes, I mean, it's not really, I don't think it's a very natural thing to do with patients, to be like: "What are your feelings about this? What are your expectations?" If you just ask the literal question, I don't think it's very smooth or real [*laughs*]. It's kind of forced. So I don't really want to ask things that way. But I also don't want to lose points on an OSCE.

These findings reinforce other studies exploring simulation as an assessment tool. In one study (Giesbrecht, Wener, & Pereira, 2014), physiotherapy students undergoing an SP-based assessment were found to have an inability to move beyond the mechanics of the SP encounter; they felt that components of their interaction were performed *only* to demonstrate competence during an assessment rather than to invest in the interactive experience from a genuine patient-focused perspective.

But does *performance* undercut being patient-centred? Atkins, Roberts, Hawthorne, and Greenhalgh (2016) aptly discuss the simulated consultation as performance, without apology, and acknowledge the role of the assessment context in shaping behaviour:

> Importantly, understanding professional behaviour as performance does not undercut its values. For example, to care for a patient may involve

244 Leanne Picketts and Anna MacLeod

> masking frustration or fatigue in order to care better. When institutions
> require this professional behaviour to be monitored or assessed, however,
> it becomes an institutional performance. (p. 4)

"Institutional performance" exists during assessment, as students are demonstrating what is institutionally and socially important. But when we deconstruct a patient interaction into discrete, isolated, and compartmentalized elements like those on an OSCE checklist, we may be unable to address the complexity of the human connection inherent in patient-centredness. Instead of assessing the authenticity and patient-centredness of the student, we may be simply assessing the delivery of FIFE, and in turn, undermining the flexibility and openness needed to achieve true patient-centredness (Hodges, 2003; Salmon & Young, 2011). It is important to consider whether assessment during simulation is teaching learners to tick boxes on a checklist, and whether patient-centredness may become so automated that it is no longer meaningful – or reconsider how the complexity of patient-centredness is assessed in a simulated environment (Gormley, Hodges, McNaughton, & Johnston, 2016).

These results underscore how curricular interventions such as FIFE can serve to reinforce ritualized patient interactions. A reliance on rigidly using interviewing frameworks as a set of acting techniques points to the need for other pedagogies beyond simulation, such as early clinical contact and work-based learning, where students have an opportunity to connect with real patients (Bokken et al., 2009; Hanna & Finns, 2006). In a clinical environment, FIFE may complement history-taking, and its use should be dependent upon individual patient needs and context.

FIFE: Authentically Performed in "Real Life"

Although there are many benefits to practising patient-centred communication in simulated clinical environments, most medical educators believe simulation does not replace direct patient contact, because it is exceedingly difficult to simulate the spontaneous and disordered practice of patient care. While SPs are an appropriate methodology for providing students with practice in history-taking and physical examination, as our study and others (Brenner, 2009; Clever et al., 2011) have shown, simulation with SPs may impact authentic and empathic patient-centredness. Hanna and Fins (2006) suggest that simulation training ought to be complemented by experiential learning with real patients, as "exclusive reliance on this pedagogic approach of simulation training may be encouraging students to become 'simulation doctors' who act out a good relationship to their patients but have no authentic connection with them" (p. 265).

Our participants discussed the difference between simulated contexts and "real life" as represented by interacting with real patients in a clinic or hospital setting. Although students might use FIFE formulaically in simulation, they understood that the intent of FIFE in actual practice is not to be used as a literal set of questions:

> It is really about weaving these questions seamlessly into the medical script ... I've seen a few medical students or doctors just kind of go through the questions and you can see, you can almost predict the next question or [what] the next two or three questions are going to be ... [*laughs*] and you wonder if they're really connecting with the patient.

These perceptions align with FIFE's original intent: to have each question integrated within the conversation when contextually appropriate (Stewart et al., 2014). Whereas in simulated environments the students we interviewed seemed focused on "performing" each step of FIFE in order to demonstrate competence, in real life the focus was on authentically engaging with the patient, which meant mediating the text to suit the context of each individual patient. One student commented:

> Sometimes I find that the interview is very structured and I follow FIFE to a tee. And then sometimes you have a patient in front of you who, you know, in the first sentence they've asked you what three words mean that you've used, and you're like: "Okay, I really have to change how this is going to go." Or you have a patient that's very distraught, and they're only going to focus on one thing and they don't want to tell you about anything else in their life. So you really have to change your approach again, based on who you have in front of you.

This approach may relate to the fact that in the clinical setting, the environment is not pre-scripted, controlled, or standardized. Relatedly, in the real world, students receive unsolicited patient feedback on their communication skills, including some of the elements of FIFE. For example, one student described asking a real patient for their feelings about their symptoms and received an unexpected response:

> I would find sometimes patients give you a bit of a sassy response back in the real world. Like when we're with SPs that's great because they know we're supposed to be using those kinds of terms and sentences and so they give you like a little spiel back about what their feelings are. But especially

246 Leanne Picketts and Anna MacLeod

my electives ... you'll say, like: "What do you think is going on?" And
they're like: "I don't know, you're the one who is supposed to tell me that."

Another student also found that real patients often don't want to be
asked exploratory questions about their perspective. She commented:
"Sometimes the patients get irritated ... because they want to be in and
out." Another student commented on his experience with patients who
defer back to the student or doctor when asked for their opinion:

> I have this joke with my friends that sometimes when you ask a patient
> what are their ideas about what's going on, they kind of stare blankly and
> go: "Oh, you're the doctor, right?" [*laughs*]. So that's been a funny one, but
> I think I've just been trying to figure out ways of better asking that ques-
> tion perhaps, rather than just being like: "So, what do you think is going
> on?" Because that just makes the patient like all: "That's not my job. That's
> why I'm here – to figure it out."

These experiences suggest that a planned simulation-based curriculum can help learners become familiar with elements of patient-centred
interviewing (like FIFE); however, it is through experiences with real
patients, in authentic clinical settings, that learners are able to refine
their patient-centred communication skills. It is important to acknowledge that this informal learning and tacit knowledge impact students'
development of patient-centredness and may be more influential than
explicit learning (Coulehan & Williams, 2001). However, students recognize the importance of the context of practice, and "what is learned
in one training or work site is not portable but is transformed and rein-
vented when applied to the tasks, interactions, and cultural dynamics
of another" (Fenwick, 2000, p. 254). This theory is known as recontextu-
alization (Bernstein, 2000); when learners apply critical thinking, their
knowledge, skills, and attitudes are transformed as they move around
and between learning contexts.

Conclusion: Learning through Practice

Medical students found both positive and unintended negative consequences to developing patient-centred communication skills in simulated
contexts. Students agreed that practising FIFE in a simulated environment was helpful when they were beginning their education and learning how to interact with patients. However, although FIFE is intended
to provide a structured framework for activating an individualized, patient-centred approach, in a simulated context students felt that their SP

interactions were sometimes artificial, that FIFE was sometimes used in a way that was performative and insincere (especially during assessment), and that their encounters were less authentic than when interacting with real patients in a clinical setting. Ritualistic performance was an unanticipated outcome of learning in simulated contexts where SP scenarios were scripted and curricular expectations were at the forefront of students' minds. Additionally, a model such as FIFE can oversimplify the complexity of doctor–patient communication. This complicates the outcomes of learning about patient-centredness in a simulated setting, as context plays a large role. It raises an important question: in a simulated learning environment, are we teaching students how to be patient-centred or how to *play the role* of the doctor (Hodges, 2003)?

Students found FIFE to be more flexible and meaningful in a clinical context with real patients, and gradually developed an understanding of how to use FIFE authentically, with humanism, intention, and meaning. Learning in a "real" setting reinforced the formal curriculum and allowed students to iteratively build their skills by strengthening and providing relevance and motivation to their learning (Dornan et al., 2006). To discourage a rote or ritualistic application of FIFE, students may benefit from early patient contact in a clinical setting in order to contextualize and integrate the framework into authentic practice, and to encourage patient-centredness to become part of a student's physician identity. It is important to include experiential learning opportunities throughout the curriculum to cultivate and retain patient-centred communication skills – iteratively with both simulated and real patients. However, it should be noted that simulation with SPs provides a safe learning environment for students, and provides essential practice prior to interactions with real patients where harm could occur.

While using FIFE may have felt awkward, hollow, and inauthentic early in students' education, comfort and expertise develop with experience. Students believed they integrated FIFE into their practice with experience, reflection, and what Ericsson (2004) refers to as "deliberate practice," gradually allowing their practice to become more authentically patient-centred, and transferable and flexible with different patients and across contexts. Experience aims to provide the motivation for learning, and reflection on experience helps to establish new knowledge and construct meaning (Fenwick, 2000; Kolb, 1984; Schon, 1983). One student acknowledged that using FIFE to elicit the patient perspective becomes more authentic and natural with practice:

> These things don't feel artificial anymore when you actually start to use
> them ... that all comes with learning and once you have this kind of in

your mind and it's part of your own way of doing an interview, you don't jump from thing to thing as obviously and it tends to flow a bit better ... At the beginning I felt that I asked them verbatim as they were written ... but as you start to go on, and you're in a conversation with a patient, and you find that there's just a natural slot to ask what that question is asking about ... so you're asking the same question but now it's so much more natural. And you're getting the same answers but it's not as verbatim and fake as it was. So I feel like that shows learning from these tools, where you learned the basics, and now you're learning to actually incorporate them in your own way, in your own practice. But before, I never would have thought to ask those questions, if we hadn't learned to do it.

We believe that simulation is an invaluable resource to prepare medical students for clinical practice; however, it is important to think critically about the behaviours enacted within the simulated learning environment. Context matters and influences learning (Billett, 2016). If patient-centredness is our end goal, we need to do the best we can to ensure our teaching strategies embrace learners' progressive development. Providing students with iterative experiential learning to practise and refine behaviour, in both simulated and real clinical contexts, and having both educators and learners transparently reflect on how specific educational contexts affect behaviour will help to ensure that simulation does not perpetuate inauthentic interactions, and will help learners integrate patient-centredness into their practice (Dieckmann, Gaba, & Rall, 2007; Schrewe, Ellaway, Watling, & Bates, 2018).

REFERENCES

Atkins, S., Roberts, C., Hawthorne, K., & Greenhalgh, T. (2016). Simulated consultations: A sociolinguistic perspective. *BioMed Central Medical Education, 16*(1), 16. https://doi.org/10.1186/s12909-016-0535-2

Barrows, H.S. (1987). *Simulated (standardized) patients and other human simulations: A comprehensive guide to their training and use in teaching and evaluation.* Chapel Hill, NC: Health Sciences Consortium.

Beach, M.C., Inui, T., & the Relationship-Centered Care Research Network (2006). Relationship-centered care: A constructive reframing. *Journal of General Internal Medicine, 21*(S1), S3–S8. https://doi.org/10.1111/j.1525-1497.2006.00302.x

Berkhof, M., van Rijssen, H.J., Schellart, A.J., Anema, J.R., & van der Beek, A.J. (2011). Effective training strategies for teaching communication skills to physicians: An overview of systematic reviews. *Patient Education and Counseling, 84*(2), 152–162. https://doi.org/10.1016/j.pec.2010.06.010

Bernstein, B. B. (2000). *Pedagogy, symbolic control, and identity: Theory, research, critique* (Revised ed.). Lanham, MD: Rowman & Littlefield.

Billett, S. (2016). Learning through health care work: Premises, contributions and practices. *Medical Education, 50*(1), 124–131. https://doi.org/10.1111/medu.12848

Bokken, L., Rethans, J.J., van Heurn, L., Duvivier, R., Scherpbier, A., & van der Vleuten, C. (2009). Students' views on the use of real patients and simulated patients in undergraduate medical education. *Academic Medicine, 84*(7), 958–963. https://doi.org/10.1097/ACM.0b013e3181a814a3

Brenner, A.M. (2009). Uses and limitations of simulated patients in psychiatric education. *Academic Psychiatry, 33*(2), 112–119. https://doi.org/10.1176/appi.ap.33.2.112

Campbell, M., & Gregor, F.M. (2008). *Mapping social relations: A primer in doing institutional ethnography.* Toronto, ON: University of Toronto Press.

Clever, S.L., Dudas, R.A., Solomon, B.S., Yeh, H.C., Levine, D., Bertram, A., ... Cofrancesco, J., Jr. (2011). Medical student and faculty perceptions of volunteer outpatients versus simulated patients in communication skills training. *Academic Medicine, 86*(11), 1437–1442. https://doi.org/10.1097/ACM.0b013e3182305bc0

Coulehan, J., & Williams, P.C. (2001). Vanquishing virtue: The impact of medical education. *Academic Medicine, 76*(6), 598–605. https://doi.org/10.1097/00001888-200106000-00008

Devault, M.L. (2006). Introduction: What is institutional ethnography? *Social Problems, 53*(3), 294–298. https://doi.org/10.1525/sp.2006.53.3.294

Dieckmann, P., Gaba, D., & Rall, M. (2007). Deepening the theoretical foundations of patient simulation as social practice. *Simulation in Healthcare, 2*(3), 183–193. https://doi.org/10.1097/SIH.0b013e3180f637f5

Dornan, T., Littlewood, S., Margolis, S.A., Scherpbier, A., Spencer, J., & Ypinazar, V. (2006). How can experience in clinical and community settings contribute to early medical education? A BEME systematic review. *Medical Teacher, 28*(1), 3–18. https://doi.org/10.1080/01421590500410971

Ericsson, K.A. (2004). Deliberate practice and the acquisition and maintenance of expert performance in medicine and related domains. *Academic Medicine, 79*(Suppl. 10), S70–S81. https://doi.org/10.1097/00001888-200410001-00022

Fenwick, T.J. (2000). Expanding conceptions of experiential learning: A review of the five contemporary perspectives on cognition. *Adult Education Quarterly, 50*(4), 243–272. https://doi.org/10.1177/07417130022087035

Giesbrecht, E.M., Wener, P.F., & Pereira, G.M. (2014). A mixed methods study of student perceptions of using standardized patients for learning and evaluation. *Advances in Medical Education and Practice, 5,* 241–255. https://doi.org/10.2147/AMEP.S62446

Gormley, G.J., Hodges, B.D., McNaughton, N., & Johnston, J.L. (2016). The show must go on? Patients, props and pedagogy in the theatre of the OSCE. *Medical Education, 50*(12), 1237–1240. https://doi.org/10.1111/medu.13016

Green, J., & Thorogood, N. (2014). *Qualitative methods for health research* (3rd ed.). Thousand Oaks, CA: Sage.

Hanna, M., & Fins, J. J. (2006). Power and communication: Why simulation training ought to be complemented by experiential and humanist learning. *Academic Medicine, 81*(3), 265–270. https://doi.org/10.1097/00001888-200603000-00016

Hodges, B. (2003). OSCE! Variations on a theme by Harden. *Medical Education, 37*(12), 1134–1140. https://doi.org/10.1111/j.1365-2923.2003.01717.x

King, A., & Hoppe, R.B. (2013). "Best practice" for patient-centered communication: A narrative review. *Journal of Graduate Medical Education, 5*(3), 385–393. https://doi.org/10.4300/JGME-D-13-00072.1

Kolb, D.A. (1984). *Experiential learning.* Englewood Cliffs, NJ: Prentice-Hall.

Laughey, W., Sangvik Grandal, N., & Finn, G.M. (2018). Medical communication: The views of simulated patients. *Medical Education, 52*(6), 664–676. https://doi.org/10.1111/medu.13547

Marinker, M. (1997). Myth, paradox and the hidden curriculum. *Medical Education, 31*(4), 293–298. https://doi.org/10.1111/j.1365-2923.1997.tb02928.x

Mayan, M.J. (2009). *Essentials of qualitative inquiry.* Walnut Creek, CA: Left Coast Press.

Mitchell, M.L., Henderson, A., Groves, M., Dalton, M., & Nulty, D. (2009). The objective structured clinical examination (OSCE): Optimising its value in the undergraduate nursing curriculum. *Nurse Education Today, 29*(4), 398–404. https://doi.org/10.1016/j.nedt.2008.10.007

Nestel, D., & Bearman, M. (2015). Introduction to simulated patient methodology. In D. Nestel & M. Bearman (Eds.), *Simulated patient methodology: Theory, evidence and practice* (pp. 1–4). Chichester, UK: Wiley-Blackwell.

Prior, L. (2008). Repositioning documents in social research. *Sociology, 42*(5), 821–836. https://doi.org/10.1177/0038038508094564

Salmon, P., & Young, B. (2011). Creativity in clinical communication: From communication skills to skilled communication. *Medical Education, 45*(3), 217–226. https://doi.org/10.1111/j.1365-2923.2010.03801.x

Sargeant, J. (2012). Qualitative research part II: Participants, analysis, and quality assurance. *Journal of Graduate Medical Education, 4*(1), 1–3. https://doi.org/10.4300/JGME-D-11-00307.1

Schon, D.A. (1983). *The reflective practitioner.* New York, NY: Basic Books.

Schrewe, B., Ellaway, R.H., Watling, C., & Bates, J. (2018). The contextual curriculum: Learning in the matrix, learning from the matrix. *Academic Medicine, 93*(11), 1645–1651. https://doi.org/10.1097/ACM.0000000000002345

Smith, D.E. (2005). *Institutional ethnography: A sociology for people.* Lanham, MD: Rowman Altamira.

Stewart, M.A., Brown, J.B., Weston, W.W., McWhinney, I.R., McWilliam, C.L., & Freeman, T.R. (2014). *Patient-centered medicine: Transforming the clinical method* (3rd ed.). London, UK: Radcliffe.

Wear, D., & Varley, J. D. (2008). Rituals of verification: The role of simulation in developing and evaluating empathic communication. *Patient Education and Counseling, 71*(2), 153–156. https://doi.org/10.1016/j.pec.2008.01.005

15 Simulation and Interprofessional Education (IPE), from Teaching Practices to Evaluation of Learning Outcomes

ALYSHAH KABA

Collaborative Practice in Healthcare and the Rise of Interprofessional Education

Healthcare practitioners work in dynamic, high-pressure clinical environments that require individuals to work collaboratively as part of healthcare teams and respond to the increasing demands of patient care needs (Bressler & Persico, 2016). Effective interprofessional collaboration has been long recognized as a means to achieve better quality of care and enhanced patient outcomes (Kaba & Beran, 2016; Peterson et al., 2014; Reeves, Perrier, Goldman, Freeth, & Zwarenstein, 2013).

In 2001 the Institute of Medicine published two seminal reports that raised awareness of the need to train healthcare professionals to work effectively as an interprofessional team: *To Err Is Human: Building a Safer Health System* (Kohn, Corrigan, & Donaldson, 2000) and *Crossing the Quality Chasm: A New Health System for the 21st Century* (Institute of Medicine, 2001). The reports commented that the decentralized and fragmented nature of the healthcare delivery system contributes to unsafe conditions for patients and called for the establishment of inter-disciplinary team education programs for providers that incorporate proven methods of team training, such as simulation-based education (Kaba, Wishart, Fraser, Coderre, & McLaughlin, 2016).

Following these seminal reports, understanding what defined the construct of interprofessional teamwork in healthcare became increasingly important. Xyrichis and Ream (2008) defined teamwork as a dynamic process involving two or more healthcare professionals with complementary backgrounds and skills sharing common health goals and exercising concerted physical and mental effort in assessing, planning, or evaluating patient care. This process is accomplished through interdependent collaboration, open communication, and shared decision-making (Xyrichis &

Ream, 2008). While interprofessional teamwork in healthcare did not begin with these groundbreaking reports, based on the frequency with which they are cited, it seems that in the 10 years that followed these publications the healthcare community took notice and responded with interventions designed to improve interprofessional teamwork in healthcare. Recommendations for education and teamwork training soon followed, fostering the development of the concept of interprofessional collaboration (IPC) (Long, 2003). IPC has been cited as being vital to patient safety and quality of care in healthcare (Hinde, Gale, Anderson, Roberts, & Sice, 2016; Kohn, Corrigan, & Donaldson, 2000; Salas & Rosen, 2013). IPC is defined as the process of developing and maintaining effective interprofessional working relationships between learners, practitioners, and patients/clients/families (Orchard et al., 2010).

Over the last 15 years there has been increased recognition and momentum in wanting to achieve IPC within healthcare and therefore a growing need for the formal development and implementation of interprofessional education (IPE). IPE is defined as an intervention where the members of more than one health or social care (or both) profession learn with, from, and about each other interactively together, for the explicit purpose of improving interprofessional collaboration or the health/well-being of patients/clients, or both (Reeves et al., 2013). One of the goals of IPE is to prepare learners for interprofessional collaborative practice. In attempts to achieve the goal of IPC, IPE has become a major focus in healthcare education curricula (Barr, Hammick, Koppel, & Reeves, 1999). Several reviews (Hammick, Freeth, Koppel, Reeves, & Barr, 2007; Reeves et al., 2013) have provided evidence that IPE interventions can improve collaboration and healthcare outcomes. For example, Barnes, Carpenter, and Dickinson (2000) emphasize that the knowledge gained from IPE includes an understanding of the differences and similarities between different professional groups. Moreover, interprofessional knowledge and understanding can help to establish the learner's own professional identity. Williamson (2012) highlights that the initial emphasis of creating IPE opportunities was to explore interprofessional attitudes and team roles. However, this report suggests that this emphasis has shifted to addressing widespread concerns of patient safety, improving communication, and working collaboratively as an interprofessional team, with the goal to reduce the risk of errors in healthcare (Williamson, 2012).

In 2010, the CIHC (Canadian Interprofessional Health Collaborative) Working Group was mandated to review the literature related to interprofessional (IP) competencies, IPE interventions, and IPC competency frameworks and develop a Canada-wide IPC framework to promote a standardized language and taxonomy for IPC. The framework provides descriptions of the knowledge, skills, attitudes, and values of the six competencies required for effective interprofessional collaboration practice, which are (1) interprofessional communication, (2) patient/client/family community-centred care, (3) role clarification, (4) team functioning, (5) collaborative leadership, and (6) interprofessional conflict resolution (Orchard et al., 2010). In response to the development of the CIHC competency framework, there were a growing number of requirements by accreditation bodies for IPE curriculum to be embedded in Canadian health professional programs (Canadian Medical Association, 2010). In addition, there have been a myriad of educational resources and modalities developed over the last 15 years targeting IPC and IPE (e.g., team training workshops, webinars, online modules, student-led clubs, orientation days, standardized patient group histories, case studies, virtual patients and simulation-based education, etc.) (Grant et al., 2016).

While the momentum for IPE as a means to achieve interprofessional collaborative practice is high, there are several barriers to successful implementation of IPE. In line with historical norms, healthcare providers continue to be largely trained in professional silos around the world (Palaganas, Epps, & Raemer, 2014). The way in which individual health professionals are socialized and trained in uniprofessional settings continues to present significant barriers to collaboration (Milne, Greenfield, & Braithwaite, 2015). A lack of understanding and knowledge of others' professional roles and perspectives, "turf" wars, and fear of "identity loss" have been cited as the main barriers to interprofessional collaborative practice (Khalili, Orchard, Laschinger, & Farah, 2013).

A problem long recognized within sociological understandings of patient safety is that those in inferior positions within the healthcare system hierarchy may have critical information, yet are unable to persuade those in more senior positions of the credibility of their knowledge or relevance of their opinions (Silbey, 2009). For example, a nurse's relationship with a patient creates an advantageous position of strength in relation to the doctor, who may be unaware of any changes in the patient's condition (Corser, 2000). Yet nurses are in a disadvantageous position within existing hierarchical relations of power and knowledge that may limit their contribution to patient care (Ceci, 2004). Despite some smoothing of the hierarchical relations between doctors and nurses in recent years, traditional relations still hold power; those lower in the hierarchy are submissive to those higher up (Sweet & Norman, 1995). These relations are not unique to nursing and medicine but occur across all health professions. In spite of general agreement about the importance of interprofessional teamwork and collaboration in the delivery of quality patient care, these critical skills are not typically emphasized in health professional education. The curricular emphasis is traditionally on dynamics within each of the individual respective uniprofessional teams (e.g., between registered nurses and licensed practical nurses). In most universities, education programs for health professional disciplines exist separately, with little opportunity for crossover (Kaba, Beran, & White, 2016).

Yet we know that creating highly reliable teams requires interactive educational experiences early in a student's career within a system that values the diversity of professional knowledge and emphasizes the breakdown of traditional hierarchies and gender roles (Zwarenstein & Reeves, 2006). Throughout each of the years of training within health professional programs, students are learning the cultural norms, attitudes, and values of their profession that will affect their future roles in interdisciplinary teams (Khalili, Hall, & DeLuca, 2014). By exposing students early to these team dynamics and also facilitating interdisciplinary educational IPE experiences, it is anticipated that they will gain improvements in knowledge, skills, attitudes, and beliefs that will enable them to work successfully within their collaborative practice environment (Robertson et al., 2010).

Simulation-Based Education as a Pedagogical Tool Supporting IPE

Recognizing the movement toward IPC and IPE, researchers have proposed simulation-based education (SBE) (Gough, Hellaby, Hones, & MacKinnon, 2012) as an emerging pedagogical tool for teaching teamwork and collaboration skills in health professional education (Reese, Jeffries, & Engum, 2010). The current impetus to explore the potential of using SBE as a pedagogical means to teach IPE mirrors the short evolution of IPE itself, with the long-term goal toward improvement in quality of patient care. The use of SBE in undergraduate and postgraduate training education has grown exponentially in the last decade. Much of the available evidence recommends that SBE be utilized for team-based education, specifically in building knowledge, attitudes, skills, and behaviours that target closed-loop communication, role clarification, situational awareness, collaborative leadership, and interprofessional conflict (Boet, Bould, Layat Burn, & Reeves, 2014; Rosen et al., 2008). SBE offers the unique opportunity for learners across the continuum of health professions education to learn and engage in reflective practice about IPC competencies and team behaviours (Reeves et al., 2013; Reeves & van Schaik, 2012).

Interprofessional simulation aims to recreate a real-life task, event, or experience, providing a safe learning environment for the acquisition of IP team' skills, knowledge, attitudes, and behaviours. The spectrum of simulation modalities used within healthcare ranges from virtual-reality-based screen interfaces and part-task trainers to full-body human patient simulators and standardized patients (Decker, Sportsman, Puetz, & Billings, 2008). Alinier et al. (2008) refer to interprofessional simulation as occurring when two or more health professions engage autonomously in highly realistic scenarios to learn with, from, and about each other in a safe and controlled manner. To be applicable, teaching IPC using simulation should be grounded in clinically contextualized scenarios (Eppich, Howard, Vozenilek, & Curran, 2011) that take into consideration the unique variances between different contents, clinical environments, and health professionals' scopes of practice.

Following the IP simulation is a structured debrief. Debriefing is a form of guided reflection and is a critical component of learning from the simulation scenario. During the debrief, learners can discuss areas for improvement as a team, which can result in potential changes in knowledge, attitudes, and behaviours (Cheng et al., 2016). Through the debriefing, behaviours are addressed in relation to the contextual and hierarchical elements that led to both strengths and challenges in team dynamics (Gilfoyle, 2017).

A common approach to teaching IPC and IPE in simulation has been the use of the crew (crisis) resource management (CRM) framework (Fung et al., 2015), which focuses on the non-technical skills required for effective teamwork in crisis situations. The core behaviours of CRM include communication, task management, decision-making, teamwork, and situational awareness. CRM was developed in the 1970s by the aviation industry, following the realization that 70% of airline crashes were due to human error (Østergaard, Dieckmann, & Lippert, 2011). Since that time, many high-risk work domains, including healthcare, have utilized the CRM framework for debriefing in SBE (O'Dea, O'Connor, & Keogh, 2014).

While CRM is an effective framework to address individual and team behaviours in SBE, the framework fails to target IPC competencies and collective team behaviours. Building on the work of Lingard and colleagues, in order to move toward IPC and collaborative care delivery, it has been recognized that health teams must be collectively competent (Lingard et al., 2012). While individual competence is necessary in today's healthcare world, collective competence is defined as team members moving away from thinking and acting as individual practitioners to thinking and acting as a high-performing collective team

(Lingard et al., 2012). SBE as a pedagogical tool is one approach that enables health professional learners to move toward collective competence as a team. Using SBE to teach collective competence allows for the deconstruction of the beliefs and assumptions underlying why a team has developed certain norms and how these beliefs and assumptions either promote or discourage IPC (Reeves et al., 2016). For example, when debriefing on role clarity following an IP simulation, the focus of the debrief moves from team members being individually competent in their given roles (e.g., giving medications, performing airway management, etc.) to understanding all roles on the team and how members can work together to achieve a common collective goal. In contrast, a lack of understanding of other roles and what they can do to support overall team functioning in a given situation limits the team's abilities to become collectively competent.

While using SBE as a pedagogical tool to move toward IPC and collective competence seems to be an intuitive approach to health professional education, it is still a relatively new approach across all levels, from undergraduates to postgraduate trainees and practising health professionals (Alinier et al., 2008). Although there has been a wealth of studies (Fung et al., 2015) and literature reviews that have indicated that SBE has become widely and effectively used to teach IPE in medicine and nursing specialties internationally (Neill & Wotton, 2011; Ricketts, 2011), it is less evident in other healthcare professions, across the continuum of care.

Given the current state of evidence of SBE, can we assume that it is a panacea for IPE? What are some unintended consequences of using SBE a pedagogical tool to teach IPE?

Social and Psychological Factors Impacting the Use of Simulation-Based Education as a Pedagogical Tool to Teach IPE

Despite the various teaching approaches and learning experiences that facilitate collaborative group learning, some interactions within these groups may interfere with appropriate knowledge and skill development. Given that a significant portion of SBE occurs in group settings (simulation labs, in situ clinical environments, etc.), it is critical to examine how interprofessional group members interact as a team within these social settings. One type of social influence that may be at risk of occurring in SBE is group conformity, whereby an individual may change their own behaviour to match the consensus of the group (Guo, Tan, Turner, & Xu, 2010). This often occurs when an individual holds an opinion that is contrary to those of the majority of group members and there is pressure to conform. This may cause distress to learners by reducing their autonomy and freedom of choice (e.g., "I disagree with others, but don't want to stand out"). The inability to speak up and the pressure to conform to the opinion of the majority group, even in situations where a diagnosis may be erroneous, may be an unintended consequence of IPE simulation (Kaba, Beran, & White, 2016). Given the pressure to conform to the views of other learners in an interprofessional simulation environment, group conformity bias may be one of a number of communication challenges associated with IPC. In practice, this may represent a factor contributing to the burden of adverse events in healthcare.

Seminal Research on Group Conformity

In the mid-20th century, social psychologists began to examine how the judgments of the majority of group members influence individual behaviours. Social influence can manifest in the act of conforming to peer views, whereby an individual provides the same response as other group members, despite possibly having a different perspective (Cappellen, Corneille, Cols, & Saroglou, 2011). This conformity may occur, moreover, when the individual recognizes that this response is incorrect. In a series of studies, Solomon Asch (1951; 1952; 1956) showed a card with a stimulus line and three additional lines of varying length to a group of four students who were instructed to select the line that matched the length of the stimulus line. The students responded in the order in which they were seated. Only one person, the "minority critical subject," was naive to the study. The others were confederates who had been instructed to give the same incorrect answer. In the first trial, the confederates selected the correct matching line, but in a subsequent trial, with a different set of lines, all confederates selected the same incorrect line. A total of 18 trials were conducted, with confederates responding correctly in some and incorrectly in others. In the control group, answers were written rather than verbalized, and thus participants did not hear the answers of other group members. Asch found that over one third (37%) of participants gave the wrong answers they had heard from the confederates, whereas only 1% of participants in the control group gave a wrong answer. Asch concluded that about a third of individuals may conform to wrong information presented by the majority of group members. In the most recent meta-analysis, Bond and Smith (1996) examined 133 studies on conformity, performed in 17 countries, that demonstrated universality of conformity across varying social circumstances. These researchers concluded that about one third of people are likely to conform to inaccurate information presented to them by group members.

Direct evidence of the potential for collaborative decision-making possibly leading to poorer decisions comes from the literature on group conformity bias. In general, when humans interact there is preference for consistency, and this may lead to individuals changing a decision to avoid inconsistency (Guadagno & Cialdini, 2010). While group conformity bias was first described by Asch more than 60 years ago in a series of psychology experiments, it has also most recently been described in the context of medical education (Beran, Drefs, Kaba, Al Baz, & Al Harbi, 2015; Kaba & Beran, 2016; Kaba, Beran, & White, 2016). There is newly emerging empirical evidence of the effect of conformity bias in interprofessional SBE, suggesting that subtle motivations and pressures within a group in a simulated environment may prevent students from challenging or questioning information that seems incorrect. In recent experiments involving nursing and medical students in an IP simulation environment, Kaba et al. found that both groups of students were susceptible to group conformity bias, although nursing students were significantly more likely to conform to the opinion of medical students than vice versa. In these experiments, group conformity resulted in incorrect interpretation of important physical findings, from which we can infer that this type of bias could increase the risk of adverse clinical outcomes. When interviewed after the experiment, three quarters of participants who demonstrated conformity bias denied conforming, suggesting that preference for consistency and pressure to conform are largely subconscious and may, therefore, be difficult to modify (Kaba & Beran, 2016; Kaba, Beran, & White, 2016). These seminal studies suggest that group conformity bias may be an unintended consequence of interprofessional SBE.

Impact of Group Conformity on Collaborative Practice Behaviours, Patient Safety, and Clinical Decision-Making

Patient safety and medical error are major concerns for the health professions and the general public. Patient care is a complex activity that requires effective teamwork and communication skills among providers to ensure patient safety and to avoid or mitigate adverse events (Leonard, Graham, & Bonacum, 2004). One source of medical errors is communication errors within healthcare teams. Practical experience in many high-stakes professions, like the health professions, has shown that optimal and efficient team communication are essential to reducing human error (Calhoun, Boon, Miller, & Pian-Smith, 2013). For example, to maintain "collaborative" relationships, health professionals reportedly do not "speak up" in an effort to avoid confrontation. Maxfield, Grenny, McMillan, Patterson, and Switzler (2005) conducted surveys, focus groups, interviews, and ethnographic observations with

more than 1,700 nurses, physicians, clinical-care staff, and administrators in 2004 in urban, suburban, and rural hospitals in the United States.
The researchers found that more than half of the healthcare workers
had witnessed their co-workers break rules, cut corners, make mistakes, and show incompetence in patient care, which had resulted in
injurious consequences. The behaviours described by these accounts,
which were a result of miscommunication, along with reports that one
in five physicians has seen harm come to patients, clearly establish the
need to examine reasons for these unsafe behaviours (Maxfield et al.,
2005). Inaccurate reporting of information and subjective normative
pressures such as group conformity bias may be among several of the
communication challenges associated with unsafe behaviours in interprofessional care.

An unintended consequence of teaching IPC in simulated environments is that collaboration may be misunderstood as consistency or
consensus across group members. If the consensus of the team is inaccurate, the inability of individuals within the team to speak up and respectfully disagree with the group may indirectly contribute to medical
errors and impaired patient care. In fact, poor communication among
nurses and physicians is reportedly responsible for 37% of all medical
errors (Henriksen & Dayton, 2006). I propose that one explanation for
this type of error is peer pressure to conform, despite inaccurate information communicated by a member of a team, which results in a condition
commonly referred to as organizational silence (Henriksen & Dayton,
2006). This phenomenon can also be seen in IP simulation learning sessions, as the pressure to perform, fear, and judgment within a group
may prevent individuals from challenging or questioning information
that may be incorrect. When translated from the simulation environment into practice, this collective implicit agreement of a non-response,
or inability to speak up, undermines a group member's ability to act
professionally and puts the safety of the patient at risk (Henriksen &
Dayton, 2006). The more cohesive the group, and the more the need
to maintain status quo, the more that communication is impaired and
silence is interpreted as consent (Millenson, 2003). For example, it has
been documented that fewer than 10% of clinical staff directly confront
their colleagues when they become aware of poor and potentially harmful clinical judgment (Maxfield et al., 2005). For simulation educators,
interprofessional SBE followed by reflection and debriefing offers the
unique opportunity to draw awareness to the phenomena of group conformity bias and organizational silence by understanding the underlying behaviours that may prevent learners from speaking up and that
contribute to these potentially harmful behaviours in practice.

Conformity Bias and Decision-Making

Within a real-life practice or within the SBE environment, humans may influence and bias each other's decision-making. Poor decision-making is not unique to the IPE and SBE context and health professional education. For example, when examining the decision-making processes during "fiascos," Janis described the process of groupthink that he felt led to poor decision-making (Janis, 1972; Rose, 2011). He defined groupthink as a mode of thinking people engage in when they are deeply involved in a cohesive in-group, when the members' striving for unanimity overrides their motivation to realistically appraise alternative courses of action. Some of the symptoms of groupthink that he identified can be observed in the context of interprofessional SBE, as members of a team may engage in collective rationalization and self-censorship, and there may be a direct pressure on dissenters to agree with the majority (Janis, 1972). Despite the ongoing debate in the psychology literature on the validity of the concept of groupthink, even those who contest the model agree that certain group dynamics may increase the likelihood of poorer decisions and that these dynamics may be a ubiquitous part of human behaviour (Zanna, 2005).

The notion that collaborative decision-making leads to better decisions is enticing because we typically seek the advice of others when faced with difficult decisions and, on a larger scale, we seek the input of many individuals when making important decisions. This can be observed in SBE; for example, in an IPE simulation session, while the team leader role is to have an overarching view of the patient diagnosis and the management and treatment plan, the leader cannot function without critical information and assessments data provided to them by the other members of the interprofessional team. In short, we have been conditioned to use social heuristics, such as the "wisdom of crowds," when making complicated decisions (Yi, Steyvers, Lee, & Dry, 2012). There is data to support the notion that under certain circumstances (e.g., when trying to estimate the number of jelly beans in a jar), taking the aggregate of opinions or brainstorming as a group is consistently better than following the advice of any given individual (Hertwig & Herzon, 2009). However, there is also a large body of literature questioning the utility of the wisdom of the crowd in health professional education and healthcare.

For example, there are several cognitive disadvantages of collaborative decision-making, which may raise potential challenges for educators teaching IPC using the pedagogical tool of SBE. There is evidence suggesting that thinking and working in groups results in fewer ideas rather than more, and hinders rather than helps productivity (Lamm & Trommsdorff, 1973). There are several possible explanations for this effect, including social loafing, where some individuals apply less effort when trying to solve problems in a group. In those who do not loaf in group activities, brainstorming may increase the risk of cognitive overload. Ideas are generated and processed in the working memory, which has a limited capacity and is, therefore, susceptible to cognitive overload (Sweller, 1988). During the process of brainstorming, while one person is proposing ideas the others must juggle multiple competing demands on the working memory, such as listening attentively and processing the ideas of others, generating their own ideas, trying to remember recent ideas, and worrying how the members of the group might judge their ideas. Thus, the cognitive multitasking involved in brainstorming may overload the capacity of the working memory, which results in fewer and less well processed ideas being generated.

Ultimately, where there are interprofessional learners and group learning environments such as SBE, there is the potential for conformity bias with respect to collaborative decision-making. Although it is desirable for learners and professionals to collaboratively make decisions as a team to follow rules, protocols, policies, and expectations, it is equally desirable that they do not follow incorrect and erroneous information, especially when it comes to patient care. The fact that there are divergent bodies of literature on the effect of collaborative decision-making on the quality of decisions and performance implies that this effect cannot be inherently good, bad, or neutral. Instead of making these assumptions, educators using SBE as a pedagogical tool to teach IPC should be discerning in recognizing some of the challenges of teaching collaborative decision-making in a simulation learning environment: in a given context, collaboration that draws upon the wisdom of crowds may improve decision-making, whereas in a different context collaboration may lead to social loafing, cognitive overload, or pressure to conform, each of which might contribute to poorer decisions and poor patient outcomes.

In addition to recognizing their limitations with respect to collaborative decision-making, we should also question whether some of the other components of the IPC and IPE might have an unpredictable effect on team performance in simulated environments. For example, does teaching IPE through SBE increase the likelihood of group conformity bias? Does mutual trust foster symptoms of groupthink, such as the illusion of invulnerability and belief in one's group's inherent morality? If we acknowledge that the impact of collaboration on performance is unpredictable (and not inherently good or bad), we can then focus on identifying contextual variables in SBE that influence the outcomes of interprofessional collaborative practice. SBE provides a safe learning environment, through reflection and debriefing, to explore potential strategies to mitigate social loafing, cognitive overload, group conformity bias, and groupthink to improve the delivery of IPC in healthcare (Packer, 2009; Pieterse & Thompson, 2010).

Currently, we know that conformity bias may creep into interprofessional SBE learning sessions and into practice (Beran et al., 2015; Beran, Kaba, Caird, & McLaughlin, 2014). Further systematic empirical research is needed to elucidate which situations in practice and in SBE pose the greatest risk for the occurrence of conformity bias and how manage to it in education and practice, as well as its potential implications for patient safety. These answers will emerge eventually through further research, although they may, unfortunately, take decades to do so.

Is All Team Learning Good? Unique Challenges for Teaching and Evaluating the Effectiveness of IPE Simulation on Student Learning Outcomes

Despite an exponential increase in interprofessional education delivered through SBE across the continuum of undergraduate, postgraduate, and continuing education, the incidence of medical error and adverse clinical events unfortunately continues to be unacceptably high, and there are data to suggest that collaborative decision-making and poor coordination of care or teamwork contribute to adverse outcomes (Chassin, Galvin, & the National Roundtable on Health Care Quality, 1998).

To understand whether using SBE as a pedagogical tool to teach IPC may or may not improve team process, performance, and learning outcomes, we need first to understand the constructs of IPC and teamwork. In the 15 years since the Institute of Medicine reports were published, there have been hundreds of publications on merits of teamwork interventions and different models and frameworks proposed describing the different constructs of IPC. There is now a growing industry that will, for a fee, import models of teamwork training developed for aviation and business into healthcare (Robertson et al., 2010). Most of these models describing teamwork acknowledge its multiple dimensions, although consensus is lacking on the precise number and descriptions of these dimensions. The framework of the Canadian Interprofessional Heath Collaborative includes six competency domains (Hewitt, Sims, & Harris, 2014). Salas, Sim, and Burke (2005) defined the "Big Five" in teamwork, which was then expanded to eight critical teamwork competencies: team leadership, mutual performance monitoring, backup behaviour, adaptability, team orientation, shared mental models, mutual trust, and closed-loop communications. These competencies have guided the content of curricula for team training interventions in education and healthcare, including TeamSTEPPS (Team Strategies and Tools to Enhance Performance and Patient Safety) (Lineberry et al., 2013). However, the evidence supporting this model (and other models) of effective teamwork comes largely from pre/post-intervention studies that do not have a comparison intervention, so the model's individual components lack experimental validation. This type of experimental validation is an important area of future research because, as reviewed in previous sections of this chapter, there is evidence to suggest that some of the proposed teamwork competencies, such as collaborative decision-making (or shared mental models) in SBE, can be positive but can also have the unintended consequence of impairing decision-making and performance.

However, there are specific aspects of SBE that, when used in the context of teaching IPE, may potentially counteract the cognitive and social biases that are ubiquitous to IPC mentioned above (e.g., groupthink, social loafing, conformity bias). In particular, debriefing, which focuses on guided and deliberate reflection following an IP simulation, is a critical component of IPE learning that can be used as a tool to address some of these challenges. There are several parts to debriefing an IP simulation to consider. The first is the timing of the debriefing. Debriefing should occur immediately following the IP simulation and be allotted two times the duration of the simulation; this is important as learners are highly activated following the simulation, and the debriefing allows them the opportunity to address their initial reactions and underlying frames (i.e., thoughts/behaviours), assumptions, and cognitive biases. The second is having trained interprofessional simulation educators co-lead the debrief (e.g., physician, nurse, and respiratory therapist) to ensure equal participation and inclusion of all members of the IP team in the debriefing session. Finally, there are several approaches to how to facilitate a debrief following a simulation. One of the most comprehensive is the PEARLS (Promoting Excellence and Reflective Learning in Simulation) framework, which utilizes a mixed method approach that is focused on the learners' needs and learning context (Eppich & Cheng, 2015). In particular, PEARLS uses the facilitation technique of advocacy inquiry (AI), which emphasizes the importance of genuine curiosity and honest feedback. For example, the person leading the debrief will describe the event/situation they observed in the IP simulation and their position (e.g., "I am concerned"), followed by exploring the drivers/frames behind the learners' thinking, and finally end the debriefing session with discussing potential learnings and strategies that can be applied in future situations.

Debriefing a simulation can facilitate focused reflection on underlying personal assumptions and beliefs specific to IPC. By using AI to facilitate an IP debrief, learners are able to reflect and talk together openly about challenges and barriers to interprofessional collaboration and decision-making within their teams and how to collectively solve them as a team. For example, following an IP debrief, a respiratory student may openly speak up and respectfully disagree with the approach to airway management suggested by the medical students, in contrast to silently agreeing with the consensus of the team, as they may feel increasingly confident to pursue open and honest communication between all team members. In spite of the critical role of debriefing in the context of IP simulation, there still remain a limited number of valid and reliable measurement tools to evaluate the effectiveness of SBE on IP student learning outcomes.

Currently, the IP simulation is most frequently evaluated by questionnaires capturing self-evaluated changes in cognitive, affective, and process outcomes (e.g., knowledge tests, attitudinal questionnaires, or teamwork scales) (Chakraborti, Boonyasai, Wright, & Kern, 2008; Salas et al., 2008; Zeltser & Nash, 2010). The explicit purpose of IPE is improving interprofessional collaboration or the long-term health and well-being of patients/clients, or both (Reeves et al., 2013). The assumption made here is that for IPE, process outcomes are either equal to or a surrogate for patient outcomes. This distinction between process versus patient outcomes is important to differentiate when considering how we can assess IP learning outcomes within SBE. In an analysis of the literature on interprofessional collaboration, Haddara and Lingard identify the emergence of two different discourses in evaluating IPC/IPE: that of utilitarian outcomes, where the value of collaboration is dependent upon demonstrating that the intervention improves patient outcomes, and emancipatory outcomes, where interventions to improve collaboration are justified if they result in flattening the power hierarchy that has traditionally existed in interprofessional care (Haddara & Lingard, 2013). Considering these results to be equal is at odds with clinical practice, where patient-centred outcomes are increasingly required to justify healthcare interventions (Selby, Beal, & Frank, 2012).

The fact that the individual components of IPC (such as collaborative decision-making) have an unpredictable relationship with performance (i.e., it can positive or negative based on the context) implies that these process outcomes cannot be considered as valid surrogates for evaluating patient outcomes in IP simulation. Consistent with the utilitarian perspective, we propose that unless we can provide experimental evidence that demonstrates that interprofessional SBE improves emancipatory outcomes (i.e., flattens the power hierarchy between health professional students), we should focus future education program research efforts on patient-centred performance measures. Interprofessional SBE should be considered effective if and when we can demonstrate an improvement in emancipatory outcomes or utilitarian outcomes in the long-term health and well-being of patients/clients, or both (Zeltser & Nash, 2010).

Developing an Educational Research Program for Evaluating IP Simulation-Based Education Learning Outcomes

Ideally, an education research program for evaluating interprofessional SBE outcomes should begin with defining the construct of interest, provide evidence to support the validity of tools assessing this construct, perform experiments to evaluate interventions that might improve important outcomes, and then design pragmatic studies to see if our interventions improve these outcomes in real life. We would then move on to studies of the comparative effectiveness and cost-effectiveness of different interventions, after which we could make evidence-based recommendations (Walsh, Reeves, & Maloney, 2014). Interestingly, IP simulations appear to have bypassed most of these steps, and many centres are already implementing the use of SBE as a pedagogical tool to teach IPE, presumably based upon the assumption of effectiveness (Hoffman & Harnish, 2007; Leasure et al., 2013). Similarly, despite limited data on interprofessional SBE effectiveness, having a formal curriculum for interprofessional SBE training of medical students is now an accreditation standard for medical schools in North America. In education and healthcare, it is not unusual for implementation to charge ahead of the evidence base, but this does not excuse us from trying to catch up.

In proposing an IP SBE research program, we are not suggesting that we halt all IP SBE activities until we have solid evidence that all outcomes are improved by these interventions. This goal is unrealistic because the effect of any intervention is modified by the persons involved, the situation, and the interaction between the persons and situation. Thus, our ambition is not to determine whether IP simulations are good or bad; instead, in designing an education research program that directly addresses simulation strategies for improving IPC, we need to first define which outcomes can be improved by which interventions in which context. Instead of interrupting current interprofessional SBE activities, which would limit our ability to gather evidence on effectiveness, we suggest that we take advantage of the momentum in these areas by incorporating assessment of patient-centred outcomes into existing and planned IP SBE. This approach would allow us to accelerate our education research agenda in these areas, including the development of assessment tools with internal structure evidence of validity (Sigalet et al., 2013) that can be used by health professional programs to assess learners' outcomes in IP simulation. Other emerging areas of research include investigating whether interprofessional SBE can be used to supplement/and or replace clinical placement experience in improving outcomes specific to IPC. Specific studies that explore the impact of IP SBE environments when compared to traditional placement alone, studying the ideal duration of the IP simulation experience, and researching the clinical benefits of interprofessional SBE for IPC are needed (Gough et al., 2012). There is still much work to be done before we have an evidence base from which to make strong recommendations on evaluating IP SBE outcomes (Thistlethwaite, 2012).

While evidence on the effectiveness of interprofessional SBE is still emerging, IPE healthcare simulation and debriefing offer a strategy to address the challenges of groupthink and conformity bias, which have been identified as an unintended consequence of the group learning environment. Given the importance of IPC for patient care, it is critical for health professional educators to harness the benefits of IPE simulation and debriefing by creating deliberate opportunities for discourse and to encourage healthy debate and dialogue among peers. It is important to recognize that trying to maintain harmonious relationships may prevent health professional students from communicating openly with their colleagues. Information may be unchallenged in a group situation where there is a strong need to "be a team player" and where being collaborative can be interpreted as agreeing and "going along with" the group consensus. IPE simulation offers the unique opportunity for learners to explore through debriefing the specific behaviours and social biases embedded in interprofessional teams that may be impairing interprofessional communication and collaborative decision-making.

In light of these complexities, we recommend that simulation educators and clinicians design IP simulations to address peer pressure and group conformity bias in debriefing by exposing learners to health professionals' communication tools (e.g., the two-challenge rule) to facilitate learning how to speak up and safeguard against peer pressure in clinical practice (Pian-Smith et al., 2009). Early exposure to communications strategies through interprofessional SBE can teach health professional students strategies to respectfully challenge one other and engage in joint clinical decisions when the patient management plan is unclear or if they have concerns. Such communication strategies also have the potential to ensure their concerns have been heard, understood, and acknowledged by the team. Educators need to also be intentional in creating SBE objectives that target social factors that may impair IP decision-making, and be open to discuss with learners clinical examples of groupthink and conformity bias that can take place in practice. Ultimately, health professional education reforms need to focus on dedicating curricular time and resources to consistent interprofessional SBE opportunities that bring consciousness and emphasis to the unintended consequences of interprofessional learning.

Summary

Contemporary healthcare is delivered by multiple professions working together, with the goal of optimizing patient outcomes. Outcomes are frequently suboptimal, and there are data to suggest that poor IPC may contribute to poorer healthcare outcomes. It seems logical, therefore, that interventions designed to improve IPC, including interprofessional SBE, should improve healthcare outcomes. However, logic is not a surrogate for better performance or improved outcomes, and the strong arguments suggesting that IPC and IPE will improve decision-making, performance, and clinical outcomes can be countered by equally strong arguments as to why these might impair these outcomes (e.g., groupthink, cognitive overload, peer pressure, and social lofting). In reality, using simulation as a pedagogical tool to teach IPE is not inherently good, bad, or neutral; instead, as with any educational intervention, the effect is modified by the individuals involved, the context, and the interaction between individuals and the context. Thus, rather than assume better outcomes with IP simulations, as clinicians and educators we have a responsibility in this emerging field to demonstrate through research that our interventions improve the delivery of healthcare and patient outcomes. According to Janis, being closed-minded and failing to criticize proposed models and interventions is one of the symptoms of groupthink (Rose, 2011). Thus, to minimize the risk of groupthink as we move forward with evaluating outcomes of interprofessional SBE, we need to critically assess our performance, and, more importantly, we need patients and clients to tell us if our approaches are effective.

REFERENCES

Alinier, G., Harwood, C., Harwood, P., Montague, S., Huish, E., & Ruparelia, K. (2008). *Development of a programme to facilitate interprofessional simulation-based training for final year undergraduate healthcare students.* Retrieved from http://uhra.herts.ac.uk/handle/2299/4573

Asch, S.E. (1951). Effects of group pressure on the modification and distortion of judgments. In H.S. Guetzkow (Ed.), *Groups, leadership and men: Research in human relations* (pp. 177–190). Pittsburgh, PA: Carnegie Press.

Asch, S.E. (1952). Effects of group pressure on the modification and distortion of judgments. In G.E. Swanson, T.M. Newcomb, & E.L. Hartley (Eds.), *Readings in social psychology* (2nd ed., pp. 2–11). New York: Holt, Rinehart & Winston.

Asch, S.E. (1956). Studies of independence and conformity: I. A minority of one against a unanimous majority. *Psychological Monographs, General and Applied, 70*(9), 1–70. https://doi.org/10.1037/h0093718

Barnes, D., Carpenter, J., & Dickinson, C. (2000). Interprofessional education for community mental health: Attitudes to community care and professional stereotypes. *Social Work Education, 19*(6), 565–583. https://doi.org/10.1080/02615470020002308

Barr, H., Hammick, M., Koppel, I., & Reeves, S. (1999). Evaluating interprofessional education: Two systematic reviews for health and social care. *British Educational Research Journal, 25*(4), 533–544. https://doi.org/10.1080/0141192990250408

Beran, T., Drefs, M., Kaba, A., Al Baz, N., & Al Harbi, N. (2015). Conformity of responses among graduate students in an online environment. *The Internet and Higher Education, 25*, 63–69. https://doi.org/10.1016/j.iheduc.2015.01.001

Beran, T., Kaba, A., Caird, J.K., & McLaughlin, K. (2014). The good and bad of group conformity: A call for a new programme of research in medical education. *Medical Education, 48*(9), 851–859. https://doi.org/10.1111/medu.12510

Bressler, T., & Persico, L. (2016). Interprofessional education: Partnerships in the educational proc. *Nurse Education in Practice, 16*(1), 144–147. https://doi.org/10.1016/j.nepr.2015.07.004

Boet, S., Bould, M.D., Layat Burn, C., & Reeves, S. (2014). Twelve tips for a successful interprofessional team-based high-fidelity simulation education session. *Medical Teacher, 36*(10), 853–857. https://doi.org/10.3109/0142159X.2014.923558

Bond, R., & Smith, P. (1996). Culture and conformity: A meta-analysis of studies using Asch's (1952b, 1956) line judgment task. *Psychology Bulletin, 119*(1), 111–137. https://doi.org/10.1037/0033-2909.119.1.111

Calhoun, A., Boon, M.C., Miller, K., Pian-Smith, M. (2013). Case and commentary: Using simulation to address hierarchy issues during medical crises. *Simulation in Healthcare, 8*(1), 13–19. https://doi.org/10.1097/SIH.0b013e318280b202

Canadian Medical Association. (2010). *Healthcare transformation in Canada.* Retrieved from http://www.cma.ca/advocacy/key-cma-reports

Cappellen, P.V., Corneille, O., Cols, S., & Saroglou, V. (2011). Beyond mere compliance to authoritative figures: Religious priming increases conformity to informational influence among submissive people. *The International*

Journal for the Psychology of Religion, 21(2), 97–105. https://doi.org/10.1080/10508619.2011.556995

Ceci, C. (2004). Nursing, knowledge and power: A case analysis. *Social Science & Medicine, 59*(9), 1879–1889. https://doi.org/10.1016/j.socscimed.2004.02.022

Chakraborti, C., Boonyasai, R.T., Wright, S.M., & Kern, D.E. (2008). A systematic review of teamwork training interventions in medical student and resident education. *Journal of General Internal Medicine, 23*(6), 846–853. https://doi.org/10.1007/s11606-008-0600-6

Chassin, M.R., Galvin, R.W., & the National Roundtable on Health Care Quality. (1998). The urgent need to improve health care quality: Institute of Medicine National Roundtable on Health Care Quality. *JAMA, 280*(11), 1000–1005. https://doi.org/10.1001/jama.280.11.1000

Cheng, A., Morse, K.J., Rudolph, J., Arab, A.A., Runnacles, J., & Eppich, W. (2016). Learner-centered debriefing for health care simulation education: Lessons for faculty development. *Simulation in Healthcare, 11*(1), 32–40. https://doi.org/10.1097/SIH.0000000000000136

Corser, W.D. (2000). The contemporary nurse-physician relationship: Insights from scholars outside the two professions. *Nursing Outlook, 48*(6):263–268. https://doi.org/10.1067/mno.2000.109154

Decker, S., Sportsman, S., Puetz, L., & Billings, L. (2008). The evolution of simulation and its contribution to competency. *Journal of Continuing Education in Nursing, 39*(2), 74–80. https://doi.org/10.3928/00220124-20080201-06

Eppich, W., & Cheng, A. (2015). Promoting excellence and reflective learning in simulation (PEARLS): Development and rationale for a blended approach to health care simulation debriefing. *Simulation in Healthcare, 10*(2), 106–115. https://doi.org/10.1097/SIH.0000000000000072

Eppich, W., Howard, V., Vozenilek, J., & Curran, I. (2011). Simulation-based team training in healthcare. *Simulation in Healthcare, 6*(Suppl. 7), S14–S19. https://doi.org/10.1097/SIH.0b013e318229f550

Fung, L., Boet, S., Bould, M.D., Qosa, H., Perrier, L., Tricco, A., ... Reeves, S. (2015). Impact of crisis resource management simulation-based training for interprofessional and interdisciplinary teams: A systematic review. *Journal of Interprofessional Care, 29*(5):433–444. https://doi.org/10.3109/13561820.2015.1017555

Gilfoyle, E., Koot, D.A., Annear, J.C., Bhanji, F., Cheng, A., Duff, J.P., ... Gottesman, R.D. (2017). Improved clinical performance and teamwork of pediatric interprofessional resuscitation teams with a simulation-based educational intervention. *Pediatric Critical Care Medicine, 18*(2), e62–e69. https://doi.org/10.1097/PCC.0000000000001025

Gough, S., Hellaby, M., Jones, N., & MacKinnon, R. (2012). A review of undergraduate interprofessional simulation-based education (IPSE). *Collegian, 19*(3), 153–170. https://doi.org/10.1016/j.colegn.2012.04.004

Grant, R.E., Goldman, J., LeGrow, K., MacMillan, K.M., van Soeren, M., & Kitto, S. (2016). A scoping review of interprofessional education within Canadian nursing literature. *Journal of Interprofessional Care, 30*(5), 620–626. https://doi.org/0.1080/13561820.2016.1192589

Guadagno, R.E., & Cialdini, R.B. (2010). Preference for consistency and social influence: A review of current research findings. *Social Influence, 5*(3), 152–163. https://doi.org/10.1080/15534510903332378

Guo, Z., Tan, F.B., Turner, T., & Xu, H. (2010). Group norms, media preferences, and group meeting success: A longitudinal study. *Computers in Human Behavior, 26*(4), 645–655. https://doi.org/10.1016/j.chb.2010.01.001

Haddara, W., & Lingard, L. (2013). Are we all on the same page? A discourse analysis of interprofessional collaboration. *Academic Medicine, 88*(10), 1509–1515. https://doi.org/10.1097/ACM.0b013e3182a31893

Hammick, M., Freeth, D., Koppel, I., Reeves, S., & Barr, H. (2007). A best evidence systematic review of interprofessional education: BEME Guide No. 9. *Medical Teacher, 29*(8),735–751. https://doi.org/10.1080/01421590701682576

Henriksen, K., & Dayton, E. (2006). Organizational silence and hidden threats to patient safety. *Health Services Research, 41*(4p2), 1539–1554. https://doi.org/10.1111/j.1475-6773.2006.00564.x

Hertwig, R., & Herzog, S.M. (2009). Fast and frugal heuristics: Tools of social rationality. *Social Cognition, 27*(5), 661–698. https://doi.org/10.1521/soco.2009.27.5.661

Hewitt, G., Sims, S., & Harris, R. (2014). Using realist synthesis to understand the mechanisms of interprofessional teamwork in health and social care. *Journal of Interprofessional Care, 28*(6), 501–506. https://doi.org/10.3109/13561820.2014.939744

Hinde, T., Gale, T., Anderson, I., Roberts, M., & Sice, P. (2016). A study to assess the influence of interprofessional point of care simulation training on safety culture in the operating theatre environment of a university teaching hospital. *Journal of Interprofessional Care, 30*(3), 251–253. https://doi.org/10.3109/13561820.2015.1084277

Hoffman, S.J., & Harnish, D. (2007). The merit of mandatory interprofessional education for pre-health professional students. *Medical Teacher, 29*(8), e235–e242. https://doi.org/10.1080/01421590701551672

Institute of Medicine. (2001). *Crossing the quality chasm: A new health system for the 21st century.* Washington, DC: National Academies Press.

Janis, I. (1972). *Victims of Groupthink: A psychological study of foreign-policy decision and fiascoes.* Boston: Houghton Mifflin.

Kaba, A., & Beran, T.N. (2016). Impact of peer pressure on accuracy of reporting vital signs: An interprofessional comparison between nursing and medical students. *Journal of Interprofessional Care, 30*(1), 116–122. https://doi.org/10.3109/13561820.2015.1075967

Kaba, A., Beran, T.N., & White, D. (2016). Accuracy of interpreting vital signs in simulation: An empirical study of conformity between medical and nursing students. *Journal of Interprofessional Education & Practice, 3*, 9–18. https://doi.org/10.1016/j.xjep.2016.03.002

Kaba, A., Wishart, I., Fraser, K., Coderre, S., & McLaughlin, K. (2016). Are we at risk of groupthink in our approach to teamwork interventions in health care? *Medical Education, 50*(4), 400–408. https://doi.org/10.1111/medu.12943

Khalili, H., Hall, J., & DeLuca, S. (2014). Historical analysis of professionalism in Western societies: Implications for interprofessional education and collaborative practice. *Journal of Interprofessional Care, 28*(2), 92–97. https://doi.org/10.3109/13561820.2013.869197

Khalili, H., Orchard, C., Laschinger, H.K.S., & Farah, R. (2013). An interprofessional socialization framework for developing an interprofessional identity among health professions students. *Journal of Interprofessional Care, 27*(6), 448–453. https://doi.org/10.3109/13561820.2013.804042

Kohn, L.T., Corrigan, J.M., & Donaldson, M.S. (Eds.). (2000). *To err is human: Building a safer health system.* Washington, DC: Institute of Medicine, National Academies Press.

Lamm, H., & Trommsdorff, G. (1973). Group versus individual performance on tasks requiring ideational proficiency (brainstorming): A review. *European Journal of Social Psychology, 3*(4), 361–388. https://doi.org/10.1002/ejsp.2420030402

Leasure, E.L., Jones, R.R., Meade, L.B., Sanger, M.I., Thomas, K.G., Tilden, V.P., ... Warm, E.J. (2013). There is no "I" in teamwork in the patient-centered medical home: Defining teamwork competencies for academic practice. *Academic Medicine, 88*(5), 585–592. https://doi.org/10.1097/ACM.0b013e31828b0289

Leonard, M., Graham, S., & Bonacum, D. (2004). The human factor: The critical importance of effective teamwork and communication in providing safe care. *BMJ Quality & Safety, 13*(Suppl. 1), i85–i90. https://doi.org/10.1136/qshc.2004.010033

Lineberry, M., Bryan, E., Brush, T., Carolan, T.F., Holness, D., Salas, E., & King, H. (2013). Measurement and training of TeamSTEPPS® dimensions using the medical team performance assessment tool. *The Joint Commission Journal on Quality and Patient Safety, 39*(2), 89–95. https://doi.org/10.1016/S1553-7250(13)39013-8

Lingard, L., McDougall, A., Levstik, M., Chandok, N., Spafford, M.M., & Schryer, C. (2012). Representing complexity well: A story about teamwork, with implications for how we teach collaboration. *Medical Education, 46*(9), 869–877. https://doi.org/10.1111/j.1365-2923.2012.04339.x

Long, K.A. (2003). The Institute of Medicine report: Health professions education: A bridge to quality. *Policy, Politics & Nursing Practice, 4*(4), 259–262. https://doi.org/10.1177/1527154403258304

Maxfield, D., Grenny, J., McMillan, R., Patterson, K., & Switzler, A. (2005). *Silence kills: The seven crucial conversations for healthcare.* Retrieved from https://psnet.ahrq.gov/resources/resource/1149

Millenson, M.L. (2003). The silence. *Health Affairs, 22*(2), 103–112. https://doi.org/10.1377/hlthaff.22.2.103

Milne, J., Greenfield, D., & Braithwaite, J. (2015). An ethnographic investigation of junior doctors' capacities to practice interprofessionally in three teaching hospitals. *Journal of Interprofessional* Care, *29*(4), 347–353. https://doi.org/10.3109/13561820.2015.1004039

Neill, M.A., & Wotton, K. (2011). High-fidelity simulation debriefing in nursing education: A literature review. *Clinical Simulation in Nursing, 7*(5), e161–e168. https://doi.org/10.1016/j.ecns.2011.02.001

O'Dea, A., O'Connor, P., & Keogh, I. (2014). A meta-analysis of the effectiveness of crew resource management training in acute care domains. *Postgraduate Medical Journal, 90*, 708. https://doi.org/10.1136/postgradmedj-2014-132800corr1

Orchard, C., Bainbridge, L., Bassendowski, S., Casimiro, L., Stevenson, K., Wagner, S., ... Sawatzky-Girling, B. (2010). *A national interprofessional competency framework.* Retrieved from http://www.cihc.ca/library/handle/10296/436

Østergaard, D., Dieckmann, P., Lippert, A. (2011). Simulation and CRM. *Best Practice & Research Clinical Anaesthesiology, 25*(2), 239–249. https://doi.org/10.1016/j.bpa.2011.02.003

Packer, D.J. (2009). Avoiding groupthink: Whereas weakly identified members remain silent, strongly identified members dissent about collective problems. *Psychological Science, 20*(5), 546–548. https://doi.org/10.1111/j.1467 9280.2009.02333.x

Palaganas, J.C., Epps, C., & Raemer, D.B. (2014). A history of simulation-enhanced interprofessional education. *Journal of Interprofessional Care, 28*(2), 110–115. https://doi.org/10.3109/13561820.2013.869198

Peterson, E.D., Heidarian, S., Effinger, S., Gunther, C., Diltz, M., Saunders, R., & Dombrowski, P.A. (2014). Outcomes of an interprofessional team learning and improvement project aimed at reducing post-surgical delirium in elderly patients admitted with hip fracture. *CE Measure, 8*(1), 2–7. Retrieved from http://www.cardenjenningspublishing.com/journal/index.php/cem/article/view/134

Pian-Smith, M.C., Simon, R., Minehart, R.D., Podraza, M., Rudolph, J., Walzer, T., & Raemer, D. (2009). Teaching residents the two-challenge rule: A simulation-based approach to improve education and patient safety. *Simulation in Healthcare, 4*(2), 84–91. https://doi.org/10.1097/SIH.0b013e31818cffd3

Pieterse, V., & Thompson, L. (2010). Academic alignment to reduce the presence of "social loafers" and "diligent isolates" in student teams. *Teaching in Higher Education, 15*(4), 355–367. https://doi.org/10.1080/13562517.2010.493346

Reese, C.E., Jeffries, P.R., & Engum, S.A (2010). Learning together: Using simulations to develop nursing and medical student collaboration. *Nursing Education Perspective, 31*(1), 33–37. Retrieved from https://oce.ovid.com /article/00024776-201001000-00009/HTML

Reeves, S., Fletcher, S., Barr, H., Birch, I., Boet, S., Davies, N., ... Kitto, S. (2016). A BEME systematic review of the effects of interprofessional education: BEME Guide No. 39. *Medical Teacher, 38*(7), 656–668. https://doi.org/10.3109 /0142159X.2016.1173663

Reeves, S., Perrier, L., Goldman, J., Freeth, D., & Zwarenstein, M. (2013). Interprofessional education: Effects on professional practice and healthcare outcomes (update). *Cochrane Database of Systematic Review, 2013*(3). https:// doi.org/10.1002/14651858.CD002213.pub3

Reeves, S., & van Schaik, S. (2012). Simulation: A panacea for interprofessional learning? *Journal of Interprofessional Care, 26*(3), 167–169. https://doi.org /0.3109/13561820.2012.678183

Ricketts, B. (2011). The role of simulation for learning within pre-registration nursing education – a literature review. *Nurse Education Today, 31*(7), 650–654. https://doi.org/10.1016/j.nedt.2010.10.029

Robertson, B.D., Kaplan, B., Atallah, H., Higgins, M., Lewitt, M.J.M., & Ander, D.S. (2010). The use of simulation and a modified TeamSTEPPS curriculum for medical and nursing student team training. *Simulation in Healthcare, 5*(6), 332–337. https://doi.org/10.1097/SIH.0b013e3181f008ad

Rose, J.D. (2011). Diverse perspectives on the groupthink theory – a literary review. *Emerging Leadership Journeys, 4*(1), 37–57. Retrieved from: https:// www.regent.edu/acad/global/publications/elj/vol4iss1/home_vol4iss1.htm

Rosen, M.A., Salas, E., Wu, T.S., Silvestri, S., Lazzara, E.H., Lyons, R., ... King, H.B. (2008). Promoting teamwork: An event-based approach to simulation-based teamwork training for emergency medicine residents. *Academy Emergency Medicine, 15*(11), 1190–1198. https://doi.org/10.1111/j.1553 -2712.2008.00180.x

Salas, E., DiazGranados, D., Klein, C., Burke, C.S., Stagl, K.C., Goodwin, G.F., & Halpin, S.M. (2008). Does team training improve team performance? A meta-analysis. *Human Factors, 50*(6), 903–933. https://doi.org/10.1518 /001872008x375009

Salas, E., & Rosen, M.A. (2013). Building high reliability teams: Progress and some reflections on teamwork training. *BMJ Quality & Safety, 22*(5), 369–373. https://doi.org/10.1136/bmjqs-2013-002015

Salas, E., Sims, D.E., & Burke, C.S. (2005). Is there a "Big Five" in teamwork? *Small Group Research, 36*(5), 555–599. https://doi.org/10.1177 /1046496405277134

Selby, J.V., Beal, A.C., & Frank, L. (2012). The Patient-Centered Outcomes Research Institute (PCORI) national priorities for research and initial research agenda. *JAMA, 307*(15), 1583–1584. https://doi.org/10.1001/jama.2012.500

Sigalet, E., Donnon, T., Cheng, A., Cooke, S., Robinson, T., Bissett, W., & Grant, V. (2013). Development of a team performance scale to assess undergraduate health professionals. *Academic Medicine, 88*(7), 989–996. https://doi.org/10.1097/ACM.0b013e318294fd45

Silbey, S.S. (2009). Taming Prometheus: Talk about safety and culture. *Annual Review of Sociololgy, 35*(1):341–369. https://doi.org/0.1146/annurev.soc.34.040507.134707

Sweet, S.J., & Norman, I.J. (1995). The nurse-doctor relationship: A selective literature review. *Journal of Advanced Nursing, 22*(1), 165–170. https://doi.org/10.1046/j.1365-2648.1995.22010165.x

Sweller, J. (1988). Cognitive load during problem solving: Effects on learning. *Cognitive Science, 12*(2), 257–285. https://doi.org/10.1207/s15516709cog1202_4

Thistlethwaite, J. (2012). Interprofessional education: A review of context, learning and the research agenda. *Medical Education, 46*(1), 58–70. https://doi.org/10.1111/j.1365-2923.2011.04143.x

Walsh, K., Reeves, S., & Maloney, S. (2014). Exploring issues of cost and value in professional and interprofessional education. *Journal of Interprofessional Care, 28*(6), 493–494. https://doi.org/10.3109/13561820.2014.941212

Williamson, I. (2012). [Review of the report *Developing interprofessional education in health and social care courses in the United Kingdom, Occasional Paper 12* by H. Barr, M. Helme, & L. D'Avray]. *Journal of Interprofessional Care, 26*(2), 161–162. https://doi.org/10.3109/13561820.2012.636965

Xyrichis, A., & Ream, E. (2008). Teamwork: A concept analysis. *Journal of Advanced Nursing, 61*(2), 232–241. https://doi.org/10.1111/j.1365-2648.2007.04496.x

Yi, S.K.M., Steyvers, M., Lee, M.D., & Dry, M.J. (2012). The wisdom of the crowd in combinatorial problems. *Cognitive Science, 36*(3), 452–470. https://doi.org/10.1111/j.1551-6709.2011.01223.x

Zanna, M.P. (Ed.) (2005). *Advances in Experimental Social Psychology, 37.* Amsterdam: Elsevier.

Zeltser, M.V. & Nash, D.B. (2010). Approaching the evidence basis for aviation-derived teamwork training in medicine. *American Journal of Medical Quality, 25*(1), 13–23. https://doi.org/10.1177/1062860609345664

Zwarenstein, M. & Reeves, S. (2006). Knowledge translation and interprofessional collaboration: Where the rubber of evidence-based care hits the road of teamwork. *Journal of Continuing Education in the Health Professions, 26*(1), 46–54. https://doi.org/10.1002/chp.50

Conclusion
Simulation-Based Education: Transdisciplinary Perspectives and Future Directions

ANNA MACLEOD, LARA HAZELTON, AND
MATTHEW A. SCHNURR

This volume is the product of and a testament to the power of informal conversations among colleagues. These contributions evolved out of discussions with faculty from multiple disciplinary backgrounds at Dalhousie University who shared an interest in innovation with respect to teaching and learning. Through these conversations, we learned that simulation-based education (SBE) offers powerful outcomes across the social, natural, and health sciences, while also presenting unique challenges and limitations.

While the value of simulation in higher education is now widely accepted in various academic disciplines, this volume has offered something different: an investigation of how simulation-based education is currently being employed, conceptualized, and studied across disciplines. With a goal of providing concrete examples and actionable advice regarding how professors are integrating simulation in a variety of contexts, from chemistry to political science to medicine, we hope to have inspired you to think about how you might move toward experiential methods, like simulation, to enrich teaching and learning in your own context.

Experiential Learning: A Rationale for Simulation-Based Education

Calls for increasing experiential learning opportunities in higher education continue to expand. With its emphasis on developing real-world skills acquired through hands-on, or applied, methods, experiential learning remains in great demand within higher education. In the global economy, universities around the world are competing for students. Innovative approaches like experiential learning can help to distinguish a particular institution among a sea of choices.

More importantly, perhaps, there are sound educational reasons for encouraging experiential learning. George Kuh's (2008) seminal work on high-impact practices has made clear that experiential pedagogies – like service learning, internships, and SBE – have a notable influence on overall student success. The Gallup Purdue Index, a measure to evaluate the long-term success of university and college graduates, examines a number of higher education factors, including experiential learning opportunities. A 2014 Gallup-Purdue Index Report found that participation in experiential learning opportunities was tied directly to greater postgraduate success and workplace engagement. A 2016 survey by the National Association of Colleges and Employers found that the most desirable qualities among new employees include leadership, being a team player, good communication skills, and the ability to solve problems – all of which may be most readily achieved in carefully conceptualized experiential learning environments (NACE, 2016).

The neuroscience of learning is helping to uncover the biophysiological benefits of experiential techniques. Research into the biological basis of learning reveals that uncertainty and ambiguity play a key role in learner engagement, that emotion and social context have a role to play in deep learning, and that review and reflection play a significant part in long-term memory acquisition (see, e.g., Ambrose, Bridges, DiPietro, Lovett, & Normal, 2010; Bransford, 2000; Caine & Caine, 1991). All of these factors are characteristic of well-designed experiential learning activities.

Despite these well-documented benefits for students, faculty, and institutions, experiential learning programs continue to exist primarily at the margins of higher education. This marginalization might be related to questions about the role of universities and their somewhat contradictory obligations of establishing a disciplinary home and a related set of critical thinking skills, as opposed to preparing a student for their eventual career. Bass (2012) describes this tension and notes that

> one key source of disruption in higher education is coming not from the outside but from our own practices, from the growing body of experiential modes of learning, moving from margin to center, and proving to be critical and powerful in the overall quality and meaning of the undergraduate experience. As a result, at colleges and universities we are running head-long into our own structures, into the way we do business. (p. 25)

Bringing experiential learning to formal university curriculum remains a challenge; however, the lines between formal and informal curriculum are becoming blurred as we recognize that learning happens all the time and everywhere. Relatedly, education research continues to reinforce the benefits of a variety of experiential pedagogical methods, forcing us to reconsider our assumptions about the value and goals of teaching and learning in higher education. We're left then with important questions: If learning happens everywhere, how does that change the way we think about pedagogy? What is the appropriate balance between experiential methods and traditional classroom experiences? How do we best engage in experiential approaches? In this volume, we've taken the perspective that simulation-based education represents an important way forward for institutions of higher education to meet student demand for experiential learning, while embracing different disciplinary takes on its conceptualization, implementation, and evaluation.

Simulations Across Disciplines: Reflections from the Social, Natural, and Health Sciences

The value of the transdisciplinary approach described in these pages is that it exposes key differences and similarities among how simulations are employed as pedagogical tools, which leads to crucial insights and unexplored possibilities.

The first insight that emerges is that the most significant distinction in how SBE is used hinges not on discipline but on degree orientation; that is, the most pronounced contrast in how simulations are used is in professional degrees such as social work, law, and medicine versus traditional undergraduate programming such as chemistry, political science, and physics.

A number of important trends are worth noting here. First, simulations in professional programs tend to focus on building specialized skills or competencies, since much of this teaching functions as a stepping stone to professional practice. In contrast, simulations in undergraduate programs tend to focus on the understanding of key concepts or more basic skills building. This leads to differences in terms of managing the complexity of SBE. For instance, contributors teaching undergraduate students – including Brynen, Sundararajan, and Ryan and Gass – crafted simulations where exploring complexity was one of the core learning objectives. In contrast, complexity is carefully managed in professional programs, where simulations are curated in order to minimize externalities and zero in on specific competencies. In these fields, simulations offer a means of isolating specific clinical scenarios or learning objectives from the messiness of the real world.

Second, the concept of authenticity is one that is differently engaged in simulations designed for professional students versus those targeting undergraduate students. Contributors recount all sorts of rigorous mechanisms for ensuring authenticity in clinical settings, including pilot testing simulations (Bogo) and employing simulated patients (McNaughton and Nestel), as well as research projects that investigate how SBE can retain authenticity without descending into ritual or performance (Picketts and MacLeod). For instructors in undergraduate classes, authenticity is not a primary consideration: their instructional context is a step removed from real-world practice, and in many cases they lack the resources – in terms of infrastructure, technology, and other accoutrements – that can help to make these representations feel real. Instructors in these contexts tend to invest more time and energy in creating the simulation setting in order to make it feel authentic to students.

This different engagement with authenticity seems to hinge upon the intended learning outcomes, which may be different across (and even within) areas of study. Within the health sciences, authenticity is primarily about fidelity, given that simulations are often linked to high-stakes assessments and are designed to lead, ultimately, to increased patient safety. Those engaging with simulations in the social and natural sciences are striving for a different type of authenticity. For example, in the natural sciences, SBE is geared toward visual representations that make hypothetical phenomena more concrete. In this case, SBE is serving several purposes, including addressing a major learning challenge in this field (making visible what cannot be seen) and helping students to develop technical skills. Thus, it appears that the concept of authenticity in SBE is distributed across a continuum. These insights suggest that, rather than focusing on how to maximize authenticity as a point of departure for a simulation, those engaging in SBE should begin with the question, "How authentic does this simulation need to be to meet desired learning objectives?"

A third distinction revolves around the use of the debrief. Contributors who teach undergraduate students tend to construct their debriefing around notions of reflexivity: What new perspectives or insights did a learner gain through SBE? Within professional degrees, debriefing tends to extend beyond the personal to encompass multiple perspectives: those of the instructor, those of the simulated patient, those of the evaluator. While the function of the debrief in undergraduate education revolves around personalizing the lessons from the immersive experience, debrief in professional degrees tends to be more pluralistic; that is, not just what did I experience, but how did my experience impact other learners, and how can I enhance my performance to ensure that other actors – patients, clients, colleagues, et cetera – have their needs met.

A fourth and final difference relates to where simulation-based education fits into the broader curriculum. In professional degrees, simulation tends to be one of the least experiential parts of a learner's education, whereas in undergraduate degrees it is generally among the most experiential part of the curriculum. For professional programs such as those in the health sciences, simulation is often designed to prepare for a transition to the immersive workplace-based learning that occurs in the clinical setting. In undergraduate programs in the social and natural sciences, experiential education is the exception rather than the norm; students will encounter simulation-based education – or other immersive opportunities such as co-ops, research assistantships, and the like – only if they are exposed to a professor who offers such opportunities.

A second set of insights relates to commonalities that cut across both disciplinary and degree lines. Take, for example, the foundational commitment to SBE as a mechanism for appreciating multiple representations of reality. Contributors in the natural sciences such as Chamberlain and Plaetkau reference this when teaching processes that are invisible to the naked eye; for example, simulations offer a means for students to visualize and interact with elements that are otherwise unable to be seen or directly experienced. But scholars across other disciplines use simulations to accomplish similar aims. For example, in the social sciences Donohue and Forcese provide an opportunity for students to take an active role in managing a national security crisis – something not many of us will have the opportunity to experience first-hand. In the health sciences, Kaba describes how learners have the opportunity to participate in interprofessional teams, assuming the identity of a different professional – providing a glimpse of the complexity and skill of other professions making up a healthcare team.

A key point here is that by changing the focal point of learning, simulation refocuses the class away from instructor-led learning toward student-centred, peer learning. Orienting higher education toward student-centred approaches, like simulation, is increasingly recognized as a key factor in authentic learning and student engagement (Brown Wright, 2011). In moving the focus away from the teacher, simulation challenges traditional classroom dynamics and associated power relations in the classroom (Baranowski & Weir, 2010). It also has a destabilizing effect of forcing students to encounter alternative viewpoints and look at the same situation from a variety of perspectives. Its ability to empower students to appreciate alternative representations of reality prompts new insights, observation, and self-reflection and amounts to one of SBE's greatest strengths.

Another theme of this volume is that of differing relationships with technology; some contributors celebrate technology's ability to enhance SBE, while others remain much more sceptical. This runs somewhat counter to the dominant line within the scholarship of teaching and learning, which tends to exalt technology as an impetus for, and sometimes amplifier of, simulation-based interventions. Contributors to this volume offer a more nuanced account. Certainly, some contributors present innovative examples of how technology can serve to enhance learning outcomes. But an equal number of cases are presented that underline the power of SBE without technology; indeed, much of the deep learning detailed in this volume stems from face-to-face as opposed to online encounters. The key message here is that simulation technology is not a panacea for stimulating deep learning – but needs to be adopted and applied in a thoughtful and deliberate way. This is an important rejoinder in higher education, where technology can be unquestionably glorified: many of us can relate to Hamstra's anecdotes about cutting-edge technologies collecting dust in the corner. The take-home message here is that pedagogy needs to come before technology, and not the other way around.

The final commonality relates to the central importance of rigorous and robust evaluation of learning outcomes associated with SBE. We work in an evidence-based industry. Yet most of the accounts of SBE rely primarily on instructor observation and student ratings of instruction. A robust evaluation of any immersive learning technique is not optional; every instructor experimenting with any new technique – SBE included – needs to have a plan for how to collect and analyse data that assess whether the intervention has achieved its desired learning outcome. Instructors need to draw on their own training as researchers and create simulation-based education that incorporates meaningful impact assessment. The answer to the question "Is the simulation achieving its learning objectives?" needs to be one that is beyond reproach.

We have attempted to demonstrate that SBE can be used in a variety of higher education contexts to consolidate knowledge, help to perfect technical skills, and even explore attitudes, providing you with discipline-specific examples of SBE from the social, natural, and health sciences. Huber and Morreale (2002) note that "each discipline has its own intellectual history, agreements, and disputes about subject matter and methods" as well as its own "community of scholars interested in teaching and learning in that field" (p. 2). This section is a first attempt to glean how SBE learning across various disciplines can be synthesized to advance teaching and learning.

Take-Home Messages: Relating Our Experiences to the Simulation Life Cycle

A key element enabling successful simulation is grounding it within a comprehensive educational framework. The simulation life cycle, introduced on page 11, provides six "steps" that represent a blueprint for operationalizing SBE across disciplinary settings. We present here an overview of the key take-home messages of each step in the simulation life cycle, along with corresponding points from our chapters.

Step 1: Conceptualization. This step begins even before the simulation takes place. An important lesson learned by our contributors is that simulation is most successful when it's approached with the end – meaning the desired learning outcome – in mind. We therefore encourage anyone interested in SBE to begin the process by asking the question "What do I hope learners will be able to 'do' as a result of participating in this simulation?" This active way of thinking helps to link the planning of the simulation activity to learning objectives and broader educational goals.

Simulations can be both realistic and practical – while still pushing boundaries and allowing for creative engagement in educational processes. Our chapters have demonstrated that there are ways to work with, and optimize, readily available skillsets and resources. An implicit, but central, connecting feature across each of the simulation projects described herein is the element of appropriate allotment of time and careful planning. In other words, a last-minute scramble is less likely to lead to an engaging and meaningful learning experience. Conceptualization and planning are critically important.

Step 2: Creating an immersive learning environment. The importance of creating an environment that enables a learner to invest in the process is a central theme across all the chapters; however, there is a significant amount of variability across disciplines and in the ways in which this process is engaged. Perhaps the most striking example of this is in the health sciences, in which simulation has become an integrated element and truly plays the role of a signature pedagogy. Along with this has come an investment in resources – both human and physical.

This investment in simulation has led to a degree of sophistication with respect to its conceptualization. In the health sciences, an entire line of inquiry addressing simulation – along with specialty journals, conferences, and products/vendors – has developed. While this degree of sophistication seems to be linked to the investment, it is worth noting that innovative work can, and does, happen even in the more under-resourced settings typical of undergraduate settings. In these cases, reflexive dialogue among teachers and learners is key.

Step 3: Integrating technology. As noted above, variability with respect to the use of technologies is significant. Our chapters have showcased an assortment of ways in which technologies have been used to structure the simulation experience, ranging from the use of computer programs designed to make microscopic processes visible, to connecting students at multiple sites through videoconferencing to simulate a multinational collaboration, to practising clinical skills with state-of-the-art manikins that can bleed, cry, or even talk. The intent of each of the technologies described herein is to improve a simulation's ability to help learners meet learning objectives by enhancing authenticity, realism, and interactivity, and in some cases, to deepen learning by going beyond the realities of space and time (Jones, 2015).

While the ways in which technologies are used are quite different across the individual chapters, what is clear is that the technologies themselves are not replacements for carefully conceptualized simulations. Hamstra notes that adding a piece of simulation technology without nesting it in appropriate curricular and pedagogical principles serves the opposite purpose. That is, the focus of learning becomes oriented around "how can we use this technology?" rather than "how can this technology help us to meet learning objectives?"

Step 4: Simulation assessment. Recent trends in assessment in higher education are moving conversations toward the idea of evaluative judgment (Tai et al., 2017), an approach that encourages us to reconceptualize the very purposes of assessment. Rather than being a process of making a judgment about knowledge or skills, evaluative judgment focuses on providing targeted, useable, and timely feedback to learners so they are able to make decisions about the quality of their work, including areas for improvement. Processes for enabling this include self-assessment, peer feedback/review, teacher feedback, rubrics, and exemplars (Tai et al., 2017).

We encourage those interested in SBE to provide opportunities for iterative engagement with the simulation itself. Conceptualizing assessment in terms of evaluative judgment – and building in opportunities for self-assessment, peer and teacher feedback, rubrics, and other examples – will ultimately support students to make effective judgments about their knowledge and skills both within and beyond the simulation.

Step 5: The debrief. Following from the concept of evaluative judgment, above, the debrief can play a central role in effective simulation. The chapters in this volume chronicle a range of debriefing approaches. The mechanisms for engaging in debrief are related to the discipline in which the simulation occurs (with those in the natural sciences being more reflexive and personal in nature, and those from professional programs being more focused on specific pieces of knowledge and/or skills).

Regardless of the approach to, or the focus of, the debrief, this step is a critical aspect of successful SBE. A good debrief helps students achieve their learning objectives (Arora et al. 2012) – some even call it the cornerstone of SBE (Lusk & Fater, 2013; Reed et al., 2013; Dufrene & Young, 2013). The other side of this coin is that poor debriefing practices may be detrimental to learning (Boet et al., 2011). Some examples of problematic debriefing practices include being overly focused on the success of the simulation itself rather than on student performance and learning (Ryoo & Ha, 2015), assigning blame for glitches in the simulation to individual participants (Rudolph et al., 2013), or rushing through the debrief (Levett-Jones & Lapkin, 2013). And, while our chapters demonstrate that there is educational value in encouraging learners to step outside their comfort zones during the simulation activities, the debrief itself needs to remain a safe and comfortable space for self-reflection (Ryoo & Ha, 2015).

Step 6: Evaluation. A key take-home message is that SBE is multilayered and complex. There are many elements to consider at each step of the simulation life cycle, and along with these elements, there are many decisions to be made. So, how do we know what's working when it comes to SBE? Engaging in some form of evaluation, ideally in the form of fully developed education research, plays a central role.

A striking theme from this volume relates to the difference in uptake of educational evaluation and/or research by discipline. Examples of SBE from the natural sciences are beginning to emerge, and simulation is becoming well recognized, and firmly entrenched, as a valuable approach in the social sciences. Despite this increased recognition, the educational scholarship investigating simulation in these disciplines is still developing. Within the health sciences, in contrast, the field of health professional education is well defined, and simulation has emerged as a signature pedagogy worthy of rigorous investigation. This commitment is visible in an abundance of specifically SBE-focused journals, like the *British Medical Journal's Simulation & Technology Enhanced Learning*, the *Journal of the Society for Simulation in Healthcare*, and *Advances in Simulation*, to name a few. In addition to journals, the field of SBE in the health sciences has a set of dedicated conferences, including the Royal College of Physicians and Surgeons of Canada's Simulation Summit, and the International Nurses Association for Clinical Simulation and Learning Annual Conference. There even exist networks of professionals working within the field of health professional simulation, including the Association for Simulated Patient Educators. SBE in the health sciences has matured as an evidence-based practice. Our hope is that SBE in the natural and social sciences will follow the example of the health sciences in developing evaluation protocols that are robust, rigorous, and embedded as a critical component of any experimental approach.

From Transdisciplinarity to Interdisciplinarity: Making a Simulation Smoothie

We have argued that there is value in thinking about SBE across disciplinary boundaries, but is there value also in thinking about SBE between different disciplines? We believe so, and here explore the possibilities for an interdisciplinary take on SBE. What do we mean by an interdisciplinary perspective? The National Academies (2005) note that work "is truly interdisciplinary when it is not just pasting two disciplines together to create one product but rather an integration or synthesis of ideas and methods" (p. 27). Thompson-Klein (2017) proposes that the value of an interdisciplinary approach is the ability to highlight the "in between" or contested space between various disciplines. In our view, the value of our individual teaching can be enhanced by broadening our use of SBE to integrate insights and practices from other disciplines.

Some scholars (Nissani, 1995) have used a fruit salad versus smoothie metaphor to present a case for taking an interdisciplinary perspective. Whereas a fruit salad might be made of a variety of separate pieces of fruit, a smoothie is "finely blended so that the distinctive flavor of each [fruit] is no longer recognizable, yielding instead the delectable experience of the smoothie" (p. 125). Recognizing that this metaphor is imperfect, this does highlight that in an interdisciplinary approach, each fruit (i.e., discipline) is purposefully selected, the act of blending (i.e., integrating) actually changes the nature of the individual contribution, and the end product of the smoothie is something entirely new.

Why are we suggesting an educational "smoothie"? Higher education continues to struggle to produce authentic opportunities for high-quality experiential learning. Taking an interdisciplinary approach has the potential to help us to rethink some of the taken-for-granted ideas underpinning our work in higher education, allowing us to move beyond the taken-for-granted restrictions of our disciplinary homes. Taking an interdisciplinary approach allows for far-reaching questioning about the nature of knowledge and the ways in which we attempt to organize, communicate, and teach it. As Moran (2010) notes, interdisciplinarity "interlocks with concerns of epistemology – the study of knowledge – and tends to be centred around problems and questions that cannot be addressed or solved within the existing disciplines" (pp. 13–14). Taking an interdisciplinary approach offers new ways to "do" teaching and learning.

We encourage educators to explore an approach to SBE that reflects the messy interdisciplinarity of the real world. Higher education works in terms of disciplines. But the real world does not. If instructors in the social, natural, and health sciences are committed to creating immersive activities that mirror real life, we can begin by breaking down these disciplinary boundaries and creating simulations that are complex enough to encompass multiple and competing perspectives. We believe simulations provide potential for authentic collaboration. We therefore encourage educators to consider shifting scales, creating SBE that is not contained within individual classes or even individual curriculum but is instead designed to replicate the scale of the problem itself. SBE is particularly well suited to addressing some of the most pressing and urgent issues of our time – climate change, terrorism, epidemics, peacemaking, poverty – each of which contains elements to be addressed through the social, natural, and health sciences. We believe that embracing the interdisciplinarity inherent in the framing of the problem will enrich the learning value of the immersive experience for students.

Faculty Development for Simulation

Faculty development programs are institutionally housed programs designed to support and prepare faculty for their various roles, including teaching. Given that experiential approaches to teaching and learning, like simulation, are often outside the typical skillset of educators in higher education, there is a clear role for high-quality faculty development to help prepare those interested in engaging in SBE and to embed interdisciplinarity as a foundational tenet of simulation-based education.

Faculty development involves training, educating, and developing teachers. Garavan (1997) defines these as related but differing activities, and it can be useful to consider them individually when identifying needs and developing programming to prepare for SBE. Training focuses on the acquisition of skills required to fulfil a specific role or task, and tends to be very context-specific. On the other hand, education produces a range of knowledge and abilities that are more likely to be generalizable across settings. Finally, development takes a more ambitious and comprehensive approach that recognizes each individual's potential and encourages personal as well as professional growth (Garavan, 1997). These three types of faculty development are increasingly intensive and transformative, with training being fairly limited to the task at hand, education improving teaching capacity more generally, and development potentially leading to changes in instructor self-perception and identity that may then facilitate leadership or creativity. As Garavan writes, development involves "expanding one's potential through conscious and unconscious learning processes with a view to enabling the individual to take up a future role within the organization" (p. 41).

When designing faculty development for SBE, it is important to consider the varied roles of those involved as well as the complexity of simulation itself. Certainly, the challenges of simulation, whether in the social, natural, or health sciences, are not uniquely related to people. Throughout this volume, our chapters have highlighted that simulation, in all its complexity, is dependent upon both people and things. These interactions can produce a plethora of challenges, many of which have been chronicled within these pages, including additional costs, intensive time investment, and unforeseen complications. Paying attention to both the social and material elements of SBE, and carefully exploring the role played by different human and non-human actors, can offer a novel perspective on SBE and help instructors to make a frank assessment of its potential costs and benefits.

We must recognize that, to some degree, the simulation activity itself is a collaborative artefact. For example, student participants may be led through the simulation by instructors who are not the same people who initially designed the activity. Simulations may involve multiple instructors, each of whom may have a different responsibility.

As an example, as described on the chapters related to simulations in the health sciences, these frequently involve a scenario related to patient care and may take place in settings that either are, or are made to resemble, clinics. In these scenarios, the instructors overseeing the exercise and evaluating learner performance may not be the same people who designed the scenario, or "wrote the case." In contrast, in the social or natural sciences, the scale of the simulation may be much smaller, with an individual instructor working on their own to conceptualize and design it. Regardless of the setting, the more people involved in a simulation, the more complex the faculty development needs become.

Consider, for example, a trauma care simulation (meaning a simulation of a traumatic injury like a motor vehicle accident or a gunshot wound) and the multiple roles of the people involved in its design and delivery. Trauma care is complex and involves a variety of health professionals and medical tools. Preparing a relatively high-fidelity simulation of trauma care would require involvement of a variety of individuals. In order to maintain accuracy, the scenario might be written by emergency room physicians or paramedics, based on their experience. It would be delivered with the help of simulated patients who had been trained by simulation specialists to portray the role of the trauma victim or, perhaps, members of their family. These simulated patients might even provide feedback to students on their performance. The simulation might be led by nurses or other health professionals who are responsible for teaching during the session, ensuring students get to practise the necessary skills during the simulation. In this situation, the people who write the case and prepare for the scenario would be the curriculum developers: the emergency medicine doctors and paramedics. Those involved in the direct teaching would be the instructors: the nurses, other health professionals, and the simulated patients.

In creating faculty development for simulation, it is important to recognize the variety of people who may be involved in SBE, and consider how faculty development might be tailored to match their respective roles. Table C.1 provides examples of components of faculty development for each role.

Using the example of the trauma simulation, the curriculum developers (emergency physicians, paramedics) might need targeted training in the areas of simulation technology, resources, institutional requirements, and learner needs. Curriculum developers would also benefit from broader education on curriculum design, principles of assessment, and best practices in simulation in order to design an effective activity. Faculty development might include leadership and managerial skills that would allow curriculum developers to function effectively as champions for simulation. The instructors (nurses, other health professionals, simulated patients) would need training to be oriented to the scenario, and any assessment tools for evaluating learner performance. Education would include skills in feedback and difficult conversation that could be used in other teaching. Finally, instructor faculty development could include increased self-awareness, and resilience as a teacher. Both the curriculum developers and the instructors could be supported to develop their identities as educators.

In providing this example, we hope to illustrate that preparing instructors for SBE is far from straightforward. There are many factors to consider, not the least of which are context and resources. We therefore propose an approach that takes into account the multiple activities in which curriculum developers or instructors might need support, including training, education, and development. We encourage those interested in giving SBE a try to engage with the variety of faculty development resources available at their own institutions, and in other locations. One such resource, described earlier in this volume, is the Simulation and Student Learning Hub (dal.ca/dpt/clt/simulation.html). The six steps of the simulation learning cycle provide

Table C.1. Approaches to faculty development for simulation

	Curriculum developers (those who are creating the scenario, interacting with instructors and administrators)	Instructors (those who are teaching in the scenario, interacting with learners)
Training (specific to role or task)	Potential uses of technology included in the simulations (e.g., manikins, diagnostic instruments), institutional requirements (curriculum map), logistical considerations (availability of resources)	Logistical aspects of implementation, content of the simulation, use of assessment tools to evaluate student performance
Education (generalizable skills)	Curriculum design, principles of assessment, creating outcomes-based objectives, best practices	Facilitating groups, providing feedback on performance, addressing professionalism concerns
Development (increased self-awareness, analysis)	Leadership skills, program assessment and continuous improvement	Self-awareness, understanding of strengths and weaknesses, building resilience as a teacher, incorporating a scholarly approach

an overview of best practices related to conceptualizing a simulation, creating an immersive environment, integrating technology, designing assessments, debriefing, and finally, evaluating the simulation itself.

Conclusion

In conclusion, we hope that this volume makes a strong case for the value of the experiential learning strategy of simulation in higher education. Our contributors have illustrated that simulation can be, and is, broadly engaged – taking a variety of forms ranging from role-playing activities, to three-dimensional modelling, to practising skills on high-fidelity manikins. And, importantly, our contributors have also demonstrated that despite a wide array of educational variables – things like differing amounts of curricular time, different course content and topics, small, large, or non-existent budgets, and newly minted versus experienced educators – SBE can be successfully used to encourage authentic engagement.

The educational literature, and the examples presented in this chapter, is clear: SBE is an educational approach that can promote deep learning. This, in turn, leads to improved mastery and retention of knowledge and skills (Hughes & Mighty, 2010). So, what should you do with this information? How might you integrate SBE into your own contexts?

We have presented an overview of how simulation is being used across a variety of disciplinary contexts in the hopes that you might become inspired to give it a try – whether that be within your own disciplinary home, or perhaps even as a strategy for tackling broader issues from a more interdisciplinary approach. We hope that whatever your role within higher education – whether as a teacher, educational developer, administrator, or policymaker – you'll feel encouraged and inspired to engage, critically, with this important pedagogical approach.

REFERENCES

Ambrose, S., Bridges, M., DiPietro, M., Lovett, M. & Normal, M. (2010). *How learning works: Seven research-based priniples for smart teaching.* San Francisco: Jossey-Bass.

Arora, S., Ahmed, M., Paige, J., Nestel, D., Runnacles, J., Hull, L., ... Sevdalis, N. (2012). Objective structured assessment of debriefing: Bring science to the art of debriefing in surgery. *Annals of Surgery, 256*(6), 982–988. https://doi.org/10.1097/sla.0b013e3182610c91

Baranowski, M., & Weir, K. (2010). Power and politics in the classroom: The effect of student roles in simulations. *Journal of Political Science Education, 6*(3), 217–226. https://doi.org/10.1080/15512169.2010.494465

Bass, R. (2012). Disrupting ourselves: The problem of learning in higher education. *EDUCase Review, 47*(2), 23–33. Retrieved from https://er.educause.edu/articles/2012/3/disrupting-ourselves-the-problem-of-learning-in-higher-education

Boet, S., Bould, D., Bruppacher, H., Desjardin, F., Chandra, D., & Naik, V. (2011). Looking in the mirror: Self-debriefing versus instructor debriefing for simulated crises. *Critical Care Medicine, 39*(6), 1377–81. https://doi.org/10.1097/ccm.0b013e31820eb8be

Bransford, J. (2000). *How people learn: Brain, mind, experience, and school.* Washington: National Academies Press.

Brown Wright, G. (2011). Student-centred learning in higher education. *International Journal of Teaching and Learning in Higher Education, 23*(3), 92–97. Retrieved from https://eric.ed.gov/?id=EJ938583

Caine, R., & Caine, G. (1991). *Making connections: Teaching and the human brain.* Alexandria, VA: Association for Supervision and Curriculum Development.

Christenson Hughes, J., & Mighty, J. (2010). *Taking stock: Research on teaching and learning*. Montreal and Kingston: McGill-Queen's University Press.

Dufrene, C., & Young, A. (2013). Successful debriefing – best methods to achieve positive learning outcomes a literature review. *Nurse Education Today, 34*(3), 372–376. https://doi.org/10.1016/j.nedt.2013.06.026

Eyler, J. (2009). The power of experiential education. *Liberal Education, 95*(4), 24–31. Retrieved from https://www.aacu.org/publications-research/periodicals/power-experiential-education

Gallup-Purdue Index Report (2014). *Great jobs, great lives: The 2014 Gallup-Purdue index report*. Washington: Gallup.

Garavan, T.N. (1997). Training, development, education and learning: Different or the same? *Journal of European Industrial Training, 21*(2), 39–50. https://doi.org/10.1108/03090599710161711

Huber, M.T., & Morreale, S.M. (2002). Situating the scholarship of teaching and learning: A cross-disciplinary conversation. In M.T. Huber & S.P. Morreale (Eds.), *Disciplinary styles in the scholarship of teaching and learning: Exploring common ground* (pp. 1–24). Menlo Park, CA: Carnegie Foundation for the Advancement of Teaching; Washington, DC: American Association for Higher Education.

Kuh, G. (2008). *High-impact educational practices: What they are, who has access to them, and why they matter*. Washington: Association of American Colleges and Universities.

Levett-Jones, T., & Lapkin, S. (2013). A systematic review of the effectiveness of simulation debriefing in health professional education. *Nurse Education Today, 34*(6), e58–e63. https://doi.org/10.1016/j.nedt.2013.09.020

Lusk, J., & Fater, K. (2013). Post simulation debriefing to maximize clinical judgment development. *Nurse Education, 38*(1), 16–19. https://doi.org/10.1097/nne.0b013e318276df8b

Moran, J. (2010). *Interdisciplinarity* (2nd ed.). London: Routledge.

National Academies of Sciences, National Academy of Engineering, & Institute of Medicine. (2005). *Facilitating interdisciplinary research*. Washington: National Academies Press.

National Association of Colleges and Employers. (2016). *Job outlook 2016: The attributes employers want to see on new college graduates' resumes*. Retrieved from https://www.naceweb.org/career-development/trends-and-predictions/job-outlook-2016-attributes-employers-want-to-see-on-new-college-graduates-resumes/

Nissani, M. (1995). Fruits, salads, and smoothies: A working definition of interdisciplinarity. *Journal of Educational Thought, 29*(2), 121–128. Retrieved from https://www.jstor.org/stable/23767672

Reed, S., Andrews, C., & Ravert, P. (2013). Debriefing simulations: Comparison of debriefing with video and debriefing alone. *Clinical Simulation in Nursing, 9*(12): e585–e591. https://doi.org/10.1016/j.ecns.2013.05.007

Repko, A. (2008). *Interdisciplinary research: Process and theory.* London: Sage.

Rudolph, J., Foldy, E., Robinson, T., Kendall, S., Taylor, S., & Simon, R. (2013). Helping without harming: The instructor's feedback dilemma in debriefing – A case study. *Simulation in Healthcare, 8*(5), 304–316. https://doi .org/10.1097/sih.0b013e318294854e

Ryoo, E., & Ha, E. (2015). The importance of debriefing in simulation-based learning: Comparison between debriefing and no debriefing. *Computers, Informatics and Nursing, 33*(12), 538–545. https://doi.org/10.1097/cin .0000000000000194

Tai, J., Ajjawi, R., Boud, D., Dawson, P., & Pandero, E. (2017). Developing evaluative judgement: Enabling students to make decisions about the quality of work. *Higher Education, 76*(3), 467–481. https://doi.org/10.1007 /s10734-017-0220-3

Thompson-Klein, J. (2017). Typologies of interdisciplinarity: The boundary work of definition. In R. Frodeman, J. Thompson Klein, & R. Pacheco (Eds.), *The Oxford handbook of interdisciplinarity* (2nd ed., pp. 21–34). Oxford, UK: Oxford University Press.

Contributors

Marion Bogo teaches direct clinical social work practice and the theory and practice of social work education in the Factor-Inwentash Faculty of Social Work at the University of Toronto. She holds an MSW from McGill University and received an Honorary Doctorate of Laws from Memorial University in 2018. She was appointed to the Order of Canada as an Officer in 2014 in recognition for her extensive research and impact in the field of social work. Her research interests focus primarily on competency for professional practice including social work education, field education, and clinical social work supervision. In her research she has developed and tested field education models and the use of simulation in teaching and assessing student and practitioner competence.

Rex Brynen is a Professor in the Political Science Department at McGill University. He recently completed a two-year placement as a Non-Resident Senior Fellow with the Atlantic Council, and he has previously acted as a consultant to organizations including the Canadian International Development Agency, the International Development Research Centre, and the World Bank. He is the author and co-author of numerous books, including *Challenges of the Developing World* (2019) and *A Very Political Economy: Peacebuilding and Foreign Aid in the West Bank and Gaza* (2000). He also acts as the senior editor of *PAXsims*, a blog devoted to conflict simulations and games.

Julia M. Chamberlain completed her PhD in solid state inorganic chemistry at Northwestern University before pursuing a postdoc in Chemical Education Research with the PhET Interactive Simulations at the University of Colorado Boulder. She is currently an Assistant Professor of Teaching in the Department of Chemistry at the University of California, Davis, where she is working to develop a new chemistry course that integrates active-learning and student-centred pedagogies. Her research focuses on the question "Why is learning chemistry hard, and how can we make it easier?" She incorporates this question into her teaching by using transformative education technologies at all levels to engage students.

Laura K. Donohue is a Professor of Law at Georgetown Law. She is the Director of Georgetown's Center on National Security and Law, and also the Director of the Center on Privacy and Technology. She has held fellowships at Stanford Law School's Center for Constitutional Law, Stanford University's Center for International Security and Cooperation, and Harvard University's John F. Kennedy School of Government. Professor Donohue is a Life Member of the Council on Foreign Relations and an Advisory Board Member of the Electronic Privacy Information Center. Her most recent book, *The Future of Foreign Intelligence: Privacy and Surveillance in a Digital Age* (Oxford University Press, 2016), was awarded the 2016 Chicago-Kent College of Law/Roy C. Palmer Civil Liberties Prize.

Craig Forcese is a full Professor in the Faculty of Law at the University of Ottawa. Craig sits on the executive of the Canadian Network for Research on Terrorism, Security and Society (TSAS), and is a Board Member and past President of both the Canadian Council on International Law and the Canadian Association of Law Teachers. In 2017, he and Kent Roach received the Canadian Civil Liberties Association Award for Excellence in Public Engagement ("for courage and commitment to human rights, human dignity and freedom"). Dr. Forcese was inducted as a member of the uOttawa Common Law Honour Society in 2016. At uOttawa, he teaches public international law, national security law, administrative law, and constitutional law. In 2014, he received the Association of Professors of the University of Ottawa Award for Excellence in Teaching, the university's highest teaching award, as well as the University of Ottawa Excellence in Teaching Award. He also co-organizes and instructs the Canadian component of Georgetown Law's National Security Crisis Law course and simulation.

Susan Gass is an Instructor and Academic Advisor in the Environmental Science Program at Dalhousie University. She received her PhD from the Scottish Association for Marine Science/Open University (Scotland). Her research interests focus on the biology, ecology, and conservation of coral reefs, including the impacts from fishing and offshore oil on coral ecosystems and conservation planning for cold water corals. She is also interested in biodiversity conservation, with particular emphasis on the public domain, urban environments, and postsecondary school campuses.

Susan P. Gentry is an Assistant Professsor of Teaching in the Materials Science and Engineering Department at the University of California, Davis. Her research interests focus on the use of simulations and experiments in materials science education. In her current position, she is integrating computer-based assignments and simulations into her teaching at both the undergraduate and graduate level. She has published a learning activity online entitled *Visualizing Crystal Structures* that uses an open-source software to help students with the three-dimensional visualization of crystal structures.

Stanley J. Hamstra is currently Vice-President, Milestones Research and Evaluation; Accreditation Council for Graduate Medical Education (ACGME), Chicago, Illinois; Adjunct Professor, Faculty of Education, University of Ottawa, Ottawa, Ontario, Canada; and Adjunct Professor, Department of Medical Education, Feinberg School of Medicine, Northwestern University, Chicago, Illinois. Originally trained in experimental psychology (human development and sensory processes), Dr. Hamstra obtained a PhD in visual neuroscience at York University, Toronto, Canada, followed by a postdoctoral fellowship in the neurophysiology of vision and auditory psychophysics at the University of Toronto. From 1997–2005, he was Assistant Professor and Director of the Office of Surgical Education in the Department of Surgery, University of Toronto. While there, he helped to establish the University of Toronto Surgical Skills Centre at Mount Sinai Hospital, Toronto, and led a program of research on the assessment of technical skills. From 2005–9, he was Associate Professor in the Department of Medical Education at the University of Michigan, where he was affiliated with the University of Michigan Clinical Simulation Center. Following this, he was Assistant Dean, Academy for Innovation in Medical Education, University of Ottawa Faculty of Medicine, and Research Director of the University of Ottawa Skills and Simulation Centre at the Ottawa Hospital, Ottawa, Canada.

Lara Hazelton is an Associate Professor in the Department of Psychiatry at Dalhousie University in Halifax, Nova Scotia. She is also the Director of Continuing Professional Development for the Department of Psychiatry, and the Director of Academic Faculty Development for the Faculty of Medicine. Her areas of scholarly activity include leadership education, faculty development, and medical humanities. She has been the recipient of the Royal College Fellowship for Studies in Medical

Education and the Dr. Gerald and Gale Archibald Gold-Headed Cane Award, awarded for excellence in the field of medical humanities.

Alyshah Kaba is the Provincial Lead Research Scientist for Simulation and Education in the Department of Quality Healthcare Improvement (QHI) within Alberta Health Services (AHS). She recently completed her PhD in Medical Education from the University of Calgary, where she also actively teaches in the Bachelor of Health Sciences Undergraduate Program. Dr. Kaba was awarded the prestigious Canada Institutes of Health Research Vanier Canada Graduate Scholarship for her doctoral research, which examined how interprofessional team decision-making impacts patient safety and medical errors among novice undergraduate learners. She has a breadth of experience as a medical educator in curricular design, instructional methods, measurement, assessment, psychometrics, and simulation-based education. As a mixed-methods researcher, she has also co-authored on a number of abstracts and peer-reviewed publications.

Vicki R. LeBlanc is an Assistant Professor in the Department of Medicine and an education scientist at the Wilson Center for Research in Education, both at the University of Toronto. She has published a number of articles on the effects of acute stressors on the responses and performance of emergency workers and physicians. She has also published a number of articles in the area of health professions education. She has been the recipient of new investigator and research presentation awards from the American Association of Medical Colleges and the Association of Medical Education in Europe.

Anna MacLeod is an Associate Professor and Director of Education Research in the Division of Medical Education at Dalhousie University. A qualitative researcher, she uses ethnographic methods to learn about distributed medical education and learning with technology. She is particularly interested in understanding the social and material influences associated with developing professional identities. Dr. MacLeod maintains a Tri-Council-funded program of research exploring the complexities of medical education in a digital age. She is currently the Principal Investigator on grants funded by the Social Science and Humanities Research Council of Canada and the Royal College of Physicians and Surgeons of Canada.

Nancy McNaughton is the Director for the Centre of Learning, Innovation and Simulation at the Michener Institute of Education. She is an active educator and researcher with over 30 years of experience in the field of simulation-based education. She designs and delivers curriculum, evaluation, remediation, and research activities for a variety of health professional trainees and practising professionals, locally, nationally, and internationally. Dr. McNaughton's research interests include exploring the role of emotion within health professional training and practice. She holds a Doctorate in Higher Education from the Ontario Institute for Studies in Education (OISE), University of Toronto.

Debra Nestel is a Professor of Simulation Education in Healthcare at Monash University and a Professor of Surgical Education in the Department of Surgery at the University of Melbourne. She is the Editor in Chief of *Advances in Simulation*, the official journal of the Society in Europe for Simulation Applied to Medicine. Dr. Nestel has published over 200 peer-reviewed papers in health professions education, published edited books on simulated patient methodology (2015) and healthcare simulation (2018), and published two edited books in 2019 on surgical education and healthcare simulation research. She has received the Ray Page Lifetime Simulation Achievement, a Presidential Citation from the Society for Simulation in Healthcare, and an Australian Government Office of Learning and Teaching program award.

Mark Paetkau is a Senior Lecturer in the Faculty of Science at Thompson Rivers University. He is also the Chair of the Faculty Council and the Physical Resources Committee. He has worked on small angle X-ray scattering experiments at Argonne National Labs. He is committed to improving physics education at the undergraduate level.

Leanne Picketts is a Graduate Student at Dalhousie University, where her research explores how we use simulated patients (SP) and formalized interviewing techniques as pedagogical tools to promote a patient-centred medical curriculum. She is also a simulated patient educator with the Centre for Collaborative Clinical Research and Learning at Dalhousie. She has presented her research at numerous conferences, including the Canadian Conference on Medical Education and the Association of Standardized Patient Educators Annual Conference. She holds a Master of Education from Acadia University.

Chad Raymond is an Associate Professor, Faculty Fellow, and Chairman in the Department of Cultural, Environmental and Global Studies at Salve Regina University. He has published several peer-reviewed journal articles on agrarian reforms in Vietnam that originated from his dissertation field research in the mid-1990s, and he has also published work on state formation and nationalism in Cambodia. Dr. Raymond is also interested in effective pedagogy and the use of simulations in international relations and comparative politics classes.

Anne Marie Ryan is a University Teaching Fellow in the Department of Earth Sciences at Dalhousie University. She is also the Coordinator of the First Year Earth Sciences Program and a Faculty Associate with the Centre of Learning and Teaching. Her research interests are focused on geoscience, in particular metals in urban soils and water, as well as geoscience education. In 2017, she was the recipient of the Anne Marie MacKinnon Educational Leadership Award, which was presented by the Association of Atlantic Universities. In recent years, she has also received the Faculty of Science Award for Excellence in Teaching, the Dalhousie University Educational Leadership Award, and the Dalhousie University Alumni Award for Excellence in Teaching – Dalhousie's highest teaching award. She believes in caring about the learner and challenging them to think critically and ask difficult questions.

Matthew A. Schnurr is an Associate Professor in the Department of International Development Studies at Dalhousie University. He is an environmental geographer with research and teaching interests in environment and development, political ecology, agricultural biotechnology, farmer decision-making, and environmental justice. He has conducted extensive research on the use of simulations in social science education. He is the recipient of several teaching awards, including the Brightspace Innovation Award in Teaching and Learning and Dalhousie University's Alumni Association Award of Excellence for Teaching.

Binod Sundararajan is an Associate Professor of Management in the Rowe School of Business at Dalhousie University. His research interests lie in organizational, professional, and business communication, computer-mediated communication, and social network analysis. He has conducted research on topics of networking technologies, social media and e-learning, leadership and sustainability, diverse areas of entrepreneurship, diversity training, and organizational theory. Dr. Sundararajan has taught and teaches courses on business communication, management skills development, corporate communication, and international & intercultural management at the undergraduate level. At the graduate (MBA) level, he has taught people management and sustainable leadership courses.

David Yaron is a Professor in the Department of Chemistry at Carnegie Mellon University. His research focuses on computational chemistry, particularly the electronic structure of large systems, including especially organic materials for electronic applications. He also works in chemical education and heads the ChemCollective, an NSF-sponsored collection of virtual labs, scenario-based learning activities, tutorials, and concept tests that helps students connect algebra with authentic chemistry and helps to bridge chemical knowledge with the real world. He has received numerous teaching awards throughout his career, including the Teaching Innovation Award in 2017 and the Award for Excellence: Post-Secondary Educator from the Carnegie Science Center in 2004.